# THE RIVER WAS DYED
WITH BLOOD

# THE RIVER WAS DYED WITH BLOOD

## Nathan Bedford Forrest and Fort Pillow

Brian Steel Wills

University of Oklahoma Press | Norman

Also by Brian Steel Wills

*A Battle from the Start: The Life of Nathan Bedford Forrest* (New York, 1992; repr. as *The Confederacy's Greatest Cavalryman: Nathan Bedford Forrest* [Lawrence, Kans., 1998])
*The War Hits Home: The Civil War in Southeastern Virginia* (Charlottesville, Va., 2001)
*No Ordinary College: A History of the University of Virginia's College at Wise* (Charlottesville, Va., 2004)
*Gone with the Glory: The Civil War in Cinema* (Lanham, Md., 2007)
(co-author) *Civil War Sites in Virginia: A Tour Guide* (Charlottesville, Va., 2011)
*George Henry Thomas: As True as Steel* (Lawrence, Kans., 2012)
*Confederate General William Dorsey Pender: The Hope of Glory* (Baton Rouge, La., 2013)

Library of Congress Cataloging-in-Publication Data

Wills, Brian Steel, 1959–
 The river was dyed with blood : Nathan Bedford Forrest and Fort Pillow / Brian Steel Wills.
   pages cm
 Includes bibliographical references and index.
 ISBN 978-0-8061-4453-5 (hardcover : alk. paper)  1. Fort Pillow, Battle of, Tenn., 1864. 2. Forrest, Nathan Bedford, 1821–1877—Military leadership. 3. Tennessee—History—Civil War, 1861–1865—African Americans. 4. United States—History—Civil War, 1861–1865—African Americans.  I. Title.
 E476.17.W55 2014
 973.7'415—dc23
                    2013036740

The paper in this book meets the guidelines for permanence and durability of the Committee on Production Guidelines for Book Longevity of the Council on Library Resources, Inc. ∞

Copyright © 2014 by the University of Oklahoma Press, Norman, Publishing Division of the University. Manufactured in the U.S.A.

All rights reserved. No part of this publication may be reproduced, stored in a retrieval system, or transmitted, in any form or by any means, electronic, mechanical, photocopying, recording, or otherwise—except as permitted under Section 107 or 108 of the United States Copyright Act—without the prior written permission of the University of Oklahoma Press. To request permission to reproduce selections from this book, write to Permissions, University of Oklahoma Press, 2800 Venture Drive, Norman OK 73069, or email rights.oupress@ou.edu.

1 2 3 4 5 6 7 8 9 10

Interior layout and composition: Alcorn Publication Design

*To the greatest of all battlefield guides,
my good friend Edwin C. Bearss,
and to my teacher and friend W. Harrison Daniel*

# CONTENTS

| | |
|---|---|
| List of Illustrations | ix |
| Preface | xi |
| | |
| Introduction: Race, War, Propaganda, and Memory | 3 |
| 1. Warrior in an Uncivil War: 1821–1864 | 18 |
| 2. Fighting for Freedom: April 1861–April 12, 1864 | 38 |
| 3. "Attending" to Fort Pillow: April 1863–April 12, 1864 | 61 |
| 4. "Will He Fight or Surrender?": March–April 12, 1864 | 86 |
| 5. "The Slaughter Was Awful": April 12, 1864 | 105 |
| 6. "Remember Fort Pillow": April 12–June 1864 | 120 |
| 7. An Election Year Gets "Massacred": April 12–November 1864 | 148 |
| 8. Reaction to Fort Pillow: 1864–1865 | 162 |
| 9. "Forrest of Fort Pillow": 1865–2014 | 184 |
| Epilogue: "War Means ... Killing" | 205 |
| | |
| Appendix A. Organization of Confederate Troops during the West Tennessee Campaign, March–April 1864 | 219 |
| Appendix B. Federal Officers at Fort Pillow, April 12, 1864 | 220 |
| Notes | 221 |
| Bibliography | 249 |
| Index | 265 |

# ILLUSTRATIONS

## **Figures**

| | |
|---|---|
| Nathan Bedford Forrest | 135 |
| James R. Chalmers | 136 |
| Charles W. Anderson | 136 |
| Tyree H. Bell | 137 |
| John Buford | 137 |
| Sharpshooters at Fort Pillow | 138 |
| Forrest's troops scaling the works | 138 |
| Benjamin F. Wade | 139 |
| Daniel W. Gooch | 139 |
| *The Massacre at Fort Pillow* | 140 |
| *Rebel Massacre of the Union Troops* | 141 |
| *Rebel Atrocities* | 142 |
| *The Modern Samson* | 143 |
| *This Is a White Man's Government* | 144 |
| *Leaders of the Democratic Party* | 145 |
| *Both Sides of the Question* | 146 |

## **Maps**

| | |
|---|---|
| Forrest's Raid into West Tennessee and Kentucky, March and April 1864 | 64 |
| The Capture of Fort Pillow, April 12, 1864 | 91 |
| Sketch of Fort Pillow | 95 |
| Battle of Brice's Cross Roads, June 10, 1864 | 133 |

# PREFACE

When I first became interested in this subject, I was a student in high school. I came to know about Confederate general Nathan Bedford Forrest and his record of military service in the American Civil War. It was impressive by any measure but all the more for his lack of formal military education and training. His martial success came less from previous experience in warfare than from his practical application of common sense and awareness of human nature. Bedford Forrest seemed to know almost instinctively what to do on the battlefield that would offer him the greatest chance for success. He particularly appeared to thrive in confrontations with West Pointers, when his combination of bluster and bluff often proved irresistible to opponents who preferred more-studied and traditional approaches to warfare.

Still, one wartime incident remained especially troubling. The 1864 attack on Fort Pillow left many of the garrison of Tennessee Unionists and black Americans dead in a confrontation widely labeled then and since as a "massacre." Detractors pounced on the incident as the ultimate illustration of the general's ruthlessness and the barbarism of the troops under his command. Even admirers of Forrest's military career have taken pains to explain or defend the actions on the apparent grounds that such a defense is even necessary. As argued herein, the facts suggest an interpretation between these extreme poles that neither exonerates Forrest nor condemns him, one that holds the Southern commander accountable for events that moved beyond his control—an offense that would have disturbed Forrest more fully than anything else.

Over the years as I have read the material made available on the events of Fort Pillow, I have found myself agreeing most with the general assessment of Albert Castel, who observed, "neither side in this controversy is altogether wrong or altogether right." He went on to say that both of these "sides" were "guilty in varying degrees of prejudice and error."[1] Likewise, I found early as an undergraduate student in a Civil War class taught by Harrison Daniel at the University of Richmond that I also agreed with the assessment of Paul E. Steiner: "To the extent that a military commander is responsible for the actions of his command, Forrest must bear the onus of this shameful affair."[2]

This is the premise from which I undertook this study, fully aware of the complexity of interpretation and the frailty of all human beings even to understand what they have seen or experienced, much less what has appeared through the eyes of others and the mists of history and time.

Many of the basic conclusions I reached in *A Battle from the Start*, published through HarperCollins in 1992 and republished as *The Confederacy's Greatest Cavalryman* by the University Press of Kansas, have remained.[3] But when a subsequent author took the tangential suggestion that Forrest may not have lead the assault himself because he hoped to preserve a sense of deniability as evidence of my own uncertainty about the general's culpability in the massacre, I realized that my final word on the subject had not been written. I knew that I had to look more closely at the events of April 1864 and Forrest's role in them as well as attempt to place them in a broader contextual framework of race, war, politics, and memory. This approach gave purpose to this volume.

Popular historian Stephen Ambrose observed in the context of a modern example of excess in war, "It is not the job of historians to condemn or judge but to describe, try to explain, and even more so, attempt to understand."[4] With Fort Pillow especially, achieving a balance between the subjective human tendency toward judgment and the need for objective, critical assessment has been difficult to accomplish. Some will not sanction any form of explanation or contextualization on the basis that these constitute nothing more than mitigation of heinous or depraved actions. Others will be adamant in equal measure that no degree of culpability can be tolerated, for that would be admission that such unsavory actions indeed took place. These extreme positions have proven formidable on a subject that continues to generate passions on all sides. Demonization of those holding variant views has become the norm under such circumstances despite running counter to the aspirations of historians for objectivity and fact-based analysis.

Such objectivity on Fort Pillow may indeed be impossible. The emotions remain so powerful that they are difficult to suppress, regardless of attention or agenda. While a student at the University of Georgia, one professor there pronounced Forrest to be "worse than Hitler." A contemporary student of Civil War atrocities observed unequivocally, "If any Southerner deserved a speedy trial and swift punishment, it was Nathan B. Forrest."[5] Whatever the validity of such views, they do not help us understand what occurred in April 1864 any better than the apologist expressions that Forrest bore no responsibility or that the members of the garrison deserved their fates because of the choices they made and the actions they took. While either position may be enough for some, neither has held here.

In addition to visiting Fort Pillow many times, in a little over a year's time, I had the opportunity to tour the sites of four engagements in which large numbers of individuals fell in combat after they were unable to render an effective defense. In the cases of San Jacinto (April 1836), the William J. Fetterman fight (December 1866), Little Big Horn (June 1876), and Wounded Knee (December 1890), much could be drawn upon for offering a better understanding of what happened at Fort Pillow in April 1864.

As with any project of this type, many individuals have offered valuable assistance and support at various levels. The University of Virginia's College at Wise was most generous in supporting the research, travel, and writing required through resources made possible from the Kenneth Asbury Chair of History. Darlene Moore in the Provost's Office was particularly helpful in this regard. Robin Benke and his excellent staff at the John Cook Wyllie Library helped with interlibrary loans and access to sources. Rhonda Bentley provided departmental support in various and important ways. Josh Jackson, an undergraduate student at the University of Virginia's College at Wise, helped with microfilm of the Memphis Daily Appeal.

Since arriving at Kennesaw State University in Georgia to assume the directorship of the Center for the Study of the Civil War Era, the same has been true of that institution. Assistance with sources through the Horace W. Sturgis Library has been superb, as has the support from former dean Richard Vengroff and Dean Robin Dorff, as well as his office personnel, and Megan McDonald of the Department of History and Philosophy. Thanks especially to former associate director Hermina Glass-Avery and the Center's assistant director, Mike Shaffer, for helping to keep the office in good order while the work on this volume progressed.

The staffs of numerous libraries and archives have also been helpful with their assistance. Visits to or contacts with the following yielded significant resources; thanks to the professionals and student assistants who worked there: the Southern Historical Collection at the University of North Carolina, the Perkins Library at Duke University, the Military History Institute at Carlisle Barracks, the Navarro College Archives, the Virginia Historical Society, Kennesaw Mountain National Battlefield Park, and the National Archives.

I have appreciated the patience and endurance Charles Rankin, editor at the University of Oklahoma Press, has exhibited as the long process has moved forward. My gratitude also goes to the other members of the press for their collaborative efforts and for the excellent editing work of Kevin Brock.

Family is always critical in such endeavors. They are the ones who endure as we scholars grapple with the process of research and publication that is frequently inscrutable to everyone else. Elizabeth and the rest of the extended family in Virginia and Georgia have aided this historical journey in every sense. I am grateful for their support.

Finally, I have chosen to dedicate this volume to two exceptional individuals: Edwin C. Bearss and W. Harrison Daniel. Ed Bearss has served as a mentor and friend. We have developed a special relationship when it comes to General Forrest, particularly in regard to the action that took place at Fort Pillow, and have tramped the ground at that site on numerous occasions. I admire this greatest of all battlefield guides tremendously. It is for this reason, as well as for the appreciation he has built within me to attempt to understand the battlefields themselves as thoroughly as possible, that I have made the dedication.

Harrison Daniel was my first Civil War professor when I attended the University of Richmond. He taught me as a history major and gently encouraged me to pursue my studies at the graduate level. His requirement of reading a cutting-edge volume called *The Confederacy as a Revolutionary Experience* by a University of Georgia professor named Emory M. Thomas steered me in that scholar's direction.

Teaching and scholarship are important professional and personal imperatives for me, though no less than the desire to come to a better understanding of the ground and conditions that relate to the events under examination. I am indebted to the influences of both of these individuals in ways that are difficult to calculate in tangible form. I hope this volume, for whose weaknesses they bear no responsibility, serves as some measure of recompense for the inspiration they have provided me.

# THE RIVER WAS DYED
WITH BLOOD

# INTRODUCTION

## *Race, War, Propaganda, and Memory*

If human testimony ever did or can establish anything then [Fort Pillow] is proved a case of deliberate, wholesale massacre of prisoners of war after they had surrendered.

*New York Tribune editor Horace Greeley, 1867*

It would be well to have the report and accompanying papers published in refutation of the slanders which have been promulgated by the Government of the enemy in relation to the conduct of our gallant and humane soldiers.

*Confederate president Jefferson Davis, August 10, 1864*

Mention of the words "Fort Pillow" has produced mental images of war in its worst incarnation since April 1864.[1] Antipathy and opportunity combined to produce what appeared to so many to be murder on a grand scale sufficient to warrant affixing the term "massacre" to the events that took place at that isolated fortification on the Mississippi River north of Memphis. Historian and Nathan Bedford Forrest biographer Robert Selph Henry terms Fort Pillow "*the* 'atrocity' of the war."[2] Clement Eaton uses the same terminology in his volume on the Southern Confederacy.[3] Writer George Burkhardt explains, "While it was not the first, last, or largest, the massacre that ensued was the only one widely and almost immediately publicized by many different sources from both sides."[4]

The Confederate commander at the engagement was himself embroiled in controversy throughout his lifetime. A prewar slave dealer, slave owner, and planter, Nathan Bedford Forrest was also closely associated with the spread of the Ku Klux Klan during Reconstruction, although not as the founder of the organization as is often popularly held. A more convenient subject for pillorying could hardly be conjured. The North at that time was not only in the midst of a war (that it would win in a year's time) but also a presidential-election year. Political figures, newspaper editors, and illustrators eagerly exploited the opportunity Forrest presented to further their own agendas.

In their examination of the "Forrest myth," Paul Ashdown and Edward Caudill observe: "The Forrest of popular memory is a character starkly drawn, the edges of his character as sharp as the cavalryman's bloodied saber. He has neither nuance nor complexity."[5] Thus, Nathan Bedford Forrest has become little more than the sum of parts that range from "untutored military genius" and "wizard of the saddle" to "slavetrader," "Klansman," and "butcher of Fort Pillow." The man became nestled somewhere beneath the popular images, the myths, and the legends.

Likewise, Fort Pillow has served as the means by which Forrest can be judged with relative ease. Writer Andrew Ward asserts that "most people who have committed a crime" spend much of their time and emotional capital denying that such a crime took place, "not because they did not commit it but because they refuse to be defined by it."[6] Of course, some figures have reveled in the notoriety produced by their misdemeanors and the definition and public reaction these acts provided.

This was true of Forrest to a point. He enjoyed notoriety of a sort, particularly when the reputation of an intimidating persona helped him achieve his aims, but not the kind that Fort Pillow generated, precisely because he did not want to be defined by a crime he did not believe he had committed. In any event, the Confederate cavalryman was neither evil incarnate, despite the popular term "devil" often applied to him, nor somehow innocent of excesses that happened within his command, not to mention his own tendency toward intemperate embellishment and justification after the fact.

Those who took positions on either side on the affair were prone to view the action on April 12 in terms that met their requirements. For the Union, election-year politicking sought a convenient Confederate scapegoat that would stir an enraged populace into greater support for a war that seemed to drag on and on with no apparent end in sight. For the Confederacy, defense of the indefensible became the norm. In the years that followed, imperatives that ranged from the desire for reconciliation among former sectional antagonists to the maintenance of white supremacy colored the views people held of Fort Pillow.

Even the terms involved in an examination of the events on the banks of the Mississippi, and elsewhere before, during, and after the Civil War, have offered their own set of challenges. In his introduction to a work dedicated to assessing "Racial Atrocities and Reprisals in the Civil War," historian Gregory J. W. Urwin identifies the "values of the Confederacy and its people." He explains, "Certain that black Union soldiers were too barbarous to abide by the rules of civilized warfare, Confederates felt absolved of observing such rules themselves," thus allowing these Southerners to become "savages themselves." Applying the brush of condemnation broadly to the individuals who wore gray or butternut, he maintains that "Confederate racial atrocities" begat Union "reprisals" so that, in effect, white Southerners bore responsibility for those actions too. Urwin recognizes that, "[f]or the most part, white soldiers tended to grant quarter to surrendering or wounded white opponents" but argues that "Confederates denied black Union soldiers the same respect and consideration, not so much for any crimes they may have committed, but for who they were and the social revolution that they represented." Even so, he insists that despite emphasizing the many "war crimes" in his work, "its purpose is not to depict the average Confederate soldier as a war criminal" and notes that while "some Johnny Rebs" demonstrated racially based ruthlessness against their opponents, "many others chose not to do so." Although commendably attempting to shed light upon the darkness characterizing portions of the Civil War and thereby debunking the myth that this war was somehow glorious, the characterization of "Confederate terror tactics" suggests a cohesiveness in policy and thought that does not actually appear to have existed.[7]

In his essay on atrocities in Arkansas, Urwin asserts, "The war crimes at Poison Spring and Marks's Mills were not isolated outbursts of senseless racial violence but part of an ongoing program of racial intimidation that took its cues from the basic values of antebellum Southern society." Yet it cannot be determined by extant evidence that Confederate leaders, not to mention the officers and men in the field, followed any defined, deliberate, and uniform "program" toward enemy combatants (or even noncombatants) they confronted at Fort Pillow or elsewhere. Complicating this assessment, when the modern historian insists upon motivation for the perpetrators of racial killings, Urwin reveals the variety of legitimate interpretations that could be employed. "As far as the men who did the killing were concerned," he explains, "they had simply made examples of some disloyal slaves to deter other blacks from betraying their masters or giving further aid and comfort to the enemy."[8] Indeed, the employment of such an object lesson in deterrence undoubtedly existed in the minds of some, if not most, of the Confederates involved. Yet anger at aiding an enemy intent upon inflicting harm was enough to stir resentments against black soldiers. This, rather than some systematic or programmatic element, was sufficient for these excesses to occur on battlefields, as they occasionally did.

The work of the joint committee of the U.S. Congress that investigated the "Fort Pillow massacre" has provided the means and context by which contemporaries and historians have viewed this event. It would be difficult to dismiss the testimony of victims regardless of its nature and circumstances, but one of the often overlooked aspects of the atrocity reports is that a long-standing tradition already existed for demonizing and dehumanizing divergent elements in American society. In his study of the literature that featured virulent attacks on excesses attributed to Masons, Catholics, and Mormons, historian David Brion Davis maintains, "The obsession with details of sadism . . . showed a furious determination to purge the enemy of every admirable quality." He concludes, "In such a role the subversive seemed to deserve both righteous anger and the most terrible punishment."[9] Detaching the opponent from his humanity could be useful in many regards, not the least in elevating one side by highlighting the depravity of the other.

Regardless of the differences in interpretation and point of view, basic facts remain indisputable. Men died at Fort Pillow who should not have been killed given the circumstances of their demise. These deaths were reprehensible, a regrettable corollary to the heat of battle, the social and racial hostilities many felt toward their opponents, and the decisions of the officers and men of both sides under the stresses and strains of death and battle. Chaos and panic were key factors in exacerbating the conditions that led to excesses once organized resistance had ceased.

Yet the facts have been equally clear that the Union soldiers who fell in the engagement were not the victims of a plot to exterminate them by a pitiless Confederate commander bent on their destruction. Defeating them was sufficient to satisfy the general, if not all of the men under his command. Fort Pillow proved to be a volatile arena of human emotions that easily got out of hand and, until the demand for violence had been satiated in blood, difficult to bring back under control, even for a force of nature as powerful as Nathan Bedford Forrest.

"Massacre" and "atrocity" have become all-the-more powerful and troubling concepts in recent years. The prolific historian Stephen Ambrose set his skills to an analysis of the My Lai incident involving Lieutenant William Calley in the Vietnam Conflict. He opens his essay on the subject by describing the "painful task—to examine a side of war that is hard to face up to but is always there." Citing the universality of the phenomenon, he determines that "My Lai was not an exception or an aberration." His conclusion is as universally applicable: "Atrocity is a part of war that needs to be recognized and discussed."[10]

Indeed, when the 1864 fighting occurred there, Fort Pillow already had an historical context. Americans in the Civil War could look back at similar events in their shared national history. Among the most powerful of these occurred in the war colonial Americans had waged against Great Britain and each other in the 1770s and 1780s. Especially in the southernmost colonies later in the American Revolution, the combat took on the qualities of civil war, pitting colonial Whigs and Tories against each other in brutal and merciless warfare.

Perhaps most symbolic of the British side of this equation was a young, ambitious, and ruthless lieutenant colonel named Banastre Tarleton. Historian Dan Morrill has termed the haughty redcoat officer the "most infamous practitioner of rampageous behavior in the Royal army during the southern campaign," pointing particularly to his actions against opposing troops at the Waxhaws, South Carolina, on May 29, 1780.[11] Coming after the fall of Charleston to British forces, the Waxhaws occurred when reinforcements meant to assist in the port city's defense began to withdraw toward North Carolina. Some 350–400 Virginia Continentals, led by Colonel Abraham Buford and encumbered with wagons, moved so slowly over indifferent roads as to allow approximately 270 of Tarleton's men to overtake them.

Buford's command proved no match for Tarleton's Legion, holding fire until the opposing horsemen were upon them and then breaking in confusion. As historian Jim Piecuch has explained, "Some of Colonel Buford's Continentals fought and some tried to surrender during this brief battle, while others fled."[12] The chaotic nature of the panic and fighting provided a potent mixture into which the redcoats blended a simmering rage at rebellion against the Crown and bloodlust. Even though some officers, including Tarleton himself, tried to reassert a sense of order, Piecuch concludes, "some British troops did not bother to make a distinction between men who had laid down their arms and those alongside them who continued to fight."[13]

At the Waxhaws, the colonial force sustained 113 killed and 150 wounded, some of whom became victims to overzealous redcoats as the fighting subsided and even after it ended. Tarleton described the furor of some of his men as indicative of a "vindictive asperity not easily restrained." Surgeon Robert Brownfield, who was present with Buford's command, recalled vividly this expression of "vindictive asperity" toward helpless Colonials: "The demand for quarters, seldom refused to a vanquished foe, was at once found to be in vain;—not a man was spared—and it was the concurrent testimony of all the survivors, that for fifteen minutes after every man was prostrate." Brownfield further asserted that some of Tarleton's men "went over the ground plunging their bayonets into every one that exhibited any signs of life," even to the extent of removing corpses from atop fallen men to finish those who lay beneath.[14] Although "Bloody Tarleton" and "Tarleton's Quarter" became popular terms for this lack of mercy, later historians have determined that the British officer deserved less personal censure for what also is known as "Buford's Massacre."[15]

Regardless of subsequent assessments, contemporary perceptions ensured that Patriot emotions remained high in the aftermath of the incident. Additional excesses occurred during the months that followed in small actions that featured fierce fighting between Patriots and Loyalists. Eventually, an opportunity for revenge on a larger scale occurred when flamboyant British major Patrick Ferguson took his command of 1,125 Loyalists into the South Carolina backcountry in October 1780. A force of backwoodsmen gathered to intercept the expedition. Aware that his opponents were closing but dismissing them as "backwater barbarians," Ferguson determined to confront them if necessary. He brought his command to the crest of Kings Mountain, near the North Carolina line, and encamped them to await developments.

The necessity for a fight arose as the determined Patriots reached the location by midafternoon on October 7, securing their animals before moving against the Loyalist position. At the start of this expedition, Ferguson had used what would be labeled at best intemperate language to motivate his supporters. Referring to "an inundation of barbarians ... who by their shocking cruelties and irregularities, give the best proof of their cowardice and want of discipline," the major admonished loyal British citizens to avoid abuse "by the dregs of mankind," who threatened them and their families. "The Backwater men have crossed the Mountain," he assured his Loyalists. "If you choose to be pissed upon forever and ever by a set of mongrels, say so at once and let your women turn their backs upon you, and look out for real men to protect them."[16] Ferguson had meant to inflame the passions of a pro-British citizenry as a call to arms but at the same time reflected the dehumanizing manner of the warfare he determined to wage.

Unfortunately for the proud Scot, clad in a bright hunting shirt, repeatedly sounding a shrill hunting whistle, and perched atop a white horse, this day at Kings Mountain was not meant to go well. Projectiles from the rifles of Patriot marksmen tore into Ferguson. The major reeled from his saddle, his foot caught in a stirrup, and he suffered the ignominious fate of being dragged along as the frightened animal galloped away.

Ferguson's second in command, Captain Abraham de Peyster from New York, recognized that the battle had turned against their forces and sought a cessation of the fighting. Many of the angry frontiersmen would accept no recognition of surrender from their opponents. Shouting "Tarleton's Quarter" as an indication of their sentiments, these men continued to fire into their enemies, even as the latter sought the presumed safety of capitulation. Colonial leader Isaac Shelby admitted: "It was some time before a complete cessation of the firing on our part could be effected. Our men had been scattered in the woods and were continually coming up and continued to fire, without comprehending in the heat of the moment what had happened." The officer added that "some" of the incensed soldiery, "who had heard that at Buford's defeat the British had refused quarters [to surrendering Americans] . . . were willing to follow that bad example."[17] Altogether, 157 Loyalists perished, with another 163 wounded, while the Patriots lost 28 killed and 62 wounded. The fallen British commander suffered the final indignity of having his earlier words turned against him as some of the militiamen relieved themselves on his corpse. One historian has concluded, "Such was the character of fratricidal conflict in the South during the American Revolution."[18]

Just over half a century later, similar emotions broiled among some Texans when Sam Houston's tremendous April 21, 1836, victory at San Jacinto avenged the earlier murders of Texan combatants and prisoners alike at the Alamo and Goliad. Once Houston's men had broken the Mexican line of defense, the fighting degenerated into individualized actions that quickly swirled out of anyone's control. Mercy depended upon the mindset of the persons involved, and many of the Texans were not in the mood to offer their defeated opponents much in the way of that precious commodity.

One Houston biographer explains, "Even though the Mexican soldiers threw down their arms and on their knees begged for mercy, the Texans shot, clubbed, and stabbed them to death—even the wounded." Then he describes a phase of the battle that eerily foreshadowed the aftermath of Fort Pillow almost twenty-eight years later. "Those who fled into the marsh were picked off from the bank."[19] The scene of slaughter continued unabated even as some Texans sought to protect prisoners or assuage the anger of their comrades.[20]

Another Houston biographer has assessed San Jacinto and the general's role in the aftermath. "It was a total rout and a gruesome disaster for the Mexican army," James Haley observes. "Once resistance was over, Houston attempted to regroup his men but was unable to stop the slaughter." Sam Houston's physically demanding day on the battlefield left him battered, weary, and wounded.[21] Bedford Forrest could legitimately make the same claim at Fort Pillow, where he experienced a similar inability to control some of the actions of his troops. Yet no one has thought to accuse Houston of attempting to carry out a deliberate policy of murdering prisoners or of tacitly approving by turning his back while such murders took place.

At Buena Vista, Mexico, in February 1847, an overriding sense of fear compounded the chaos and confusion of the ebb and flow of battle to create conditions that produced panic among some of the American combatants. These men poured into a deep ravine hoping to find either cover or an opportunity for escape only to learn that they were trapped. Heavy Mexican fire pinned them to their locations while lancers threatened to impale those who tried to find egress. One of the participants, a future Union general named William H. L. Wallace, expressed his surprise that greater casualties did not ensue. "They are most miserable shots," he concluded of his adversaries, "or they would have killed every one of us huddled as we were in the utter confusion."[22] He ultimately made a successful dash to safety, but many of those who had been with him were not so fortunate, Mexican lancers having the tendency to offer little pity to those who could be run down.[23]

If previous experiences in the Revolutionary War South, Texas, or Mexico could provide context, it should not be surprising that contemporary references to the savagery displayed at Fort Pillow were also meant to evoke popular conceptions of conflicts with Native Americans. Tales of scalping, kidnapping, slaughter, and torture had permeated the American psychological landscape since the days of colonial settlement and provided easy, immediately understood reference points for examples of uncivilized warfare.

During the Civil War and a month before Fort Pillow, there were indications elsewhere that racial antagonism would exacerbate emotions triggered as white Confederates confronted armed black Federals. At Suffolk, Virginia, in March 1864, a running fight occurred between North Carolinians and former slaves, many of whom came from the surrounding region. Captain Henry Chambers of the 49th North Carolina recorded in his diary that a rider approached the Confederates as they neared Suffolk urging them to hasten their pace if they were going to catch a Union patrol before it could depart. "Colonel for God's sake hurry your men on or you will be too late," he implored. Then the messenger turned to the soldiers themselves, calling to them, "Run boys, run, and we will catch the G—d d—d niggers yet!" Chambers noted, "We were nearly exhausted with our long double quick but when told 'that the hated negroes had been encountered,' we received as it were renewed vigor and on we pushed." Civilians along the route likewise encouraged the men. "Do hurry friends or they will get away." But even with the ability to lob shells from the artillery that accompanied them, the Confederates could not prevent the majority of Union troops from withdrawing. "We could see the negroe cavalry scatter when the shells would fall in their midst," Chambers observed, but the Southerners' lack of mounted troops hampered further pursuit.

Yet even as the main body slipped away, not all of the bluecoats in Suffolk managed to elude their Confederate pursuers. Chambers happened upon the scene of fighting that engulfed a residence on "the eastern edge of the town." Told that the structure contained "negroes," the diarist matter-of-factly recorded, "This house was set on fire and burned before the negroes could be gotten out and killed." The defenders had resisted, and it was unclear from Chambers's account if he meant that they had died in the fire before they "could be gotten out" for capture or that they would have been "killed" regardless.[24]

Another participant offered his view of Confederate motivations toward these Union opponents, who he insisted had occupied the building "for the purpose of picking off our officers."

> Soon the fire and smoke had its effect—suffocation commenced—one of the infernals leaped from the window to escape the horrible death of burning; a minute more and a dozen bayonets pierced his body; another and another followed, and shared the same fate. Three stayed and met their doom with manly resolution. They were burnt to cinders. After the flames had enveloped the house and immense clouds of smoke were issuing from the burning building, where nothing could be seen from within, the crack of a rifle was heard above, and one of the artillery men fell severely wounded in the knee. This was the last fire from the house. See with what determination they continued their work. Twas worthy of a better cause. But death was their doom, and the flames were their choice.[25]

In the aftermath of the engagement, Confederate lieutenant Angus McDonald informed his mother, "General Ransom ... had a fight day before yesterday at Suffolk & killed a bout thirty negrows but took no prisoners." Rather than condemn the practice, the Southerner added, "But that Is something that our soldiers are apt not to do to take any negro souldiers [as captives]."[26] Another boasted subsequently: "We did not take any prisoners. Officers and men were perfectly enthusiastic in *killing* the 'd—d rascals' as I heard many call them. Ransom's brigade never takes any negro prisoners." Of course, the fact was not lost upon him that should the fortunes of war change, the ramifications could be dire. "If some of us should be captured by them, our fate would be hard."[27]

The characteristics of the Suffolk encounter were different in many respects from those seen in western Tennessee a short time later. The Civil War engagement that most approximated Fort Pillow also took place in April 1864 and came when Confederates confronted the Union defenders of Plymouth, North Carolina. These forces included black recruits and noncombatants as well as North Carolina Unionists, or "Buffaloes." Just as in Tennessee, the attacking Confederates threatened "no quarter" as one of the means of producing the surrender of the Plymouth garrison, suggesting that such capitulation would "spare the effusion of blood." But if compelled to attack, "the responsibility for the terrible consequences must rest" on the Union commander's head.

Even with Union brigadier general Henry W. Wessell's determination to surrender, elements of the extended Federal forces continued to resist for a time, adding to the chaos and casualties. Then in the course of the fighting, at least a portion of the African Americans and Buffaloes present fled from the front lines and attempted what one historian has labeled "a desperate rush for the swamps." Confederate troops "intercepted" these "fugitives," killing many of them indiscriminately. A New Yorker who participated in the defense recorded in his diary the next day, "Last evening the Rebs went gunning for the colored troops, who when the 'jig was up' ... broke over the works and took to the woods." He observed conclusively: "They were shot down at sight. It was a massacre."[28]

Nor were all such actions limited to Confederates. Seven months after Fort Pillow at Sand Creek in Colorado Territory, militia under the command of Union colonel John Chivington demonstrated merciless ferocity against Native American opponents that included women and children in an attack that featured stories of butchery and mutilation. Four years later George Armstrong Custer carried out a brutal assault on a Cheyenne camp along the Washita River in November 1868. Frustration, chaos, and opportunity in that instance produced a substantial level of indiscriminate killing among the Cheyenne of all ages and regardless of gender. Custer took steps to limit the killing of noncombatants before breaking off what he termed "a regular Indian 'Sailor's Creek,'" alluding to a disastrous defeat for Southern arms in the latter stages of the Civil War.[29]

Subsequently at Little Big Horn in 1876, in what proved to be Custer's final campaign, the nature of some of the deaths and the treatment of many of the slain soldiers challenged the sensibilities of individuals who knew only what newspapers and stories told them of native culture and customs. While an assessment of the engagement illustrated the effects of the breakdown of unit cohesion as panicked troopers either sought to ward off their attackers in small defensive knots or scattered for what they hoped would be an opportunity for salvation. Instead, the circumstances limited the effectiveness of any defense and led to these soldiers being overwhelmed.[30]

A few years later at Wounded Knee, an attempt to disarm and over-awe Sioux warriors led to a brutal demonstration of power. As individuals sought cover in a nearby ravine, U.S. troops poured a murderous fire upon combatants and noncombatants alike. One historian, who compared warfare in southern Africa with that on the American plains, concludes that whether the incident was a regrettable corollary of frontier fighting or "a deliberate massacre" depended "to some extent on one's point of view."[31]

Examples from international conflicts exemplify the ways in which combatants caught up in the fury of combat exhibited chilling behaviors toward enemies who had ceased to resist effectively. At Majuba Hill in southern Africa in February 1881, surprised and poorly positioned British troops fought and then fled from their Boer attackers. "Soldiers were shot down like bolting rabbits," one historian notes of the lopsided affair.[32]

Only two years earlier such a startling defeat had come at the hands of Zulus in the Battle of Isandlwana, where a vainglorious commander named Lord Chelmsford lost a significant portion of his command. The collapse of the defense of the British camp there resulted in widespread carnage. "Soon the track was blocked by panic-stricken men, many of them wounded, screaming for help," a student of the engagement has explained. Most of these desperate refugees "had no chance," he notes, and perished in the effort.[33] A subsequent campaign allowed British forces to bring the full brunt of modern weaponry and a desire for vengeance over this humbling defeat to bear in fighting around Ulundi. Those soldiers exacted their revenge with artillery, Gatling guns, and lances, exhibiting little compassion toward their adversaries and a disdain for taking prisoners.[34]

Perhaps no cruelty in the period matched the German policy toward the Herero people of southwest Africa, which featured driving them into the desert and sealing off the wells in what was ostensibly a military operation. Vowing that every Herero man, woman, or child found in the region "will be shot," General Lothar von Trotha took such decisive and ruthless steps to rid the German colony of native peoples. The architect of what amounted to an extermination program received the Order of Merit for his efforts.[35]

For Americans in the early part of the twentieth century, there was probably no warfare more brutal than that which occurred in the Philippines in the aftermath of the war with Spain in 1898. Unharmed captives were luxuries on either side of what developed into a vicious guerrilla-style war. Some of the American forces skirted with the edges of brutality as they applied programs to encourage prisoners to divulge useful information, including the "water cure." This procedure called for the forced introduction of copious amounts of water into an individual's system and then the dramatic release of the same by stomping on the stomach. Circumstances were hardly better for U.S. troops taken captive, for whom torture and death were likely outcomes, including the staking out of prisoners.[36]

Some of the terminology emanating from soldier correspondence might easily be mistaken as coming from the conflict of the 1860s rather than the one of the early 1900s. Writing about how he had advanced through muddy water, one combatant insisted, "we did not mind it a bit, our fighting blood was up, and we all wanted to kill 'niggers.'" Comparing the experience favorably to sport—"beats rabbit hunting all to pieces"—the same man concluded: "We charged them and such a slaughter you never saw. We killed them like rabbits; hundreds, yes thousands of them." Almost nonchalantly he added, "Every one was crazy."[37]

Another incident in the Philippine War reflects similarities with what had occurred to the defeated combatants at San Jacinto and Fort Pillow. Trapping an enemy force against a river, one man recalled, "many were shot down like sheep" as they attempted to swim for safety. "It was a glorious victory but a horrible slaughter," the U.S. soldier observed.[38]

A guerrilla assault on an American unit reflected the vicious nature of warfare on both sides, with the bolo, or sharpened machete, frequently being the Filipino weapon of choice. The deaths that resulted were gruesome, with mutilations another common and effective psychological element. As one historian describes the fate of some of the U.S. troops in the final stages of one particular attack, "A few who sought flight in the water nearby were hunted down in boats and boloed to death."[39]

British historian John Keegan selected several examples of the deaths of men after fighting had subsided to describe inhumanity under the stresses and strains of war. Two of these incidents occurred during World War I, at the Third Battle of Ypres and at the Somme. In each instance men acted under circumstances that could not be attributed to battle but were direct corollaries of it. A third example came from the Italian front during World War II, when men in the "Irish Guards" killed Germans "who delayed their surrender" with the admonition, "Too late, chum."[40] Keegan recognizes that behaviors on the field and those dictated in training manuals do not always coincide. "For if one admits that the behaviour of a group of soldiers on any part of the battlefield ought to be understood in terms of their corporate mood, or of the conditions there prevailing at the time, indeed in terms of anything but their willingness to do [only] as duty, discipline, and orders demand, then the whole idea of the outcome of a battle being determined by one commander's defter manipulation of his masses against his opponent's crumbles."[41]

During World War II, an American officer was concerned that in the charged atmosphere of the aftermath of the Normandy invasion, excesses were bound to occur. "We needed prisoners for interrogating," he recalled afterward, "so I ordered the men not to shoot."[42] That at least this individual felt the necessity to issue such orders, then later to register such concerns, is telling. He certainly believed that if he did not require that his soldiers make a concerted effort to obtain prisoners of the Germans they encountered, there might be none to question afterward for intelligence purposes. An officer in the famed 101st Airborne Division let the gesture of offering cigarettes to captive Nazis turn into a gruesome demonstration of callousness when he suddenly gunned the men down as they smoked. The soldier then continued his duties as if nothing had been amiss.[43]

The situation was even more troublesome in the Pacific Theater of Operations. In what one author terms "war without mercy," antagonists on both sides demonstrated little compunction to spare prisoners. "Of greater interest," John W. Dower writes, "is what the reminiscences [of some of the Allied soldiers] reveal: that many men in the field participated in or at least witnessed the killing of helpless, wounded, or captured Japanese."[44]

The latter examples occurred in the context of a war in which the sides were clearly defined between the forces of democracy and those of totalitarianism. How much more difficult to label such extremes when Americans fought Americans, both sides claiming the same democratic roots, historical heritage, and divine guidance.

Battle fury and chaos, panic and pursuit, racial and sectional antagonism, all were present as factors at Fort Pillow. The results of this combination of elements on the field added to the intensities and uncertainties of a world in transition and an election through which war-weary Northern voters appeared to require motivation to support the Lincoln administration. Americans in blue and gray actually needed little encouragement to place the events of April 12, 1864, into contexts that fit into their notions of what society and warfare ought to be.

For *New York Tribune* editor Horace Greeley, who had taken Abraham Lincoln to task for not moving more swiftly on emancipation, the evidence of a massacre at Fort Pillow and the moral indignation it engendered were unmistakably clear. "If human testimony ever did or can establish anything then [Fort Pillow] is proved a case of deliberate, wholesale massacre of prisoners of war after they had surrendered."[45] Many white and black Americans shared this view and the sense of outrage that accompanied it.

On the other side of the dividing line, in late August 1864 Jefferson Davis, as was his habit, appended a short notation to correspondence related to Fort Pillow for Secretary of War James A. Seddon. "It would be well to have the report and accompanying papers published in refutation of the slanders which have been promulgated by the Government of the enemy in relation to the conduct of our gallant and humane soldiers." The Confederate president's conclusion was certainly self-serving, except for the fact that it was intended as a private communication with his war secretary and not for public consumption or posterity's approval. "Instead of cruelty," he noted carefully, "General Forrest, it appears, exhibited forbearance and clemency far exceeding the usage of war under like circumstances."[46]

Davis labeled his postwar assessment, found in his 1890 edition of *A Short History of the Confederate States of America,* "Fort Pillow" and included no references to excesses or massacres. In it he provides a brief, antiseptic overview of the engagement, arguing that the loss of life came when the garrison rejected a demand to surrender, thus necessitating an assault. Furthermore, when the attack occurred, the chaotic conditions of the retreat produced the casualties, which only Southern restraint prevented from being greater.[47]

These disparate views of the same event illustrate the difficulty that has existed in arriving at a balanced view of the action at Fort Pillow. Obviously, contemporaries on either side of the conflict found common ground difficult to locate. Likewise, many historians have fared little better in avoiding extremes. Some of these have condemned Forrest and his men out of hand for what happened, stridently ignoring factors that suggest otherwise; others have defended the general and the troops without a great deal of reservation or qualification, insisting that the members of the garrison or their commanders brought on the dire consequences that befell many of them. While either of these positions could be sustained to a point, the truth of what happened on April 12, 1864, lies somewhere between them, incorporating elements of both.

History is less the determination of absolute certainty or truth about any person or event than it is the construction, or reconstruction, of that subject based upon the available evidence. The difficulty always arises from the attempt to create a plausible and convincing explanation that is as objective as human interpretation will allow. The fact that others will disagree and offer viewpoints of their own is a welcome and necessary part of the process.

As is true with all things historical, the story of Fort Pillow is much more complex than the extreme views of either side have allowed. A thorough analysis demonstrates that the engagement that took place in April 1864 was indicative of neither a policy of "massacre" carried out "deliberately" by the Confederates nor a wholesale Northern fabrication meant to discredit Nathan Bedford Forrest and the Confederate States of America. Evidence indicates that elements of both extremist perspectives have worked in shaping and explaining events for the convenience of their respective point of view.

In the final analysis Fort Pillow is a study in race, war, and the roles of propaganda, interpretation, and memory regarding an understanding of the events that took place on that field. The most significant aspect of the story is its context in a world under the pressures and transitions attendant to war. For this reason as much as any other, the events that occurred on the banks of the Mississippi River in April 1864 can really only be understood by peeling away multiple layers, often produced simultaneously, of shared historical and cultural experiences, political imperatives and opportunities, and the nature of human beings in wartime conditions.

If, as historians Paul Ashdown and Edward Caudill observe, "[w]hat happened there [at Fort Pillow] would become the most important element of the Forrest Myth," then it becomes all the more incumbent to come to grips with that engagement and its aftermath. Of course, no single study will provide all of the answers and settle the debate on what happened at Fort Pillow and why. As will be seen, it is impossible to separate any, much less all, of the complex motivations from which individuals, past and present, have viewed the actions in far western Tennessee. Perhaps the best that can be done is to raise points that will help clarify those events and provide a greater understanding of one of the Civil War's darkest chapters.

CHAPTER 1

# WARRIOR IN AN UNCIVIL WAR

## 1821–1864

I did not come here to make half a job of it. I mean to have them all.

*Nathan Bedford Forrest at Murfreesboro, Tennessee, July 13, 1862*

Whenever you see anything blue, shoot at it, and do all you can to keep up the scare.

*Forrest in pursuit of Abel Streight, May 1863*

I'm tired of sacrificing lives, and I offer you a chance to stop it. If you don't, I won't be answerable for the consequences.

*Forrest to Streight, May 1863*

[M]y idée is, to always git the most men thar fust, and then, ef you can't whup 'em, outrun 'em.

*Forrest to fellow generals, September 1863*

The man who led his men in the action at Fort Pillow, Tennessee, on April 12, 1864, was a product of the Tennessee backcountry. Nathan Bedford Forrest began his life on July 13, 1821, near the small hamlet of Chapel Hill.[1] He grew up in an isolated environment that required self-reliance at an early age. Forrest quickly learned the harsh lessons of life in the hinterlands from the dangers that required prompt action to overcome. For a youth with only six months of formal education, these lessons came largely from his life experiences rather than through the classroom, although Bedford Forrest demonstrated himself to be a quick and able learner as he matured.

Forrest's world inured him to hardship and danger. He responded to these elements by attacking them head on, his compensation no doubt for the fear that lay deep inside. He illustrated this himself with the story of a routine event that nearly led to disaster. Apparently, one of young Forrest's chores included watering the family's animals. In the process he passed a cabin whose occupants owned dogs that enjoyed the diversion of chasing after the horses. The boy thrilled in the game as well, tossing sticks and rocks at the pursuers from the supposed security of the saddle until he was out of their range. Unfortunately, on one occasion the horse on which he rode did not properly appreciate the arrangement, and when the dogs came roaring after them, the frightened animal bolted and bucked his rider from his perch. Forrest recalled that as he hurled through the air and then plummeted toward ground, he expected to be torn to shreds but was determined to sell his life as dearly as possible. Yet instead of perishing at the fangs of vicious canines, he noticed that the dogs were racing in the opposite direction. In the common practice of the chase, they had never experienced a rock as big as a boy.

On that day Bedford Forrest learned that his opponents in any clash were as afraid of him as he was of them. He came to understand how to turn their fear to his advantage while simultaneously harnessing his own. By mastering himself, he hoped to control a situation and defeat any foe that might rise to challenge him. "Get 'em skeered and then keep the skeer on 'em," he observed as his unique articulation of that principle.[2] Consequently, in scrapes throughout his life and in virtually every circumstance he faced on the battlefield, Forrest emerged successful more often than not through sheer grit and determination.

Forrest's penchant for pursuing a defeated foe remained a hallmark of his Civil War experience. He understood that broken units might rally and prove formidable on different ground. In this sense Bedford Forrest shared the outlook of his celebrated comrade from Virginia, Thomas J. "Stonewall" Jackson. "Always mystify, mislead, and surprise the enemy if possible;" Jackson once observed, "and when you strike and overcome him, never let up in the pursuit as long as your men have strength to follow; for an army routed, if hotly pursued, becomes panic-stricken, and can then be destroyed by half their number."[3]

As a soldier, Forrest adapted this aggressiveness to the battlefield with ease. "Whenever you meet the enemy," he liked to say, "no matter how few there are of you or how many of them, show fight." Forrest knew that to exhibit weakness or indecision was tantamount to inviting attack. "If you show fight," he explained, "they will think there are more of you, and will not push you half so hard."[4] In his pursuit of Union raiders across northern Alabama, the Confederate admonished his men, "Whenever you see anything blue, shoot at it, and do all you can to keep up the scare."[5] At Brice's Cross Roads, Forrest's greatest victory, he described the advantages of a man "in motion" as being "worth two standing."[6] The benefit to be derived from such displays would be twofold: aggressive action would mask one's own vulnerabilities at the same time it kept an adversary off balance and tentative. The result would be to obtain, or retain, the initiative in any confrontation. Again, in his own words, he would often say that his object was to get "the bulge" on his opponent.[7]

In addition to a confidence that came from self-reliance and a tendency toward action rather than passive contemplation, Forrest learned and utilized other skills that served him well. It is difficult to say with any exactitude at what point he took up what became a lifelong interest in gambling. Forrest was proficient at riding and liked to race horses. It was a logical progression for him that wagers entered into the process, and as he began to play cards for money, that aspect of competitive engagement occupied a larger place in his life and thoughts.[8] A contemporary account asserts the extraordinary claim that "although he seldom gambled, he never left a race-course or a card table a loser."[9]

As a soldier, Bedford Forrest was able to apply the skills these games of chance perfected in him to situations in combat with consistent success. It is clear that his opponents in battle, as well as those who competed against him over the poker table, faced a formidable foe. Indeed, as one of Forrest's commanding officers assessed after the war, "He was a great poker player and illustrated some of its principles and technicalities on the battle-field."[10] Another source from the period notes simply, "He seldom gambled with [the lives of] his men, if I may appropriate the term, unless, as he expressed it, he thought he 'had a dead thing.'"[11]

To these characteristics Forrest added an almost innate understanding of human nature. He knew how to motivate people when he wanted them to follow a particular path. He knew just as well how to intimidate them when they interfered with a course he had set for himself. Bedford Forrest honed the personal tools that rested on these instincts through his practical experiences in the backcountry and his earliest interactions with other human beings. He recognized the basic truth that when an individual or individuals have entered into a combat situation, or other life-threatening circumstance, the prime motivation would be survival.[12]

Throughout his life, Forrest also exhibited a temper that was legendary in its proportions and its effect on those around him. One devoted staff officer, D. C. Kelley, noted that circumstances could easily determine his chief's state of mind. "When the Battle was over," he explained of Forrest, "he was like a tiger at bay untill he got a good sleep and during that time we always kept out of his way."[13] At Brice's Cross Roads Forrest's trusted artillery chief, John Morton, issued the cavalry commander orders without initially realizing the implications of his actions. As a searing sweep of recognition overcame him, the cannoneer recalled that he "apologized, but expected, nevertheless, to be invited to attend to his own 'd—d business.'" There was no such response from his volatile chief on that occasion, but Morton knew he was fortunate to have avoided one.[14]

At other times Forrest was less muted in his reactions. At various points in the war, he clashed with superiors and subordinates, sometimes reaching the point of exchanging blows, before calming down and surveying the differences between them.[15] Unfortunately in the case of Andrew Wills Gould, a violent interaction took place at Columbia, Tennessee, regarding artillery lost during the pursuit of Streight's raiders in April–May 1863 that ultimately cost the young lieutenant his life and nearly ended Forrest's as well.[16] In another instance, only a staffer's timely intercession prevented the general from shooting a private who ran by them toward the rear. "Oh, general, think," the aide called out as Forrest drew his weapon and prepared to fire, causing him to let the fellow go on his way unharmed.[17]

In his early adult years, Forrest went to live and work with a relative in Hernando, Mississippi. He soon found himself embroiled in an argument that resulted in the death of his uncle, Jonathan. But Bedford held his ground and turned back the four attackers, winning the approval of the community.[18] In their appreciation of his courage in the face of long odds, Hernando citizens made young Forrest their coroner, the man who bore the responsibility for collecting local fees.[19]

One individual who had a tremendous calming influence on Forrest was his wife, Mary Ann Montgomery. When they had first met, he knew immediately that she should become his bride and pursued that result with the single-minded determination that he brought to all his serious endeavors. He recognized that her temperament and upbringing differed from his in significant ways. Her guardian balked at Forrest's request for her hand. "You cuss and gamble, and Mary Ann is a Christian girl," the Reverend Samuel Cowan explained. Straightforward in his logic as well as his approach, even with regard to affairs of the heart, Forrest responded: "I know. That's why I want her."[20] An aide later noted simply, "When out of temper he would say 'send for "Old Miss,"'" and Mary's presence would have the desired effect.[21] Mary Ann Forrest's example was so powerful a force in her husband's life that near the end of the war, when he could not be certain about his fate, Forrest sent instructions to his son in which he admonished the young man to "[t]ry to emulate her noble virtues." Candidly, he observed, "If I have been wicked and sinful myself, it would rejoice my heart to see you leading the Christian life which has adorned your mother."[22]

Having married despite the difficulties that faced them, the couple settled down to raise a family in the bustling river town of Memphis. It was here that Bedford Forrest embarked in a serious way on the line of employment that offered him and his family a sense of financial security—the slave trade. Of these activities, Thomas Jordan and J. P. Pryor explain, in a volume that the general critiqued and revised personally, that Forrest was one of "many dealers who overcame the prejudice [against slave traders] by their individual worth and standing."[23] A contemporary summarized Forrest's commercial philosophy succinctly: "His business had been that of a speculator in lands, in negroes, in horses, in cotton, and in fact every thing which was likely to prove lucrative."[24]

Always a man of contradictions, Forrest accepted the practices of others without necessarily indulging in them himself. "My staff does my drinking for me," he once explained when declining the offer of alcohol.[25] In his youth Forrest had survived an encounter with a demijohn that had left him dangerously ill for a time and afterward diminished the desire to repeat the experience.[26] Consequently, he never developed sophistication in his tastes, a comrade noting that the general "did not know whiskey from brandy, but called everything liquor." The same individual remarked that while Forrest "would occasionally swear at my pipe, he never failed to get me a good pouch of tobacco if it came his way."[27]

When it came to his involvement in the slave trade, much would be made by apologists to note the relatively humane way Forrest was supposed to have treated slaves who passed through his mart.[28] As a businessman it was certainly in his best interest to maintain such a reputation, for to have done otherwise would have adversely affected his ability to consummate sales. As an entrepreneur he had known both success and failure, and his hardscrabble background reminded him constantly of the struggles that awaited if his capitalistic ventures proved unsuccessful. "General Forrest is a hard worker," a wartime associate observed. "Everybody about him must be busy."[29] But this driving force existed long before the war and must account in large measure for the dedication with which he approached every task.

As a young man, Forrest usually remained aware of how he presented himself to others. He took care with his appearance and worked diligently to project himself favorably to those he wanted to impress.[30] These early habits persisted through his life and reflected his desire not only for order and control but also for acceptance among his peers. "Few men were neater in personal appearance or his surroundings than General Forrest," one colleague recalled. "He abhorred dirt and disorder," preferring when necessary to "take the broom himself and never stop until things were neat and clean."[31]

Zeal and determination helped make him successful in most of his endeavors, but underlying these traits was more than a hint of intimidation. An assessment at the time of his death reveals insight into his character offered by neighbors in Memphis. "There is no instance of any slave taking advantage of the permission [to go freely into the city] to run away," writer Lafcadio Hearn notes. "Forrest taught them it was in their interest not to abuse the privilege; and as he also taught them to fear him exceedingly, I can believe the story."[32] Despite the implications of physical force suggested in the usual application of such lessons, Forrest seemed to combine an understanding of human nature and the use of reward to achieve his goals rather than rely solely on abject brutality. Fear of his mighty wrath had a controlling effect on more than a few persons, black or white, throughout Forrest's life and could not be discounted.

In any case, when it came to his civilian pursuits, Bedford Forrest continued to make his mark wherever he could. He developed his plantation property in northern Mississippi and plied his trade, becoming the largest slave dealer in Memphis, with a trading network that extended across substantial portions of the South. An individual who knew him during this period observed that Forrest established a business reputation that enabled him to become successful. "He grew rich apace," he recalled in an 1864 sketch of the general, and by the start of the war, Forrest "was one of the wealthiest planters whose home was in Memphis." Most importantly, from a capitalistic or entrepreneurial perspective, "His credit with merchants and bankers was limitless."[33] Forrest also obtained a level of legitimacy in Memphis, where he served as an alderman for two consecutive terms from 1858 to 1860.[34]

Forrest was not averse to exhibiting an image of determination when he felt that circumstances warranted. Just prior to becoming an alderman, he became involved in an incident that revealed a great deal about his character, especially with regard to his public persona. The story involved the "rescue" of a young man named John Able who was about to be lynched by an enraged mob of Memphians in 1857. The situation developed after Able had killed a fellow gambler who was trying to collect a debt.[35]

According to the version presented by the general's earliest postwar biographers, only Forrest's vaunted courage stood between the alleged murderer and eternity for the young man at the hands of a lynch mob.

"Pressing through the turbulent masses with much difficulty up to where Able was standing with the rope around his neck, his mother and sister by his side making piteous, tearful appeals to the implacable throng around for the life of their kinsman," the stalwart backwoodsman girded himself to save the fellow. "But Forrest, drawing his knife, with a swift sweep severed the rope, and, taking Able by the arm, announced aloud his intention to remand him to the custody of the rightful authorities."

Once more at the jailhouse to which he had managed to bring Able safely, Forrest had to confront the angry mob. The soon-to-be alderman "presented himself upon the steps of the prison, drew a revolver, and declared it to be his determination to shoot the first man who approached to the door." Forrest's resolve, no doubt underscored by his piercing gaze and emblazoned features, convinced the crowd that he meant business, and it slowly melted away before him. John Able would have his day in court, apparently thanks only to Nathan Bedford Forrest.[36]

Such displays of bravery and boldness were indeed indicative of Forrest. His willingness to undertake action, even in the most extreme circumstances, was likewise a part of his makeup. But these were not the personality traits that the Able incident exposed. Rather, it was Bedford Forrest's penchant for embellishment and exaggerated storytelling that was apparently at work, for he actually played little more than a tangential role in the entire affair. Contemporary newspaper accounts do not credit him with rescuing John Able at rope's end or jail's door with knife or pistol in hand.[37] By the time the Jordan and Pryor biography appeared, Forrest was struggling with postwar fiscal and emotional realities that must have proved daunting to one who thrived so heavily on controlling circumstances around him. Perhaps the intervening decade had dulled his memory, or more likely, he simply recalled the events as he had grown accustomed to telling them, with his role and its centrality to the story having grown over time.

A former Confederate colleague and superior recalled that Forrest relished recounting the stories of his wartime exploits. Dabney Maury explained that the Tennessean had his favorite subjects and was "most fond of relating the incidents," doing so "with much enjoyment." The Able story may well have been another case of a tale "which pleased him greatly" as did others he shared with whomever would listen.[38] His desire to relate a tale, and particularly his fondness for putting himself at the center of it, would not always bode well for Bedford Forrest or his reputation, as he would learn after Fort Pillow.

Yet the war that would bring him especial notoriety had not begun as Forrest served out his terms as alderman. But in the wake of the election of

Abraham Lincoln to the presidency, the secession of the Deep South states from the Union, and the formation of the Confederate States of America, hostilities opened in Charleston Harbor, South Carolina, in April 1861. Lincoln's call for 75,000 militia to suppress the rebellion prompted other states to leave the Union rather than supply their quota of men against their Southern sisters. Bedford Forrest followed Tennessee out of the Republic. He and his fifteen-year-old son, Willie, joined a regiment as privates. But Bedford Forrest's leadership potential and friendship with Governor Isham Harris quickly elevated him to the rank of lieutenant colonel.

In raising a command, Forrest would appeal to his fellow countrymen. Yet an unusual aspect of his recruiting tactics was not aimed at family members, neighbors, or business associates but directed at his slaves. In testimony before a congressional committee after the war, he related his initial interactions with his bondsmen. "I said to forty-five colored fellows on my plantation that it was a war upon slavery, and that I was going into the army; that if they would go with me, if we got whipped they would be free anyhow, and that if we succeeded and slavery was perpetuated, if they would act faithfully with me to the end of the war, I would set them free."[39] Forthright in a way that most of his compatriots would have deemed impossible, Forrest demonstrated a practical awareness of the manner in which he could extract loyal service while maintaining control over individuals who would otherwise have no reason to respond as he wished.

From the start of the conflict, Nathan Bedford Forrest understood the basic elements of war. In his recruitment advertising he made this awareness abundantly clear. "I wish none but those who desire to be actively engaged," he explained. "Come on boys, if you want to have a heap of fun and kill some Yankees," one of the notices proclaimed.[40] It was vintage Forrest, an in-your-face appeal that distilled war to its simplest common denominator. You had to be willing to be the cause of your opponent's demise, or at least be willing to shed his blood, to avoid death yourself.

Forrest issued his call for those who, like himself, wished "A Chance for Active Service." They could expect close-quarters fighting in which "shotguns and pistols" would be "preferable" as weapons.[41] Nor did he apparently lose his taste for this type of warfare. In March 1862 an officer observed in correspondence with Secretary of War Judah Benjamin, "Colonel Forrest, the most efficient cavalry officer in this department, informs me that the double-barrel shotgun is the best gun with which cavalry can be armed." Forrest exuberantly attested to the effectiveness of the weapon based upon his combat experience at Fort Donelson, Tennessee, when the Confederates had tried (more successfully than they realized) to shatter Ulysses S. Grant's right flank.[42]

Colonel Forrest soon had his men outfitted, relying largely upon his own funds and his network of prewar trading contacts to accomplish the task. In December 1861 the command also experienced its first real combat, a running fight at Sacramento, Kentucky, where the cavalryman demonstrated that he would lead from the front and engage the enemy personally in hand-to-hand fighting. The command endured a taste of defeat the following spring as it participated in the defense of Fort Donelson. After a furtive effort at breaking through an encircling Union army, Confederate commanders John B. Floyd, Gideon Pillow, and Simon B. Buckner determined to surrender the fort and its garrison to General Grant. Forrest angrily demurred, insisting that his own probes indicated that the army could save itself. When he failed to convince his superior officers, the cavalry commander obtained permission to take his troops out of the works. In characteristic take-charge fashion, he did so before the white flag appeared that sealed the remaining garrison's fate.

The riders proceeded to the Tennessee state capital, where a fellow Confederate recalled that in the chaos that was Nashville after the fall of Fort Donelson, Forrest stepped forward to assume control. "I well remember how he looked," Basil Duke related, "his resolute face seeming to subdue all he gazed on to his will and his tall powerful form towering above the mob which, in its most furious moments, gave way before him."[43] The cavalryman used more than sheer force of will, even employing fire engines to pump icy water from the Cumberland River when necessary to disperse the crowds.[44] Duke was suitably impressed. "I rather think that a number of those with whom he came in contact did not soon forget it."[45]

In April Forrest and his men participated in the Confederate counterstroke at Shiloh, or Pittsburg Landing, by which they sought to recoup their previous losses in Tennessee. The initial attacks proved successful, although Forrest chafed at the lesser role he had been assigned in guarding the Confederate right flank. Finally, his impatience got the best of him, and he entered the vicious fighting in the vicinity of the Hornets' Nest.

As the fighting settled down on this first day, Grant's lines held a position anchored along the Tennessee River, fronted by steep ravines, and bristling with artillery. Skulkers crowded the landing itself, but the situation was not as tenuous as it might have appeared. Throughout the night, Forrest tried to encourage his superiors to launch an attack or to pull back to more-defensible positions. Although night assaults were typically chaotic and ineffective affairs, he knew that Federal reinforcements were arriving that would enhance Grant's ability to reclaim what had been lost in the previous day's fighting. Forrest complained that if nothing were done to prepare for, if not to try to prevent, the arrival of additional Union troops, the Confederate army "will be whipped like hell before ten o'clock to-morrow."[46]

The next morning, with those fresh troops to augment his command, Grant shoved the Confederates back over the ground they had so recently won. Colonel Forrest's last fighting of the Shiloh Campaign came in a rear-guard action at Fallen Timbers in the retreat toward Corinth, Mississippi. There, he rode into the Union lines when the rest of his men broke off the attack and became surrounded by Federals intent on not letting him out of their grasp alive. Despite a disabling wound, the colonel grabbed one of the Union soldiers, hoisted him on the horse behind him as a shield, and rode back to his lines before dumping the hapless man on the ground.

The Shiloh/Fallen Timbers story has all of the hallmarks of fiction. Historians Paul Ashdown and Edward Caudill have assessed it as such in their examination of the myth of Nathan Bedford Forrest, with the visualization of the Confederate snatching a "bantling in blue."[47] Yet Forrest's impetuosity and the wound he suffered on the occasion were real enough. Minimizing the incident also did not credit the exertions that a person pumping with adrenaline might be capable of performing under the threat of imminent death. The Jordan and Pryor biography neglects to mention the soldier-as-shield aspect of this story. But the omission may be explained by the authors' observation that Forrest "did not have the opportunity to revise the chapter of [the book] which touches upon the battle of Shiloh."[48] If so, the general missed a wonderful chance to indulge in his penchant for storytelling for the benefit of a postwar audience.

Forrest had to take some time to recover from the severe wound he had suffered. When he attempted to return to active duty too soon, he reaggravated the injury. But by the summer of 1862, Bedford Forrest was back in the saddle in time to launch a lightning raid against the Union supply depot at Murfreesboro, Tennessee. The moment would do much to define the officer and his techniques for securing victory in the face of unexpected adversity.

At least initially, the chances for Confederate success appeared bright. The raiders benefited from a spat between local Union commanders that caused the defenders to locate units in separate sectors. Inexplicably, the cavalry patrols meant to offer a measure of security to the post also pulled back each evening. Thus when Forrest arrived on the scene, his men achieved the surprise they desired. But matters quickly became complicated as the Federals regrouped and began to resist in a more organized fashion.

Forrest moved from point to point to provide his firm hand of leadership only to find the defenders clinging more stubbornly to their ground than he had anticipated.

As the attack slowly unfolded, some of the Southern cavalry commander's subordinates felt uncomfortable concerning the prospects for victory if they lingered in the vicinity too long. Forrest expressed his determination to see the operation through to the ends for which he had come. "I did not come here to make half a job of it," he told officers who worried that Union reinforcements might be closing in on them. "I mean to have them all."[49] Having "them all" was to be a key ingredient to Forrest's approach to the battlefield. No half-measures would suffice as long as they could be prevented.

In the Murfreesboro Raid Forrest also exhibited two forms of psychological warfare to accomplish his goal of capturing the town and the men guarding it. These methods recalled his days as a gambler, winning, or at least attempting to win, hands by bluff. In the first instance Forrest used deception to inflate the numbers of his command so as to impress his opponent with his apparent numerical superiority. In the second he sent in a surrender demand that called for the capitulation of the defenders in order to avoid the further effusion of blood. Employing language that would take on even greater meaning in combat situations to come, the gambler Forrest also sought to stack the deck in his favor by adding a warning. If the Federals refused his demands, he explained ominously, "I will have every man put to the sword."[50]

Of course, his purpose in making the threat was to "have them all" by surrender if possible, not to wipe out the garrison in some unbridled display of bloodlust or vengeance. Nathan Bedford Forrest was no Old Testament warrior bent on illustrating God's wrath through the indiscriminate slaughter of those opposed to him. Nor was he a backwoodsman run amuck in a civilized world, not understanding the rules of warfare or the strictures of human society. He was, both in the simplest and most complex ways, a soldier trying to win an engagement and willing to use nonlethal, as well as lethal, means to do so. His threat of "no quarter" was a device to win a given battle, and when Forrest found that it could achieve, or at least help to achieve, this goal at Murfreesboro, he clearly decided to use it again wherever he considered the method promising.

The raid ended as the total victory that Bedford Forrest had envisioned when he vowed to "have them all." The Murfreesboro depot and 1,200 men of its garrison as well as wagons and supplies lay in his hands. Twenty-nine of the Federal defenders were dead and 120 of their comrades had suffered wounds, but their resistance had inflicted twenty-five killed and forty to sixty wounded on the ultimately successful Southerners.[51]

This determination to win a complete victory was already the standard operating procedure of Nathan Bedford Forrest and would remain so for the rest of his military career. Contrary to those who assumed that he simply wanted to kill in order to obtain his objectives was the fact that in many instances he depended on that very assumption to prevent, or at least minimize, the bloodshed necessary to achieve the preferred results. If he could convince opponents that he would destroy them, such a threat based upon the fierceness of his reputation might prevent the need to do so in actuality. Either way, through fighting an enemy or outfoxing him, Forrest would accomplish his task. After all, a successful conclusion was all that he desired.

Victory achieved through less lethal methods did not prevent Bedford Forrest from demonstrating a sense of frontier justice during the raid when he felt the situation warranted it. As the Confederates approached Murfreesboro, he detailed one force to go to the courthouse and surrounding buildings to isolate any defenders there and free a number of individuals from the area being held in the jail. In the chaos that filled the streets, several of the panicked Federals shot into the cells as they departed. One of them took the additional step of starting a fire before leaving, and only strenuous exertions by the arriving Confederates allowed the prisoners to avoid incineration.

Bedford Forrest soon appeared, inquired about the captives, and received assurances that despite efforts to burn the jail they were safe. When he learned that the culprits had sought refuge in the courthouse, he observed quietly, "Never mind, we'll get them." Once the fighting had subsided, the Confederates gathered the Federal prisoners. Forrest approached one of the Southerners who had almost perished in the fire. "They tell me these men treated you unhumanely while in jail. Point them out to me." The rescued person identified the arsonist, and when a roll call came a few hours afterward, that individual failed to respond. "Pass on," Forrest remarked nonchalantly, "it's all right."[52] There was no direct evidence that the Confederate commander had exacted a deadly price for the soldier's earlier actions toward defenseless prisoners, but the phraseology suggested that he had accounted for the missing man by another means.

Forrest also experienced race and war firsthand at Murfreesboro when, according to biographers Thomas Jordan and J. P. Pryor, a "negro camp-follower" shot at him. The commander instantly returned the fire "with his pistol at the distance of thirty paces" and killed the man. The implication from this source is clear that this was a killing done in self-defense, not motivated by prejudice or malice.[53]

Another account, provided by Union general David Stanley, offered a different interpretation of this event. Although the matter had come to his attention at third hand, Stanley explained that the original source was a reputable one, "an officer serving under FORREST." According to this individual, the killing occurred when the mulatto servant of a Union officer appeared before Forrest, who "inquired of him, with many oaths, what he was doing there." When the man responded that he "was a free man" serving the Union officer at his pleasure, Forrest "deliberately put his hand to his holster, drew a pistol, and blew the man's brains out." According to Stanley, even the Southerner who had passed the story along condemned Forrest's "act as one of cold-blooded murder" and "vowed not to serve under him again."[54]

One of the participants in the raid recorded a different incident in which that soldier encountered "a fine big Buck Negro dressed in federal uniform" and "started to hunt up Gen. Forest" to present him with the prize. The fellow was astounded that when he found his commanding officer "[s]iting on his horse his eyes blazing fire ... instead of complimenting me he gave me a Cussing that still amuses me when I think of it[.]" Colonel Forrest apparently failed to appreciate the captive's attire, for when the Confederate tried to explain that he saw the man as "a Very Valuable nigger," Forrest retorted that "a Dead nigger in federal uniform was more valuable to the Confederacy than a live one[.]" Of course, had the story ended there, it would have served as early corroboration of Forrest's ruthlessness toward blacks in uniform. Instead, the commander's bluster aside, the soldier recalled, "He ordered me to turn himover [sic] to Col Morrison who had charge of the prisoners and he finally Sent the Negro home to his owner Dr. Rucker of Rutherford Co Tenn[.]"[55]

For his military success at Murfreesboro, Nathan Bedford Forrest received a promotion to brigadier general on July 21. The Confederate Congress also belatedly bestowed its "thanks" to the enterprising commander and his men a year later, "especially for the daring and skill exhibited in the capture of Murfreesboro, on the 13th of July last, and in subsequent brilliant achievements."[56] Among these "achievements" was a bold raid through western Tennessee that resulted in the capture of railroad depots and the destruction of trestles and bridgework in the region. Coupled with an operation against the forward Union supply base at Holly Springs, Mississippi, conducted by Earl Van Dorn, the two expeditions disrupted Grant's initial overland push toward Vicksburg.

Near the conclusion of that foray, Forrest found himself in a particularly tight spot, caught between two Union forces at Parker's Crossroads. Despite the appearance of Federals in his rear, he managed to extract his force. Once again, myth combined with reality as the general was supposed to have stood high in his stirrups and announced that he was going to "Charge them both ways." But whether or not Forrest uttered those words, his actions on the field mirrored them by using a portion of his men to hold one enemy force in place while he struck the other. With both Federal commands momentarily neutralized, he slipped through with the bulk of his command and made it to safety.

By the spring of 1863, Forrest returned to Middle Tennessee to strike blows against isolated Union garrisons in the vicinity of Franklin and Nashville. Once more, his work illustrated both a penchant for quick slashes behind Union lines and a willingness to resort to stern measures to achieve his aims. To the stubborn defenders of a fortification guarding a bridge over the Harpeth River, he sent in his aide Charles Anderson with a chilling message: "Major, take in a flag of truce, and tell them I have them completely surrounded, and if they don't surrender I'll blow hell out of them in five minutes and won't take one of them alive if I have to sacrifice my men in storming their stockade." A white shirt substituted for a handkerchief, and 230 Union officers and men from the 22nd Michigan Infantry became prisoners.[57] Forrest's tactic of bluster had succeeded once again.

While Forrest excelled at raiding himself, in April the Confederate took up the trail of a Union force under Colonel Abel Streight as it worked its way across northern Alabama. The Federals hoped to reach Rome, Georgia, and beyond to cut the Western and Atlantic Railroad between Chattanooga, Tennessee, and Atlanta, Georgia. Forrest doggedly chased the raiders, finally running them to ground on May 3 near the Alabama-Georgia line in the vicinity of Gaylesville, Alabama. The Confederate general used his wits and a generous supply of bluff to prompt the harried bluecoats to surrender 1,600 men to his much smaller force.[58]

Several distinct versions detailed the manner in which the drama might have unfolded. A common element of each of these was Forrest's willingness to use bluff to exaggerate the size of his forces to his exhausted opponent. One staff officer related how his chief fascinated friends with the tale of Streight's capture. "Forrest came into the editorial room of the Rebel at Chattanooga, where three or four of his old friends were collected, and gave us a minute narrative of the recent campaign," the staffer explained. "His descriptive powers are naturally very good, and on this occasion he was full of his story, and spoke with enthusiasm." The general confessed to a sense of vulnerability as he confronted Streight: "'I wasn't certain,' said Forrest, 'when I demanded his surrender, which would have to give in, him or me. But it was just like a game of poker, I called him on a single pair to his 'full [house]' trusting to luck. He seemed, at first, to have very little confidence in my hand; but I said: 'I give you five minutes to decide. I've followed you and fit you for two weeks, and now I've got you just where I want you. I'm tired of sacrificing lives, and I offer you a chance to stop it. If you don't, I won't be answerable for the consequences.'" Forrest was obviously pleased with the outcome and determined that Streight had been "fairly bluffed." The Union commander belatedly recognized the situation and understandably inquired, "Where is the rest of your command General?" Forrest took the matter in stride, "smiled grimly, and made no reply."[59]

The bulk of the variations in descriptions of the raid's final moments concern Forrest's meeting with Streight to discuss the Federals' surrender. "I seen him all the time we was talking, looking over my shoulder and counting the guns," Forrest recounted in one of these. "Presently, he said: 'Name of God! How many guns have you got? There's fifteen I've counted already!'" Trying to avoid overplaying his hand at such a critical juncture, Forrest replied simply, "I reckon that's all that has kept up." Phony couriers reporting the arrival of nonexistent units added to the uncertainty in his opponent's mind. Yet Streight insisted that he be told the size of the force he faced before agreeing to submit. Forrest was equally determined to prevent the colonel from gaining that vital intelligence. Finally, he decided to force the issue, calling out the command, "Sound to mount!" The threat of facing such a seemingly overwhelming force and the pressure to capitulate from his own subordinates proved too great for Streight to resist, and at last he reluctantly agreed to surrender. Forrest instructed him to have his men stack their arms and, when they had done so, ordered his men forward to seize them. Only then did Streight begin to realize that he had been duped and demanded his weapons back.

By this account, Forrest indicated that he took the Union colonel's demeanor—"he did rear!"—and his demand for his weapons to be returned good naturedly. "I just laughed at him and patted him on the shoulder, and said, 'Ah, Colonel, all is fair in love and war you know.'"[60] But in another version, the Confederate answered more testily to his irate adversary, "Dry those tears or you'll be drying them in hell."[61]

In a fourth variation of the interchange between the commanders, a prewar associate of Forrest suggested that the Confederate offered to return the stacked weapons to his opponent. "'Here, are your arms...' said Forrest, 'there is an open field; we can soon settle the question of valor—numbers are nothing!'"[62] Certainly, Forrest the realist and pragmatist would have been least likely to follow such a course, unless it was after the fact, when only comrades who were fascinated to hear his recounting of the tale surrounded him. Indeed, one can almost imagine the story evolving with each retelling, although the ultimate result of the capture of the colonel and his raiders remained the essential fact.

Following his apprehension of Streight, General Forrest participated in Braxton Bragg's retreat from Middle Tennessee and performed with distinction at the Battle of Chickamauga, Georgia, on September 19–20, 1863. Historian David Powell has taken Bedford Forrest to task for errors he committed in the course of the Tullahoma and Chickamauga Campaigns, arguing effectively that these failings stemmed from his tendency to want to "go where the action was," even if his presence as a commander would have been more useful elsewhere. Still, as Powell assesses, "To his credit, Forrest did not repeat [the] mistake" of allowing an inexperienced officer to move without his direct supervision and assistance for the remainder of these campaigns. The general's desire to place himself in tactical positions occasionally limited his broader command capabilities, particularly when situations demanded attention at widely scattered points along his lines.[63] Despite the horseman's occasional miscalculations over these hectic days, Powell credits Forrest for actively seeking to fulfill his duties as he transitioned from "a partisan raider into a more complete cavalry general."[64]

Whatever his leadership shortcomings, Bedford Forrest generally enjoyed accolades from his superiors for his performance on the battlefield and obtained subsequent promotion on December 4 to the rank of major general.[65] One of his troopers wrote his father anticipating the promotion for his cavalry chief: "Genl Forrest has been ordered to the Command of all the Troops in Middle Tennessee, and is now acting Major Genl. And I presume will soon be Commissioned as Such." For William T. Howard, such recognition would not be surprising. "[H]e certainly deserves it—if Courage Caution and untiring energy entitle him to it. I have never followed a more gallant man in the field, and I have been with him in many close places, where it seemed almost impossible to get out, without being cut to pieces—and yet we came Safely through." The volunteer staffer thought his commander was also beginning to demonstrate a bit more wisdom when it came to engaging personally in combat. "Though as dashing and gallant as ever, he acquires more prudence, with increased experience—and I think will whip every fight he makes—his determination is—never to be whipped."[66]

Service under Bedford Forrest was arduous and demanding. Although he routinely gave his men and mounts as much time to recover from a previous expedition as he could before undertaking another, circumstances often dictated that the chance for rest and refitting was limited. His troopers uniformly recalled the whirlwind of riding and fighting with a justifiable sense of pride. Tennessean Robert Milton McAlister recalled: "The experance of a Calvery Man is some what complicated. Hear to day. There to morrow. Most all ways on the go."[67] Forrest would certainly have appreciated what fellow veteran H. C. Coles remembered of his wartime service under the general: "We eat what we could get, slept wherever we stoped or on our horses.... Our necesities were principally supplied by our foes."[68]

Nor were these strictly the views of individuals looking back with some sense of nostalgia upon the days of their youth. Robert E. Corry's wartime letters home to his wife reflected the same sentiments of the postwar veterans concerning Forrest and the cavalry service under him. In November 1863 he recorded the results of "a consultation" his commanding officer had made with the general. "[Forrest] says that our field of operations will be between the Miss. and Tenn. rivers and that he don't want any man to go with him unwillingly, and that everything that will add to our comfort shall be supplied—blankets, shoes, and all that is necessary for a soldier and also that all we capture will be ours."[69] Four days later he warned Lizzie, "Tomorrow we have to start with I suppose about 1500 men and we will be lucky if some of us don't pay a visit to Alton [Prison in Illinois] or some other miserable prison for I know that our leader the great go ahead Forrest is a rash man and fond of going into danger."[70]

By early 1864, Nathan Bedford Forrest had established himself as a more-than-capable cavalry commander and one of the finest mounted raiders on either side in the war. On more than one occasion, he was supposed to have attributed his success on the battlefield to getting there "first with the most men." He particularly liked to say this to people he wanted to impress—John Hunt Morgan was one of them. Dashing and popular, Morgan had established himself as a figure of near-legendary status.[71] Thus, when Forrest had the opportunity to spend some time with the Kentuckian, they began, according to Basil Duke, "comparing notes of their respective expeditions made about the same date in the summer of 1862, the one into middle Tennessee and the other into Kentucky." For once, Forrest the storyteller gave way to Forrest the soldier, anxious to learn how another practitioner applied his craft. "Each seemed far more concerned to learn what the other had done and how he did it," Duke remembered, "than to relate his own performances; and it was interesting to note the brevity with which they answered each other's questions and the eagerness with which they asked their own." When the topic turned to Murfreesboro, Morgan's inquiry as to Forrest's success there led the Tennessean to respond, "Oh, I just took the short cut and got there first with the most men."[72]

In the aftermath of Chickamauga, Forrest made a similar point to "a group of Confederate officers" as they discussed "the recent engagement and of military subjects generally." Knowing the accounts of the "remarkable exploits" associated with their colleague, the "West Pointers, who were curious to know what tactics the great raider had used and what systems he had followed that enabled him to be eminently successful, plied him with question after question." One specifically wanted to know what Forrest considered "the most important principle to be adopted in active operations against an enemy in the field." In what the writer recalled was a "broad, uncouth dialect," Forrest responded eagerly: "'Wall, General, if I git youah idée, you want to know, sah, what I considah the main pint. Wall, now, I don't know what you all think about it, but my idée is, to always git the most men thar fust, and then,' he added, 'ef you can't whup 'em, outrun 'em.'" Aside from its practical application, the general's observation reflected time-honored martial wisdom. The witness concluded simply, "It must be conceded that Forrest's way of putting the Napoleonic maxim to 'converge a superior force on the critical point at the critical time,' was forcible and intelligent, if inelegant."[73]

Forrest's experiences for the remainder of the war apparently created no sense of altering that formula. He had continued to enjoy successes, including Fort Pillow and Brice's Cross Roads, as well as enduring setbacks, such as at Harrisburg or Tupelo, to allow for reconsideration, but he remained wedded to the notion he had expressed to other colleagues on earlier occasions. Near the end of the war, Forrest employed the same maxim to define his many victories in his communications with Union cavalry counterpart James Harrison Wilson: "But I always make it a rule to get there first with the most men."[74]

To be sure, Bedford Forrest's military career was a litany of tremendous feats of arms, though rarely because he possessed the larger battalions. Dabney Maury later recalled, "His successes were achieved with forces much inferior to his enemy."[75] It is clear that Forrest exaggerated in using this maxim as a way of impressing those with whom he was speaking, not as a genuine reflection of his military record. Perhaps in that light, it would have been more accurate for him to have applied the sense that he reached the battlefield "on-time with enough men."

Theatrics also remained a vital part of the Confederate cavalryman's personal arsenal in the early months of 1864. His awareness of motivation and bluff found new elements for display at Okolona, Mississippi, when a Union raiding force penetrated the northern portion of that state. In the course of a running fight, Forrest had occasion to be "approached by several ladies, wringing their hands and imploring him to tell them what to do." The general was not about to chastise their actions, but he was prepared to use them to his advantage. After quickly surveying the scene, he admonished them, "When the bullets begin to whistle, jump in the stumps, wave your bonnets and shout hurrah boys!"[76] He understood that the perception created would be of civilians cheering the arrival of reinforcements. Forrest had used the same logic with a young soldier he approached at Parker's Crossroads the previous year. "That doesn't make any difference," the cavalry commander blurted to the fellow's remonstrance about being unarmed, "get in line and advance on the enemy with the rest; I want to make as big a show as possible."[77]

Forrest was more than capable of producing dramatic moments in critical situations and employing these devices to turn even adverse conditions to his benefit. This frequently also meant generating the stories that could become fodder for later recollections of those harrowing and exhilarating events. But Forrest's tendency toward after-the-fact embellishment and his need for inhabiting the heart of any story returned poor dividends for him after Fort Pillow. Bedford Forrest was proud of his martial accomplishments prior to April 12, 1864, and never expressed regret for any of them after that date. But his initial terminology regarding Fort Pillow would prove particularly problematic as, indeed, would his use of the Murfreesboro-style ultimatum in the attempt to induce a quick capitulation of the garrison.

As his own men and his opponents understood, Forrest continued to have a reputation for fearsomeness in combat. Yet he would have ample opportunity to prove that bloodlust was not uppermost in his mind or in his military strategy. Ironically, the place that would offer an illustration of the complexity of his motivations would also represent the most controversial combat action associated with him: the assault on Fort Pillow.

Nathan Bedford Forrest and his men were also confronting historic changes during this period that had altered the nature of the conflict they were fighting. Both the Confederate States and the United States were undergoing transitions in their social systems wrought by the war. By the time Forrest's command rode into West Tennessee in April 1864, the most significant of these developments was the introduction of African

American soldiers into the Union forces. The path for these men had been no easy one to follow, and the outcome of the alterations remained unsettled, but the events at Fort Pillow would provide another important milepost in the journey.

CHAPER 2

# FIGHTING FOR FREEDOM

### April 1861–April 12, 1864

And I further declare and make known that such persons of suitable condition will be received into the armed service of the United States.

*Abraham Lincoln, Emancipation Proclamation, January 1, 1863*

We are coming Father Abraham.

*James S. Gibbons, 1862*

"Freedom." This most powerful word associated with the American Civil War came in many incarnations during that conflict. For supporters of the Confederacy, it meant not having to exist under a government that did not protect a way of life and the values they held dear. For many white Northerners, the concept offered the opportunity for them to decide for themselves what they would do or become in their lives. For many blacks in the South, it meant an end to the "peculiar institution" that had controlled their people's lives for the hundreds of years since the arrival of the first enslaved Africans in the English colonies along Chesapeake Bay. All of these "freedoms," though, could not be realized at the same time. War would decide which of them prevailed.

Frederick Douglass thought he understood which version must succeed. A former slave and one of the greatest orators of his or any time, Douglass carried a rhetorical flag that he hoped he could use to rally a nation to its highest moral duty. But to be truly effective, he knew that he had to reach one person in particular—Abraham Lincoln.

For his part, President Lincoln evolved (painfully slowly in Douglass's estimation) in his political position from "gradual compensated emancipation" to finally putting his administration on record for the freedom of those enslaved in areas that stood in rebellion against the United States. Grappling with what he saw as the political realities of a national "house" that had indeed "divided," as he had feared it would, the Illinois Republican adhered to a position that refused to accept the spread of slavery under any conditions while searching for some conciliatory gesture significant enough that it might end the crisis. He abhorred the institution of slavery personally but elevated the political imperatives above its immediate eradication. Initially, he thought that external colonization for freed persons was a viable alternative if slave owners would accept emancipation with compensation. That position proving inadequate, a steady stream of events slowly drove the process toward emancipation during the first two years of the conflict. Whether anyone realized it fully or not, American society was undergoing a transition away from slavery as the antebellum world had known it.

Even so, such an important alteration would not occur seamlessly. At just about the time the combatants clashed in the vicinity of Manassas Junction in Virginia, President Lincoln reiterated his intention to follow a constitutional course when it came to the peculiar institution. "Would it not be well to allow owners to bring back those which have crossed [the Potomac River]?" he queried in mid-July 1861.[1]

Later that same month, a communication from Union general Benjamin F. Butler put the issue squarely before the government. Noting the presence of large numbers of black men, women, and children who had come into his lines on the Virginia Peninsula, Butler understandably asked the War Department for clarification of their legal status. Applying the phrase "contraband of war" to such individuals, he asserted that they were "[n]o longer under ownership of any kind," and thus the circumstances of war and rebellion had altered their former "state and condition" as slaves.[2]

In August the U.S. Congress passed the First Confiscation Act. In an effort to deprive the South of a valuable resource, the bill provided for the seizure of property, including slaves, being used to further the Confederate war effort. Confiscation challenged the foundations on which the fugitive-slave law had rested since the drafting of the U.S. Constitution in 1787 and augmented by its emphasis under the Compromise of 1850. Now, slaves who had assisted the Confederacy were not to be considered fugitives to be returned if they removed themselves, or the circumstances of war removed them, from their master's control. Even so, the measure left crucial aspects of a slave's status unclear. "They no longer owed labor to their owners, but the act did not explicitly emancipate them," historian Eric Foner has noted of the legislation's ambiguities.[3]

Later that same month, a former Republican presidential standard bearer and current commander of the Department of the West, Major General John C. Frémont, issued a proclamation from his headquarters at

St. Louis, Missouri. Under the aegis of martial law, which he declared to exist throughout Missouri, Frémont called for the seizure and emancipation of the slaves of anyone who "shall take up arms against the United States, or who shall be directly proven to have taken an active part with their enemies in the field." Any slaves belonging to these individuals would be "hereby declared free men."[4]

This declaration put enormous pressure on Lincoln.[5] The commander in chief informed Frémont that he would prefer that the general adhere to the language of the First Confiscation Act. The president was also clear as to his motives for taking a slower, more conservative approach when it came to slavery. Among his reasons for the request, Lincoln stated, "I think there is great danger that the closing paragraph, in relation to the confiscation of property, and the liberating slaves of traitorous owners, will alarm our Southern Union friends, and turn them against us—perhaps ruin our fair prospect for Kentucky."[6]

To his friend and political associate Senator Orville Browning of Illinois, Lincoln shared his thoughts on the subject in a "Private & Confidential" communication in September 1861. "Gen. Fremont's proclamation, as to [the] confiscation of property, and the liberation of slaves, is *purely political,* and not within the range of *military* law, or necessity [emphases his]," the president observed. Employing the analogy of a commander using private property for military purposes, he explained that Frémont "has the right to do so, and to so hold it, as long as the necessity lasts; and this is within military law, because [it is] within military necessity." Such usage was not meant to be permanent, however, or to abrogate the rights of the owners to their property. "And the same is true of slaves," Lincoln added, pointing out: "If the General needs them, he can seize them, and use them; but when the need is past, it is not for him to fix their permanent future condition. That must be settled according to laws made by law-makers, and not by military proclamations."

In the same letter Lincoln spelled out the fear he had earlier mentioned to Frémont in trying to convince him to modify his edict. The concern was that precipitate action with regard to slavery would alienate those Unionists who would otherwise support the administration and the war. "I think to lose Kentucky is to lose the whole game," the president told his friend, citing that loss as adversely affecting the ability to hold on to Missouri and Maryland. "These all against us, and the job on our hands is too large for us," he concluded plainly.[7] Lincoln avowed that he would have reached the same conclusion in any event, but clearly he had the continued support of Unionists in the border areas uppermost in his mind.

He would not sacrifice that support for what he deemed to be hasty action regarding the peculiar institution.

President Lincoln remained busy in the latter part of 1861 trying to keep a war going and at the same time to find some measure of compromise that might bring the already bloody contest to a close. Through his December message to Congress, and even more specifically in a special address the following March, he laid out his ideas on such thorny issues as emancipation and the colonization of freed slaves.

In his message to Congress on March 6, 1862, Lincoln provided language for a joint resolution that would offer the cooperation of the U.S. government "with any state which may adopt gradual abolishment of slavery, giving such state pecuniary aid, to be used by such state in it's discretion, to compensate for the inconveniences public and private, produced by such a change of system." The president insisted that the "measure [was meant] as one of the most efficient means of self-preservation." He was convinced that any slaveholding state that remained in the Union and availed itself of this opportunity would also be sending a clear message through the "initiation of emancipation" that it had no intention of joining the rebellious states "in their proposed confederacy." He ended unequivocally by observing that "in my judgment, gradual, and not sudden emancipation, is better for all." Lincoln maintained that the expenditures for war would quickly dwarf what could be spent to compensate owners for freeing their slaves "in any named State," and he offered a bow to states' rights through his preference for leaving the decision on this matter to the states themselves. Beyond his broad statement on the subject, the president did not offer further specifics on how he expected the national government to implement such a policy.[8]

Lincoln's proposals were not without their critics, even among friends and supporters, and he took the opportunity to respond to one of them on March 9. Henry Jarvis Raymond had been a journalist when he founded the *New York Times,* later also serving as lieutenant governor of New York. The president sought to apply the most practical of terms relating to gradual compensated emancipation. "Have you noticed the facts," Lincoln observed to Raymond, "that less than one half-day's cost of this war would pay for all the slaves in Delaware, at four hundred dollars per head?—that eighty-seven days cost of this war would pay for all in Delaware, Maryland, District of Columbia, Kentucky, and Missouri at the same price?"[9]

By now, the U.S. Congress was engaged in a full-blown debate over war policies that promised to alter the institution of slavery irrevocably. March 13, 1862, marked a day in which that legislative body insisted that Union army officers would no longer be allowed to return fugitive slaves to their owners, regardless of loyalties. "Having built up a head of steam," historian James M. McPherson notes, "Republicans pressed ahead: from April to July they enacted and Lincoln signed legislation to abolish slavery in the District of Columbia, to prohibit it in the territories, and to confiscate the slaves of Confederate owners."[10]

President Lincoln was acting in the manner he felt offered the best opportunity for achieving positive results for the war effort, but some of the generals in the field were not shy in adding complications to his delicate task. Union major general David Hunter took an initial step on April 13, 1862, with General Orders No. 7, to declare martial law and freedom for all "persons of color held to involuntary service by enemies of the United States in Fort Pulaski and on Cockspur Island, Georgia."[11] He followed this limited effort with a broader one a month later aimed at persons in Georgia, Florida, and South Carolina "heretofore held as slaves," now, on his own authority, "declared forever free."[12]

Facing the potential of a backlash in the Border States that remained in the Union, and irritated that Hunter had acted without consulting him, Lincoln issued a revocation order of his own. The president observed that he had not known that such an action was pending, then added decisively: "I further make known that whether it be competent for me, as Commander-in-Chief of the Army and Navy, to declare the Slaves of any state or states, free, and whether at any time, in any case, it shall have become a necessity indispensable to the maintenance of the government, to exercise such supposed power are questions which, under my responsibility, I reserve to myself, and which I can not feel justified in leaving to the decision of commanders in the field." Lincoln remained hopeful that a reasoned approach to the situation could prevail and repeated the argument he had presented before Congress embracing gradual compensated emancipation. Indeed, he considered the idea, "adopted by large majorities of both branches of Congress" in the form of a joint resolution, to represent "an authentic, definite, and solemn proposal of the nation to the States and people most immediately interested in the subject matter." Those sympathetic to the Confederacy or supportive of slavery need not solely take him at his word that a transition could be undertaken in a manner he hoped they might find more palatable.[13]

The president saw the fate of slavery as one weapon in his arsenal for ending the rebellion, but he had yet to demonstrate publicly a position beyond its slow demise. The seeming uncertainty came less from any moral failing than from the practical realities of waging a war to save the Union. Precipitate action might prove counterproductive and, in the end, backfire.

Lincoln had absolute clarity concerning the basis for war itself, as he indicated to Congress in the wake of its censure of former secretary of war Simon Cameron. "The insurrection which is yet existing in the United States, and aims at the overthrow of the federal Constitution and the Union, was clandestinely prepared during the winter of 1860 and 1861, and assumed an open organization in the form of the treasonable provisional government at Montgomery, in Alabama, on the 18th day of February, 1861," he explained. The conflict's origins were likewise definitive. "On the 12th day of April, 1861, the insurgents committed the flagrant act of civil war by the bombardment and capture of Fort Sumter, which cut off the hope of immediate conciliation." All subsequent actions came in the administration's effort at suppressing these treasonous elements and restoring the Union to a state of tranquility.[14]

In remarks to a visiting delegation of Progressive Friends on June 20, President Lincoln intimated the continuing progression of his thought concerning slavery. "If a decree of emancipation could abolish Slavery, John Brown would have done the work effectually," he observed. "Such a decree surely could not be more binding upon the South than the Constitution, and that cannot be enforced in that part of the country now." Always practically minded, he concluded, "Would a proclamation of freedom be any more effective?"[15]

In the meantime, the U.S. Congress took a further step regarding slavery and rebellion in July 1862 by passing the Second Confiscation Act. Any slaves seized under the provisions of this legislation would be "forever free of their servitude, and not again to be held as slaves." The same political issues and military imperatives already noted very nearly caused Lincoln to veto the measure.[16]

Tuesday, July 22, marked another distinctive point in the process by which President Lincoln linked slavery to a successful prosecution of the war. Employing a constitutional and legislative framework, he continued to advance the notion of gradual compensated emancipation while applying the threat of "forfeitures and seizures" as punishment for "treason and rebellion," already stipulated by Congress for those who did not "cease participating in, aiding, countenancing, or abetting the existing rebellion, or any rebellion against the government of the United States, and [thereby do not] return to their proper allegiance to the United States." Finally, as concomitant of confiscation, the president announced that he was prepared, "as a fit and necessary military measure ... as Commander-in-Chief of the Army and Navy of the United States[, to] declare that on the first day of January in the year of our Lord one thousand, eight hundred and sixty-three, all persons held as slaves within any state or states, wherein the constitutional authority of the United States shall not then be practically recognized, submitted to, and maintained, shall then, thenceforward, and forever, be free."

During the cabinet meeting in which the president made this proposal, Postmaster General Montgomery Blair argued that the move would prove detrimental to elections in the fall, while Secretary of State William Seward insisted that the administration would be best served to wait for a military success to announce the policy. Secretary of the Treasury Salmon Chase offered support for a measure that would also allow for the arming of the freed slaves, but Lincoln was unwilling to embrace that step at this point.[17]

In a private letter on July 26 to Reverdy Johnson, who served as a special State Department agent investigating irregularities in New Orleans, Lincoln revealed the internal juggling he had to endure to take measures sufficient to achieve success while not alienating those upon whom he believed such success, at least partially, rested. "You are ready to say I apply to *friends* what is due only to *enemies*. I distrust the *wisdom* if not the *sincerity* of friends, who would hold my hands while my enemies stab me. This appeal to professed friends has paralyzed me more in this struggle than any other one thing." He concluded: "I am a patient man—always willing to forgive on the Christian terms of repentance; and also to give ample *time* for repentance. Still I must save this government if possible. What I *cannot* do, of course I *will* not do; but it may as well be understood, once for all, that I shall not surrender this game leaving any available card unplayed."[18] The question was less what card would be played as when it would be tossed on the table and under what conditions.

At the end of the month, New York financier August Belmont forwarded a portion of a letter in which an unknown author chided the president for his policies heretofore: "The time has arrived when Mr. Lincoln must take a decisive course. Trying to please everybody, he will satisfy nobody. A vacillating policy in matters of importance is the very worst." The argument cut to the heart of the matter regarding the unsettling, transitional nature of the conflict. "Now is the time, if ever, for honest men who love their country to rally to its support. Why will not the North say officially that it wishes for the restoration of the Union as it was?"

Lincoln responded that the writer did not seem to have understood what he had said previously on numerous occasions before asserting strongly: "Broken eggs cannot be mended.... This government cannot much longer play a game in which it stakes all, and its enemies stake nothing." The war could not be allowed to continue indefinitely without significant consequences to those the president felt were responsible for inaugurating and carrying it forward. "Those enemies must understand that they cannot experiment for ten years trying to destroy the government, and if they fail still come back into the Union unhurt. If they expect in any contingency to ever have the Union as it was, I join with the writer in saying, 'Now is the time.'"[19]

This incremental approach to the fundamental issues was not new for President Lincoln. In his "Message to Congress in Special Session" on July 4, 1861, he had noted plainly, "The people of Virginia have thus allowed this great insurrection to make its nest within her borders; and this government has no choice left but to deal with it, *where* it finds it."[20] There might still be hope that some gesture could find traction that would end the national trauma sooner, but Lincoln was clear in his assertion that time for something short of comprehensive measures was running out.

Pressure for more-direct and immediate action came from newspaper editor Horace Greeley in a piece entitled "The Prayer of Twenty Millions," which appeared in his *New York Tribune* on August 19. Greeley had once suggested that the seceding Southern states be allowed to go their own way, but in the wake of Fort Sumter and the outbreak of hostilities, he took the side of those who quickly lost patience with Lincoln's prosecution of the war. His opening salvo included, in the name of those "who desire the unqualified suppression of the rebellion now desolating our country," how the people of the North were "sorely disappointed and deeply pained by the policy you seem to be pursuing with regard to the slaves of rebels." Blaming the "timid counsels" that threatened Lincoln's presidency and the nation, Greeley lodged complaints against current policies as he understood them, insisting "that every hour of deference to Slavery is an hour of added and deepened peril to the Union."[21]

A few days later, on the twenty-second, President Lincoln produced a response that captured his desire to assert the paramountcy of restoring the Union. His words reflected the maximum flexibility he hoped to maintain even as he moved to a more decisive and definitive position on the future of slavery in America:

> I would save the Union. I would save it the shortest way under the Constitution. The sooner the national authority can be restored; the nearer the Union will be "the Union as it was." If there be those who would not save the Union, unless they could at the same time *save* slavery, I do not agree with them. If there be those who would not save the Union unless they could at the same time *destroy* slavery, I do not agree with them. My paramount object in this struggle *is* to save the Union, and is *not* either to

save or destroy slavery. If I could save the Union without freeing *any* slave I would do it, and if I could save it by freeing *all* the slaves I would do it; and if I could save it by freeing some and leaving others alone I would also do that. What I do about slavery, and the colored race, I do because I believe it helps to save the Union; and what I forbear, I forbear because I do *not* believe it would help to save the Union. I shall do *less* whenever I shall believe what I am doing hurts the cause, and I shall do *more* whenever I shall believe doing more will help the cause.

In concluding, Lincoln thought better of including a passage he had employed on an earlier occasion, crossing out these words from his draft: "Broken eggs can never be mended, and the longer the breaking proceeds the more will be broken."[22]

The president's focus on saving the Union first and foremost was rapidly reaching a point of no return with regard to slavery in the rebellious regions. Southern sympathizers and Northern Democrats might challenge his point concerning the constitutionality of his actions, but Lincoln wanted as many options available for as long as possible. His top priority remained as it had since the inauguration of his presidency, and all other concerns were meant to be secondary to that purpose. Obviously, Lincoln understood that he could have no effect on the institution of slavery in the South if the Confederacy succeeded in winning its independence.

He also was aware enough of the lessons of history, as indeed were many of his fellow citizens North and South, to realize that republics were vulnerable enterprises. There was no guarantee in the best of times that this republic would fare any better than others that had come and gone before it. The president recognized early in the conflict what historian James McPherson has asserted about the importance of Union victory in settling "two fundamental, festering issues left unresolved by the Revolution of 1776: whether this fragile republican experiment called the United States would survive, and whether the house divided would continue to endure half slave and half free."[23] Abraham Lincoln also understood that the war the nation had embarked upon was bound to have profound effects on that nation, one way or another.

Obviously, the Union leader now realized, as he had suggested to Greeley, that slavery would have to be sacrificed to save the Union. But the metaphor he chose to illustrate his position this time was appropriate to the battlefield. "In our case, the moment came when I felt that slavery must die that the nation might live!" Lincoln recognized that without the removal of slavery, something akin to a gangrenous infection might set in to kill the Union in the future. In effect, the patient had to be saved from himself.[24]

The importance of accepting such a remedy was what Lincoln told his cabinet when he broached the subject of issuing a statement on emancipation. By July 1862, freeing the slaves, at least in those areas that remained in rebellion against the government, had become in Lincoln's mind "a military necessity, absolutely essential to the preservation of the Union."[25]

Many of Lincoln's generals in the field recognized the evolving nature of the conflict and the ramifications its continuation had on the peculiar institution. Hardly an advocate of racial progress, William T. Sherman nevertheless understood that rebellion must exact a price from those engaged in it. To an old school friend living in Coahoma County, Mississippi—Nathan Bedford Forrest's prewar home—near Memphis, the fiery Ohioan explained: "You ask me of your negroes, and I will immediately ascertain if they be under my Military Control and I will moreover see that they are one and all told what is true of all—Boys if you want to go to your master, Go—you are free to choose. You must think for yourselves, Your master has seceded from his Parent Government and you have seceded from him—both wrong by law—but both exercising an undoubted right to rebel. If your boys want to go, I will enable them to go, but I wont advise, persuade or force them."

Sherman understood that his friend wanted to protect his propertied interests as they had existed under the old order, but the nature of that relationship had changed:

> The Constitution of the United States is your only legal title to slavery. You have another title, that of possession, & force, but in Law & Logic your title to your Boys lay in the Constitution of the United States. You may say you are for the Constitution of the United States as it was—You know it is unchanged, not a word not a syllable....But your party have made *another* and have another in force. How can you say that you would have the old, when you have a new. By the new if successful you inherit the Right of Slavery, but the new is not law till your Revolution is successful. Therefore we who contend for the old existing Law, contend that you by your own act take away your own title to all property save what is restricted by *our* constitution, your slaves included.

As a soldier, Sherman maintained, "You know I don't want your slaves, but to bring you to reason I think as a Military Man I have a Right and it is good policy to make *you all* feel" the effects of rebellion, "and that by Rebelling you risk [all]." Under the circumstances he felt that his conclusion was inescapable: "Even without the Confiscation Act, by the simple laws of War we ought to take your effective slaves, I don't say to free them, but to use their labor & deprive you of it."[26]

For his brother, John, a senator in Washington, Sherman addressed the matter of emancipation. He was convinced that freeing substantial numbers of slaves would only prove to be "an incumbrance" to an army that would then have to assume the care for not only the able-bodied men among them but for their dependents as well. "Where are they to get work, who is to feed them, clothe them, & house them[?]," the general inquired. "We cannot now give tents to our soldiers, and our wagon trains are now a horrible impediment, and if we are to take along & feed the negros who flee to us for refuge, it will be an impossible task." At any rate, he concluded, "You cannot solve this negro question in a day."[27]

Reaction among Confederate leaders in the regions affected by these policy shifts reflected the building intensity of emotions. Brigadier General M. Jeff Thompson withheld little in his response to Frémont's declaration of martial law and confiscation in Missouri, threatening to "hang, draw, and quarter a[ny] minion of said Abraham Lincoln" who was responsible for the death of any of his men "in pursuance of said order of General Frémont." Thompson insisted, "While I am anxious that this unfortunate war shall be conducted if possible upon the most liberal principles of civilized warfare and every order that I have issued has been with that object yet if this rule is to be adopted (and it must first be done by our enemies) I intend to exceed General Frémont in his excesses and will make all tories that come in my reach rue the day that a different policy was adopted by their leaders." He concluded emphatically, "Should these things be repeated I will retaliate ten-fold, so help me God."[28]

Threats of retaliation had existed from early in the war. Historian Lonnie Speer notes that the Civil War devolved rapidly: "Within months of its beginning this conflict was anything but 'civil' and conducted by anyone but 'gentlemen.'" Regarding this "war of vengeance," he maintains, "There is ample documentation to suggest that both sides quite commonly practiced retaliatory measures against each other for real or imagined wrongs."[29] Such harsh deeds could come from soldiers and officers in the field or from authorities in Washington or Richmond, but they served as additional evidence that the war was spiraling out of control, with the most vulnerable persons, from civilians to prisoners of war, caught in the middle and suffering the direst consequences.

Individuals in the higher echelons of the Confederacy took cognizance of these developments as well. In late July and again at the beginning of August 1862, President Jefferson Davis ordered an investigation into reports of Union misdeeds against Confederate civilians based upon the threats of John Pope and the actions of David Hunter. On August 1 he reminded

Robert E. Lee that he wanted an immediate response and, presumably, a repudiation of these activities in the field by the Lincoln government. Basing his information on Northern newspaper reports, the Confederate president particularly condemned the arming of "slaves for the murder of their masters" and the "inauguration of a servile war," which he believed such actions would instigate." Davis offered the Lincoln administration fifteen days in which to respond and promised to view silence as tacit admission of support and thus, guilt. "In such an event," he assured his trusted advisor and field general, "on that Government will rest the responsibility of the retributive or retaliatory measures which we shall adopt to put an end to the merciless atrocities which now characterize the war waged against us."[30]

Pursuant to this course of action, on August 21, General Orders No. 48 emanated from the Confederate War Department with the approval of Jefferson Davis. Aimed primarily at General Hunter, the edict employed the term "outlaws" and threatened to condemn any "commissioned officer employed in drilling, organizing, or instructing slaves, with a view to their armed service in the war." For Confederate officials, the historical connection to slave rebellion was impossible to avoid, and the proscriptions for such activity were time tested. Such an officer was "not [to] be regarded as a prisoner of war, but held in close confinement for execution as a felon at such time and place as the President shall order."[31]

In September Lincoln offered an extended statement on the subject of emancipation in response to pressure from a public meeting held in Chicago, Illinois. It is likely he would have felt the need to reply in any case, but with this "memorial" having come from an ecumenical group out of his home state, Lincoln probably felt he had little choice. Averring that the subject had been on his mind "much for weeks past," he assured the petitioners that he only wanted to take steps that would have meaning and legitimacy. In the course of his response, Lincoln displayed the humor for which he was famous: "I do not want to issue a document that the whole world will see must necessarily be inoperative, like the Pope's bull against the comet!" Turning serious, the president laid his case carefully for what he had done thus far and why he might seem to have reticence in acting as he personally wished to do. His final comments were more heartfelt than utilitarian: "Do not misunderstand me, because I have mentioned these objections. They indicate the difficulties that have thus far prevented my action in some such way as you desire. I have not decided against a proclamation for liberty to the slaves, but hold the matter under advisement. And I can assure you that the subject is on my mind, by day and night, more than any other. Whatever shall appear to be God's will I will do."[32]

Amid this discourse, military events furnished opportunity for action on the question. September 17, 1862, proved to be a crucial day for Lincoln and the emancipation process. General Lee had moved northward into Maryland only to have a crucial set of directives lost near Frederick that imperiled the scattered elements of his Army of Northern Virginia. The "Lost Orders" emboldened George B. McClellan and led to sharp fighting at South Mountain and Crampton's Gap. Although Stonewall Jackson successfully subdued the Union garrison at Harpers Ferry, Lee's position along Antietam Creek, near the little village of Sharpsburg, Maryland, was tenuous at best. The fighting that occurred there produced such horrific casualties as to present the seventeenth with the dubious distinction of being the bloodiest single day of the war. Lee held the field at the end of the day, but he could not remain in the North and retreated to Virginia the following evening. President Lincoln used the opportunity to issue a preliminary version of the Emancipation Proclamation.[33]

In the aftermath of Antietam, Lincoln's course would appear to have been set. Yet with the deadline approaching for his proclamation to go into effect, he held out one last gesture to the rebellious states through a special message to Congress in December 1862. The president had outlined a proposal for gradual compensated emancipation in March. Now he sought to establish the specific parameters for this proposal. Undoubtedly, he hoped to demonstrate his sincerity in offering any slave state that wished to do so a chance to experience a slower-paced transition from slavery to freedom.

As a way of bringing a close to "our national strife," President Lincoln suggested the adoption of amendments to the Constitution allowing for gradual compensated emancipation. He set January 1, 1900, as the date by which all slaves ought to be freed and offered owners recompense through the sale of Federal bonds for the liquidation of their assets in human property. "Without slavery the rebellion could never have existed," he contended, "and without slavery it could not continue."[34]

Of course, these words fell on at least two sets of deaf ears: those of Confederates who did not trust or believe him or any offer he might make and those of the Radical Republicans in Congress and abolitionists elsewhere who saw the war as an opportunity to strike a decided death blow to the scourge of slavery once and for all. The president recognized that his proposal would be unsatisfactory to those wanting to retain the institution indefinitely or to end it immediately. He sought a middle ground, but an already long and bloody conflict made this at best a tenuous foundation on which to stand.

Events through the autumn of 1862 had already proven challenging, if ultimately successful, for Lincoln and his administration. In addition to Lee's penetration of Maryland, Confederates under Braxton Bragg and Edmund Kirby Smith had threatened Union control of Kentucky. Despite momentary victories in the Bluegrass State at Richmond (August 29–30) and Munfordville (September 14–17), a pitched battle over the rolling hills and fields near Perryville on October 8 forced matters decisively and turned back the gray-and-butternut tide. In Mississippi a victory at Iuka on September 19 by William Rosecrans and an ill-fated and costly Confederate assault on the stout defensive works at Corinth a month later left Union fortunes enhanced and the Southern commands of Sterling Price and Earl Van Dorn demoralized and in disarray.

Under the stresses and strains of continuing warfare, both sides were increasingly employing extreme language in their descriptions of their opponents. Noting the inflamed rhetoric of Pierre Gustave Toutant Beauregard and John C. Breckinridge concerning the "violation of the usages of civilized warfare," including the arming of slaves and the destruction of private property, historian Dennis Frye concludes: "Such merciless language from *military men* had little previous parallel during the Civil War. All knew the meaning: no mercy for the vanquished; no surrender for the loser; only death for those defeated." By the same token, the "language of conquest poured forth" from Northern sources toward their Confederate adversaries.[35]

Soldiers in the field at this time experienced alterations in the conditions of warfare and responded to them in myriad ways. Retribution, retaliation, and reprisal were becoming familiar concepts as warriors confronted the changing landscape of combat. Whether prompted by mistaken assumptions about the duration of the fighting, the degree to which Confederate Southerners embraced their national enterprise, or the virulence of guerrilla activity, Union troops turned invariably to a form of "punitive war" that encouraged their opponents to respond in kind.[36]

The targets of such retribution were not always white Southerners. In distant Minnesota the complaints of disgruntled settlers and a desire by some Union veterans there to regain their stature after earlier embarrassments elsewhere led to decisive campaigns against Native American warriors. Subsequently, a tribunal in the region passed judgments of death on more than three hundred defeated Dakotas. Amid his positioning for emancipation, President Lincoln reviewed the cases and commuted most of the sentences. But on December 26, 1862, the remaining thirty-eight condemned men met summary justice on the gallows in Mankato, Minnesota, in what historian Alvin Josephy terms "America's largest public mass execution."[37] The action demonstrates that Lincoln could exhibit both individual compassion and harsh determination regarding opponents of the Union. But the moment became lost in the arrival of a new year and the implementation of the president's program of emancipation.

When it went into effect on January 1, 1863, the Emancipation Proclamation illustrated that it was a military, rather than a moral, measure. It did not extend freedom to every enslaved person wherever he or she might be found. Instead, the measure freed the slaves in the areas that remained in rebellion when it went into operation. But it did more, for it put the administration squarely on the side of freedom. President Lincoln realized as much as anyone could that the government could not free just some of the slaves and "leave others alone," as he had implied to Greeley might be possible. Once assaulted in a direct way, the peculiar institution would have to go completely. The president made that clear by taking the next and, given the attitudes of the day prevalent in both the North and South, extraordinary step of opening the military widely to black enlistment.

Regardless of its manifestation, "freedom" required men willing to fight to obtain or maintain it. Yet between the influx of recruits the wave of patriotism after Fort Sumter produced and the realization that more than the initial 75,000 militia would be needed to suppress this rebellion, President Lincoln faced inordinate manpower demands to wage war successfully. To meet this requirement, he had issued a call for 300,000 more men in the summer of 1862. Poet James S. Gibbons wrote the words at the time that reflected the sentiments of many Unionists. The same words could now apply to blacks who answered the nation's summons to military service. Put to music, they became one of the North's most popular wartime songs.

> We are coming Father Abraham, three hundred thousand more.
> From Mississippi's winding stream and from New England's shore.
> We leave our plows and workshops, our wives and children dear,
> With hearts too full for utterance, with but a silent tear;
> We dare not look behind us, but steadfastly before,
> We are coming Father Abraham, three hundred thousand more.[38]

Lincoln's proclamation opened the door for black men to step forward to stake their claim in the fight as soldiers. "And I further declare and make known that such persons of suitable condition will be received into the armed service of the United States," he asserted, "to garrison forts, positions, stations, and other places, and to man vessels of all sorts in said service." Such persons already had helped the Union armies and navies function, largely through noncombatant support roles. Now that service would come in the form of brothers in arms. As a result of the opportunity thus presented, some 200,000 "men of color" would stake their lives on the cause of freedom by becoming soldiers and sailors themselves.[39]

Yet Lincoln's proclamation still envisioned the placement of these troops in largely support-oriented positions. "The practical result" of the Emancipation Proclamation in Tennessee, according to one historian, "was that most [black] units raised there wound up guarding the rail lines, supply posts, and other such points, which were generally isolated and vulnerable to enemy raiders." Noah Andre Trudeau considers this set of circumstances tailor made for Forrest in early 1864, and so they were.[40]

The president's action presented further evidence of the evolving nature of the conflict, to which the men in the field had to contend and adjust. In General Orders No. 12, issued in the Department of the Gulf from his headquarters at New Orleans, Major General Nathaniel Banks authorized a clarification of Federal policy for his officers and men. Lincoln's proclamation had complicated matters by leaving portions of Louisiana "not to be affected by its provisions." While Union troops could not, by law, return fugitive slaves to their masters or act upon the claims of those persons, they also could not remove them from such service. "Officers and soldiers will not encourage or assist slaves to leave their employers, but they cannot compel or authorize their return by force."[41]

Whatever limiting factors the Emancipation Proclamation might include, Frederick Douglass was not deterred. Instead, he immediately turned his redoubtable talents to the recruitment of black soldiers and sailors. The ex-slave and outspoken abolitionist called upon the members of his race to shoulder the fight for their interests in equality as well as liberty.[42] Nor did he refuse to experience personal sacrifice when calling upon others to do so. Douglass sent his own sons into the service as part of the celebrated 54th Massachusetts Regiment. His eldest son, Lewis, experienced the bloody and futile fighting that cost his commander, Colonel Robert Gould Shaw, and many of his comrades their lives before Fort Wagner, outside Charleston, South Carolina, in July 1863.

Although there was a sense of joy to Lincoln's actions in many circles, the reaction to the change in emancipation policy was not universally well received, even in the North. Some Union soldiers expressed a desire to leave the service. They had not gone to war to free anyone, especially if those who might be granted this boon would become competitors in the work force of the free-labor North. Others took the president's actions as a clarion call to arms, feeling that they now had a moral reason, as well as a philosophical or constitutional one, for waging war. Most importantly, Great Britain and France might keep the South permanently at arm's length in a war to end slavery.[43]

Still, some prominent British voices reacted to the Emancipation Proclamation with skepticism and contempt. "Where he has no power Mr. LINCOLN will set the negroes free," the *Times* of London editorialized, "where he retains the power he will consider them as slaves." Derisively, the newspaper writer compared the exercise, as he saw it, "more like ... beating two swords together to frighten his enemy than like an earnest man pressing his cause." Others were more ominous in their prognostications of "horrible massacres" and pronouncements that the administration "would league itself with Beelzebub" to achieve victory.[44] The British minister in Washington, D.C., described the measure as a "brutum fulmen" and derided it as having "no pretext of humanity." As he read the document, the diplomat deemed it as "merely a Confiscation Act, or perhaps worse, for it offers direct encouragement to servile insurrection."[45]

Sir John Tenniel of London's *Punch* used his illustrator's pen to comment on the proclamation. In *Abe Lincoln's Last Card; Or Rouge-Et-Noir,* he depicts a dyspeptic Lincoln flinging an ace of spades into a game being played atop a keg of gunpowder. The opposing player, ostensibly Jefferson Davis, keeps his hand close to the vest and wears a smirk that suggests he is untroubled by the gesture.[46]

If to some Lincoln was playing a last desperate card in a vain attempt to achieve victory, others saw opportunity in the enlistment of blacks to aid in delivering a blow against the rebellion. Virginia-born George Henry Thomas, whose sword and service remained with the Union in the conflict, viewed the usefulness of employing black troops in multiple fashions. "The Confederates regard them as property," he explained in a communication with the War Department in November 1863. "Therefore the Government can with propriety seize them as property and use them to assist in putting down the Rebellion." Although such views were not a departure from the foundation of the confiscation acts already enacted, the general held a broader vision too. "But if we have the right to use the property of our enemies," he added, "we share also the right to use them as we would all the individuals of any other civilized nation who might choose to volunteer as soldiers in our Army." Thomas had experienced firsthand the development of the raw material of white volunteers into soldiers and thought the same could be true of blacks. This course would also have the advantage of easing their transition from slavery to freedom while they trained to become soldiers and learned to fend for themselves.[47] Left unsaid in this context was the benefit to be derived by the augmented numbers of troops thus brought to bear in the service of the Union.

In July 1863, the same month that Colonel Shaw and his regiment proved themselves in the sand dunes near Charleston, Lincoln signed an order that labeled the enslavement of black Union soldiers "a relapse into barbarism and a crime against the civilization of the age" and promised protection of these individuals while in the nation's service. He also addressed the topic of retaliation for Confederate transgressions toward any man who bore arms in defense of the Union: "It is therefore ordered that for every soldier of the United States killed in violation of the laws of war, a rebel soldier shall be executed; and for every one enslaved by the enemy or sold into slavery, a rebel soldier shall be placed at hard labor on the public works and continued at such labor until the other shall be released and receive the treatment due to a prisoner of war."[48]

Yet if the president appeared ready to back his new troops with the full force of the Federal government, the use of them also exposed internal social rifts that remained to be addressed. Racial antipathy among disgruntled white Northerners could trigger strong emotional responses, the worst of which occurred in New York City on July 13–16, 1863, when antidraft outbursts reached a fever pitch, and the bitterness of class warfare turned into racial violence. Throngs of angry citizens clashed with police and rampaged against the symbols of their perceived disaffections, looting and vandalizing widely. Veteran troops, some of whom had served in the Gettysburg Campaign, were diverted to assist the local authorities in quelling the mayhem. The mob at length gave way, though not before the charred ruins of numerous structures smoldered as reminders of the rioting. The toll in lives lost has been impossible to verify accurately, although eleven black men were lynched and estimates of more than a hundred civilians killed. Many more people were injured in the worst of the bloody disturbances that shook the city.[49]

Some Southern civilians saw the violence of the New York City Draft Riots as providing Northerners with a taste of the upheavals they were experiencing regularly. As news reached her, South Carolinian Emma Holmes, who frequently departed Charleston for safer regions of her state, noted sardonically,"I'm glad the Yankees are suffering a touch, even though such a faint one, of the horrors they have committed or tried to execute in our midst."[50]

For individuals like Holmes, the threat to society included not only the depredations of the enemy against innocent civilians but also the danger to the South's racial order. Yet President Lincoln's policy transformation regarding slavery and black military service was hardly satisfactory to those who championed full racial equality. Frederick Douglass applied considerable pressure on the president on matters related to the black soldiery, meeting with him personally at the end of August 1863. But Lincoln deflected issues such as distinctions in pay levels by reminding the strident advocate that "the employment of colored troops at all was a great gain to the colored people—that the measure could not have been successfully adopted at the beginning of the war." The war itself had changed the social dynamics, and they were bound to change again until black servicemen "shall have the same pay as white soldiers."[51]

President Lincoln was willing to offer assurances of his commitment to freedom, telling General Banks, "For my own part I think I shall not, in any event, retract the emancipation proclamation; nor, as executive, ever return to slavery any person who is free by the terms of that proclamation, or by any of the acts of Congress."[52] At the same time he encouraged Ulysses Grant to support "the raising of colored troops" in the area near Vicksburg. Lincoln insisted of the use of black soldiers generally: "I believe it is a resource which, if vigorously applied now, will soon close the contest. It works doubly, weakening the enemy and strengthening us."[53] Grant reacted enthusiastically to the directive. "I have given the subject of arming the negro my hearty support," he explained. "This, with the emancipation..., is the heaviest blow yet given the Confederacy."[54] At the very least, these exchanges illustrate the degree to which the Lincoln government had proceeded following the Emancipation Proclamation.

The Confederates were experiencing difficulties of their own with developments that challenged the foundations of their society as they struggled for independence. The Confederate Constitution had explicitly upheld the institution of slavery, offering guarantees and protections for its existence in articles throughout the document.[55] Furthermore, many whites in the South, including nonslaveholders, viewed slavery as an immutable part of their social system. Lincoln's words mattered little to such people at the beginning of 1863. But those words began to have increasing consequence as the year wore on. The Confederate government could no longer ignore the changes being wrought to the peculiar institution the Southern states had seceded from the Union to uphold and ultimately gone to war to defend.

The first reaction of many Confederate leaders to the enlistment of African Americans as military personnel was to look to the past. Men such as Vice President Alexander H. Stephens could see no reason to alter the assessment that race-based slavery was the "cornerstone of the Confederacy." Therefore, any assault on the institution would threaten to crumble the new nation's foundation.[56]

Being accused of inciting servile insurrection was serious business in the slave South, as John Brown had learned after his actions at Harpers Ferry in 1859. The efforts of the Lincoln administration could certainly be interpreted as engaging in similar activity on the grandest scale. Consequently, the Confederate Congress passed a measure that equated black military service in the Union armed forces to insurrection and held those responsible for it to those penalties. From the white Southern conservative point of view, the ideal outcome for the ex-slaves would be to return them to the authority and control of their masters.

Blacks captured in uniform would fit into one of two identifiable categories: either they were slaves—the property of others—to whom they should be returned if claimed or they were free men and subject to enslavement or punishment for inciting servile insurrection. There was no middle ground from the proslavery Southern perspective; indeed, there could be none. Slave rebellion had to be crushed in any form in order to discourage it among others.

The Davis administration had struggled with the thorny issue of black military service under white Union officers through the latter portion of 1862. In the case of the officers, Adjutant and Inspector General Samuel Cooper produced an unmistakable directive in August. General Orders No. 60 specified that "any ... commissioned officer employed in drilling, organizing or instructing slaves with a view to their armed service in this war, he shall not be regarded as a prisoner of war but held in close confinement for execution as a felon."[57] Concerning any black prisoners, Secretary of War James A. Seddon advised General Beauregard in November to turn them over to "civil tribunals" for dispensation. "They cannot be recognized in any way as soldiers subject to the rules of war and to trial by military courts."[58]

President Davis made his position on the subject clear when he signed a December 23 proclamation. General Orders No. 111 specified "[t]hat all negro slaves captured in arms be at once delivered over to the executive authorities of the respective States to which they belong to be dealt with according to the laws of said States." Furthermore, white officers commanding these troops were to be treated in the same manner "when found serving in company with armed slaves in insurrection against the authorities of the different States of this Confederacy."[59]

In a strongly worded "message" to his Congress issued on January 12, 1863, Davis condemned Lincoln's proclamation of emancipation. "Our own detestation of those who have attempted the most execrable measure recorded in the history of guilty man is tempered by profound contempt for the impotent rage which it discloses," he asserted. The Confederate president expected the individual states to address related issues that arose, including "the punishment of criminals engaged in exciting servile insurrection." Enlisted personnel could be exempted "as unwilling instruments in the commission of these crimes," but offending Union officers must be held to account.[60]

After six months, the Confederate chief executive's ire had not abated. In a call for absentees and deserters to return to the ranks following the horrific bloodletting at Gettysburg, Davis sought to place the national situation in an appropriate context. "You know too well, my countrymen, what they mean by success. Their malignant rage aims at nothing less than the extermination of yourselves, your wives, and children. They seek to destroy what they cannot plunder." The president accused their Federal opponents of deliberately attempting "to incite servile insurrection and light the fires of incendiarism wherever they can reach your homes" and charged them with an "inability to prevail by legitimate warfare." In the face of those who failed in "conducting the war according to the usages of civilization," there could be "no alternative … left you but victory or subjugation, slavery, and utter ruin of yourselves, your families, and your country."[61]

Some citizens saw the evolution of the conflict in similar terms. When she heard the stories of "the awful barbarities committed in Mississippi" two weeks later, Emma Holmes concluded, "Humanity sickens at their demoniacal brutality & far better would it be for South Carolina to become a wilderness and desolation, one vast sepulcher & heap of smoldering ruins, than to be cursed for one brief moment with their power to wreak evil."[62]

Confederate war clerk John B. Jones illustrated the conflicting attitudes between the combatants on war and slavery in mid-1863 with an incident that occurred near Fredericksburg. Southern pickets "whistled a horse, drinking in the Rappahannock, and belonging to Hooker's army, over to our side of the river." Declaring the animal "a very fine horse," Jones observed that "Federal Gen. [Marsena R.] Patrick sent a flag demanding him, as he was not captured in battle." The Confederate bureaucrat noted: "Our officer sent back word that he would do so with pleasure, if the Yankees would send back the slaves and other property of the South not taken in battle. There it ended."[63]

Yet the Confederate States of America faced significant challenges in waging a successful war for independence. One of its outstanding fighting generals, Irish-born Patrick Ronayne Cleburne, certainly understood that in a protracted conflict, his country did not have the manpower to sustain its armies in the field against a numerically superior foe. His solution to the problem placed patriotism over any desire to leave the peculiar institution inviolate. If the armed forces of the Confederate States employed blacks as combatants, he felt that not only would the disparity in numbers be addressed but also slavery would become an asset to the South rather than a liability. Freedom at the conclusion of honorable service to the Confederacy would offer a choice other than insurrection or escape and enrollment in the Union military for slaves who wished to exert some measure of control over their lives. But there was no time to lose. "Negroes will require much training, training will require time, and there is the danger that this concession to common sense may come too late."[64]

As it turned out, in the early days of 1864, the plucky Irish Confederate was ahead of the political curve, and his "memorial" found itself buried in desk drawers or suppressed rather than being officially discussed, much less implemented.[65] Whatever the merits of Cleburne's proposal, as one biographer of President Davis has observed, "having blacks don the gray was one experiment that Confederates were not yet ready to try."[66]

Some of the rank and file were less circumspect about what the changes wrought by war and emancipation might mean. William Nugent's rhetoric in his letters to his wife matched the August heat in Mississippi. "There is a probability that the war will not be conducted altogether in a civilized way hereafter," he speculated on the fifteenth. "Lincolne demands that we treat the negro soldier upon an equality with our *whites* & threatens retaliation if we do not." Predicting "dire results," Nugent was certain that such policies would lead to extreme reactions from Northerners and "may provoke the abolitionists to a ferocity unparalleled."[67]

Nugent's pen had hardly cooled twelve days later when he offered his wife his notions of the response Confederates should make to recent developments. He thought Northerners might yet "avoid" the costs of irregular warfare "by a different policy, but their maxim is rule or ruin and they haven't the judgment enough to pursue a different course." Nugent believed that there was a simple solution to the issues at hand. "If they respect private rights & private property, abolish their unholy alliance with our negroes, put them back upon the plantations and make them work as heretofore, they would do more to end this war than by five years hard fighting."[68]

Nathan Bedford Forrest's frame of mind toward the status of slaves and armed black Union soldiers would become an open question in 1864, but he revealed elements of his thinking in the aftermath of the capture of Abel Streight's raiders. On October 22, 1863, he corresponded with John H.

Winder from Dalton, Georgia, on the subject. "There were quite a number of negroes with the command when I first overtook Streight," he noted of the April–May campaign. "Most of them escaped and returned to their masters." Of those who did not follow what Forrest would have considered the appropriate path, there was no indication of summary punishment or any other reaction than rather mundane reporting of the facts. "I found some of the negroes in arms," he added. "Indeed, very few (not exceeding fifteen) were with Colonel Streight's command at the time of the surrender."[69]

Perspectives were changing as to the nature of the war in 1863–64, but in many ways General Forrest confronted race and war in much the same way as he had done from the start of the conflict. Whatever course individual slaves might choose for themselves, he looked at those persons in a context that prevented them from challenging his notion of societal norms. These individuals continued to be the property of owners to whom they remained connected and to whom, by law, they should be returned, if possible.

When the spring campaigning got underway, two very divergent positions were in place concerning the use of "men of color" as combatants. Such completely opposite policies ensured that the North and South would not easily resolve the status of blacks as soldiers and the white officers who led them if and when they should be captured. Re-enslaving blacks and hanging their white officers as the leaders of slave rebellion would surely invite retaliation from the Union government and elevate the intensity of the conflict for the troops on both sides. Whatever might transpire between the combatant governments and their political representatives, the time was rapidly approaching when the soldiers—both black Union troops and white Confederates—would collide at a small, isolated fortification north of Memphis.

CHAPTER 3

# "Attending" to Fort Pillow

## April 1863–April 12, 1864

Such conduct [by Union colonel Fielding Hurst] should be made known to the world.

*Nathan Bedford Forrest, March 21, 1864*

There is a Federal force of 500 or 600 at Fort Pillow which I shall attend to in a day or two, as they have horses and supplies which we need.

*Report of General Forrest, April 4, 1864*

[Fort Pillow] is perfectly safe.

*Major Lionel Booth to Major General Stephen Hurlbut, April 3, 1864*

Nathan Bedford Forrest was not the type of person one would think would be deeply affected by close combat and death. Indeed, if anything, exposure to such elements of war would seem to have hardened him to mortality and inured him to suffering. Yet Forrest's frequent brushes with death on the battlefield and his willingness to risk personal danger obscured the toll that war had already exacted from him.

By the spring of 1864, Forrest could look back on a year of personal losses that must have had a profound effect on him. The first of these concerned the killing of his artillerist, Samuel Freeman, by a Union captor near Franklin, Tennessee. The second struck even closer to home with the death of his beloved youngest brother, Jeffrey, at Okolona, Mississippi.

Captain Freeman was a favorite of Bedford Forrest. As Forrest's artillery chief, Freeman liked to say that he would go as close to the enemy as the general would let him. In April 1863 the Confederates were reconnoitering toward Franklin, when a Union force under Major General David Stanley sliced into the flank of Forrest's command. A courier raced to impart the unhappy news to the Confederate commander, who characteristically replied with a show of bravado that masked his genuine concern: "That's where I've been trying to get him all day, damn him! I'll be in *his* rear in about five minutes."[1] Unfortunately, five minutes was an eternity, especially for the men captured when the Federals struck. Among them was Sam Freeman.

As the Confederates reversed themselves to respond to the threat, the cannoneer's captors began to worry that they might become prisoners themselves if they did not hasten away from the scene. They urged the artillerist to pick up his pace. Whether Freeman failed to do so deliberately, to allow his comrades time to reach and rescue him, or because he was unable to run faster, a Union officer guarding him decided not to take any further chances. He shot his prisoner through the head before riding on to the safety of his own lines.[2]

The loss of his friend affected Forrest deeply. When he rode up to where the artillerist lay, he repeated the phrase "None braver." Biographers Thomas Jordan and J. P. Pryor note the long-lasting effects of this killing on some of the general's troops. "The men of Forrest's Tennessee regiments were greatly incensed by this act, who at once expressed their determination to inflict complete vengeance upon the Fourth [U.S. Cavalry] Regulars for it."[3] The intensity of their feelings did not dissipate over time, and they eventually got the opportunity for retribution in Mississippi in early 1864 and again in Alabama in 1865.

The first chance to strike a blow at the 4th U.S. Cavalry came in a running battle near Okolona, Mississippi. Here, Forrest suffered his second personal loss. As he led a charge, Colonel Jeffrey Forrest took a round in the throat that felled him from his saddle. Bedford Forrest rushed to his side, but there was nothing he could do. Jeffrey's life ebbed away as the general held him in his arms. Bedford Forrest cradled the brother he had raised as a son after the death of their father, then left the care of his remains to a subordinate before hurling himself back into action with a heightened ferocity.

Although not noted for indulging in solemn introspection, Forrest expressed indications of sensitivity at times. He tended not to brood over losses, even such personal ones, yet displays of emotions not typically seen in battle were common for the fierce warrior too. "Forrest himself was by no means immovable," an aide remembered. "I have often seen him give way to the most uncontrollable grief." When the general received an earlier, erroneous report of his youngest brother's demise, he had been inconsolable. "He spoke of his misfortunes," the same staffer recalled, "declared that this was the sorest of them all; told how he had tried to educate Jeffrey so that he might not have to contend against the obstacles which had beset his elder brothers; dwelt upon the promise which his young life had revealed; and finally broke down entirely whilst the tears streamed over his face."[4]

However much Forrest mourned the actual loss of his youngest brother, he also knew Jeffrey had died in combat at the head of his troops. Freeman's killing at the hands of men who held him after he had surrendered, though, was much less palatable. Jeffrey Forrest had taken his chances in battle; Sam Freeman had never had a chance. This was a distinction that Bedford Forrest would surely have made. The men he faced in battle were, like his brother, placing themselves at risk by participating in the fighting. Men like Freeman, captured and disarmed, were nothing more than victims, having no fair chance to defend themselves. The lesson would be reemphasized in another way when the Confederate cavalry commander and his men faced a new opponent on the battlefields of 1864 at such places as Fort Pillow, Tennessee, and Brice's Cross Roads, Mississippi.

Forrest had driven a Union force from northern Mississippi at a high cost to himself. Now in early March, he enjoyed the rare boon of reinforcements. Kentuckians arrived from Bragg's Army of Tennessee, and although their numbers had been whittled terribly by losses, the plan was to put them under Forrest to replenish their ranks with recruits while raiding in western Kentucky.

Prominent among these new arrivals was an enigmatic figure. Brigadier General Abraham Buford was a substantial physical specimen of some three hundred pounds. Before the war he had made a reputation for himself in raising and racing Kentucky thoroughbreds. Now he joined Forrest's command in West Tennessee with the expectation of raising cavalrymen instead.

Forrest prided himself on his ability to fill his ranks with fresh bodies. Buford would give him the opportunity to tap into Kentucky. William T. Sherman thought the Southern recruitment effort at best a neutral factor. He believed it would take one good man to watch every conscript that Forrest forced into the ranks through one of his many dragnets. The Union general had not reckoned on his opponent's ability to mold those who served under him into a cohesive and effective fighting force.

Forrest intended to scour the western portions of Tennessee and Kentucky for these men as well as for fresh animals and supplies. Any harassment of Union forces, both of a conventional and less conventional nature, would be welcome too, of course. The Confederate cavalry commander found that he had scores to settle as he rode into West Tennessee in the spring of 1864. As he pushed his troops into that area in mid-March, the effects of the conflict in the region were painfully obvious. "The whole of

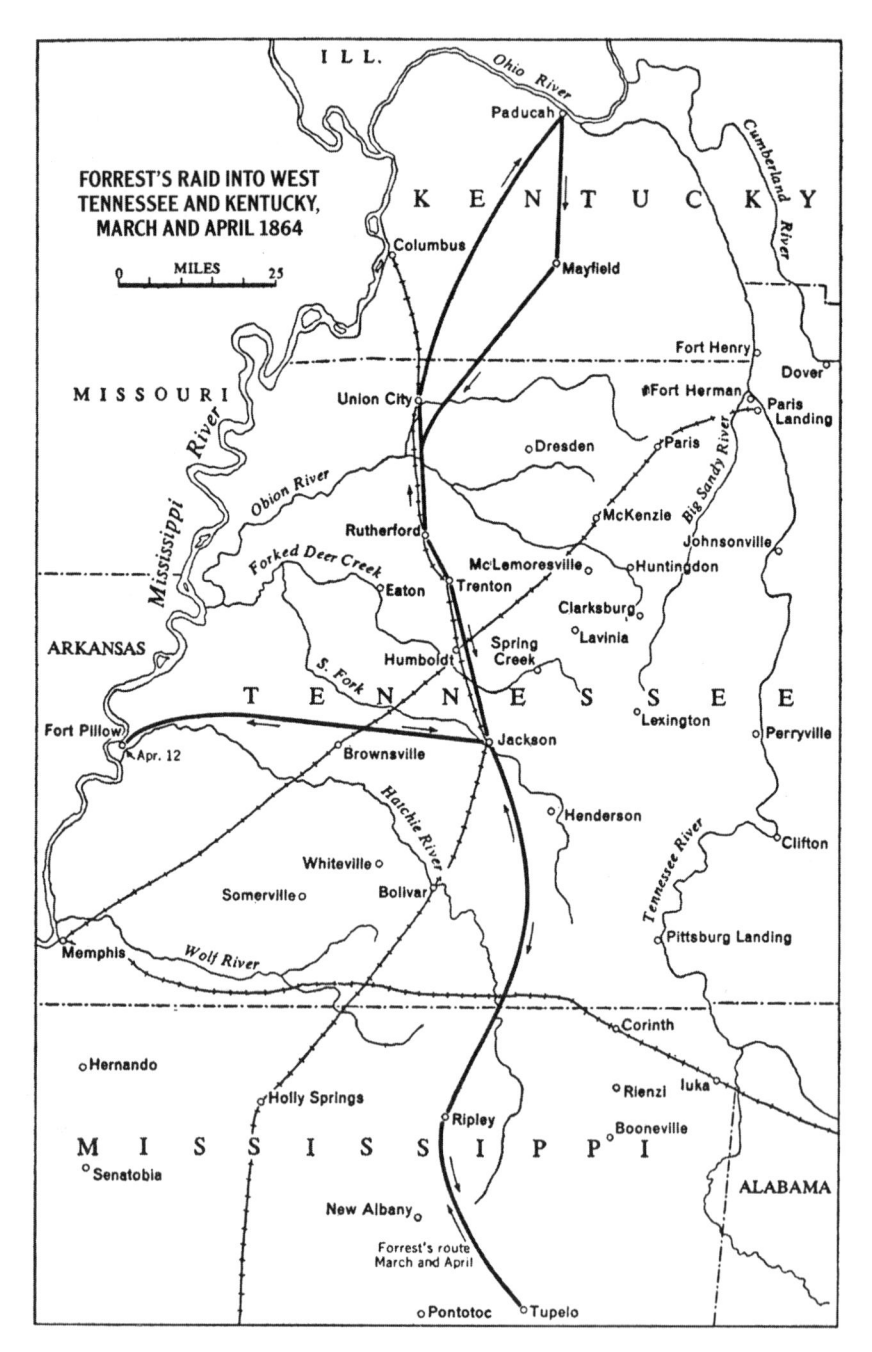

Forrest's Raid into West Tennessee and Kentucky, March and April 1864. Wyeth, *Life of Forrest*.

West Tennessee is overrun by bands and squads of robbers, horse thieves and deserters, whose depredations and unlawful appropriations of private property are rapidly and effectually depleting the country," he reported on the twenty-first.[5] Even more disturbing than this were the accounts from the distressed citizenry of the region. His response to what he would hear speaks volumes about Forrest's personality and the expectations with which he waged war.

Anyone prepared to dismiss Nathan Bedford Forrest as simply a merciless killer should first consider the contradictory evidence of his attitudes and expressions regarding the actions of some of his enemies. The most troublesome for Forrest seemed to have been those associated with Colonel Fielding Hurst. The general used Hurst as a moral counterpoint to what he understood as the legitimate methods of waging war, demonstrating that he held himself and his command to a standard of conduct that at least some of his opponents, he believed, did not attain.

A complicating factor was that Colonel Hurst was a Unionist in the deeply divided state of Tennessee. He had expressed these sentiments openly from the outset of the war, incurring the wrath of his pro-Confederate neighbors. Nor was he alone in holding such views. By one account, as many as twenty-three members of his extended family joined him in the Union ranks.[6] Labeled by one historian "a vengeful partisan in his mid-fifties," Hurst commanded the 6th Tennessee Cavalry (U.S.). He had accepted a Federal commission and quickly established a reputation for suppressing Southern sentiment and activities in western Tennessee.[7] Another historian has noted that even legitimate military activities had a tendency to go awry in the field when associated with the Unionist's command. "As Hurst's cavalry patrolled areas of West Tennessee," Gary Blankinship explains, "his men had a bad habit of leaving the regiment to go on private raids of their own."[8] Apparently, the colonel's men demonstrated this annoying tendency to scatter and reassemble at their pleasure from the earliest days of their service, prompting one Union commander to observe, "If I got into a fight I hoped it would be about noon so I could have the services of his regiment."[9]

The unit originally organized in McNairy County in August 1862 but found adequate arms and equipment difficult to obtain. Even so, it mustered additional companies in the following months and, by the fall of 1863, was in the area of Jackson, Tennessee.[10] In October explicit orders advised against "plundering or pillage by men or officers" of the regiment.[11] Yet the unit's reputation for order and discipline suffered early on in the eyes of its superiors. Brigadier General John D. Stevenson complained to Major General Stephen Hurlbut that he could not locate Hurst's regiment to bring it under his authority.[12] Hurlbut replied emphatically that he should "[t]ry and find out where Hurst is and get him under your command." Interestingly, for an officer who had his own tendency to skirt regulations when it suited him, Hurlbut added, "Both the 6th and 7th Tennessee have behaved badly."[13]

Forrest's command experienced one confrontation with Hurst and his men in December 1863 that offered an indication of what might be expected if they met again. One participant remembered that the colonel was in the town square of Somerville, Tennessee, when Forrest and his men, many of whom were unarmed recruits, suddenly appeared. "My God boys! Yonder comes Forrest!" Hurst was supposed to have proclaimed as he tore out from the scene. At least some of his troopers were not so fortunate in escaping and may well have been shown no mercy by their agitated adversaries.[14]

Certainly, a considerable amount of animosity existed between the commands. Furthermore, pro-Confederate civilians in the region would have agreed that Hurst's Tennesseans "behaved badly" when it came to them too. Yet whatever issues the colonel's enemies, as well as his Unionist colleagues, might have had with him, his superiors gave his men a relatively free hand in West Tennessee. On January 11, 1864, Hurst was told to "proceed to the destruction of all armed enemies of the United States Government."[15] His scope of operations was sufficiently large to make an impression on a restive population. "This order is not intended to confine you to any particular locality, but you will move your command in any part of West Tennessee where, in your judgment, it can be used most effectively."[16] Nine days later he received an additional directive. "You will gather all serviceable stock on your route," his orders of January 20 read, "and subsist your command upon the country."[17]

For Union brigadier general William Sooy Smith, these instructions meant that Colonel Hurst had "a roving commission with his regiment (the Sixth Tennessee Cavalry) and directed him to 'grub up' West Tennessee." Smith, who had recently had his own run in with Forrest, concluded in his communication with U.S. Grant, "I think he will reduce that district to order."[18] It might have been more accurate to say "in short order," for Hurst was soon "roving about," much to the chagrin of Southern sympathizers in Jackson.

It was Hurst's activities in and around Jackson that so incensed Forrest. The stories he heard prompted the most strongly worded and determined dispatches of protest that would emanate from the general's headquarters regarding the difference between acceptable and unacceptable practices in warfare. That the Confederate would even have a code of ethics that could be offended might surprise some. It would not have surprised those who knew the cavalryman well. Forrest had a finely tuned sense of what should or should not happen in war, all of his bluff, bluster, and intimidation to the contrary. There was right and wrong. He felt clearly that he, at least, recognized and understood the difference and adhered to the proper side of the line.

Fielding Hurst was another matter. The Union commander had committed "outrages" of the first magnitude and had to be held to account for them. "I respectfully demand," Forrest asserted in one piece of correspondence with his Union counterparts, "that restitution be made by the U.S. authorities in the sum of $5,139.25 to the citizens of Jackson, Tenn., the amount extorted from them by Col. Fielding Hurst, on or about the 12th day of February, 1864, under threats of burning the town."[19] To make matters worse, Hurst had extorted the ransom payment and set fire to the town anyway. As many as fourteen structures were consigned to the flames before his Union troopers departed. Obviously, the adherence of the people of Jackson to the colonel's demands had availed them little.

It was not so much that Forrest objected to Hurst's use of a threat to accomplish his ends. The general had used such tactics himself with consistent success. But he had done so to subdue military opponents, not to extort money from civilians on pain of arson. Forrest also never shied away from taking such war materiel as might prove useful to himself and his command. Yet Hurst's actions had amounted to nothing more than robbery and blackmail disguised as legitimate military activity. Bedford Forrest would have none of it. Yet this was not the worst crime for which he believed Hurst and his men bore responsibility and guilt.

The more serious offense to Forrest was not arson, but murder. In this instance, atrocity begat atrocity between Hurst and his enemies. When Confederates captured and executed his nephew William, the Union colonel responded with a single-minded ruthlessness, killing as many as thirteen Southern prisoners in retaliation, then displaying their remains openly as warnings for others.[20]

In a sense General Sherman had predicted this type of excess when in September 1862 he communicated with Confederate major general Thomas Hindman over the appropriate application of "the usages of civilized warfare." Hindman protested the degree to which the Federals exhibited their frustrations over Southern guerrillas. Admitting that the two examples he cited were based upon reports received of the proposed execution of one prisoner and the murder of another, the Confederate commander in Little Rock, Arkansas, nevertheless threatened retaliation, insisting, "Efforts to induce your army to conform to the usages of civilized warfare have thus far failed."[21]

Sherman found no evidence that such excesses had even occurred, but he considered the notion of taking lessons from Confederates on such matters amusing. "Of course I mentioned incidentally the ridiculous feature of his communication," he explained to department commander Samuel Curtis, noting that Hindman's assertion was faulty in "claiming the rights of civilized warfare for ununiformed cowardly guerrillas firing from ambush on unarmed steamers loaded with women and children."[22] Hindman had not broached with Sherman the steamer incident that resulted in the virtual destruction of the town of Randolph, Tennessee, as an object lesson for the price of engaging in such activity, but the Union general focused on this incident as illustration of the absurdity of the Confederate position.[23] The fiery warrior concluded disdainfully, "You know full well that it is to the interest of the people of the South, that we should not disperse our troops as Guerillas, but at that game your Guerillas would meet their equal and the world would be shocked by the acts of atrocity resulting from such warfare."[24]

Sherman later observed to the Confederate general, "It should not be that men of enlarged intelligence should make civil war more desperate than it is" at the hands of unrestrained forces. "If we allow the passions of our men to get full command then indeed, will this war become a reproach to the names of liberty and civilization." Nevertheless, the Union general stood prepared to take whatever measures his understanding of circumstances required. He added ominously for Hindman and any future opponent, "for every grade of offence there is a remedy."[25]

In his communications in late 1862, Sherman focused on guerrilla activity threatening the movement of vessels in his jurisdiction. Less than a year later, Nathan Bedford Forrest indicated his desire to harass, if not interdict entirely, Union shipping on the Mississippi River. He forwarded such a plan to Adjutant General Cooper on August 9, 1863. "I respectfully lay before you a proposition which, if approved, will seriously if not [entirely] obstruct the navigation of the Mississippi River," Forrest pledged. He could accomplish this, starting with only a small nucleus of troops, by being given the freedom to form a command "of all the forces I may collect and organize" between Vicksburg, Mississippi, and Cairo, Illinois. "I have resided on the Mississippi River for over twenty years," Forrest explained. "Was for many years engaged in buying and selling negroes, and know the country perfectly from Memphis to Vicksburg on both sides of the river." The general added that he was "also well acquainted with all prominent planters in that region as well as above Memphis." What he did not know personally of the area and its inhabitants the men on his staff, "who have rafted timber out of the bottom," would know. "With the force proposed" and the accumulated knowledge of the region and its terrain features, the cavalryman forthrightly predicted, "I am confident that we could so move and harass and destroy boats on the river that only flats heavily protected by gun-boats would be able to make the passage."[26]

It was a tempting proposal, but it was not to be. For the moment, General Bragg could not spare Forrest and did not yet want to be rid of him. To the original proposal, the commanding general noted, "I know of no officer to whom I would sooner assign the duty proposed, than which none is more important, but it would deprive this army of one of its greatest elements of strength to remove General Forrest."[27]

Forrest tried to nudge the issue along with a letter sent directly to President Davis on August 19. The cavalry general deliberately chose to bypass the proper channels to make his appeal to the Confederate commander in chief because he did not believe that Bragg would forward the request and thought the matter "of sufficient importance to merit the consideration of your excellency." Forrest argued that he should be allowed to "go where (as I believe) I can serve my country best."[28]

Despite the unorthodox approach, Davis concurred with the sentiment. In a note to the secretary of war, the president observed, "The services of Brigadier-General Forrest would no doubt be valuable in that portion of [the] country to which he refers, and in the character of service that he describes."[29] But Davis deferred to his commanding general on the matter, and Bragg's earlier endorsement spoke for itself. Bragg had demonstrated the "propriety of a postponement" in such a reassignment for Forrest, the president noted, but he believed the delay would not be indefinite. "Whenever a change of circumstances will permit, the measure may be adopted."[30] Forrest would have to stay, at least for the time being.

Bragg had been correct in his assessment of his colorful subordinate's capabilities as a cavalry commander. At the Battle of Chickamauga, Forrest demonstrated that he could render valuable service to the Army of Tennessee in the traditional cavalry roles of screening and scouting.[31] But an impasse was rapidly approaching between the rigid army commander and his fiery lieutenant. Forrest dictated a letter in which he used, as the aide who wrote it for him termed, "plain, straight language" to condemn his superior as duplicitous and deceitful. "Bragg never got such a letter as that before from a brigadier," the Tennessean commented as an aside.[32]

Whether propelled by a rash display of insubordination and a lack of professional decorum, an expression of Southern honor by which one man sought satisfaction from another, or some combination of these and other factors, Forrest was not likely to remain content with a piece of correspondence to make his point. A personal confrontation was probably inevitable, and it came when the frustrated subordinate stormed into Bragg's tent and launched into a powerful diatribe against his commander. Following a torrent of accusations of the abuse he felt he had suffered at the general's hands, Forrest finished with a flourish. "You have played the part of a damned scoundrel and are a coward," the cavalryman blasted. "If you were any part of a man I would slap your jaws and force you to resent it." Forrest then warned his meddling superior to leave him alone and promised that if Bragg ever crossed his path again, "it will be at the peril of your life."[33]

Forrest's kinsman, Dr. J. B. Cowan, had accompanied the angry general and thought that the tirade would produce a negative response on Bragg's part. "No," Forrest assured him calmly now that the storm had passed, "he'll never say a word about it; he'll be the last man to mention it, and mark my word, he'll take no action in the matter." Then the cavalryman reached the heart of the issue as he saw it. "I will ask to be relieved and transferred to a different field, and he will not oppose it."[34] Forrest may well have embellished the nature of his encounter with his unpopular superior in subsequent retellings, but the outburst fit the cavalryman's personality and ultimately produced the outcome he preferred. More importantly, from the Tennessean's perspective, Bragg made no official reference to the incident as Forrest was supposed to have predicted.

By October 9, President Davis had arrived in the volatile western theater to assess the command situation in the Army of Tennessee for himself. With Bragg's acquiescence, Forrest finally secured his transfer, but he had to content himself with raising a new command rather than threatening the Mississippi and its defenders with the one he had led in northern Georgia. As far as his superiors were concerned, Forrest could raid as much as he pleased as long as he recruited a new and effective force to do so.[35]

Thus, Forrest headed back into West Tennessee, which in the past had proven so lucrative to him in men, horses, and supplies. His forces had met with mostly positive results when roaming that area. Now came the time to take advantage of the regional Union commander's dispersal of troops to isolated locations like Fort Pillow. For Forrest, in addition to separating himself from a troublesome superior, the potential for expropriating any U.S. government assets gathered there as well as the benefit of defeating yet more Federal forces were the desirable corollaries of returning to this area of operations.

Forrest's appropriation of resources from the Federal government and its supporters rankled those who saw such efforts as little more than plundering, but those activities fit legitimately into the context of warfare. White Southerners did not countenance the measures taken against them by Union forces either. But in early 1864 it was Bedford Forrest's turn to protest what he viewed as unacceptable Northern excesses. "It appears that within the past two months," he alleged, "seven cases of deliberate murder have been committed in this department, most of them known and all of them believed to have been perpetrated by the command of Colonel Hurst." Such circumstantial evidence notwithstanding, Forrest was convinced that the perpetrators of these crimes must answer for them. To the Confederate general this meant "the surrender of Col. Fielding Hurst and the officers and men of his command guilty of these murders." Once in custody, they would be "dealt with by the C.S. authorities as their offenses require."[36]

The most vicious of the acts concerned the "death by torture" of Lieutenant Willis Dodds. The officer had been busy attempting to round up deserters and absentees when Federal troops captured him at his family residence in Henderson County, Tennessee. A witness reported seeing Dodds's remains shortly after "his murder." The result was representative of the brutality that too often characterized the ruthless and merciless nature of the war in the backcountry, from Virginia, Kentucky, and Tennessee to Kansas and Missouri. The witness observed that the lieutenant's corpse "was most horribly mutilated," with "the face having been skinned, the nose cut off, the underjaw disjointed, the privates cut off, and the body otherwise barbarously lacerated and most wantonly injured." Whether or not Dodds had been living when all of these violations occurred, it was certain to this individual "that his death was brought about by the most inhumane process of torture."[37] Forrest had taken the war to opponents in the most personal fashion possible and was himself ultimately responsible for killing thirty men by his own hand by the end of the war, but he had done so in the heat of battle. Apparently, his subordinate had not been so fortunate.

If nothing could be done with regard to Hurst by Union authorities, Forrest was prepared to "declare the aforesaid Fielding Hurst, and the officers and men of his command, outlaws." In his eyes this meant that they would no longer be "entitled to be treated as prisoners of war [when] falling into the hands of the forces of the Confederate States."[38] The declaration was tantamount to a death sentence for the Tennessee Unionist.

Forrest was also determined to make such enemy excesses as widely known as possible. "I desire, if it meets with the approval of [Stephen D. Lee,] the lieutenant-general commanding, that this report may be sent to some newspaper for publication," he explained. Exactly what news organ he had in mind for exposing Hurst's actions he did not indicate, but Forrest was convinced that such excesses demanded full public exposure as well as any censure that might result. "Such conduct should be made known to the world," he concluded.[39]

That Forrest should have been more aware of the perceptions others might have of excesses attributed to him and his men ought to have been clear to him. Regardless, the Union commander had crossed the line as far as the Confederate was concerned, and he was prepared to expose these transgressions to a discerning world. Even so, the general remained highly sensitive to the type of criticisms he leveled so easily at Hurst. After the war that sensitivity spilled forth in a letter to a friend. "I took particular pains when I entered the army," Forrest wrote in November 1868, "to make myself fully acquainted with all rules and usages pertaining to civilized warfare." The implication was clear, but he added as a matter of emphasis a denunciation of anyone "who says I ever overstepped the bounds of civilized warfare during my career in the Army."[40] Nevertheless, he should have realized that if he used limitations in reference to his opponents' actions, others would apply them to him too.

Antagonism was certainly not difficult to find between the Tennesseans in blue and those in gray. The relations between those under Forrest and those under Hurst mirrored the bitter divisions in the state as a whole and exacerbated feelings of hatred and hostility that often predated the war. The same would be true of the Tennesseans under Major William F. Bradford stationed at Fort Pillow.

Even more ominous for these acerbic intrastate opponents was the degree to which each regarded the other as devoid of any civilizing effects in combat. Killings without regard to formalized rules of warfare seemed to dominate their encounters. In late February 1864 Colonel William B. Stokes of the 5th Tennessee Cavalry (U.S.) complained that Confederates had "made a dash on one of my picket-posts," with some of these men dressed in Union uniforms while others pretended to pursue, calling on their disguised comrades to surrender. Observing that "the story appeared very plausible," Stokes noted that the ruse cost four genuine Union pickets their lives—"3 after they had surrendered and the other after he had been captured." Similarly, a Federal patrol along the Calfkiller River had come under attack from Confederates, "many" of whom were "dressed in our uniform at the time ... and several of my men were killed after they were captured." Stokes recognized that his counterpart, Colonel John M. Hughs of the 25th Tennessee Infantry (C.S.), "does not allow this barbarity, but his subordinate officers practice it." The nature of this style of warfare was exasperating and infuriating. "I have to fight for every ear of corn and blade of fodder I get," the Union officer bemoaned, then adding, "I have to fight rebel soldiers and citizens, the former carrying the arms and doing the open fighting; the latter, carrying news and ambushing."[41]

Bradford and Forrest had something in common besides the fact that they carried Tennesseans on their rosters and called Bedford County, Tennessee, home. Both men planned to use their time in West Tennessee to augment their commands through recruitment. Forrest never passed on the opportunity to send out agents to scour the region for individuals he could return to the service or add to his units. Likewise, when Bradford's men reached Fort Pillow on February 8, 1864, they were expected to use the post as a base for raising troops in addition to other duties.[42]

Major Bradford operated under instructions similar to those given Hurst. Sooy Smith named Fort Pillow as "your recruiting rendezvous for the present." While there, the major was to make his post "a good defensible position" and "scout the surrounding country thoroughly." In the process Smith wanted him to "hunt up and destroy guerrilla parties," which would undoubtedly please local Unionists. "You will subsist your command upon the country as far as possible," the Federal commander insisted, "and take the stock necessary to keep it well mounted, giving vouchers to loyal men only." The general expected the garrison to be ready for action whenever called upon and instructed his subordinate to draw conventional resources from Memphis.[43] This meant that Bradford had a free hand to requisition supplies as he saw fit to maintain his command. Drawing subsistence in this manner would obviously fall most heavily on those he deemed disloyal, further aggravating the relationship between his soldiers and area civilians.

One factor exacerbating the situation was that some of the Union troops were former Confederates. Historian Gregory Macaluso's analysis of Bradford's roster reveals that "at least sixty-four men" of the 268–272 who composed the unit had been "former Confederate soldiers."[44] Even if these men had entered Southern service under less than voluntary circumstances, their erstwhile colleagues in gray were unlikely to welcome their new allegiances.

Forrest could expect, perhaps should have expected, that trouble would occur when these antagonists met in the field. Indeed, he may have counted on it as a motivational tool to enhance the performance of his troops. Bedford Forrest was certainly not one to fail to give psychology a chance to work in his favor. "You d—n boys have been bragging you could whip half a dozen Tennessee Yankees," he told some of his Tennessee troops as encouragement. "You are the 7th Tennessee Rebs, the 7th Tennessee Yanks are at Union City. I am going to send you there to clean them up, if you don't, never come back here."[45] If his men thus were determined to give a good account of themselves against this particular opponent, then so much the better, although adequate supervision would have to be used to keep the situation from spiraling out of control. "Boys," one of the Southerners recalled saying to his comrades, "maybe we have been talking too strong. But Forrest has called our hands."[46]

In the meantime, the general also had a military operation to prepare to undertake, along with the various ancillary activities of recruitment and procurement of supplies. He saw little contradiction in requisitioning local resources on his behalf, including sending an officer out specifically to locate "the finest horse he can find in the state" as a personal mount. Forrest maintained that the loss of animals he had endured at Okolona "in defense of the state," as one officer described it, meant that the commander "justly felt that he has the right to impress the finest horse that could be found within its limits for his individual use."[47]

As was his usual style, Forrest spread his forces broadly across the region. The effect was to maximize results and magnify his presence. General Sherman confirmed that this part of his opponent's strategy was working. In communications from his headquarters in Nashville, Sherman noted reports that Forrest seemed to be everywhere at once. To George H. Thomas he observed that the Confederate raider "seems to be omnipresent."[48] Subsequently, he confessed to John A. Rawlins incredulousness as well as grudging respect of Forrest: "I admire his great skill, but he can't do all that."[49]

In a sense, of course, Sherman was correct. Forrest could not be everywhere simultaneously and often appeared only as a product of a worried commander's imagination. But when sending out detachments, as he did frequently, the Tennessean exhibited a range that exaggerated his numbers and his presence wherever they went. Again, Forrest the gambler was playing his hand in such a way as to keep his opponents off balance by constantly forcing them to guess where he really was and what he intended to do. He had victimized enough Federal commanders who had neglected to exhibit the appropriate amount of vigilance as to make their successors extremely wary of being caught in the same manner. In that sense his previous successes based upon bluster and bluff would make future such victories even more difficult to attain. Nevertheless, as he prepared to undertake another raid, Forrest expected to use these tried-and-true tactics.

Thus, on March 22, 1864, the general reached Trenton, Tennessee, and prepared to deploy his men so as to create the greatest consternation among Union garrisons in the region. The next day he detailed the responsibility for leading a strike against the railroad and depot at Union City, just below the Kentucky line, to Colonel William L. Duckworth and a detachment of approximately five hundred troopers.[50]

Duckworth's command arrived before its intended target early on March 24. The Confederates drove in the pickets at approximately 4:00–4:30 A.M., killing two and wounding several others. The remainder scampered back and found refuge in the fortifications. As the Southerners converged on the position, they discovered the presence of hundreds of entrenched Federal troops.

At 5:30 the Confederates made a bold but ill-advised mounted dash on the Union works. The Federals turned this back easily, but the Southerners regrouped for another try, this time on foot.[51] A participant recalled that the men used fallen timber for cover as they advanced, taking care not to expose themselves too recklessly and firing at any Union target that appeared over the defensive works.[52] Two more dismounted probing assaults, the last one coming at about 8:00 A.M., indicated the strength of the position and convinced Duckworth to choose a different approach. While Confederate sharpshooters harassed the garrison, the colonel pondered a new scheme that, if successful, would garner him the position without risking additional troops in frontal assaults.[53]

The lightness that allowed the column to move so swiftly also mitigated its effectiveness against strongly held defenses, for Duckworth had no artillery with which to threaten his opponents or intimidate them into surrender. But even this limitation did not deter the officer, who had watched his commander employ bluff in similar situations so effectively. Forrest's penchant for winning bloodless battles was about to pay dividends for his lieutenant.

It probably did not hurt that the commander of the Union City garrison had been an earlier victim of Forrest's psychological warfare. Colonel Isaac R. Hawkins had fallen prey to the Confederate during the Southerner's foray into West Tennessee in December 1862. He had been part of the command of Colonel Robert G. Ingersoll when the Confederates compelled his surrender near Lexington. A contingent of 272 soldiers from the 2nd West Tennessee Cavalry under Hawkins was among the 773 Federals who became Forrest's captives that day.[54]

Even so, Duckworth could not be sure how his counterpart would react this time. Either Hawkins would prove a patsy, easily gulled into folding rather than playing his hand in combat, or he had learned a lesson from his experience and would be tougher than ever to deceive. Duckworth thought it worth testing. Trying to fool the Federals would certainly do no harm, given that the Confederates were not going to be able to overrun the position without artillery or more men.

Consequently, about midmorning Duckworth sent in what had become the standard "Forrest" call for surrender.[55] Hawkins responded by asking for time to consider the demand. He also made the request to meet with the general, his former adversary, personally. Perhaps he doubted Forrest's presence or was simply stalling for time until he could determine what else he could do. At any rate, Duckworth quickly closed this course of action by denying the request peremptorily. "I am not in the habit of meeting officers inferior to myself in rank under a flag of truce," the colonel replied, still posing as Bedford Forrest, "but I will send Colonel Duckworth, who is your equal in rank, and who is authorized to arrange terms and conditions with you under instructions."[56]

To be sure, Duckworth had instructions, though not from Forrest on the scene. Still, Hawkins did not know that the general was not present, but the Southern colonel employed his wits to create and maintain the bluff just to be sure. Duckworth did not rely solely on the Union commander's history or his mindset to accomplish the capitulation of the garrison. He also began moving his command around, just clearly enough to be seen from a distance, so that his numbers appeared much greater than they were in reality. Of particular benefit in the charade were the horseholders, the one man in four who normally remained in the rear with the mounts while the other three troopers went forward on foot to fight. Producing a timely shout as if they were welcoming the arrival of fresh reinforcements, and their subsequent deployment from point to point to substantiate the illusion, these men were effective in helping swell the Confederate ranks in the minds of their Union opponents.[57] The ruse was complete when a telegraph operator informed a collection of Federal officers that the Confederates "had two pieces of artillery; that he had seen them."[58] This last piece of disinformation was likely the one that made the difference, for artillery meant that the Southerners could blast their opponents into submission if they chose. Hawkins now figured that the outcome was assured. In a sense it was.

The Union commander later explained that under the impression of his opponent's capabilities, "it would save a great many lives if we surrender." His mind made up, Hawkins met with Duckworth at about 11:00 A.M. and consummated the arrangement. Ten minutes later Union City was in Southern hands.[59] The day's work by Forrest's subordinate netted the Confederates nearly five hundred officers and men, including "the renegade Hawkins," as well as 200–300 horses, the latter an important commodity in a fast-moving raid that broke down mounts and required ready replacements.[60]

By noon, the Southerners had torched the barracks and begun to march away with their cache of prisoners. Union captain John W. Beatty reported that the Confederates seemed especially happy to have confronted the Tennessee Unionist Hawkins, although not for the bloodthirsty reasons that one might surmise. "The rebel officers told me that they knew they would get our regiment when they were 400 miles south of Union City, Tenn. They also said they were willing to parole Colonel Hawkins and let him get some more horses and arms, and then they would come and get them."[61]

Unfortunately, the defeat was even more personal for Hawkins and his fellow officers and men. They had on their persons some $60,000 they had recently drawn from the paymaster for "over a year's service." A prisoner later recalled that as their captors herded them into a line before the courthouse, they "searched each man as he went in, robbing them of their money, blankets, etc."[62] Hawkins was himself a victim and protested to his Confederate counterpart, but Duckworth could do little to prevent such abuses by these enterprising Rebels.[63] Most noteworthy was the fact that for all of the indignities they felt they had endured at the hands of Duckworth's men and the underlying hostilities that existed, the Unionists left no record of life-threatening treatment from their captors.

Unfortunately, there remained much worse circumstances for the men to experience when they entered Southern prison compounds. Many of these Tennesseans in blue found themselves in Camp Sumter or Andersonville, the notorious facility in Georgia, whose inmate death rate was among the highest in the Confederacy.[64] According to one historian, "Almost 66 percent of the enlisted men, or two out of every three who had been captured at Union City that day in March of 1864, never made it home."[65]

Even while in the saddle, General Forrest realized that others would be watching and assessing his command's actions from afar. He may have been limited in formal education, but he understood the value of the printed word and became an avid reader of newspapers.[66] He developed a useful method of disseminating information to various news organs so that the exploits of his command might be known to a wide readership. George W. Adair, for a time editor of the *Atlanta Southern Confederacy* and a prewar friend, was then a member of the general's staff and remained busy supplying fresh information from the front.[67] In turn, other newspapers picked up the reports and reprinted them so that the news truly traveled widely across the Deep South. For instance, the *Augusta [Ga.] Chronicle & Sentinel* announced to its readers twice in the early part of 1864 that Captain Adair "of Forrest's staff" had provided "some interesting news" to several papers that the editors were happy to pass along.[68]

While in the course of the raid through western Kentucky and Tennessee, Adair drafted a letter designed for publication that appeared in the itinerant *Memphis Daily Appeal*. The writer informed his readers that at Columbus, Kentucky, the Confederates also secured "a large quantity of hats, boots, clothing, etc.," which surely came in handy for replacing items worn out through the winter months and the hard riding and campaigning of the spring. Then, he noted, the Southerners returned with their "prisoners and supplies, and Col. Faulkner moved on towards Hickman, tearing up the railroad, burning bridges, etc."[69] This was the kind of raiding at which Forrest and his men excelled.

While Forrest's subordinate met with unqualified success at Union City, the general was enjoying less of it himself as he threatened the river town of Paducah, Kentucky. When the Confederates arrived there in the early afternoon of March 25, they found the area well defended.[70] The garrison of 665 men under the command of Colonel Samuel G. Hicks consisted of both white and black soldiers from the 122nd Illinois Infantry (120 men), the 16th Kentucky Cavalry (271 men), and the 1st Kentucky Heavy Artillery (274 black troops). These Federals had the additional benefit of a strong earthwork called Fort Anderson, located on the western side of town, and the presence of two gunboats, the *Peosta* and the *Paw Paw*, on the Ohio River.[71] Forrest's men poured through the outskirts of Paducah, driving the Federals into their fort and occupying nearby houses from which they could lay down a harassing fire.

As was his custom on any battlefield, Bedford Forrest immediately scouted the situation for himself. It became readily apparent, to him at least, that assault alone would not win the day. As part of this reconnaissance, the cavalry commander instructed his able lieutenant General Buford to send a small force forward, as one Southerner reported, "to examine the condition of the fort." The Kentuckian selected a man who must have seemed perfectly suited for the task, Colonel A. P. Thompson, a native of the city and a well-known attorney there before the war.[72]

Unfortunately for the colonel, the bold approach seemed to hold out the greatest chance for success. He thought the desired outcome might still be achieved by a dash at Fort Anderson. "I am going to take that fort!" Thompson proclaimed as he lined his men up for an assault.[73] The move was certainly daring but extraordinarily reckless, as subsequent results made horrifyingly clear. Leading his men in the furious charge, Thompson was waving his cap in encouragement when, as one of the troopers with him noted, "he was struck by a shell, which exploded as it struck him, literally tearing him to pieces and the saddle off his horse."[74] Another witness observed even more graphically, "His head was knocked off his shoulders." Then, the same fellow added, with an unintended dual meaning regarding the vessels whose fire had most likely cost the colonel his life, "The gunboats did good execution."[75]

The Kentuckian may have had another motivation that prompted him to risk the attack that cost his life. "When he approached the fortifications" on his scouting mission, according to one account, Thompson "saw the negroes in Federal uniform within, [and] he became so indignant that he took parts of three regiments, and without orders, attacked the fort, and was shot dead in the front of his men, within forty yards of the works—thus losing his life through impatience and indiscretion."[76]

By this account, Colonel Thompson exhibited a racial animus that was surely not confined to him alone. His death prevented any postaction confirmation of any specific motivation on his part, much less an indication of how this particular combat experience might have shaped any subsequent encounters with black Union troops. No contemporary evidence has appeared to suggest that the Confederates who survived the assault looked upon the loss of their leader or the makeup of the opposing force in any manner inconsistent with the reactions they would have had to any other similar events. Defeat at the hands of former slaves or Southern Unionists would have been galling for Forrest's Confederates in any instance and certainly must have been so at Paducah.

As it was, the attacks on Fort Anderson came in several waves, with Thompson being struck down in the final attempt to storm the Federal works. Two Confederate staff officers also fell at the colonel's side in the ill-fated charge.[77] Thus, having lost their commander so dramatically, the assaults ended, and the survivors hobbled back to their lines. Confederate sharpshooters remained busy peppering the Union position, but Forrest undertook no further aggressive efforts against Fort Anderson. Any additional price was simply too steep to be paid, especially for questionable results.[78]

The gunboats provided Colonel Hicks with a considerable boost of confidence. The deck log of the *Peosta* indicated the effectiveness of the fire from the river as the gunboat first "steamed to the upper end of the city where the enemy being seen we opened on them with our starboard & bow guns." The *Paw Paw* joined in the barrage, and both vessels soon "droped [*sic*] along down to the foot of broadway" and fired their pieces "as fast as possible," causing the Confederates to retreat to cover.[79] Working in tandem with the other gunboat, the *Paw Paw* also raked the streets and open ground "above and below the Fort."[80]

Forrest had been on his intelligence-gathering ride when Thompson went forward, and the general certainly regretted the impetuosity that led to the colonel's death. He had not ordered an attack, but at least one Confederate thought that he had authorized it. Captain Henry A. Tyler later recalled, "Supposing that the charge had been ordered by General Forrest," he had sought and obtained permission from Thompson to join it.[81] Tyler's assumption, erroneous as it turned out, would not be the last time individuals in Forrest's command assumed they knew what their general intended or invoked his name on behalf of actions they undertook by their own authority.

In the meantime, Forrest's personal observations and Thompson's rash demise convinced the general to try another tactic to take the fort and its garrison. Just as Duckworth had done at Union City, Forrest sent in a demand to Hicks that he hoped would convince him of the futility of further resistance. "Having a force amply sufficient to carry your works and reduce the place, and in order to avoid the unnecessary effusion of blood, I demand the surrender of the fort and troops, with all public property." As additional encouragement, the Confederate cavalryman promised, "If you surrender, you shall be treated as prisoners of war; but if I have to storm your works, you may expect no quarter."[82] Now the decision rested in the Union commander's hands.

Hicks considered the demand and dismissed it, perhaps sensing that the threat of "no quarter" masked a weakness. Unlike his comrade at Union City, he would not be so easily swayed. "I can answer that I have been placed here by my Government to defend this post," he replied, "and in this, as well as all other orders from my superiors, I feel it to be my duty as an honorable officer to obey. I must, therefore, respectfully decline surrendering as you may require."[83] Forrest would have to do more than issue threats to convince Hicks of the futility of his position. The general would have to demonstrate to the colonel's satisfaction that he, Nathan Bedford Forrest, could back up his words.

That satisfaction would not come by virtue of the sustained firepower the Federals were able to bring to bear against the Confederates. When fighting resumed at 4:45 P.M., the fire from the gunboats was less in defense of the Union position than to dispel the parties of Southerners who were ranging through the town looking for spoils of war. The *Peosta* "opened on the Rebels again who were plundering the city and advancing on the Fort." But the naval gunners had new targets too. "In consequence of the heavy fire of musketry directed against us from Rebels in the buildings we opened on them, demolishing the City Hotel & Brewery and setting fire to other houses."[84]

Such collateral damage was impossible to avoid, with Confederate sharpshooters, ensconced in the structures nearest the river, attempting to silence the gunboats by aiming at the portholes through which the cannon fired. The *Peosta* reported being struck "about 200 times with musketry. Some entering the Ports and a few penetrating the sides." This damage, except for a gunner wounded in the hand, was largely cosmetic. Both gunboats expended a considerable amount of ammunition, most of it in the form of explosive rounds such as shell, canister, and grapeshot. Altogether, the *Peosta* sent 328 rounds hurtling into Paducah; while the *Paw Paw* added another 127, to the discomfiture of Confederate soldiers and city residents alike.[85]

In his report on the expedition, Forrest put the best interpretation on events. He recorded the outcome at Paducah as more successful than Thompson's ill-advised attack might indicate. "I drove the enemy to their gunboats and fort, and held the town for ten hours; captured many stores and horses; burned sixty bales of cotton, one steamer [the *Dacotah*], and a drydock, bringing out fifty prisoners." He indicated that it was the news of an outbreak of smallpox that convinced him to abandon any further efforts to capture the garrison.[86]

Colonel Adair delighted in recounting the spoils the Southerners obtained in the Paducah raid: "Four hundred fine horses, several ambulances, quartermaster stores, medicines, etc., fell into our hands. The Yankee papers admit a loss of fourteen whites and eleven negroes, killed and many wounded." But he seemed particularly to have enjoyed the extent to which these same sources exaggerated the admittedly heavy Confederate losses. "They also report," he wrote near the end of April, "Gen. Forrest's loss at twelve hundred, which is equal to the entire detachment carried to that place."[87] In truth, whatever the extent of his gains and losses in the affair, Forrest had done about all that he could against a determined foe stubbornly holding his ground, whatever odds might be brought against him.

Author Ronald Huch discerns greater ramifications for future Confederate actions from the setback at Paducah. He insists that the defeat "served to intensify the fury felt by the Rebels toward Northern troops in general, and black soldiers in particular." Huch believes that these Confederates sought to avenge the sense of "humiliation" they had experienced, declaring that "the setback at Paducah was probably sufficient cause to turn Forrest and his men from angry, battle-weary warriors into mass murderers at Fort Pillow."[88]

Forrest's men may well have felt the need for avenging "the setback at Paducah" as they would for any defeat. They undoubtedly found the presence of black troops among the garrison vexing to their notions of social order and racial subordination. But Forrest seemed to hold the opinion that now these African Americans only operated under the control of different masters, ones who deluded and manipulated them for their own purposes. Of course, according to the extant records, the one man who may have been most clearly affected by the existence of black defenders at Fort Anderson perished in the assault. In any case, if Huch's Paducah thesis prevailed, then Forrest missed the best opportunity to use racial animus to avenge his fallen subordinate when he allowed the Kentuckians to disperse on brief furloughs immediately following the fight, thus preventing them from being present at Fort Pillow, where they could have exacted retribution and asserted their notions of racial superiority.

It was always possible that Forrest realized that his troops would want revenge against black opponents in particular and thus detailed the soldiers most likely to engage in such activity on other duty to avoid any future criticism or culpability. But the calculations that made most sense for the general to employ were in meeting the demands of his forces amid an active and grueling campaign. As such, he would not furlough the Kentuckians in order to prevent possible retaliation or to mitigate charges that might someday be leveled against him; the move was a basic one to replenish recruits and mounts while the detailed units were close to home and could more readily obtain them. Vengeance for Paducah might still have been present in the minds of some when they reached Fort Pillow and found black soldiers there, but the general responsible for assembling an assault force against the garrison was more interested in practical realities than anything else.

As the Confederates slipped off to the south, away from the short, sharp bloodletting at Paducah, Forrest paused at Dresden, Tennessee, to catch his breath. He directed the composition of a report to his superior, Leonidas Polk, that outlined the successes he had achieved thus far and his aspirations for the remainder of the campaign. "I hold possession of all this country except posts on the river," he explained, perhaps already eyeing one of them for personal attention. "Think if I can remain unmolested here fifteen days I will be able to add 2,000 men to my command."[89]

Certainly, as he had demonstrated with his newly acquired Kentuckians, Forrest understood the need to maximize the chance the raid gave him for replenishing his forces. The general did the same for the 7th Tennessee, giving the men in that unit instructions to reassemble after they had fulfilled their assigned tasks and enjoyed the brief opportunity to renew contacts with family.[90] Benjamin Bondurant of Bell's Brigade recalled that after the fighting at Paducah, he and his comrades "wer[e] furloughed to go home for about 20 days."[91]

Although he had not been very successful in Kentucky, Bedford Forrest could boast of one additional, and most welcome, victory over a well-known nemesis at the end of March. On the twenty-ninth Brigadier General James Chalmers reported that Confederates under Colonel J. J. Neely had "met the traitor Hurst at Bolivar, [and] after a short conflict, in which we killed and captured 75 prisoners of the enemy, drove Hurst hatless into Memphis." The capture of "all his wagons, ambulances, and papers" and the abandonment of "his mistresses, both black and white," proved to be additional embarrassments for the hated Unionist.[92] Another account noted the victory over "about six hundred of the enemy, near Bolivar, under the notorious Tennessee tory and robber, Col. Hurst" had resulted in "killing twenty two, capturing thirty five and wounding a great number." The writer happily recounted that the remainder of the Federals fled "in the wildest confusion toward Memphis, losing their entire wagon train and sixty-five thousand rounds of ammunition." He took particular pleasure in observing, "Col. Hurst led the inglorious retreat, bare headed and wild with fright."[93]

Another Forrest subordinate, Lieutenant Colonel Crews, also enjoyed success against a Union detachment as he kept an eye on the roads from Memphis. His opponents, horsemen under Union brigadier general Benjamin Grierson, numbered some four hundred men. Although the Confederate officer had only seventy-five men, he adopted his commander's aggressive style and charged on the Somerville Road near Raleigh, Tennessee. The tactic worked, inflicting over twenty casualties on Grierson's command and netting Crews and his men some six Union prisoners. The assault also had the desired result of causing the rest of the force to retire to Memphis, where it would not have the opportunity to interfere with further Confederate activities in West Tennessee. In the process the Southerners suffered only light losses of two men wounded.[94]

On April 4 Forrest paused in his active operations to report his accomplishments to his superiors. Establishing his own casualties to date at fifteen killed and 42 wounded, he put those of his opponents at seventy-nine killed, 102 wounded, and 612 captured.[95] Earlier he had set his losses from Union City and Paducah at twenty-five killed and wounded.[96] A Union officer noted that although the Confederates spent considerable time using wagons to gather their dead and wounded, they had been unable to retrieve the bodies of fifteen of their slain in the vicinity of Fort Anderson, suggesting that the total Forrest reported was low.[97] It is indeed telling that the cavalry commander offered no number of missing in either of his casualty assessments.

The bloody repulse at Paducah aside, the raid into West Tennessee had thus far generated positive results. But Forrest was not finished, considering the greater spoils to be had for the taking. "There is a Federal force of 500 or 600 at Fort Pillow," he explained in his report, "which I shall attend to in a day or two, as they have horses and supplies which we need."[98] The acquisition of such resources was critical to maintain the raid's effectiveness, and the source of supply fit well with Forrest's pattern. As one of his men later recalled, with more than a hint of proud adornment: "In fact the Federals were largely our commissary, blankets, etc. and part of [our] clothing and much that we ate" came from the U.S. government's largess.[99] There was no reason to think this would not be the case with Fort Pillow too. In addition, the fort contained artillery, and one could never have enough of that commodity.

Despite Huch's conclusion that the repulse by black artillerymen at Paducah would subsequently "turn Forrest and his men ... into mass murderers at Fort Pillow," nothing in the general's report indicates that this frame of mind dominated his thoughts after the earlier setback. Astoundingly, Huch goes on to conclude, "If Forrest had gained the surrender he sought at Paducah, there would probably have been no Fort Pillow massacre."[100] Bedford Forrest would certainly not have shied from insisting that his opponents be obliterated if he had held such intentions, whatever had taken place on other fields.

In Richmond, news of Forrest's exploits in West Tennessee lifted spirits. On the same day the general made his report, Ordnance Chief Josiah Gorgas recorded his impressions of these exploits in his journal: "The news from Forrest to-day is very good. He attacked Union City on the 25th & took 450 prisoners." Gorgas noted that the raiders had also "captured" Paducah, "but did not hold it, the Small pox being prevalent." But to the Confederate official, Forrest had achieved remarkable results with relatively few losses of his own. "He returns about 600 prisoners who are on their way to Demopolis. He states his loss at only 25 killed and wounded, while the Yankee accounts had made it as high as 1300!"[101]

In the meantime, Forrest rode south with the intention of "attending" to Fort Pillow. He continued to order units to fan out across the region to mask his intentions. Perhaps they would achieve additional successes as well. But General Forrest had his sights set on another tempting target: the isolated fortification on the Mississippi River above Memphis, with its garrison of Tennessee Unionists and black troops and the "horses and supplies which we need."

CHAPTER 4

# "WILL HE FIGHT OR SURRENDER?"

## *March–April 12, 1864*

We will not surrender.
> Major William Bradford to General Forrest, April 12, 1864

Superficially at least, Fort Pillow looked like a formidable position. The Confederates had initially constructed the work as part of a system of defenses to protect Memphis from Union riverine assault. It contained three sets of works stretching inland from the Mississippi River. The innermost of these overlooked the river from a steep bluff. This interior line featured a parapet six to eight feet high and four to six feet across constructed of dirt shoveled out of a ditch to its front eight feet deep. The half-circle-shaped work lay 125 yards in length, with its rear, toward the river, opened to the bluff. Two ravines flanked the position, having been cut into the rolling hills of loess soil as water ran from the higher elevations to the river.

The Confederates had not held the post since abandoning it in 1862 around the time of Memphis's capture. The Federals incorporated it into a system of works that was supposed to protect their river communications and the flow of supplies and commerce on the Mississippi. General Sherman made the importance of this abundantly clear to Major General James McPherson in early March 1864, when he observed, "The river Mississippi must be held sacred, and any attempt of the enemy to make a lodgment anywhere on its banks must be prevented by any and all means." He pointed out that the river's "peaceful navigation must be assured," with harsh retaliation for the "molestation" of any "legitimate and licensed traffic."[1]

Yet Sherman also seemed anxious to consolidate the positions from which the river would be defended, focusing his efforts on Memphis as a base of operations. With troops concentrated in that city, they could be sent in any direction in which a Confederate threat materialized with sufficient force to eliminate or drive off the challenge without too great a risk of a military disaster. Isolated posts like Fort Pillow not only would offer no material benefit to this strategy but also would serve as tempting targets of dispersed forces, which was precisely what Sherman did not want to happen in his rear as he prepared to move against Atlanta.

Largely for this reason, debate has continued to rage as to whether or not Fort Pillow should have been defended in the first place. General Sherman, whose area of authority included the fort and its garrison, was determined to abandon it.[2] But his subordinate in Memphis, Stephen Hurlbut, had other ideas. His reasons for disregarding his superior's instructions were tied to the interests he had developed in a local, and what one historian has deemed, "lucrative trade in confiscated cotton." Historian Noah Trudeau explains that under these circumstances, the Union officer "needed the fort for the conduct of his illegal dealings."[3]

The first Union troops reassigned to Fort Pillow in the spring of 1864 were white Tennesseans under Major William F. Bradford. They were soon joined by black cannoneers from the 6th U.S. Colored Heavy Artillery under Major Lionel F. Booth, a former noncommissioned officer from the antebellum Regular Army, who assumed command of the post. In addition, members of the 2nd U.S. Colored Light Artillery received orders to augment the garrison. One author has speculated that "the best runaway slaves" would likely not wish to risk Southern retaliation by enlisting, although they might be tempted by better army pay for laborers than for its black soldiers. At any rate, the 2nd Light Artillery had existed for only a short time.[4]

Still, the ex–Old Army sergeant had his charges busy prowling for Southern soldiers and sympathizers or improving the defensive works. Throughout February and March, Major Booth employed the gunboat *New Era* to ferry small detachments of troops from the fort, and occasionally they returned with prisoners, who were routinely "put in Irons for safe keeping," a practice that no doubt galled the captives and any sympathizers who learned of it.[5]

The soldiers of the garrison also spent a great deal of their time strengthening Fort Pillow. They erected and improved an earthwork capable of holding artillery, one that would be significant enough to give the garrison a sense of security against any attacking force, should one materialize. The *New Era* was instrumental in helping perform this work by bringing in fresh provisions as well as the necessary building materials. Only two days before Forrest's Southerners arrived, the deck log recorded that the vessel had "landed at Fort Pillow and discharged lumber which was for strengthening fortifications."[6]

On April 10 Forrest set his men in motion. Fifteen hundred troops under General Chalmers headed for Jackson, Tennessee, preparatory to moving against the fort, while two other columns headed for other destinations in a combination of opportunity-seeking expeditions and diversions. Forrest would have the Federals believe that he was again everywhere at the same time, which might delay or diffuse any effort to concentrate against him. And there might also always be another Hawkins present somewhere, waiting to accept surrender as the most attractive option when facing the "Wizard of the Saddle" and his troops.

An ominous sign that trouble was approaching Fort Pillow took place that same day, when the *New Era* accepted several Confederate captives. There would be no chances taken with these men either, as the logbook indicates. "Three prisoners from Gen. Forrest['s] Command were sent aboard in double irons for safe keeping."[7] But if this development alarmed anyone on the vessel or in the fort, there was no mention of it.[8]

Indeed, Forrest's Confederates were closing in on Fort Pillow. The movement required some of these men to traverse a significant amount of territory, though. Captain Elisha Hollis of the 20th Tennessee Cavalry had participated in the Paducah raid and was now hastening toward Fort Pillow. In his diary entry for Sunday, April 10, he noted, "After night we mounted our stock and marched all night in the direction of Brownsville." The following night he was back in the saddle again after a daylong ride: "Marched all night, dark night, awful march" was all he could bring himself to write.[9] Another of the Southerners wrote his family about the grueling march, "all day monday and all night monday night," that put them in the vicinity of Fort Pillow early on the twelfth.[10] Yet another elaborated on the conditions as special correspondent for the *Mobile Advertiser and Register*. "We arrived in a few miles of the fort by three o'clock in the morning, having traveled all night long through a slow rain, and halted for the appearance of day."[11]

Forrest biographers Thomas Jordan and J. P. Pryor note that the Confederates benefited enormously from the assistance of a local citizen who helped guide them "to the rear of their [the garrison's] picketpost." The resident's help nearly secured all of the soldiers manning the outpost, although "at least one man escaped" to give the Federals warning of the Southerners' approach.[12]

In addition, W. J. Shaw's aid was nothing less than providential for the Confederates. Arrested and held in Fort Pillow, he had remained in Union hands until managing an escape on April 11, the eve of Forrest's arrival.[13] The timing and the information he was able to provide, in addition to his work as a guide, was of incalculable value to the attacking columns as they sought to invest the Union position he knew and could describe to them so well.

Even so, the approaching troops had not been able to corral all of the pickets and prevent some of them from spreading the warning that an attack was imminent. Confederate general Tyree Bell recalled rather incongruously, "Before daylight all the outside pickets were taken in and the others escaped to the fort."[14] Another participant observed, "Learning where the pickets were posted, Gen. Chalmers sent a squad ahead, under a guide, to surround, and capture them." Like Bell, he was inconsistent in recording the outcome. "The surprise was perfect, but three out of the seven escaped, the remaining four were brought in."[15]

James Marshall, the acting master of the gunboat *New Era*, noted that Major Booth "sent me word that the rebels were advancing on us" at 6:00 A.M., and "I immediately got the ship cleared for action."[16] In his after-action report he explained, "At 6:30 A.M. the firing had commenced on all sides, we moving up and down, and firing as signaled from the fort."[17]

Other individuals learned of the Confederate advance as well and moved immediately to the fort to gain protection or to join in the defense. Vermonter Edward Benton, who had relocated to the area to grow cotton "just outside the fortifications," received from one of his hands the shocking news that Forrest and his men had arrived. He later recalled, "I got out of bed and looked out of the window towards the fort" and watched as hundreds of cheering Confederates passed. "I put some things in my valise and started for the fort in a roundabout way, and got in, by running the pickets, about six o'clock, and went immediately to Major Booth, and asked for a gun, and took my stand with the soldiers inside the breastworks, where I remained." Benton remembered that as the fighting progressed, he "shot at every person of Forrest's men that I could get a chance at, firing forty-eight shots in all."[18] Hotel owner John Nelson and his cook, a former slave named Jacob Thompson, as well as storekeeper Eugene Van Camp and clerk James R. Brigham all dispensed with their civilian roles to grab muskets for service. A photographer from Minnesota, Charley Robinson, and his friend George Washington Crafts not only took up weapons but also donned uniform "blouses" to assist in the defense of the post.[19]

Southerner Alex Jones was one of the men who "was thrown [out] as skirmishers[, and] after advancing about half a mile we came in view of their outer fortifications."[20] The Confederates then moved into positions surrounding the fort. While positioning his troops, Bell recalled, "I deployed a lot of sharp-shooters and set them at work, they crawling and getting behind every chunk as they went and the enemy were firing on them rapidly from the fort." The benefits to be derived from these dispositions immediately became apparent. Bell noted that the sharpshooters "continued this

90  THE RIVER WAS DYED WITH BLOOD

movement until they got position where they were securely covered and commanded the fort completely."[21]

The marksmen selected the *New Era* as a prime target too. Marshall reported that he moved his vessel according to "previously established signals" from the fort's commander and "commence[d] firing up what we call No 1 ravine, just below the quartermaster's department.... Then he signalled [sic] me to fire up Coal Creek ravine No. 3, and I then moved up there." The gunboat captain added, "Before I left down here at ravine No. 1 the rebel sharpshooters were firing at me rapidly."[22] Forrest, whose bouts with gunboats stretched back to 1861 Kentucky and included the memorable engagement on February 14, 1862, at Fort Donelson, had learned that one way to keep such a vessel occupied and minimize its firing effectiveness was to cover the gun hatches with aimed fire.[23]

In overall command until Forrest could reach the scene, Chalmers sent Colonel Robert McCulloch's brigade to the left, with Bell's to the right. Colonel George Adair described the terrain advantages the Southerners enjoyed, also attributing Chalmers's initial dispositions to General Forrest. "The surrounding country is undulating and presents a series of ravines and intervening hills, of which circumstances Gen. Forrest took advantage in bringing his forces through ravines and behind hills until they were quite under the range of the guns [in the fort.]" These sharpshooters kept the garrison under fire by "occupying safe positions on the surrounding eminences, from which they were able to pick off the enemy's gunners if they should attempt to use, or alter the range of their guns."[24] This tendency to credit Forrest with the actions of his subordinates would have different implications as the attack on Fort Pillow progressed.

Situated as they were on ground overlooking the interior of the fort and comparatively free from harassment, the marksmen had no difficulty picking targets as they became available. "We commensed fighting and advancing," a Southerner explained, "slowly taking advantage of the ground as we moved up placing out sharp shooters to keep their heads down when we had to pass exposed points."[25]

The fort's defenders had the earthen parapet wall for protection and had constructed a firing step on which they could quickly rise to shoot over it; as soon as they had discharged their weapons, they could drop back down and be safe from enemy fire. Of course, for the few seconds a soldier emerged above the wall, his upper extremities would be exposed.[26] Confederate sharpshooters would have those same seconds to pinpoint their targets and fire. Forensic reports are not available for the Union troops beyond those for wounded men taken to hospitals in Mound City, but

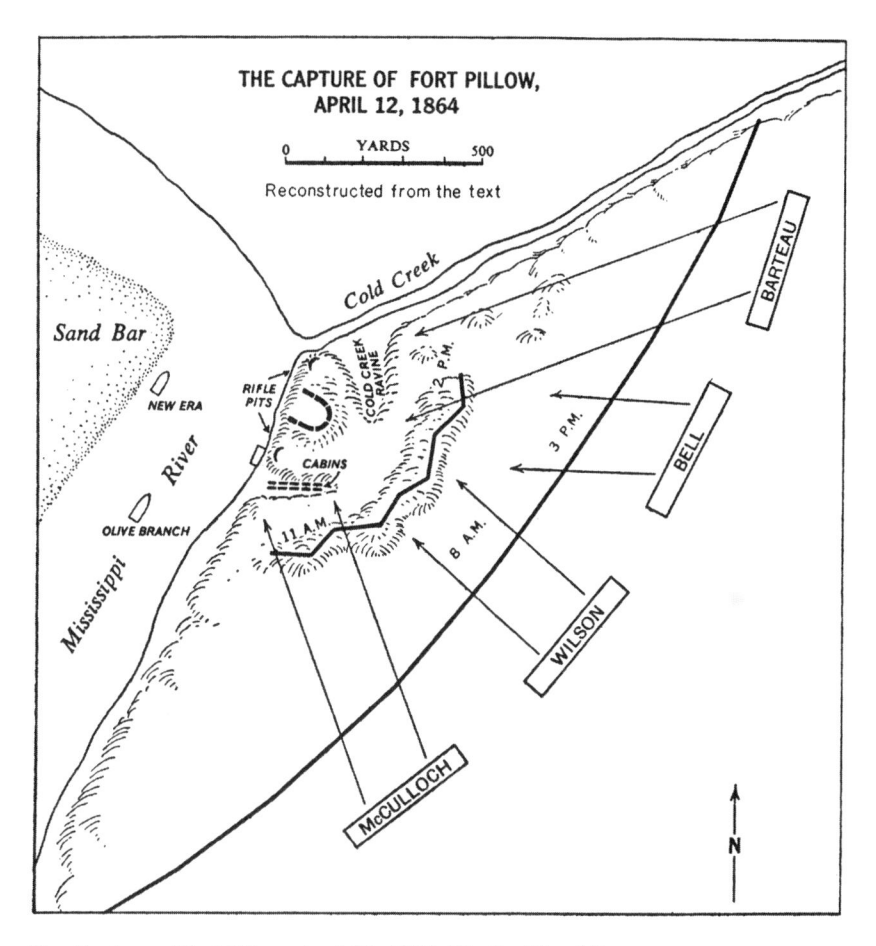

The Capture of Fort Pillow, April 12, 1864. Wyeth, *Life of Forrest.*

aimed shots by marksmen to the head and chest surely must have resulted in more deaths than any general fire on an open field would have produced. As constructed and positioned, the works meant to provide protection actually put the defenders in a shooting gallery in which any exposure could prove fatal.

Unfortunately for the fate of the garrison, at approximately 9 o'clock that morning, one man who unwittingly exposed himself to this fire was the fort's commander, Major Booth. Perhaps as much to inspire his troops as to assist with an artillery piece, Booth placed himself behind the embrasure at porthole number two. From some distance, a sharpshooter drew a bead on the Union officer, and lingering too long in the opening, he took a round in the chest and died instantly.[27] The Confederates did not realize it, but the fort now had a new commander, Major Bradford.

The marksmen's fire was having a galling effect on the Union defenders and would profoundly affect the outcome of the battle in other ways. After Sergeant Wilbur Gaylord helped carry his slain commander's body to the rear, he rejoined his comrades at the wall. "As soon as I returned Captain Epeneter, Company A, was wounded in the head while standing at port-hole No. 4."[28] Union lieutenant Mack J. Leaming observed that "under the unerring aim of the rebel sharpshooters," the garrison "suffered pretty severely in the loss of commissioned officers."[29] Such casualties, difficult at any time to absorb, were particularly critical now, depriving the fort's defenders of the experience of their senior commander and undoubtedly demoralizing the soldiers as they suffered further, steady losses. The carnage would be especially disturbing to men who had heretofore only experienced the relative quiet of garrison duty.

Like the officers, the artillerists suffered inordinately from Forrest's sharpshooters. As much to suppress the occasionally heavy artillery fire as to exploit the openings through which the guns operated, the marksmen focused on the men serving the pieces. Henry Weaver testified that in the course of the fighting, "The cannoneers were all killed or wounded at my place except one or two, and also at Lieutenant Hunter's gun."[30]

The cannon fire from Fort Pillow and the *New Era* remained general despite the harassment the gunners endured. Confederate Charles Anderson recalled that he was riding with Forrest when, "within eight or ten miles of the river we heard the first cannonading at the fort, and knew then that Gen. Chalmers was at work." They accelerated their pace and had cut the distance to the fort in half when a courier met them with the news that Chalmers had forced the Federals into their works, though the brigadier expressed his doubts as to whether the Confederates might succeed in capturing the position without severe casualties. The hesitation reflected in the message prompted Forrest to redouble his efforts to reach the scene and examine the situation for himself. "This dispatch put us in a trot," Anderson noted, "and Gen. Forrest was soon on the ground and in command."[31]

When Forrest arrived at midmorning, he found the fort surrounded and his troops deployed.[32] Never content to accept another individual's responsibility for such dispositions, he examined the men for himself and personally repositioned sharpshooters as he saw fit. In the process the general exposed himself unnecessarily to enemy fire. Adair recorded, "When near the outer fort, the Federals having all fallen back to the principal fort on the bluff, as the general rode in range of a battery on a magnificent charger captured at Paducah, a cannon ball struck the horse, and passing through his body, cut the stirrup leather and grazed the general's leg."[33] Forrest's harrowing near miss might have made another man more circumspect. It did not have that effect on the general.

Still undoubtedly dazed and certainly battered from the resultant fall from the saddle, Forrest gathered his wits and called for another horse in order to complete his inspection of the lines. Wright Whitlow, a twenty-seven-year-old slave, hastened forward with an animal. In a postwar application that he submitted for a pension from the state of Tennessee, Whitlow observed, "I witnessed the battle of Fort Pillow and at one time during the battle I held the horse of General Forrest while he mounted his new one after the first had been shot from under him."[34]

Biographer John Allan Wyeth noted that in one instance the new mount reared "and fell over upon the general, who was badly bruised by the accident." At one point an aide brought Forrest another horse but quietly suggested that he might prefer to conduct the remaining work on foot. The cavalryman shrugged off the idea with the observation that he "was just as apt to be hit one way as another, and that he could see better where he was."[35] General Forrest was right about the vantage point, but his subordinate was equally correct about the danger.

Colonel Adair concurred that Forrest was taking quite a physical beating. "Later in the day, he had a second horse killed under him, and was knocked down twice—once by a spent canister [round] that struck him in the breast." Even then the general was not spared from further threats to his health and safety. "Again, a piece of timber, thrown by a bursting shell, struck him on the back of the neck, which stunned him for some time." Adair concluded of these myriad near misses, "If a protecting angel is not ever near him, by the prayers of his pious and devoted wife, then there is naught in the teachings of spiritual philosophy."[36]

Forrest's injuries were significant enough that speculation ran rampant for days afterward that he had been killed. The editor of one newspaper concluded, "The reckless daring of Gen. Forrest, and the constant exposure of his person in the thickest of the fight on all occasions where his command is engaged, renders such a result as his death by no means improbable."[37] Bedford Forrest survived his encounters with Union fire at Fort Pillow, but he had clearly come under duress and suffered effects that lingered for some time afterward.

It is unclear whether the general experienced fire from the fort's or the gunboat's batteries or both. The *New Era* was expending a considerable amount of ordnance against the Confederates. Master Marshall recorded that his vessel fired some "282 rounds of shell, shrapnell, and canister."[38] In a subsequent report the gunboat commander specifically enumerated, "Amount of ammunition expended in the engagement of the 12th instant: 191 rounds of shell, 85 rounds of shrapnel, 6 rounds of canister, 375 rounds of rifle cartridges, 96 rounds of revolver cartridges."[39] A Confederate witness bore testament to the effectiveness of at least some of this effort by *New Era*'s crew. Texas lieutenant T. T. Hopkins observed in gruesome detail: "At the battle of Fort Pillow, Tenn., the 1st Lieutenant of this company was killed. A shell from a gunboat exploded in our midst, tearing his head to pieces."[40]

When not dodging enemy fire or shaking off the effects from it, Forrest had to like what he saw. He already understood the decided advantage that the elevated ground gave his men. Using tree stumps as protection, they could fire independently at targets of opportunity or in concert with the final push when it came, forcing the defenders to hug the parapet walls in any case. Forrest did not know that this had already paid handsome dividends with the death of the Union commander before the general had even arrived.

Other Confederates on the scene were less sanguine of success. General Chalmers insisted from the outset that the defenses appeared too strong to be breached by assault without producing a prohibitive number of Southern casualties. Before Forrest had reached the field, Chalmers remarked to fellow brigade commander General Bell, "If he does not get here, we cannot take that place as it is too formidable."[41] Perhaps with the lessons of previous frontal assaults in the teeth of enemy defenses, most recently reinforced by Colonel Thompson's deadly experience at Paducah, Chalmers was wise to be hesitant.

Facing an entrenched opponent with six pieces of artillery, consisting of two 10-pounder Parrott rifled guns, two 12-pounder howitzers, and two 6-pounder rifled field pieces, as well as the supporting fire of the *New Era*, Forrest could only answer with four small mountain howitzers of his own.[42] Yet while the Federals had an earthwork brimming with artillery, ravines on either side of the fort gave potential attackers cover for assembling in close proximity to its walls. The same geographical features provided access to the landing below the bluffs. Any retreat, or the arrival of any reinforcements, could be cut off at that point by relatively small flanking forces sent below the bluffs. With the sharpshooters doing their work and the Southern artillery placed to keep the gunboat at bay, the situation did not look quite so hopeless to the much more optimistic commanding general. Consequently, and with his personal, although painful,

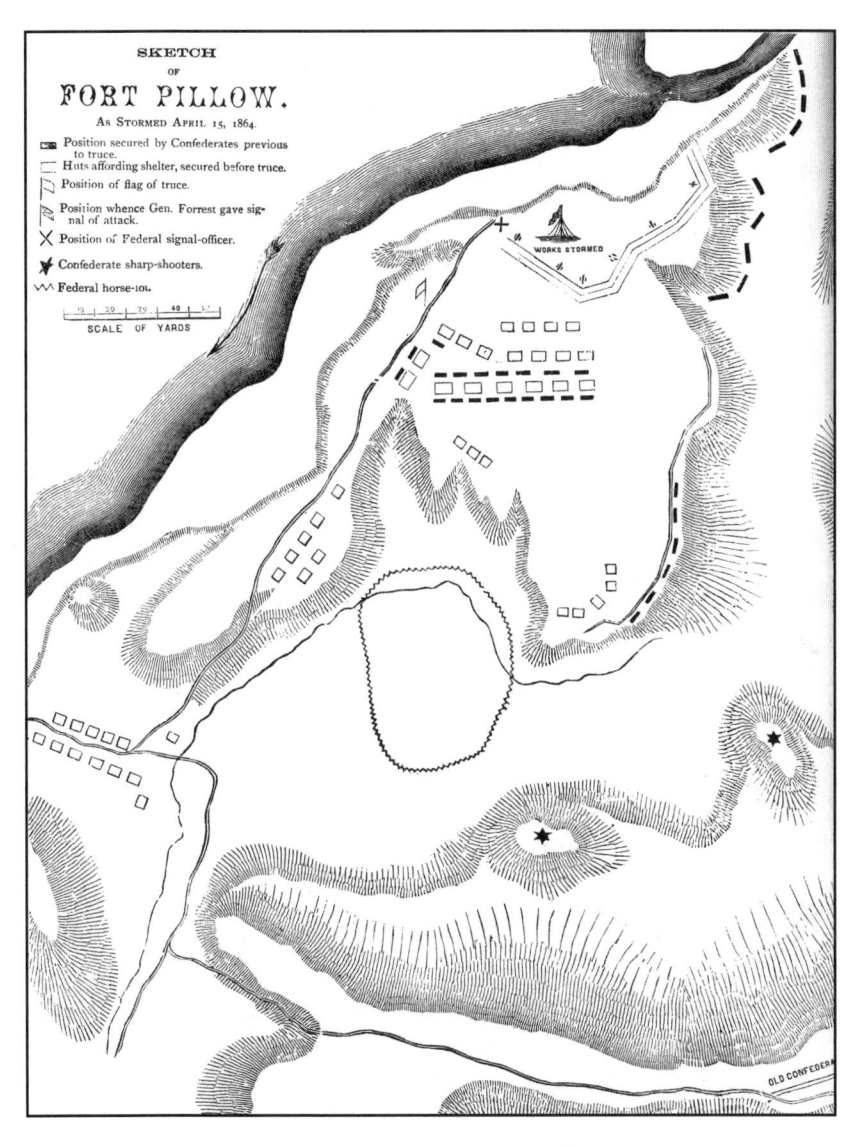

Sketch of Fort Pillow. Jordan and Pryor, *Campaigns of Forrest*.

reconnaissance to sustain him, Forrest remained undeterred in his determination to take Fort Pillow and its defenders.

Nathan Bedford Forrest had another very significant asset in his favor. His enthusiasm on the battlefield was infective. Adair depicted the "towering form, blazing eyes, and the clarion voice of the fearless leader," calling out along the line for the men to "move up, move up," as sufficient "inspiration" to alter the mood of men and commanders alike.[43]

Ironically, the layout of the military grounds at Fort Pillow also favored the attackers. Several rows of buildings that served as storehouses and barracks offered the Confederates additional cover tantalizingly close to the enemy position. Forrest recognized this too and immediately sought to incorporate it into his thinking. When he met with Robert McCulloch after completing his reconnaissance, he asked the colonel if he had noticed the structures and wanted to know what he "thought of capturing the barracks and houses which were near the fort and between it and my position." McCulloch saw the advantages for himself and observed that if he succeeded in taking them intact, his men could use the cover to "silence the enemy's artillery." This was all Forrest needed to know, replying that the colonel should "go ahead and take them."[44]

The Federal leadership seemed initially not to appreciate the dangers these buildings posed or the advantages they offered the Confederates. But at least one private of the 6th U.S. Colored Heavy Artillery recognized their significance. Thomas Adison later ventured an opinion for investigators from the Joint Committee on the Conduct of the War. "The rebels never would have got the advantage of us if it had not been for the houses built there, and which made better breastworks for them than we had," he explained. "The major would not let us burn the houses in the morning. If they had let us burn the houses in the morning, I do not believe they would ever have whipped us out of that place."[45]

Too late the Federals sought to fire the structures, but the Southern sharpshooters were already in place to make such work truly hot. The Union troops managed to destroy the row nearest the fort before Confederate fire drove them back into the confines of the earthworks. Even so, a portion of the buildings remained beyond their reach. A Union officer explained, "From these barracks the enemy kept up a murderous fire on our men despite all our efforts to dislodge him."[46]

Forrest continued his probing, looking for other weaknesses in the Union position that would give him an advantage and simply testing the defensive capability of the garrison. Employing his longstanding policy of "Let's give 'em a dare anyhow," the Confederate commander turned to General Bell to select a small group of volunteers to conduct a mission.[47] Captain James Stinnett of the 16th Tennessee offered to command the patrol of fifty-two men, including two junior officers. As he prepared to lead them out, he spoke plainly: "Boys, this is a pretty tight pill, some of us will be hurt and some probably killed. But that is what we bargained for when we joined the army."[48] There was nothing of false bravado in the captain's words or of feelings of antagonism toward the enemy troops. It was a dangerous mission to be sure, but it was another one like others they might be called upon to make on any field and against any opponent.

Stinnett's words of encouragement offered, the captain and his men sprinted from cover toward the Union earthwork. The seconds must have seemed interminable as the soldiers raced across the open space before reaching the relative security of the ditch. When they jumped in, apparently unscathed, they found that the Union gunners could not depress their weapons sufficiently to hit them, and any Federal riflemen who might try to shoot at them would be exposed to the sharpshooters brimming the nearby heights. The general now had his answer.

Forrest was growing impatient. Never one to exhibit too much deliberation in any case, he worried that Union reinforcements might arrive to snatch the garrison from his grasp. He had endured such a surprise at Parker's Crossroads as he waited for one command to surrender when another unexpectedly materialized in his rear. He had thought then the matter secure, with his best man, brother William Forrest, supposed to be guarding the road along which any enemy reinforcements might come. Only the legendary command to "Charge them both ways" had extricated him from that trap. But the white flags of the first column disappeared as fast as the arriving column drove Forrest's troopers from the field that day. He would not allow anything similar to happen here.

The Confederate leader was certainly correct to worry about the reinforcement of the beleaguered garrison. In his report of the action, James Marshall indicated that he and Major Booth had formed a plan for cooperation in the event of an attack on the fort. "We had previously arranged signals with the commander of the post, so that in case he was attacked he would give us by signal the position of the enemy." With these methods providing directional guidance for his guns, Marshall supported the fort throughout the morning until the gunboat's firing halted about 1:45 in the afternoon.[49] By that time he felt that the heavy rate of fire required him to disengage to give the men rest and to clean the guns, already beginning to foul with powder residue.[50]

Confederate accounts suggested that before this time Southern fire had already rendered the *New Era* largely ineffective. Anderson credited the placement of artillery with compelling the Union vessel to pull back from the fight. Another Confederate corroborated the point. "We now drove the Gunboat from the only position in which it could do us any injury,"

DeWitt Clinton Fort recalled. "That made the task much easier. The danger now was all from one direction, The gunboat was silent and as useless to the enemy as it was harmless to us on thro' the balance of the fight."[51]

The stage was set for the final blow. A comparatively short dash would put any attackers against the parapet wall, where the boost from a friendly set of hands would hoist them over and into Fort Pillow itself. Utilizing the lay of the land and the covering fire of the marksmen, one of the men due to make the advance explained, "[we were] moving up in that way until we got within twenty steps of the fort when there was a flag sent in demanding a surrender."[52] Obviously, Forrest felt that there was still the possibility that this prize might be won rather easily, especially if the garrison's commander could be made to understand his desperate straits. The general planned to give him that chance.

Bedford Forrest had no doubt as to the conclusion of the martial drama unfolding before him: it would rather be a question of how that end—the capitulation of the garrison—would be achieved and at what cost. As he had done before, the Confederate commander sought to bring the matter to a close through negotiation and in doing so displayed a tone that was uncharacteristically conservative and laudatory. "The conduct of the officers and men garrisoning Fort Pillow has been such as to entitle them to being treated as prisoners of war," he dictated to an aide to write on his behalf. "I demand the unconditional surrender of the entire garrison, promising you that you shall be treated as prisoners of war."[53]

These were important and symbolic words. Many of Forrest's Confederates felt an intense antipathy for the soldiers who made up the Union garrison. But the general's message was clear. He felt that the defenders, white and black, had conducted themselves like soldiers through the morning's engagement and as such they had "entitled" themselves to treatment as prisoners of war, not as renegades or war criminals. Forrest wanted the garrison's commander to be sure of that distinction as further inducement for him and his troops to lay down their arms.

Still, if a fight were to become necessary, Forrest wanted his adversary to know that he was ready to conduct it to a successful conclusion. Having "just received a fresh supply of ammunition," he expected, or at least wanted his adversary to believe, that he could "easily assault and capture the fort." Of course, if this logic did not move the Union commander to yield under the circumstances, there were liable to be dire results. "Should my demand be refused," Forrest insisted, "I cannot be responsible for the fate of your command."[54] Perhaps he would have been better served in that case to say that he would not necessarily be able to control the conduct of some of his troops, but Nathan Bedford Forrest would never have admitted that to himself, much less to an opponent.

Of particular interest in light of the events that followed was the general's decision not to include the direct threat of obliterating the garrison if the Union commander failed to comply with his surrender demand. In July 1862 at Murfreesboro, where there were no black troops or Tennessee Unionists, this was the style of language Forrest had employed. "I will have every man put to the sword," he had assured Lieutenant Colonel John G. Parkhurst.[55] The spectacular results of that raid seemed to speak for themselves in encouraging him to use such language again if the situation required.

With Abel Streight in North Alabama in May 1863, he dispensed with the menace of "no quarter." Forrest recognized that the situation differed from Murfreesboro enough to encourage him not to issue exaggerated threats. Streight's exhausted men could still put up a fight, and so he explained that he sought their surrender only to "avoid the further effusion of blood."[56] The implication also must have been clear that he would shed that blood if required to do so.

Following Streight's capitulation, Forrest communicated with the Confederate provost marshal of Richmond, Brigadier General John H. Winder, on the subject of the black prisoners who had fallen into his hands. Although he had "found none of the negroes in arms," the presence of such men with the Union column represented a challenge to the social order white Southerners accepted and wanted to maintain. Forrest's conclusion regarding the slaves who managed to elude him revealed his mindset in mid-1863 concerning such persons when he assumed that "most" of these men had simply "returned to their masters."[57] Furthermore, his letter contained no particular animosity toward the "very few" captives taken as a result of this military action.

Before Fort Anderson at Paducah, Forrest employed the same type of threat he had now come to use as standard operating procedure. In an address after the war on the general and his campaigns, James Chalmers observed, "It was said that Forrest's demand for a surrender at Paducah, coupled with an implied threat that he could not be responsible for the consequences if compelled to take the place by assault, showed a predetermination to cold-blooded murder." Chalmers knew better. "This was the form of his first demand for surrender made at Murfreesboro, and he practiced it afterwards just as he practiced his flank attack, and for the same purpose, and with the same effect, to intimidate his adversary."[58]

The argument could certainly be made that due to his limited education, Bedford Forrest did not author these surrender demands himself and thus bore no responsibility for the wording used in them. But this was not the case either. To be sure, he had the benefit of only six months of formal education, but he had spent a lifetime in business in which he had taught himself enough to function more than adequately in communicating his thoughts and ideas. One of his staffers recalled, "Precision in the camp and in council, not less than decision on the field, was one of his most striking traits; and, although his education had been wholly neglected, he has made me write the same letter or order three times over; and I am bound to say that I think the last copy was invariably an improvement on the first."[59]

A young clerk who served with Forrest during the last stages of the war proclaimed his superior to be "a hard worker" who remained actively engaged in processes at headquarters. "I think he calls for 'them clerks' a dozen times a day," George Cable remembered. "He attends to everything himself, sits and talks to everyone, knows everyone by name, tells everything he intends to do, and tells the same instructions over fifty times in half an hour." But his apparent garrulousness did not obscure his capabilities. "His brain, however, is as clear as crystal & he seems to think of a dozen things at once."[60] Cable added of Forrest's headquarters habits, "When he dictates a letter or a telegram he labors for good language," although the clerk thought that the general tended to use "many words to say but little."[61]

Particularly for his official communications, Forrest preferred to turn to others. Yet the words they chose to use on his behalf were indicative of his meaning. "If it doesn't have the right pitch," Forrest once explained, "I give it a new tune."[62] The message had to be true to what he wanted to convey, even if the words being used were not in his usual vocabulary. He reprimanded one staffer for changing his word choice: "Leave the message as I dictated it. If you use the word 'bring,' they will take several days in reaching me, but if I say 'fetch,' they will come at once with what they can carry and I want them now."[63] "You write very well," another aide quoted Forrest as saying when he contemptuously tossed a message back to him for revision, "but you don't seem to see what I'm driving at. I want you to recollect that it ain't your letter, but my letter. All I ask of you is to see that the spelling an' grammar are right. I'll furnish the words and ideas."[64] Chalmers recollected of his superior, "It has been said that Forrest was uneducated, and this is true, but his ideas, when properly clothed in correct language, were pointed and strong, and he was exceedingly tenacious that his own ideas, and not those of the writer, should be expressed by those who wrote for him."[65] His words were meant to have consequences, this time in the form of compelling a surrender that he believed would be self-evident.

For his surrender demand at Fort Pillow, Bedford Forrest drew on all of his previous battlefield experiences, his skills at psychological warfare, and his understanding of human nature. It was up to the Union commander to determine the risk he was willing to undertake in rejecting or ignoring it. But in any case, General Forrest was not about to let his quarry escape. He watched with dismay as smoke rose from the Mississippi, a sure indication that there was the presence of riverine traffic and the possibility of Union reinforcements. Forrest was determined to stop that from happening and, despite the truce, took steps to prevent it.

First, he shortened the time for the Union commander's consideration of his demand from an hour to "twenty minutes." If his counterpart was stalling in the hope of succor, Forrest was not inclined to accommodate him. Even if this was not the case, the Confederate wanted an answer before any potential help could arrive.

Second, as the vessels approached without any apparent signal from the fort that a truce was in place, Forrest sent two columns to secure the landing below the bluffs against any eventuality. Captain Charles W. Anderson took some 200 men with him to the left of the Confederate position, while Colonel Clark S. Barteau led a like number to the right. Forrest's instructions to Anderson were unmistakably clear. He was expected to maintain his position along the river and thereby "prevent any escape of the garrison" by water, "to pour rifle-balls into the open ports of the *New Era* when she went into action," and to "fight everything 'blue' between wind and water until yonder flag comes down."[66] The latter was a reference to the fort's standard, which presumably would be lowered upon the surrender or capture of the position.

Perhaps unaware of their cause, the Federals could see these movements and considered them violations of the truce. Neither command was supposed to improve their positions during the pause, although Forrest contended that this was precisely what the Union vessels were doing and that he had every right to counter such actions.

As with so much that has to do with Fort Pillow, there was some truth on both sides of the equation. Forrest biographers Thomas Jordan and J. P. Pryor insist that during this period, "the smoke of several steamers was discovered ascending the river; and speedily one, crowded with troops, and her lower guards filled with artillery, was distinctly seen approaching, near at hand, and manifestly bearing directly for the beleaguered fortress." Consequently, Forrest took steps to prevent any reinforcements from landing by sending out Anderson and Barteau. Anderson declined the opportunity to fire on the loaded craft beyond a few warning shots at the pilothouse, which convinced the master of the *Olive Branch* to "sheer off to the opposite shore, and pass on up the river."[67]

Union brigadier general George F. Shepley was aboard the *Olive Branch* at the time, returning from New Orleans as the outgoing military governor of Louisiana. Although he subsequently insisted that the vessel "was incapable of rendering assistance" to the garrison, "being entirely defenseless," he noted that he had considered bringing "a section" of one of the two batteries he had at his disposal "to go to Fort Pillow." He had learned of Forrest's attack from civilians who hailed the vessel from shore and received confirmation from the steamer *Liberty*, also carrying troops, which had just passed the site going south and indicated that it was safe to proceed "up there" since *New Era* lay just "off the fort." As the *Olive Branch* approached the scene of action, it received the fire aimed at her pilothouse, though Shepley added: "There was no firing at the fort at this time. The Union flag was flying, and after we passed the fort we could see a 'flag of truce' outside the fortifications." The vessel paused only long enough to allow an assessment of the situation and receive a request from *New Era* for authorities at Cairo, Illinois, to send "400 rounds of ammunition" to replenish that gunboat's depleted stores.[68] Forrest could not have known the extent of capabilities from either *Olive Branch* or *Liberty* for offering aid to the garrison, but certainly he did not want to accept the risk without making a response of his own.

Confederate participants and sympathetic chroniclers have insisted that no violation of the truce at Fort Pillow occurred from Forrest's movements to prevent reinforcements from landing, but at least one action must be construed otherwise. As an unintended corroboration to one Union accusation, a participant in Captain Stinnett's probe of the defenses recalled that this activity actually occurred during the negotiation period.

The lull in the fighting, or more precisely the cessation of sharpshooting fire under the truce, also allowed the members of the garrison to relax. The toll of the marksmen had been severe, especially among the officer corps. But with the firing halted, the defenders exposed themselves without fear. This opportunity seemed to have emboldened some of them to the point of recklessness. Undoubtedly feeling secure in their works, some of the Federals began to taunt the Confederates. "During the truce," one Southerner recalled later, "they openly defied us from the breastworks to come and take the fort."[69] With so many officers down and the new commander engaged in determining his reply to Forrest's ultimatum, discipline in at least a portion of the garrison appears to have broken down. Those who engaged in such activity would not have imagined how this defiance could turn against them when the final assault took place.

One other explanation for the garrison's behavior, offered from Confederate sources, was the supposed presence and availability of alcohol.[70] Although not present himself at Fort Pillow, one of Forrest's men maintained, "There was much talk when we got quietly settled in camp at Verona, Miss., about the capture of Fort Pillow." Based upon what he was hearing, John M. Hubbard observed "that the garrison had been lavishly stimulated with whisky, as was evident from the fact that a number of barrels of whisky and beer with tin dippers attached were found by the Confederates."[71] General Bell insisted that he turned over barrels containing spirits when he entered the fort at the end of the fighting.[72]

Such testimony did not guarantee that one or more of the Confederates fabricated or exaggerated the matter for self-serving purposes, but the simple fact was that whether through other influences or not, a good portion of the defenders felt a sense of security within their earthworks and from the supporting artillery pieces at hand and aboard the *New Era*. They saw the likelihood as remote that their Southern antagonists could reach them before being decimated, but even should the attackers succeed, a retreat to the riverbank under the protective covering of the gunboat would prove sufficient for salvation. Of course, should the Confederates both capture the fort and neutralize the *New Era* successfully, this would alter that calculation and have an unnerving, if not devastating, effect on the morale of the remaining bluecoated soldiers.

Discipline, or the lack thereof, may have been an open question for the Confederate forces too. It was during the initial truce that Forrest experienced the first indication of a breakdown in discipline in his command. Captain Marshall on the *New Era* noted that at this time, "Some of the officers came to me and told me the rebels were robbing the quartermaster's department." They suggested that the gunboat lob some rounds at the plunderers, who offered such easy and available targets. Marshall demurred, considering such action on his part inappropriate under the flag of truce, with the admonition that "two wrongs did not make a right."[73]

The post quartermaster, Lieutenant John C. Ackerstrom, was connected to these events and, in the course of his actions, may have drawn upon him unwanted Confederate attention. One Union participant recalled, "Mr. Akerstrom was in his office down under the hill after the flag of truce was [sent] in, and made some signs for us to come to him."[74] The fate of the quartermaster was of particular interest, for Confederate atrocities at Fort Pillow included allegedly nailing and burning that Union officer after the fort had fallen.

Others recalled seeing Southerners plundering the stores as well. James McCoy of the 13th Tennessee (U.S.) observed, "I saw them gathering around there [outside the fort] all the time [during the truce], and all the time they were stealing from the commissary's stores blankets and everything else they could get at. I reckon I saw 200 men climbing the hill with as much as they could carry on their backs, shoes, etc."[75]

Apparently, Forrest was aware that some of his men were taking advantage of the opportunity to fill their personal larders. Although requisitioning supplies from the Federals was a fact of life with his command, this was not the time to engage in the practice or, as commander, for him to allow his men to indulge in it. When asked by a colleague after the war, "I hear you shot some of your own men at Fort Pillow, how was that?" Forrest responded, "Well, I'll tell you how that was." He related that when the firing on the line had died down unexpectedly, he went to investigate the cause, "and there was the sutler's store just broken open, and as I rode up one of the boys came out with his arms full of dry goods. I was so mad I dropped him with my pistol; right behind him came another, and he was a captain, and he, too, was loaded with plunder, and I shot him, too." The summary action had the desired effect, for Forrest concluded, "They all went on fighting after that."[76]

Whatever Forrest felt about the actions of these men, he was growing increasingly tired of waiting for a Union response to his ultimatum. When it finally came, the reply was, to say the least, cryptic. "Your demand does not produce the desired effect." Forrest must have scratched his head as he tried for a moment to decipher what Bradford-as-Booth was trying to say. It did not take him long to decide, however, for he told one of his subordinates: "This will not do. Send it back, and say to Major Booth that I must have an answer in plain English—Yes or No!"[77] In a subsequent after-action report, Forrest explained that the message he conveyed was, "Will he fight or surrender?"[78] Whatever the precise words, the effect was the same—the Union commander had to make his decision, and he had to make it now.

Major Bradford could delay no longer. Finally, he sealed the fate of his command with a direct response: "We will not surrender."[79] Forrest scanned the message and turned his horse back toward his own lines. His bluff, the bloodless way to secure the fort and its garrison, had failed. It was time to have done with this business. It was time to make an all-out assault. The general called for his bugler.[80]

CHAPTER 5

# "The Slaughter Was Awful"

## April 12, 1864

Boys, save your lives!

*Major William Bradford*

The slaughter was awful—words cannot describe the scene.

*Confederate sergeant Achilles V. Clark to his sisters, April 14, 1864*

It is hoped that these facts will demonstrate to the Northern people that negro soldiers cannot cope with Southerners.

*Nathan Bedford Forrest, April 15, 1864*

General Forrest issued the orders that would culminate in the assault he had tried to avoid. Of course, the "effusion of blood" that he most wished to mitigate was that of his own men and not necessarily that of the opposing Federals. He was confident that his men could overwhelm the Union garrison at Fort Pillow with relative ease, but as recent experiences at Paducah must have reminded him, all the élan in the world could not prevent casualties from occurring in the ranks of even the most determined assaulting force or ensure success as palliation for the lives lost. The best way to take the fort and evade great losses, aside from the relatively bloodless victory he had hoped his surrender demand would procure, would be a sudden attack that would carry the works as swiftly as possible. His sharpshooters could keep the defenders pinned down while his assaulting troops raced across the narrow open plain and scrambled into the ditch fronting the earthworks.

Forrest sought to amplify his chances for success by using psychology to motivate his men to do their utmost. "I dispatched staff officers to Colonels Bell and McCulloch, commanding brigades," he stated later in an after-action report, "to say to them that I should watch with interest the conduct of the troops; that Missourians, Mississippians, and Tennesseans surrounded the works, and I desired to see who would first scale the wall."[1] A participant recalled that the Confederate commander expressed this competition as concern that the Mississippians "might feel slighted." Therefore, he instructed his commanders to "tell them ... I want them to be first into the fort, tell the Missourians not to be behind them, and the Tennesseans that I expect them to do their duty."[2]

It was telling that the motivation he employed did not include the racial or sectional identification of the garrison troops. Confederates from various state-oriented units would vie with each other in doing "their duty" to subdue the Federals and capture the fort. There was no spontaneous or emotionally charged admonition to destroy hated opponents or a calculated call to impart a lesson in blood on former slaves or Unionist neighbors who now bore arms against the South. Bloodthirsty harangues would not have been out of place were the goal of the general to be the deliberate massacre of the defenders.

Also unusual for him, given his intensely personal style of leadership and previous combat record, Bedford Forrest chose not to lead the men on this final assault of Fort Pillow.[3] When Jacob Gaus sounded the charge, the general remained in the secondary line, some four hundred yards outside of the fort. It may well have been that he was simply too battered by the spills he had taken earlier as he improved the positions of sharpshooters and scouted the enemy's works. He wrote his superior several days later that he had hoped to report in person "but am now suffering from exhaustion, caused by hard riding and bruises received in the late engagement."[4] It may also be that General Forrest did not expect a garrison comprised of men for whom he had little or no respect as soldiers to be so great a challenge as to require his presence to overcome them.[5]

Certainly, had Forrest's primary intention been to massacre the garrison, he would have forsaken his own injuries and led the men himself to ensure that they carried out the bloodletting to the fullest extent. The same man who had proclaimed on another battlefield that he meant "to have them all" would have demonstrated no hesitation here. To be sure, Forrest was bound to be angry that the Union commander had made a final assault necessary, but he realized equally that any attack against an entrenched position, no matter how much success might seem foreordained, was a serious and deadly undertaking for those involved. Any lives lost in such an effort would be the bitterest to sustain. Still, Forrest left the fighting to others, with every expectation that they would succeed, even without his immediate presence to inspire them. He was not mistaken.

When the call came to advance, the Southerners sprinted across the open ground for the relative security of the ditch. Defensive fire felled some of them as they crossed even this rather narrow killing zone. The tall figure of Lieutenant Colonel Wiley M. Reed, a former minister of the First Cumberland Presbyterian Church in Nashville, was among the most obvious targets in the onrushing ranks. A contemporary account noted that Reed "was shot while waiving [sic] his sword over his head, far in advance, urging his men to follow." As inspiring as he meant the gesture to be for his men, it also made him stand out all the more to defending riflemen. At least three rounds tore through the soldier-cleric, hitting him "in the leg, spine, and breast."[6]

Officers and men fell in the short, sharp fight, an indication that the initial defense against this final assault was not inconsequential.[7] Nevertheless, the remaining attackers swarmed into the ditch, where they gained the twin advantages and disadvantages of proximity to their opponents. It would be more difficult for defenders to hit them now without exposing themselves to Confederate covering fire, but retreat back across the open ground would only result in additional casualties. Both sides had reached a tipping point in the engagement from which neither could hope to find an easy path of departure—that moment had passed when the sounds of Gaus's instrument wafted across the field.

Quickly, some of the attackers hoisted themselves or their comrades onto the parapet. "In an instant a crop of armed men sprung from the walls of the fort," a writer explained, the soldiers "screaming and yelling" as they dropped into the Union works.[8] Another noted, "With the first that scaled the parapet wall the fighting was hand-to-hand, several being knocked off by the clubbed muskets of the enemy."[9] Another of the advancing Confederates described his experiences to his wife a few days later. "[W]e were ordered to charge the fort when the work of death commenced, them in side and we a crawling up the embankment on the outside fighting near a nough to nock our guns to gether Kiling and capturing evry man in the plase."[10]

In the case of Fort Pillow's defenders, the ferocity of the attack had an enervating effect. Disintegration developed quickly under the pressure exerted by the assault. The earthworks that had earlier appeared to be a safe haven now took on the grim aspect of a death trap. The open area to the rear and the bluff that dropped off to the river seemed to beckon as logical escape routes. There was also the tantalizing promise of protection from the salvos of canister that the *New Era* would ostensibly unleash on the pursuing Confederates.

Consequently, some of the defenders now fled in terror, though others held their ground and tried to continue their resistance. Nobler instincts might suggest the latter were attempting to buy time for their comrades to escape, but the nature of the fighting, devolving as it did into hand-to-hand combat, offered the lingering men little other choice. As one student of soldier psychology concludes, in such instances there were going to be those who would "break and flee in panic and disorder occasionally with—but usually without—any significant resistance [on their parts]. With or without individual resistance, flight is perceived as a means of survival."[11] As terror and panic took hold, the prime directive became escape.

The situation mirrored what had happened and would happen on other battlefields under similar circumstances. Self-preservation prevailed in all forms, from fight to flight, as it had at the Waxhaws and Kings Mountain in the American Revolution, at San Jacinto and Buena Vista in Texas and Mexico, and at numerous other engagements during and after the Civil War. Vicious personal combat and the chaos and confusion defined the fighting as resistance ebbed and flowed and combatants exhibited every form of reaction to the events unfolding around them.

At Fort Pillow one of the Southern attackers noted that the defenders "soon broke in wild confusion, running, jumping, tumbling, rolling down the bluff, pursued with mad yells by our boys."[12] Another recorded, "Then the work of slaughter and death commenced." Noting that some of the Union soldiers "kept firing upon and killing our brave boys," the writer explained that the attack continued unabated. "The sight was terrific—the slaughter sickening." At the same instance, the cohesion of the assault itself fell apart, and the combat disintegrated into patches of men fighting and swarms of others running for their lives. The killing was beginning to take on a life of its own, marked by a particularly vicious intensity and ruthlessness. Pent-up anger against Tennessee Unionists and former slaves bearing weapons against them prodded men in the Confederate ranks toward a blinding rage that exhibited itself in a pitiless and continuous barrage of gunfire. "Wearied with the slow process of shooting with guns, our troops commenced with their repeaters, and every fire brought down a foe, and so close was the fight, that the dead would frequently fall upon the soldier that [had] killed [the man]."[13]

How much genuine resistance the Confederates now faced is impossible to say. The Union troops who recognized that the fight was over made gestures to surrender; others turned to run for whatever safety they might be able to find on the river landing below. "For ten minutes death reigned in the fortification, and along the river bank," a Confederate summarized. "Our troops, maddened by excitement, shot down the retreating Yankees, and not until they had attained the water's edge and turned to beg for mercy, did any prisoners fall into our hands." Even then the treatment of the soldiers differed according to their race. "Thus the whites received quarter, but the negroes were shown no mercy."[14] The presence of black troops was particularly galling to some. One participant admitted, "The sight of negro troops stirred the bosoms of our soldiers with courageous madness."[15]

William Bradford must have experienced many emotions as the Confederates poured into the works, but he most assuredly felt first apprehension and then abject fear. A day of reckoning had come, and although he had spared himself the humiliation and opprobrium of Isaac Hawkins by refusing to surrender, he was clearly not going to enjoy the success of Samuel Hicks either.

Major Bradford appeared to believe that under any circumstances the *New Era* or some other vessel could prove to be the garrison's salvation. A Minnesotan explained in a letter home: "After our men had been fighting about four hours, and were pretty well tired out, the smoke of a steamboat was seen by the river. The commander came around & said, 'You have done well my boys. Hold out a little longer for there is a boat coming with reinforcements & if we can hold the place a little longer we will have plenty of help as there is a thousand soldiers on the boat.'"[16]

The Union commanders of the fort and the gunboat apparently had such a last-ditch arrangement to succor the garrison if that extremity manifested itself. Even as the defense broke down all around him, evidence exists that Bradford still counted on help from outside the post to save it. In later testimony James Marshall, commander of the *New Era*, divulged such a plan. "Major Bradford signaled to me that we were whipped," he explained. "We had agreed on a signal that, if they had to leave the fort, they would drop down under the bank, and I was to give the rebels canister."[17] By raking the shoreline, theoretically at least, the Union gunboat could hold the Southerners at bay until the garrison could be rescued or reinforced.

Such a rescue mission failed to materialize. Confederate countermeasures prevented the gunboat from approaching closely, particularly once the fort fell and the attackers could turn the captured artillery on it. Marshall noted that as "shell[s] were falling over and around us," he moved the vessel "upstream out of range."[18] *New Era* was also suffering from an apparent shortage of ammunition.[19] The expenditure of only six rounds of canister suggests that contrary to plan, any scheme to save the garrison by raking the Confederates as they descended upon the retreating soldiers essentially went unimplemented.[20]

Major Bradford may have been attempting to buoy his men's spirits for the trial to come with his statement about possible reinforcements from the river. The irony, though, was that the potential threat of such assistance also made Bedford Forrest more resolved than ever to end the standoff and complete the task before any intervention. This erroneous insistence on salvation was bound to backfire as reality set in for the remaining Federals. Perhaps most critically, the decision to remain and fight in the hope of relief diminished the likelihood of surrender before the final assault occurred. However, without the help they believed was coming, there would be less chance for a determined defense or a positive outcome.

At the same time, Bradford was demoralized by the total disintegration of his command before his eyes. The situation deteriorated instantaneously, with such a shocking suddenness that the major's confidence swept away on a tide of chaos and panic. One participant explained, "During the last attack, when the rebels entered the works, I heard Major Bradford give the command, 'Boys, save your lives.'" The soldier implored, "'Do not let the men leave the pieces; let us fight yet;' but the major, turning around and seeing the rebels coming in from all sides, said, 'It is of no use anymore.'"[21]

One of the Federals summarized what he witnessed as the Southerners stormed over the works. "As soon as the rebels got to the top of the bank there commenced the most horrible slaughter that could possibly be conceived. Our boys when they saw they were overpowered threw down their arms and held up, some their handkerchiefs & some their hands in token of surrender, but no sooner were they seen than they were shot down, & if one shot failed to kill them the bayonet or revolver did not."[22]

In a letter to his sisters only days afterward, Sergeant Achilles V. Clark was still troubled, although he "was quite well" and had "just passed safely through the most terrible ordeal of my whole life." Clark wanted his siblings, and presumably anyone else who would read his letter, "to judge whether or not we acted well or ill." The taunting that Forrest's Southerners had endured from their opponents during the truce and other lulls in the action had increased their desire to respond. "Our men were so exasperated by the Yankee's threats of no quarter," Clark explained, "that they gave but little. The slaughter was awful—words cannot describe the scene." Amid the anarchy attending the storming of the fort, few attackers seemed to have exercised restraint. "The poor deluded negros would run up to our men, fall upon their knees and with uplifted hands scream for mercy," Clark related to his sisters, "but they were ordered to their feet and then shot down. The white men fared but little better." The result was a bloodbath of frightful proportions. "Their fort turned out to be a great slaughter pen—blood, human blood stood about in pools and brains could have been gathered up in any quantity." After what must have felt like an eternity, the Confederate sergeant observed that he and "several others tried to stop the butchery." These individuals "had partially succeeded but," in what became the strongest indictment of the Confederate cavalry commander, "Gen. Forrest ordered them shot down like dogs and the carnage continued. Finally, our men became sick of blood and the firing ceased."[23]

Clark did not say that he actually saw Forrest issuing orders to continue the killing. Indeed, he simply may have thought that this course of action would be what his commander desired. Perhaps unknown to the sergeant, Forrest was not in Fort Pillow when it fell to his troops. The general had remained some four hundred yards in the rear, along the second line of the Union defenses. Once the attackers scaled the ramparts and entered the fort, Forrest rode forward.

Tyree Bell was already over the earthworks, his attention drawn to several barrels of whiskey, "with the heads knocked out and tin cups scattered about and the first thing I did, was to turn these barrels over." Perhaps Bell spilled their contents out of concern that his own troops might take advantage of the chance to quench their thirsts, but he was not alone in identifying the potential for trouble from this source. "About that time," he recalled, "Gen. Forrest came in a gallop from the direction where they [the Confederate attackers] came in [to] the fort, jumped off his horse and turned over one barrel at least."[24]

Confederate Samuel H. Caldwell was also taken aback by the scenes that confronted him in the fort. "It was decidedly the most horrible sight that I have ever witnessed," he told his wife a few days later. "They refused to surrender—which incensed our men & if General Forrest had not run between our men & the Yanks with his pistol and saber drawn not a man would have been spared."[25]

Fort Pillow would not provide the only instance in which white Confederate anger could be associated with murderous excess against opponents for their political or racial distinctions. The dean of Civil War soldiery, Bell I. Wiley, argues that the "antipathy" of white Confederates toward black troops far exceeded any such feelings that Johnny Rebs harbored toward Billy Yanks. "The mere thought of a [former slave] in uniform was enough to arouse the ire of the average Reb; he was wont to see in the arming of the blacks the fruition of oft-repeated Yankee efforts to incite slave insurrections and to establish racial equality."[26] In his study of the common soldiers, historian James I. Robertson, Jr., notes, "Southern troops often reacted with cold fury when they encountered former slaves fighting against them."[27] At Fort Pillow the Federals who were spared proved to be the fortunate ones. General Forrest could intervene to see that at least some of them were not harmed; others never had the chance for his intervention as actions developed beyond his ability to control them.

By this time, the action had swept over the heights to the landing below. From his vantage point below the bluffs and to the south of the fort, Charles Anderson heard the assault begin, illustrated by the shouts of attacking graybacks and the defensive artillery and small-arms fire. "In a few moments," he noted later, "a portion of the garrison rushed down toward the river, and upon them we opened a destructive fire." More soldiers , thoroughly demoralized, soon followed, "rushing down the bluff toward the water with arms [weapons] in their hands." Instead of any relief that might have been expected from the gunboat, these men found themselves subjected to a withering fire from Anderson's Confederates. The unexpected fusillade produced "unutterable dismay and confusion" among the Union troops as the retreat turned to rout, and chaos reigned supreme. The captain observed that the fire from his troops and other Confederates from the main assault "was, for the few moments it lasted, most destructive and deadly," but he insisted that as soon as "the Federal colors came down, I ordered firing to cease at once, and it was promptly done."[28]

Most of the accounts, Union and Confederate, mark this stage of the battle as the most vicious and chaotic. Federal defenders were running, shooting, or trying to escape or surrender, often at alternate intervals as they determined the conditions around them. Confederate pursuers reacted to what they encountered with responses that ranged from ruthless killing to acts of mercy. The photographer Charles Robinson was in a prime position below the bluff to witness the "horrible slaughter" that was taking place around him. In addition to the pre-positioned Confederate units on either flank of the retreating garrison, some of the men who had overrun the fort lined the bank overlooking the landing or followed their adversaries down to the water's edge. Hunkered behind a "high log," the Minnesotan could see the effects of the combat—"our poor fellows bleeding"—and "hear" the brutal indifference with which some Confederates responded to cries for surrender or mercy. He recalled vividly of the assailants: "One of them soon came to where I was laying with one of [the] 'Co. C' boys. He pulled out his revolver and shot the soldier right in the head[,] scattering the blood & brains in my face & then putting his revolver right against my breast he said[,] 'You'll fight with the niggers again will you? You d—d yankee.'" Only an empty chamber saved Robinson from death, although the same man who had wanted to kill him prevented others from doing so once the Minnesotan became a prisoner.[29] Although offered from the perspective of an individual with strong antislavery views, Robinson's graphic account mirrors that of Confederate sergeant Clark.

As a commander, Bedford Forrest preferred to at least appear to have control of his actions and of those around him. When he led from the front, the men had little choice but to follow, and as he waded into personal combat, his focus could remain riveted upon the immediate opponents that confronted him. At Fort Pillow his choices remained cloaked in the chaotic circumstances of the final struggle in which he did not play his customary personal role. That he resorted to descriptions afterward that conveniently minimized his loss of control over events and attempted to place himself in a better light once criticism developed was as much a part of Forrest's nature at Fort Pillow as it had been with the John Able rescue, the aftermath of the Gould shooting, or the outcomes of engagements such as Dover and Parker's Crossroads that had not gone as he had hoped. Consequently, the general could remember cutting down a flag or turning over a barrel of whiskey, which more likely were added to his accounts after the fact to make it appear as if he could exert the power of his presence amid the chaos inside Fort Pillow.

Whatever Forrest's actions were as he rode up, he became too preoccupied with potential threats from the river to pay as much attention to what was happening outside his scope of vision as he should have, however much he may later have wished that he had done so. His paramount concern quickly became securing the position so that his victory could not be threatened, and he allowed himself to be drawn into activities he could easily have delegated to a subordinate. Forrest's encounter with a Union physician illustrates the degree to which the general abrogated his role as overall commander at a critical point in the engagement. Not unlike the criticism historian David Powell has leveled against his performance at Chickamauga, Bedford Forrest was behaving at Fort Pillow in the intensely personal level he preferred against the danger he considered most clear and present. It could not be known what his influence would have been on the unnecessary killing that was taking place just out of his range of vision, but Forrest's penchant for hands-on involvement limited his choices in any regard.

Surgeon Charles Fitch had been attending previously wounded soldiers below the bluff when he noticed the victorious Confederates in pursuit of the broken garrison, many of the Federals discarding their weapons "as they came." He managed to survive the onslaught, but as excessive actions began to occur around him, Fitch quickly determined that his best chance for personal safety lay in returning to the fort itself. He sidled up to a Confederate who was taking his horse back to the top of the bluff. "Who [is] in command?" the doctor inquired, and "a soldier replied Gen. Forrest. I asked where is he? he pointed to Forrest saying that is him sighting the Parrott Gun on the Gun boat." At the time, Fitch recalled, this artillery piece "was not over forty feet from me." The doctor remembered that he "sprang instantly to Forrest addressing him, are you General Forrest? He replied yes sir, what do you want?"

The conversation that then ensued revealed the thinking of both men. "I told him I was the Surgeon of the Post, and asked protection from him that was due a prisoner." Of course, the fact that Fitch made such a request at all indicates that what he had witnessed happening at the river's edge made him fearful for his life and desirous of the general's intervention.

Forrest's response to the surgeon's request was surely not what he had hoped to hear. "He said, you are Surgeon of a Damn Nigger Regiment." The implication was clear that as such Fitch should not expect the protection he sought. "I replied, I was not." The general was undeterred. "You are a Damn Tenn. Yankee then." But Fitch's reply to this obvious conclusion no doubt confounded the Southern commander totally. "I told him I was from Iowa. Forrest said what in hell are you down here for? I have a great mind to have you killed for being down here." The surgeon's approach might not seem to have been the best policy when confronting Bedford Forrest, but the Confederate took no hostile action against this utterly defenseless Federal. Rather, he offered an astute observation. "He then said if the North west had staid home the war would have been over long ago."

Then, as Fitch explained, the general instructed a nearby soldier "to take charge of me and see that I was not harmed. For which I thanked him." It was not clear that the Confederate commander understood that more than the ordinary dangers of the battlefield existed from which Fitch sought protection. Indeed, Forrest may still have been wondering how an Iowa doctor got into a Union fort in West Tennessee in the first place. But he did not have time to consider these questions for too long before his gaze and attention refocused on the *New Era* in the river below.[30]

Ironically, another recipient of Forrest's attention in the confusing aftermath of the battle was William Bradford. According to Tyree Bell, the Union commander was among a great number of men who had fled into the river and "staid there until he was nearly froze." Finally coming out of the water, the major reached the fort. "He asked for Gen. Forrest and I carried him up to where Gen. Forrest was and told him 'Here is Col. [*sic*] Bradford, who had command of the fort.' Forrest spoke to him and told him to go into the tent and get some dry clothes on."[31]

General Forrest later claimed that his men lowered the colors and thus brought the remainder of the action in and around Fort Pillow to a halt. He would assert to a former comrade that in regard to the excesses, "there has been a great deal of exaggeration and misrepresentation about that, and I'll tell you how that was." Dabney Maury listened intently enough to remember what the cavalryman said. "When we got into the fort the white flag was shown at once, and the Negroes ran down to the river," Forrest explained, "and although the flag was flying, they kept turning back and shooting at my men, who consequently continued to fire into them crowded on the brink of the river, and they killed a good many of them in spite of my efforts and those of our officers to stop them."[32]

Even if Forrest made an effort to end the firing once he had turned his attention to it, the damage was done. The majority of the killing, especially along the riverbank, had already taken place. He may well have taken steps to prevent further carnage inside the fort, where he could witness it, but considerable blood, a great deal of it unnecessarily and brutally, had already been shed.

The final tally of Union casualties at Fort Pillow was inordinately steep by anyone's assessment, particularly regarding the number of killed or mortally wounded. Of the approximately 585–605 men who made up the garrison, historians John Cimprich and Robert Mainfort, Jr., conclude that those who suffered death on the battlefield or from wounds sustained there amounted to 277–297, or 47–49 percent of the total involved in the affair. Of these the Tennessee Unionists lost some 31–34 percent of their number, while the largest percentage of deaths and mortal wounds fell to the black troops, at 64 percent.[33]

Since most soldiers initially survived their battle wounds in Civil War engagements, the high mortality rate for the black troops at Fort Pillow indicates an anomalous outcome in which deaths exceeded wounds significantly. Although the Southerners took prisoners, including blacks, they clearly could have taken more. As it was, Confederate losses were significantly lighter, especially considering that they were the attacking party and had carried out at least three separate assaults. Forrest would lament the twenty killed and sixty wounded in his command, particularly among the officers, but he would have had to admit that in the face of the Union losses, his were considerably less.[34]

Several factors accounted for the disparities in these numbers. One was the nature of the battle itself. Confederate marksmen picked off Union troops, especially officers, throughout the morning with deliberate, aimed fire from elevated positions. The targeted nature of that effort was bound to produce a disproportionate number of deaths in the process. Likewise, the close-hand fighting at the ditch and the walls was particularly vicious and deadly once the attackers reached that location. But perhaps more than any other factor, the positioning and close proximity of the Southern flanking forces below the bluffs was especially devastating to the disorganized and demoralized mass of Union soldiers seeking safety for themselves. As these men instinctively crowded together at the water's edge, seeking the false sense of protection the massed numbers seemed to offer, or plunged into the murky Mississippi to flee the deadly melee, the Confederates needed little precision to generate casualties among their blue-coated opponents.

No one recorded until after the fact that the continued appearance of the flag in the fort had any bearing on what was happening in the shooting gallery along the river. The men engaged there were unlikely to look above the smoke and confusion of the fray to find cues that the fighting should be suspended or curtailed in any case.

Within a matter of weeks, Chalmers attempted to clarify the question of Union resistance at Fort Pillow in a May 7 report. "The enemy made no attempt to surrender, no white flag was elevated," he observed, apparently referring to the lack of a collective effort rather than the individual ones that had taken place. "Nor," the general maintained, "was the U.S. flag lowered until pulled down by our men."[35] Almost five years later Forrest insisted similarly: "The fort never hauled down the flag. I cut it down with my own hands, and did all I could to stop the firing."[36] Both statements were self-serving, but Forrest's words were the most problematic. Like his account of his role in the Able rescue in prewar Memphis and other recollections of dramatic events during the war itself, this one smacked more of revisionism than reality.

Aside from the fairly well established facts that Forrest came into the fort only after it had fallen, became preoccupied with the gunboat in the river, and at best had acted to stop excessive killing only after he became aware of it (and then only in his immediate vicinity), any other involvement on his part remains speculative. Forrest was not shy about wading into the fighting and dying; indeed, he took inordinate pride in his personal success against individual opponents. Had he added to the macabre total on that day, he would have certainly credited himself with the results. Nor was he the type of person to direct others to do his work for him—he could do his own killing if the situation warranted.

Another contributing element to the bloody aftermath of the engagement was the racial and sectional bitterness that prevailed among the antagonists. The attackers gained the distinct advantage as the battle unfolded and appeared to use it to the fullest. Soldiers who might have shown mercy under different circumstances were disinclined to do so here, swept by the rush of combat and no doubt feeling that these adversaries deserved the outcome now being visited upon them. Until cooler heads could prevail as the heat of battle subsided, killing was bound to persist unchecked and unabated.

In assessing the results for the sake of his superiors, Bedford Forrest did not dictate his earliest reports on Fort Pillow with posterity in mind. If he had done so, he would certainly have demonstrated more of the dispassionate discourse that marked his subsequent communications on the subject. As it was, he submitted three separate reports from his headquarters in Jackson, Tennessee, on April 15, 1864.

To Lieutenant General Leonidas Polk, the cavalry commander noted that he and his 1,500 men had driven "the enemy, 700 strong, into the fort, under the cover of their gun-boats." Following the rejection of his surrender demand, "I stormed the fort, and after a contest of thirty minutes captured the entire garrison, killing 500 and taking 200 horses and a large amount of quartermaster's stores." He noted that during the battle, the "officers in the fort were killed, including Major Booth," and reported his own losses as "20 killed and wounded." Apparently, the Union fatalities included noncombatants as well. "Over 100 citizens who had fled to the fort to escape conscription ran into the river and were drowned." At any rate, the brief report concluded, "The Confederate flag now floats over the fort."[37]

In a longer and more detailed assessment afterward, Forrest lost some of the initial restraint and allowed his exuberance to get the better of him. "The victory was complete," he recorded in this second April 15 dispatch, "and the loss of the enemy will never be known from the fact that large numbers ran into the river and were shot and drowned." Again establishing the garrison's numbers at 700 men, "about 500 negroes and 200 white soldiers (Tennessee Tories)," he added coldly: "The river was dyed with the blood of the slaughtered for 200 yards. There was [also] in the fort a large number of citizens who had fled there to escape the conscript law. Most of these ran into the river and were drowned."[38]

The scene was no doubt reminiscent of what had happened some twenty-eight years earlier in Texas as the frightened Mexican troops of Santa Anna fled from the fighting at San Jacinto, with many of them dying while they flailed through a swampy bayou trying to escape the wrath of their opponents.[39] Interestingly, Union major general Cadwallader Washburn made such an historical reference in correspondence with Forrest in June 1864, reminding the Confederate that the Texans had cried

"Remember the Alamo!" seeking retribution for the killings there, as they struck at San Jacinto.[40]

Bedford Forrest could certainly be chided for his choice of phrasing, or at least the acceptance of the words used in his report, but as unfortunate as they later proved for the general, they were not out of line with similar expressions used by others on previous occasions. Following his lopsided victory at Camden, South Carolina, in 1780, British officer Banastre Tarleton exuded, "After this last effort of [the] continentals, rout and slaughter ensued in every quarter."[41]

Descriptions concerning the inflicting of enemy casualties in the Civil War employed this same type of language, including reports associated with the Union disaster at Ball's Bluff in 1861 and at Shepherdstown in 1862. In the case of the latter, Major General Ambrose Powell Hill sounded exactly as Forrest would later in reporting that after driving the Federal defenders "pell-mell into the river," there "commenced the most terrible slaughter that this war has yet witnessed. The broad surface of the Potomac was blue with the floating bodies of our foe." Then, Robert E. Lee's subordinate concluded, again in a manner not dissimilar from that associated with Forrest at Fort Pillow, "But few escaped to tell the tale."[42]

Had Nathan Bedford Forrest intended to use the elimination of the Fort Pillow garrison as an object lesson, there was nothing to prevent him from saying so in his written reports. There was also always the possibility that he wanted to send a broader message by deliberately letting some survive while others perished. But the general who had urged his command at Murfreesboro "to have them all" was disinclined to promote half-measures or orchestrate objectives in such a limited fashion if he could help it. He was the type to exert a "knife to the hilt" approach unless bluff or intimidation rendered that application of warfare unnecessary.[43]

Indeed, General Forrest drew larger lessons from the Fort Pillow experience. "It is hoped that these facts will demonstrate to the Northern people that negro soldiers cannot cope with Southerners." Yet in this statement he seemed mostly interested in illustrating that such troops as garrisoned the Union fort were no match for his men, not that a massacre of them was necessary to make the point. Defeating the garrison illustrated that "fact" quite sufficiently, regardless of the nature and number of associated casualties. Indeed, Bedford Forrest's concerns following Fort Pillow were less with imparting lessons than in his utilization of "the guns recently captured" at the fort to interrupt the "enemy's navigation of the rivers" and cause the Federals as much aggravation as possible.[44]

In a third dispatch on the same day meant to be hand delivered by special courier to President Davis, Forrest returned to a more circumspect tone. He indicated the gunboat rescue plan and downplayed the rhetoric regarding Union casualties. "The enemy attempted to retreat to the river," he explained, "either for protection of gun-boats or to escape, and the slaughter was heavy [there]." Here, he attempted to clarify the earlier numbers he had provided to General Polk. "It is safe to say that in troops, negroes, and citizens the killed, wounded, and drowned will range from 450 to 500." Forrest reiterated that he considered the victory a "complete" one, but there was no mention of a river stained with their blood. Perhaps in a moment of hyperbole, considering the negative outcome of events at Paducah in particular, the cavalry commander observed inaccurately of his enemy encounters, "I am glad to state that in all the engagements I have had with them since I re-entered West Tennessee we have been successful."

The general explained to the chief executive that he had remained too occupied to conscript as thoroughly as he desired, although he assured Davis that he would do so when the opportunity presented itself. For the time being, he had to be vigilant against attack while simultaneously continuing to carry out offensive operations. In any case, the region and the Southern sympathizers in it had benefited from his activities there.

Forrest could not close his communication with Davis without also availing himself of the opportunity to repeat his charges against Fielding Hurst and to note with satisfaction the defeat of the commands of Isaac Hawkins, William Bradford, and Hurst. These victories had "broken up the Tennessee Federal regiments in the country," he explained to the president. "Their acts of oppression murder & plunder made them a terror to the whole land."[45]

Given the environment, it is likely that even had Forrest not given rein to his propensity for exaggeration, that Fort Pillow would have been fodder for election-year propaganda. But his need to be at the center of every story, and his willingness to embellish any story of which he was a part, in this instance did more to harm his reputation than to help it. His name would forever be associated with a battle that he had not controlled and "a massacre" that he neither needed nor appeared to have wanted.

CHAPTER 6

# "Remember Fort Pillow"

## *April 12–June 1864*

Mr. Forrest ought not be so *bloody.*

*Nathaniel Cheairs, May 1, 1864*

I have come to the conclusion that Confederate Guns won't wound negro troops. They either kill them or miss them entirely.

*Confederate soldier D. C. Jones, June 13, 1864*

As General Forrest and his tired but victorious troopers rode toward Brownsville and away from the bloody field of Fort Pillow, it is difficult to imagine what was going through their minds. Undoubtedly grateful that they had survived a brush with a foe that, given their political and racial preconceptions, they felt they had no choice but to defeat, the Confederates could now count their spoils and their costs. One of the men, Alex Jones, who had emerged from the fighting unscathed, paused a few days later to inform his wife, Sallie, "I did not get hurt for which I feel thankful to god."[1]

To attend to those left behind, the general designated his aide Captain Anderson to remain at the fort to supervise the final details, which called for him to "make some disposition of the wounded Federals, and see that the dead were buried, etc." Anderson made contact with the *Silver Cloud*'s acting master, William Ferguson, who soon had a shore party on site to assist with these necessary arrangements. In his commander's name, Anderson informed Ferguson, "I am authorized by Major-General Forrest to say that he desires to place the badly wounded of your army on board of your boat, provided you will acknowledge their paroles." Forrest left no instructions to exclude anyone from the offer, regardless of what they might say about what they had seen or experienced. Indeed, Anderson added, "I shall send all, white or black, who desire to go."[2]

The naval officer acquiesced to the terms, which called for a cessation of any hostile action in the area "until 5 P.M. for the purpose of burying our dead and removing our wounded." For the moment at least, Forrest was undoubtedly pleased to have the wounded Federals taken off his hands rather than sustain the burden of caring for them. The Confederates did nothing to hinder the process; in fact, as William Ferguson reported, "Details of rebel soldiers assisted us in this duty."[3]

Following the burials and the retrieval of the wounded and prisoners, Ferguson submitted a report on April 13 that acknowledged his acceptance of three junior officers, "43 white privates, and 14 negroes."[4] Two of these officers, Lieutenants John H. Porter and M. J. Leaming, were members of Bradford's 13th Tennessee (U.S.). The other, Lieutenant H. Lipsett, belonged to the 6th U.S. Colored Troops.[5]

If Forrest felt guilty for having carried out an atrocity, he certainly did not act like it. Furthermore, his humanitarian gesture, while meeting his short-term interests of divesting himself of caring for these captives, created no small future inconvenience for him. Perhaps he did not expect these men to tell others what they had witnessed, but Bedford Forrest was too smart a person and too prone to storytelling himself not to be aware that this could happen. One can only surmise that he did not think he had anything for which he would have to answer or apologize. Regardless, he would have the rest of his life to regret that decision.

Even as the hostile forces left the scene, the aftermath of Fort Pillow continued to play out. The last shots of the affair came as the Confederates carried their able-bodied prisoners with them. Among this number was the unfortunate final commander of the garrison, William Bradford. Tyree Bell noted that the panicky major had run to the river below the fort before finally surrendering himself.[6] Bradford's good fortune at not being killed in the chaotic immediate aftermath of the battle did not last. A fellow prisoner explained that the major was "under guard, as a prisoner of war, and was reported as such," although he "had tried to conceal his identity as much as possible, by putting on citizen's clothes." W. R. McLaglan observed that a detail of five Confederates "took Major Bradford out about fifty yards from the road" and shot him.[7]

Union general Cadwallader C. Washburn brought the matter of the post commander's death to Forrest's attention. The Confederate cavalryman denied knowing what had happened to Bradford until more than a week after the fact and insisted that in any case his information differed from Washburn's on more than detail. By Forrest's version, Bradford had violated a parole given him to attend the burial of his brother, Captain Theodore Bradford, who was killed in action at Fort Pillow. According to Forrest, the major abused this favor when he "changed his clothing and started for Memphis" instead of adhering to the terms of his temporary release. The Union officer had the misfortune of running into some of Forrest's men who were combing the area for deserters. Inadvertently swept up in their dragnet, Bradford "attempted to escape, and was shot." Remembering his own condemnation of Hurst, Forrest assured his counterpart, "If he was improperly killed nothing would afford me more pleasure than to punish the perpetrators to the full extent of the law, and to show you how I regard such transactions I can refer you to my demand upon Major-General Hurlbut (no doubt upon file in your office)."[8]

Forrest and his men certainly did not have any lost love for Unionist Tennesseans. Bradford's death would be little mourned by them. Yet if the general planned to eliminate all such individuals, especially among the officer ranks, he already had failed to complete the task by turning over Lieutenants Porter, Leaming, and Lipsett. Regarding enlisted personnel, Gregory Macaluso notes that of 142 whites captured in the battle, "at least 17 men [10 of them Tennesseans and 7 Kentuckians] can be positively identified as having deserted from various Confederate units."[9] Bedford Forrest could be merciless and callous to men from his command who deserted or fled in the face of the enemy, but there was no indication that applying such a standard to these prisoners was a priority to him or these seventeen captives surely would have suffered a different fate.

The argument could certainly be made that Forrest was selective in applying his sense of vengeance by killing some opponents and sparing others. The Confederate cavalryman was capable of nuance, despite a ruthless temper that he found difficult to curb in the heat of battle or in personal confrontations. But in weighing the fate of these prisoners, the most logical conclusion would seem to be that if his men had standing orders to take no such prisoners or if he had wanted them summarily shot when captured, the Confederates would have done so without pause or regret.

Indeed, Bedford Forrest had enjoyed opportunities to contradict his ruthless reputation in his treatment of other captives. When a Union chaplain appeared before his tent as a prisoner, the Confederate asked the minister to provide the blessing for their meal. Taken aback by a request that did not fit the personality of the opponent he had expected, the preacher expressed his "gratitude" for "being thus considerately treated." The next day Forrest offered the man an escort to his lines, insisting as they parted, "Parson, I would keep you here to preach for me if you were not needed so much more by the sinners on the other side."[10]

When later Forrest brought his command through Fielding Hurst's hometown of Purdy, he took the precaution of sending his trusted lieutenant Charles Anderson (now a major), and a small squad to secure the Unionist's property from any potential retribution by his men. Furthermore, he reassured local residents that while he did not blame his men for wanting to express their antagonisms tangibly, he would not allow them that opportunity. Even so, the gesture should not be misconstrued. Should his command face the Tennessee Unionists again on a battlefield, Forrest intended to make every effort to "wipe them off the face of the earth." He considered these particular opponents "a disgrace to the Federal army, to the state and to humanity."[11] Clearly, even in the aftermath of Fort Pillow, Bedford Forrest had not changed his opinion as to who he believed were renegades. But neither had he reached the conclusion that wholesale destruction was warranted against anyone associated with them simply because of their family or social connections.

In the meantime, the general had further military operations to oversee and an extended raiding campaign to bring to a successful close. As part of this effort, Abraham Buford detached 150 men under Captain Henry A. Tyler to test the defenses at Columbus, Kentucky. Evoking his commander's name as Duckworth had done previously, Tyler called on the garrison to surrender. The captain added a warning as a means of intimidating the Union commander into adhering to his demand: "Should you surrender, the negroes now in arms will be returned to their masters. Should I, however, be compelled to take the place, no quarter will be shown to the negro troops whatever; the white troops will be treated as prisoners of war."[12] These were ominous words in the context of what had just occurred at Fort Pillow. Certainly, if Forrest planned to unleash a war of extermination against black Union troops, it would seem to corroborate the charges that many in the North would soon level against him.

But in the case of Columbus, Captain Tyler did not have the strength to carry out his demand. He issued it with the intent of overawing the Federal commander into capitulating without a fight. Given the circumstances, bravado was about the only chance for success Tyler had in an operation that was meant as a diversion anyway. He never intended a continuation of a policy to kill armed black soldiers, if one had ever existed in the first place.

Nor was Tyler alone in his mission or his method. After detaching the small strike force for Columbus, Buford rode on to Paducah, perhaps hoping to surprise a Union command that might not expect the Confederates to return so soon after their previous visit. But when he reached the river town on April 14, Buford found the garrison once again prepared in its defense. The Kentucky Confederate sent in his demand, under his own name, and the antagonists agreed to give civilians an opportunity to remove themselves from harm. "After that time," Colonel Hicks noted in his reply to the Southerners, with justifiable confidence based upon the earlier repulse of the Rebel raiders, "come ahead; I am ready for you." Like Tyler's message the day before at Columbus, Buford's was essentially a bluff. Keeping the garrison pinned in their works would give his men free rein to range the area for whatever supplies remained. Northern newspapers had boasted that in their first appearance in Paducah, the Confederates had missed 140 good horses; they did not overlook them this second time.[13]

Forrest's men continued to roam through portions of West Tennessee, scouring the region for recruits or conscripts, requisitioning horses and supplies, and attempting to suppress Unionist activities. Colonel Duckworth kept his column busy through the latter part of April "scouting from Ripley to Fort Pillow and in conscripting."[14] On the twenty-seventh, members of Forrest's command seized approximately two hundred dollars' worth of corn, bacon, and flour from a Benton County farmer who later sought and obtained restitution from the Tennessee state government.[15]

Bedford Forrest had left an indelible mark on the western portion of his home state. Ironically, no one knew this better than his Tennessee Unionist nemesis, Fielding Hurst. In a communication with Andrew Johnson on April 29, 1864, the colonel of the 6th Tennessee Cavalry (U.S.) drew the governor's attention to "the deplorable State of affairs which now exist in West Tenn." He wanted Johnson to understand that while he and his men had been faithfully serving the U.S. government, their homes and families had been left to the mercies of an implacable foe. "Forrest is now and has been for forty days in the counties between the Mississippi and Tennessee Rivers," he explained, "carrying devastation and destruction as he goes."

It was bad enough that "the military authorities" had been able to "do nothing to alleviate their Suferrings [sic], but on the contrary, frequently taunt us with being 'Conquered Rebels' and *insinuate* that they had just as leave have us on the other Side as not." Clearly smarting over such insults from those whom he felt should have supported them, Hurst assured the governor: "This does not at all suit me. I don't like to be compelled to keep my Regiment where a Rebel has more influence over the authorities than a loyal man, neither do I like the idea of guarding Rebel property, whilst the owners of Said property are living luxuriantly under the protection of *my* Government and at the same time plotting treason against that Government." Perhaps with his former commander in mind, the colonel added icily, "neither do I like to be under the *immediate* command of men who have 'Cotton on the brain' to Such an extent as to cause them to neglect their duty to the Government." Hurst closed the letter with the assurance that he had assembled "nearly a full Regiment" of almost a thousand men but had to admit, "we have been in Several engagements, in one of which the loss was forty and three officers."[16]

Hurst's letter sounded remarkably like one that Forrest might have dictated in his place. Perhaps that similarity in outlook, if not their shared Tennessee heritage, was one of the reasons the two men clashed so bitterly. In the short term the Confederate had gotten the best of his Union counterpart. But the war would not end in the short term.

The effects of Fort Pillow were not always immediately clear to audiences at some distance from Tennessee. In Great Britain at least one newspaper thought that Forrest's capture of the fort had a greater strategic significance than it actually did. "The repossession of Pillow by the Confederates again closes the Mississippi," the *Miner and Workman's Advocate* argued at the end of April.[17] But Forrest would have had to remain in the vicinity of the river to accomplish such dramatic results, a capability he did not have with the numbers of men he had available.

In the meantime, the Northern press was busy alternately predicting doom and advising readers that the Confederate cavalryman's days were numbered. The *Boston Post* informed its patrons, "There seems to be a Forrest in the lower part of Kentucky that needs clearing." The *Louisville Journal* expanded on the image, promising, "Col. [Sam] Hicks has been blazing away at it, and [Benjamin] Grierson is out on a survey and will girdle it, if possible." But the *Memphis Daily Appeal,* exiled in Atlanta, Georgia, and quoting the other references, assured its readers, "Our Forrest has not been disturbed." The paper then sarcastically offered, "Send out the rail splitter [Lincoln] himself next."[18]

Historians Paul Ashdown and Edward Caudill have accurately concluded, "With great reliability, the lens through which Fort Pillow was viewed in the press could be predicted by geography."[19] Headlines from the major dailies in New York City told the story at a glance. The *New York Times* of April 16, 1864, opened with a powerful flourish: "The Black Flag. Horrible Massacre by the Rebels. Fort Pillow Captured after a Desperate Fight. Four Hundred of the Garrison Brutally Murdered. Wounded and Unarmed Men Bayoneted and Their Bodies Burned. White and Black Indiscriminately Butchered. Devilish Atrocities of the Insatiate Fiends."[20] For several days, the *Times* continued to trumpet "The Massacre at Fort Pillow" on its pages.[21] Its rival, the *Tribune*, spread the garish headlines even further, assuring its readers of a story that was "Shocking from the Mississippi" and adding similarly styled running titles: "Men Shot While in the Hospital. The Hospital Burned. Negroes Buried Alive but Escaped." For his role in the "Shocking Scenes of

Savagery," the newspaper concluded that "Forrest has placed his name side by side in infamy with that of the butcher of Lawrence[, Kansas, William Clarke Quantrill]."[22]

New York's *Army and Navy Journal* made an attempt at evenhandedness in covering the events at Fort Pillow. "Making due allowances for the exaggeration incident to excited statements," an editorial noted, "it can hardly be hoped that the particulars of the affair will receive any essential modification from official reports and investigations." There was the sense that other than slight alterations in numbers that might "soften details," any examination "can scarcely be expected to completely set aside the evidence of the damning fact that soldiers of the Republic, surrendering to superior numbers, disarmed and helpless, have been deliberately shot down while entreating for that mercy which the most savage of modern soldiers does not refuse to a helpless enemy."[23] The implication was clear that the Confederates who stormed Fort Pillow were the "most savage" perpetrators of a "massacre" of "helpless" soldiers who had ceased to resist.

In early May the *Chicago Tribune* sought to inform its readers of the type of individual capable of perpetrating these atrocities. "The Butcher Forrest and His Family: All of them Slave Drivers and Woman Whippers" offered a capsule history of the Forrests that had an original dateline from Knoxville, Tennessee, and had appeared in the *New York Tribune*. This piece would help explain the general's wartime "record of infamy," including "the cowardly butchery" that followed the fall of Fort Pillow. His prewar years demonstrated that he was a "mean, vindictive, cruel, and unscrupulous" creature who "had two wifes [sic]," with children by each. Maintaining that a "universal sentiment" existed for showing Forrest's command "no quarter," the author of the sketch concluded, "Such are the appropriate antecedents in the character of the monster who murdered in cold blood the gallant defenders of Fort Pillow."[24]

On May 14 William G. "Parson" Brownlow's newspaper, *The Knoxville Whig and Rebel Ventilator*, forwarded a piece that had originally appeared in the *Cleveland Herald*. The short editorial drew a direct "parallel" between Fort Pillow and the 1836 battle of San Jacinto, Texas. It noted that the "brutality" of the "no quarter" policy exhibited by the Mexicans toward the defenders of the Alamo, particularly to the "six of their number remaining alive," had "aroused a fire in the hearts of the Texans." It noted the battle cry then of "Remember the Alamo!" and suggested that the new one now should be "Remember Fort Pillow!"[25]

Generally speaking, Confederate editors had a different take on Fort Pillow. But newspapers like the *Mobile Advertiser and Register* illustrated the difficulty the Southern press found in responding to their Northern counterparts' charges of massacre. On May 6 the *Advertiser and Register* reprinted material from "a private letter" that had appeared in a New York newspaper. Widely quoted then and since, "an intelligent Irishman" was supposed to have spoken firsthand with survivors of the fighting at Fort Pillow. Ironically, this individual concluded that officers of both sides had failed "to control their men" or "lost all control over them." Although the Southern journal touted this version as "a rational and probably a very correct account of the affair," the letter writer's conclusion was not entirely favorable to the Southern cause. "After the surrender the rebel officers, with but few exceptions, did what they could to control their men," he explained. "They could expect nothing if the defence failed from the rebels, who entering the fort sword in hand would probably refuse quarter, which I am informed the laws of war permit in cases where the place is taken by assault."[26]

Five days later the Mobile daily presented its readers with the April 20 address of Brigadier General Chalmers to his command at Oxford, Mississippi. That officer certainly expressed no remorse for anything that had happened at Fort Pillow. "I congratulate you upon your success in the brilliant campaign recently conducted in West Tennessee, under the guidance of Maj. Gen. Forrest, whose star never shone brighter, and whose restless activity, untiring energy and courage, baffled the calculations and paralyzed the arms of our enemies." To such hyperbole on his commander's behalf, Chalmers offered to "review the part taken by the soldiers of this Division in this decisive campaign."

After recounting the successes of Colonels Duckworth and Neely, at Union City and Bolivar, respectively, the general turned to Fort Pillow. While not referring to the actions that took place following the fall of the post, Chalmers was unequivocal concerning the results, explaining that the Confederates had "taught the mongrel garrison of blacks and renegades, a lesson long to be remembered."[27] Even in the days before a twenty-four-hour news cycle and the indulgence in "spin" to manipulate information, the Confederate in charge at Fort Pillow before Forrest arrived and who participated in a primary leadership capacity throughout the engagement would have had difficulty explaining these words to a skeptical audience.

From Johnson's Island, Ohio, on April 16, John M. Porter recorded in his diary, "Ft. Pillar has fallen—garrison put to the sword." Then he added without further editorial comment, "Negroes murdered."[28] In early May Confederate major Nathaniel F. Cheairs was languishing in Camp Chase in Ohio as a prisoner of war when word reached him of what had happened at Fort Pillow. His words reflected the understandable angst of one worried that the repercussions of what had occurred in Tennessee would eventually affect the nature of his confinement. "We now have some prospect of being exchanged soon," he speculated hopefully, "provided the *bloody Massacre* of the *Colored troops* by Forrest at Fort Pillow don't interfear with the Cartell."[29]

Nat Cheairs had first been a prisoner at the surrender of Fort Donelson and then a volunteer aide to Bedford Forrest following his exchange and release. Now in his second stint as a captive of the Federal government, he commented on the news he had learned regarding his old chief.[30] Although the officer may have been writing his sister with a message he knew would pass any censor, his feelings concerning Fort Pillow bear the ring of sincerity. "The public accounts which I have seen makes it a horrid, dreadfull affair," he explained. "Mr. Forrest ought not be so *bloody*. Hope he will act with more humanity in the future."[31]

Forrest may have felt that he had done nothing for which he should apologize or answer. Still, the general was sensitive enough to the firestorm of protest that he made an unusual request of his senior commander. On May 16, from his headquarters at Tupelo, Mississippi, Forrest asked for Stephen D. Lee's assistance in obtaining information on "the so-called massacre" by having a third party, Judge P. T. Scruggs, interview captured Union officers "in regard to the matter." He felt that under the circumstances, it would behoove him to gather "all the facts" and make them available to the Confederate War Department.[32] It seemed not to have occurred to him that the circumstances of these interviews could be questioned as having taken place under the duress of captivity.

Three days later one of these men, Captain John T. Young, authored a letter from the prison at Cahaba, Alabama. He corroborated Charles Anderson's account. "I saw no ill-treatment of the wounded on the evening of the battle or next morning," Young explained.[33] Of course, it would be hard to imagine that as a prisoner of war the Union officer would have felt able to write freely about what he had seen or experienced.

Indeed, Young was apparently not above suspicion at the time. The *New York Times* published a scathing indictment of the Union soldier's loyalty. Appearing in the form of a letter from Cairo, Illinois, on April 14, a correspondent of the *Missouri Democrat* chastised the captured Federal for his apparent friendly relations with the Confederates. "It was a subject of considerable remark that Capt. YOUNG was treated by the rebels with so much favor," the writer noted, before postulating, "and it is said that his brother, who has been in the rebel army, kept a grog shop at the fort and was a rebel sympathizer."[34] Certainly, the idea that a former Confederate was now serving beverages to Union personnel despite his own pro-Southern proclivities sounds, on the face of it, preposterous. But at least one modern author saw favoritism for the Union captive even in the selection of prison accommodations. "Most of the Federal prisoners were sent to the dreaded Andersonville prison which was substantially larger and not as well administered as the Cahaba detention facility that housed Young," Richard Fuchs noted.[35] The fact that the Cahaba "detention facility" routinely flooded and contained its own special brand of misery for its occupants seemed not to have been considered important when weighing the relative prison conditions.[36]

Operations of his own occupied William T. Sherman's attentions when Forrest's men assailed Fort Pillow. By early April, he was in Chattanooga discussing future operations with George H. Thomas and inspecting the Division of the Mississippi, the Ohioan's new command. His focus had become riveted on preparations for an invasion of Georgia, to be carried out in conjunction with an offensive by Ulysses Grant in Virginia, that he hoped would do much to determine the outcome of the war.[37]

To his credit, Sherman never allowed Forrest's successes to affect his strategic vision. Just days after Fort Pillow, as he wrote admiringly of the Confederate to John A. Rawlins, Sherman demonstrated that he would not lose sight of the bigger picture. "I am willing he should continue to attack our forts," he observed of Forrest, "and he may also cross the Tennessee," thereby threatening Sherman's attenuated line of supplies from Nashville to Georgia. But the Union commander would not be pressured into altering his larger plans. "We have plenty of stores here," he noted, adding, "we are pushing them to the front as fast as possible. I will not let Forrest draw off my mind from the concentration going on."[38]

Sherman had what he thought was a clear understanding of the role that cavalry could play in the conflict. Even before Forrest had set out on the operation that included the assault on Fort Pillow, the Union general informed his favorite lieutenant, Major General James McPherson, that he was not concerned with "marauding cavalry, that can in no wise influence the course of the grand war." Therefore, he claimed at that earlier stage, "I would heed this cavalry little."[39] Sherman would quickly change his tune, largely in response to Forrest's successes, first in western Tennessee, then in northern Mississippi, instructing two of his commanders to "follow Forrest to the death if it costs 10,000 lives and breaks the treasury." He rightly came to understand that as long as the Confederate and his troopers traversed the region, they would constitute a disruptive force that could not be ignored. "There will never be peace in Tennessee," Sherman finally concluded, "till Forrest is dead."[40]

But Bedford Forrest was not alone in preoccupying the Ohioan's thoughts. In the immediate aftermath of the events of April 12, Sherman remained perplexed as to why a garrison was located at Fort Pillow, where it would even be possible for it to be obliterated. Across a period of several days, he sent out a steady stream of correspondence on the subject, searching for answers.

When Brigadier General Mason Brayman, commanding the military district headquartered at Cairo, Illinois, informed him that the fort had fallen and a terrible massacre of the black troops there had taken place, Sherman was incredulous.[41] "Fort Pillow has no guns or garrison," he replied. "It was evacuated before I went out to Meridian."[42] Nevertheless, the facts seemed to speak for themselves. Forrest had attacked the post and defeated its garrison, with fearsome results. "I don't know what these men were doing at Fort Pillow," Sherman explained to Grant in distant Virginia the next day. "I ordered it to be abandoned before I went to Meridian, and it was so abandoned. General Hurlbut must have sent this garrison up recently from Memphis."[43] To General McPherson, Sherman reiterated the point as if to establish it clearly in his own mind: "I don't understand it, as the place was long since abandoned by my order."[44]

Then there was Stephen Hurlbut himself. "I don't know what to do with Hurlbut," Sherman confessed to Grant. "I know that Forrest could pen him up in Memphis with 2,500 men, although Hurlbut has all of Grierson's cavalry and 2,000 white infantry, 4,000 blacks, and the citizen militia [of] 3,000."[45] Busy with plans of his own in Virginia, the general in chief was less uncertain as to what course to follow. "Relieve Maj. Gen. S. A. Hurlbut," Grant directed unequivocally. Furthermore, if atrocities had occurred at Fort Pillow, Sherman should be prepared to respond. "If our men have been murdered after capture, retaliation must be resorted to promptly."[46]

Sherman still had the matter on his mind the next day. Regarding Hurlbut, he concluded: "In making up our fighting force we have left inferior officers on the river. General Hurlbut has full 10,000 men at Memphis, but if he had a million he would be on the defensive." That was why Cadwallader Washburn was on his way to Memphis at that time to assume command. As for the Fort Pillow defenders, "The force captured and butchered at Fort Pillow was not on my returns at all." Still, that force had been there, and perhaps valuable lessons could be learned and benefits derived from the bitter experience. "It is the first fruits of the system of trading posts designed to assist the loyal people of the interior." Although this assistance was desirable, it constituted a luxury that the Federal government could not easily afford. Isolated posts were simply too vulnerable to lightning cavalry raids. "All these stations are a weakness, and offer tempting chances for plunder," the Ohioan observed.[47]

Sherman was equally convinced that such isolated outposts as Fort Pillow and the men assigned to garrison them were part of a larger policy he could not bring himself to endorse. "Of course, Forrest & all Southerners will kill them and their white officers," he insisted of the black Union soldiers to his brother John. "We all knew that, and should not expose small detachments" for the Confederates to threaten. He thought the "policy" of employing such troops ill advised and considered the motives of Northern state politicians, using Massachusetts as an example, to "dodge their share" of white recruits by filling their quotas with former slaves. "We ought not to engraft a doubtful element in any army *now*, it is too critical a period," he closed ominously.[48] Among its many faceted lessons, Fort Pillow had exposed a flaw in the system that Sherman thought needed to be addressed.

New commanders might certainly help. Washburn reached Memphis on April 22. The next day a new cavalry commander, Brigadier General Samuel D. Sturgis, arrived as well. A frustrated Sherman had been infuriated that Hurlbut had allowed Forrest to move so freely outside the well-protected environs of the city. This would not do to continue. "I have sent Sturgis down to take command of that cavalry and whip Forrest," he informed Grant through his chief of staff.[49] Hurlbut had commanded enough troops to take on Forrest if he had wished to do so. Washburn would be allowed no such luxury. "I know there are enough troops in Memphis to whale Forrest if you can reach him," Sherman stated pointedly.[50] "Don't let Forrest insult you by passing almost in sight of your command."[51]

Again, to General Washburn, Sherman painted the bigger picture so that his subordinate would be clear on his responsibility. "We are now all in motion for Georgia. We want you to hold Forrest ... until we strike [Joseph E.] Johnston. This is quite as important as to whip him."[52] The new Union commander in Memphis surely understood the implication: he had better find a way to "reach" Forrest or at least keep him occupied well away from the supply lines that would feed Sherman's pending operations or he would incur the wrath that had lost his predecessor his job.

Throughout the summer, Sherman ordered forces out of Memphis to try to locate and eliminate the Forrest threat. Sturgis tried his hand unsuccessfully and humiliatingly at Brice's Cross Roads in Mississippi in June. Andrew Jackson Smith almost succeeded in July at Harrisburg, or Tupelo.

Later, only a dramatic surprise dash by Forrest into the streets of Memphis prevented Smith from doing so in August. Nevertheless, as Sherman had so fervently wished, the Confederate cavalryman remained busy in Mississippi, prevented from harassing Union supply efforts in Middle Tennessee or North Georgia despite the calls from prominent Southern political leaders that he be turned loose to do so.[53]

Not surprisingly, Fort Pillow continued to have ramifications on Forrest's command long after the troops had left the banks of the Mississippi River. In the engagement against the Federals on June 10 at Brice's Cross Roads, Forrest faced Sturgis's 8,300 Union infantry and cavalry and twenty-two artillery pieces. The Federal command contained black troops under Colonel Edward Bouton who had sworn vengeance for Fort Pillow and promised no quarter to any of Forrest's Southerners who fell into their hands. Bouton's men had taken this oath upon bended knee before setting out on the campaign, supposedly adorning their uniforms with badges that carried the slogan "Remember Fort Pillow."[54]

Although these black troops performed heroically in the retreat from the June 10 fight, the rout and the associated panic that swept through the entire Union command affected them too. Some of the men began to strip off their uniforms and discard the Fort Pillow badges lest they be overtaken wearing them and subjected to wrathful retaliation by Forrest's Confederates. One Southerner recalled years later, "The negroes throwed their guns down and then their coats and last of all their shoes and run back towards Memphis much faster than when they come out to meet us." When in his mid-seventies, Solomon Brantley added gleefully, "I venture to say that if any of those negroes are living today they will tell you that they dident even have time to start a crap game in Miss. [in the course of the campaign.]"[55]

But ridding themselves of items Confederates would find offensive did not necessarily guarantee safety. A local witness recorded that the Southerners were "incensed" at the black troops and "relentlessly shot them down."[56] One of these Confederates recalled that when they had learned that black troops would again face them, the soldiers could not wait to confront "the damned Negroes."[57] Another participant wrote to his sister in Memphis of the aftermath of the battle: "The negro troops suffered severely. I saw a great many dead on the field—all in Yankee uniform fully equipped with gun and cartridge box." The scene left a strong impression upon the man: "After walking over the field I have come to the conclusion that Confederate Guns won't wound negro troops. They either kill them or miss them entirely."[58]

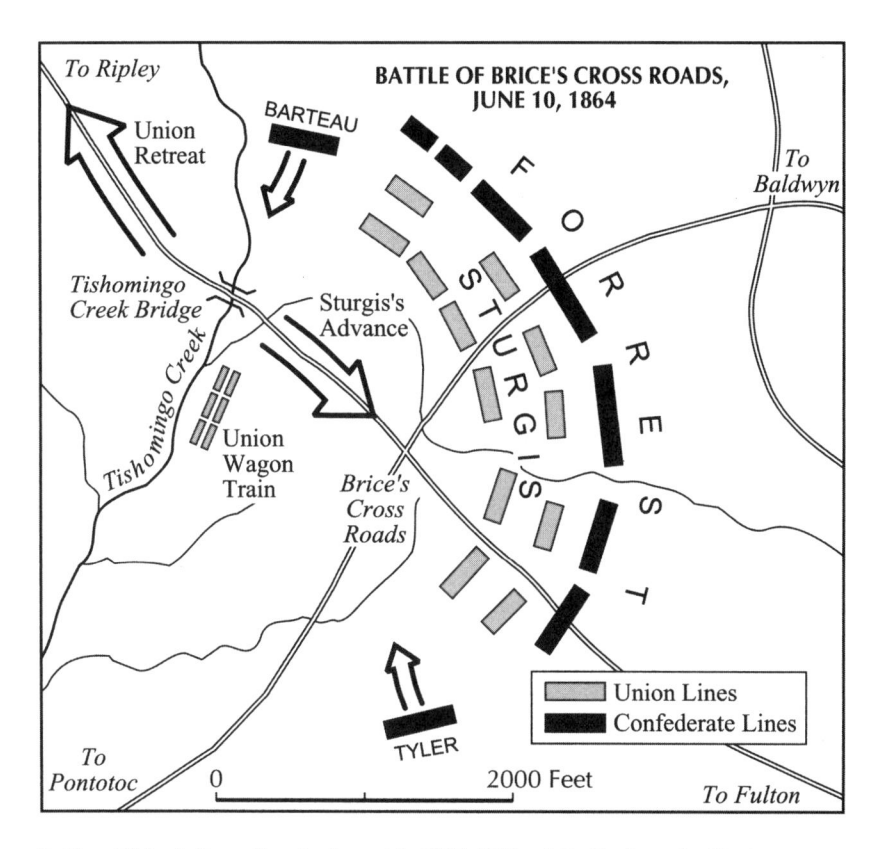

Battle of Brice's Cross Roads, June 10, 1864. Wills, *A Battle from the Start*.

Years later Brantley observed succinctly, "We capture[d] white prisoners all along [the retreat route] but no negro prisoners were taken."[59] Although it might have been possible that his unit never saw African Americans who could be taken captive, Brantley's phrasing undoubtedly meant that he and his comrades did not allow any black Union soldiers to surrender. In a very real sense, based upon this interpretation of such evidence, the aftermath of Brice's Cross Roads was Fort Pillow all over again on a different scale.

Forrest had proven difficult to defeat in combat since the war began, and in the summer of 1864, he surely seemed more invincible than ever to the "military authorities" of the North. But in the aftermath of Fort Pillow, the Federals were finding out that there were ways of beating the Confederate other than on the battlefield. They could take him on with greater chances for success in the newspapers of the North and the investigative arm of the U.S. Congress. After all, the general had handed them a golden opportunity based upon what had occurred at Fort Pillow in April. With a critical election year cranking up, the situation was right for exploiting the "Fort Pillow massacre."[60]

Termed alternately as the "Wizard of the Saddle" and "That Devil Forrest," Major General Nathan Bedford Forrest commanded the troops who overran Fort Pillow, a name that afterward entered the lexicon of excesses that occurred during the American Civil War. COURTESY OF THE U.S. ARMY MILITARY INSTITUTE, CARLISLE, PA.

Brigadier General James R. Chalmers deployed the Confederate forces that threatened Fort Pillow's garrison and defended the actions of the attackers in the years that followed. Wyeth, *Life of Forrest*.

Captain Charles W. Anderson (shown here later as a major) served as one of Forrest's principal aides and helped seal the Union garrison's fate by moving troops through one of the ravines to cover the landing below the fort. Wyeth, *Life of Forrest*.

Brigadier General Tyree H. Bell participated in the final Confederate assault and purported to see barrels of liquor inside the fort after it had fallen. Wyeth, *Life of Forrest*.

An intrepid Kentuckian, Brigadier General John Buford joined Forrest in his raid of West Tennessee and Kentucky in 1864 but missed the action at Fort Pillow while recruiting men and securing mounts in his native state. Wyeth, *Life of Forrest*.

Confederate sharpshooters assumed a critical role at Fort Pillow by pinning down the garrison and killing the Union commander, Major Lionel Booth, while he stood near an artillery piece before the final assault. Wyeth, *Life of Forrest.*

Having failed to secure a surrender of the garrison, Forrest sent his troops forward to scale the works and overwhelm the defenders of Fort Pillow. Wyeth, *Life of Forrest.*

Senator Benjamin F. Wade of Ohio provided the principal leadership for the congressional Joint Committee on the Conduct of the War, which investigated the excesses that had occurred at Fort Pillow. COURTESY OF THE LIBRARY OF CONGRESS.

Representative Daniel W. Gooch of Massachusetts joined Wade as a subcommittee to examine survivors of what quickly became known in Union circles as the "Fort Pillow Massacre." COURTESY OF THE LIBRARY OF CONGRESS.

*Harper's Weekly* produced *The Massacre at Fort Pillow* to introduce readers to the events that had occurred in West Tennessee from a Northern perspective. COURTESY OF THE LIBRARY OF CONGRESS.

*Frank Leslie's Illustrated Newspaper* also focused on the affair in a manner calculated to appeal to its readership in *The War in Tennessee—Rebel Massacre of the Union Troops after the Capture of Fort Pillow, April 12th, 1864.* PHOTOGRAPH COURTESY OF THE HARGRETT RARE BOOK AND MANUSCRIPT LIBRARY, UNIVERSITY OF GEORGIA.

Emphasizing President Lincoln's vow to exact retribution for "Rebel atrocities," this Thomas Nast *Harper's Weekly* illustration, published on May 21, 1864, features several wartime incidents that involved Nathan Bedford Forrest, including Fort Pillow.
AUTHOR'S PERSONAL COLLECTION.

After the war, Thomas Nast aimed his work at Democrats and enjoyed using Forrest and Fort Pillow as symbols, with the Confederate general torching the U.S. Constitution in *The Modern Samson* (October 3, 1868). COURTESY OF THE LIBRARY OF CONGRESS.

Nast's *This Is a White Man's Government* (September 5, 1868) employs Forrest, displaying the badge of Fort Pillow, an Irish brute from New York City, and a prominent Democratic financier as foils to a prostrate African American soldier reaching for a ballot box. COURTESY OF THE LIBRARY OF CONGRESS.

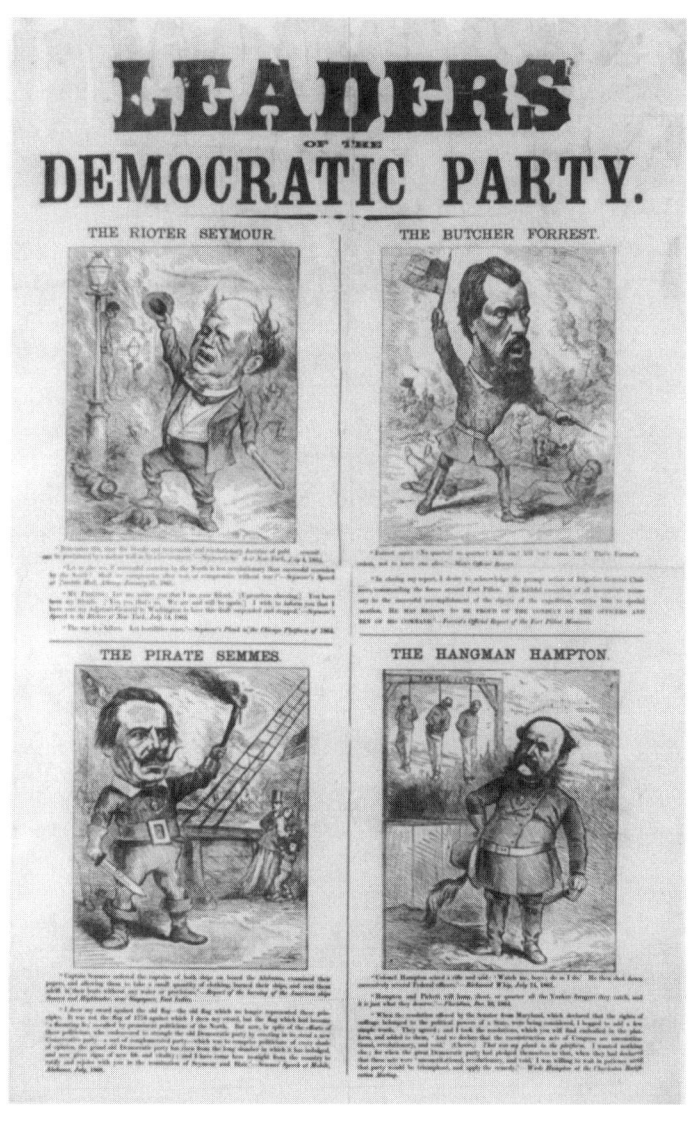

"The Butcher Forrest" joins Democratic candidate Horatio Seymour (*top left*), Raphael Semmes of the CSS *Alabama* (*lower left*), and fellow former Confederate Wade Hampton (*lower right*) as the *Leaders of the Democratic Party* (ca. 1868). COURTESY OF THE LIBRARY OF CONGRESS.

The impressive array of figures in blue and gray adorn competing sides as Ulysses Grant and Schuyler Colfax confront Horatio Seymour and Francis Blair in the election of 1868.

Forrest is positioned prominently on the Democratic side under a banner that extols Fort Pillow in *Both Sides of the Question* (October 24, 1868). AUTHOR'S PERSONAL COLLECTION.

CHAPTER 7

# AN ELECTION YEAR GETS "MASSACRED"

## April 12–November 1864

> The atrocities committed at Fort Pillow ... were the results of a policy deliberately decided upon and unhesitatingly announced.
>
> No cruelty which the most fiendish malignity could devise was omitted by these murders.
>
> *Joint Committee on the Conduct of the War,* Fort Pillow Massacre, *1864*

Abraham Lincoln did not think he would be reelected in 1864. This is an astounding conclusion given the stakes, as he saw them, of the great conflict that embroiled the nation. But there were in reality few viable candidates to replace him, and he vowed, in any case, that even if turned out of office, he would help the president-elect try to resolve the war before taking his final leave of the presidency.[1]

Of course, between the spring and the autumn of 1864, much could happen to shape the November election. Perhaps better than anyone else, Lincoln knew this. He might go or remain in office based upon the perceptions voters had about how the war was going and the prospects for victory in the foreseeable future.

In the meantime, the president had to admit that his decisions and the course of the war left much to be desired in political terms. He had issued the Emancipation Proclamation and watched as it went into effect, but not all Northerners cheered. Disgruntlement mounted in Democratic circles, where "Copperheadism" seemed rampant, but more ominous were such signs among some supporters of the administration, including in the armed services themselves.

Although his political instincts were virtually unmatched in his time or any other, Lincoln recognized the dangers of the course he had taken from the days of gradual compensated emancipation to the proclamation that had taken effect on January 1, 1863. Before the summer was out, there would be severe outbursts of disaffection, particularly in Democratically significant New York City. Lincoln was correct to worry.

Ironically, one of the Republican's greatest gifts may have come not only from someone outside of his party but also an unlikely source who would claim not even to be part of the Illinoisan's country. That source was Nathan Bedford Forrest, by virtue of the military action taken at Fort Pillow. Through the events that occurred there in April, Forrest offered the president an issue that his supporters, if not Lincoln himself, could utilize effectively throughout the remainder of the year to the polls. As historian William Marvel has observed, "The defeat at Fort Pillow therefore presented the Northern war party with some much-needed moral ammunition that spring."[2] In a sense the political prosecution began building its case against the Confederates almost as soon as the news of what had transpired on the banks of the Mississippi River became known.

Lincoln's instincts in the public arena were well honed. Famously, he had tussled with the "Little Giant," Stephen A. Douglas, during their famous debates for a U.S. Senate seat from Illinois in 1858. During their initial verbal jousting match, at Ottowa, Illinois, the lanky politician from Springfield exposed insights into his understanding of the importance of mass opinion. Maintaining that "public sentiment is everything" in politics, Lincoln argued, "With public sentiment, nothing can fail; without it nothing can succeed."[3] Battlefield success would tilt that equation dramatically, but the assessment was sound and would apply amply to the engagement at and aftermath of Fort Pillow.

Lincoln first spoke out publicly on that event in a Sanitary Fair speech in Baltimore, Maryland, on April 18, 1864. His primary concern was to address the government's apparent lack of ability to protect its black soldiers in the field. Accepting responsibility for the implementation of the policy that put such men in uniform, Lincoln resolved to stand behind them now. Citing the "painful rumor" of a "massacre, by the rebel forces, at Fort Pillow ... of some three hundred colored soldiers and white officers, who had just been overpowered by their assailants," Lincoln built upon a metaphor of the government as a "shepherd [that] drives the wolf from the sheep's throat." He confronted the underlying concern directly. "There seems to be some anxiety in the public mind whether the Government is doing its duty to the colored soldier," he told the audience. "Upon a clear conviction of duty I resolved to turn that element of strength to account; and I am responsible for it to the American people, to the Christian world, to history, and on my final account to God."

Now the task was to determine what had actually occurred at Fort Pillow. The president spoke to this as well. "We do not to-day *know* that a colored soldier, or white officer commanding colored soldiers, has been massacred by the rebels when made a prisoner. We fear it, believe it, I may say, but we do not *know* it." If, as he was also suggesting in the speech, there might be a requirement for Federal retaliation, the facts had to be clear and unmistakable. Therefore, he assured the listeners, "We are having the Fort Pillow affair thoroughly investigated; and such investigation will probably show conclusively how the truth is." Should the investigation substantiate that a massacre had indeed taken place, Lincoln underscored, "the retribution ... must come."[4]

One factor was certain in the days ahead as assessments of the "Fort Pillow affair" took place: those evaluations would not occur in a vacuum. Other incidents might have drawn similar attention, but this "massacre" held an unchallenged position of importance. As historian Greg Urwin concludes, "Fort Pillow was not the first racial massacre of the Civil War, nor was it the largest, but politics invested it with a prominence that overshadowed all other outrages of its type."[5] The central problem for any investigative body was going to be separating cold facts from the sensational reports that were already emblazoning headlines across the North.

The Joint Committee on the Conduct of the War was responsible for carrying out the investigation to which the president referred in his speech. Headed by Senator Benjamin Franklin Wade of Ohio, the committee had already engaged in two investigations in 1864, but these were hardly of a nature to appeal to a wide national audience. Historian Hans Trefousse notes that "few people could understand the highly technical problems of heavy ordnance or the irregularities in the awards of government ice contracts." The committee needed something with more flair, for the right story could garner headlines and raise not only its profile but also that of Congress. "In April, all that changed," Trefousse adds, "and the enemy presented Wade with a splendid opportunity to put his propaganda machine into action."[6]

The committee's specific charge was to "inquire into the truth of the rumored slaughter of Union troops, after their surrender, at the recent attack of the rebel forces upon Fort Pillow."[7] The larger body named a special subcommittee to sift through the available evidence and determine the truth surrounding the allegations of atrocity. Senator Wade and Representative Daniel Gooch of Massachusetts, both Republicans, constituted that subcommittee.[8]

The two men had ample credentials for the job. Ben Wade had been born in Massachusetts before moving westward as young man. He settled in Ohio, opened a law partnership there, and quickly made a reputation for his antislavery views. An early stalwart of the Republican Party, he became the nemesis of all things Southern and Democratic.[9] His views were so intensely held, asserts historian T. Harry Williams, that the politician expected to use the committee as an "engine of destruction" for the institutions he loathed.[10] Williams labels the congressional report produced on Fort Pillow as one of the "most expert propaganda productions of the war."[11]

Wade's partner in the enterprise was twenty years his junior. A native of Maine who had attended Dartmouth College and established a law practice in Boston, Daniel Wheelwright Gooch became increasingly active in Republican politics. He had been in Congress since placed there through a special election in 1858.[12] Labeled by historian Bruce Tap as "the legal expert on the committee," Gooch occasionally differed from his colleagues to the point that some of them considered him to have a more conservative bent.[13]

It was nearly inevitable that an attempt to arrive at an objective conclusion would prove difficult for these two men. Aside from their roles in the radical wing of the Republican spectrum, Wade and Gooch would also have to rely on the testimony of participants. Receiving such evidence from one side without being able to contrast it with the other would make it hard to arrive at a close approximation of what actually happened at Fort Pillow. Since there was no reasonable way to call Confederate witnesses or obtain Southern reports, it was unlikely that the investigators would be able, even if they had been willing, to weigh matters from both sides evenly. Injecting leading questions designed to extract specific responses would also mean that objectivity and truth would give way to subjectivity and bias.

Still, the testimony had to be collected, and Secretary of War Stanton did his part to clear the path for the investigators. On April 18 he notified Union commanders "at Cairo, Memphis, and all other military posts of the Ohio and Mississippi Rivers" to prepare to receive the visitors. Noting that the politicians "have been designated to inquire into and report upon the attack, surrender, and massacre at Fort Pillow," the secretary instructed the officers at the various posts to "provide quarters, subsistence, and transportation as might be required."[14] A subsequent order included stenographer William Blair Lord in the arrangements to be made for the investigative team.[15]

Historian Derek Frisby notes that "Wade's atrocity propaganda" had a powerful effect, having "dehumanized the Southern enemy and prepared the country for hard war."[16] There is no way to measure the success of the

Joint Committee's efforts to bolster morale by exposing and attacking Confederate atrocities. Did any single individual respond to what he read by enlisting or reenlisting for the service? Did someone decide not to shirk his duty? Such answers will always be, at best, anecdotal. Yet it can be said that it made much more sense for the committee and its reports and public accounts to target Confederates for blame rather than Union generals, no matter how much the latter might have deserved it.

Bruce Tap has argued that the "Republican members of the Committee on the Conduct of the War were convinced that Union battlefield defeats in part resulted from insufficient morale among northern soldiers." As such, these individuals felt that they could play critical roles in building that morale and thus "demonstrated that the power of disclosure could be used in a positive way to aid the war effort."[17]

So much the better to turn what many saw as a liability—the emancipation and arming of slaves—into an asset. But the benefit would not come from the moral uplift provided to those who were helping a downtrodden people be free. It would come by detailing the inhumanity and barbarity of their opponents toward the weakest and most vulnerable—black Union troops and prisoners of war. This would excite a war-weary nation that could only be moved to depression when the focus rested on the incompetence and mistakes of their own generals, the disheartening realities of corruption and wartime profiteering, or the terrible costs in lives and treasure associated with making war.

By the time the Fort Pillow investigation had closed, its results were already a foregone conclusion. A resolution passed on May 6 that "forty thousand copies of the Report of the Joint Committee on the Conduct of the War, etc., with the accompanying testimony, in relation to the late massacre at Fort Pillow, be printed for the use of the members of this house." Thus, established at the outset was the indisputable fact that Forrest and his men were guilty of perpetuating a "massacre," and that the results of the investigation must be disseminated widely. The document supplies straightforward conclusions: "It will appear, from the testimony thus taken, that the atrocities committed at Fort Pillow were not the result of passions excited by the heat of conflict, but were the results of a policy deliberately decided upon and unhesitatingly announced."[18]

The opening narrative reflects an unmistakable tone as it describes the aftermath of organized resistance within the ramparts. "Then followed a scene of cruelty and murder without parallel in civilized warfare," Wade and Gooch explain, "which needed but the tomahawk and scalping-knife to exceed the worst atrocities ever committed by savages." At Fort Pillow the Confederates had engaged in "an indiscriminate slaughter, sparing neither age nor sex, white or black, soldier or civilian. The officers and the men seemed to vie with each other in the devilish work." Highlighting the catalog of crimes to which the attached testimony would allude, the authors conclude for effect, "No cruelty which the most fiendish malignity could devise was omitted by these murderers."

The principal charges laid at the feet of the Confederates are that they had violated a flag of truce in order to obtain positions from which to more easily capture the post; killed large numbers of the defenders after they had ceased to resist; murdered civilians, including women and children; buried individuals while they were still living; and tortured garrison members, often when they were wounded and unable to save themselves, by burning them to death, even nailing at least one man down to ensure his demise in the most gruesome manner possible. The phrasing of the opening section is clear in that the Confederates "deliberately shot,…butchered, …shot them down in cold blood,…brutally shot down,…had their brains beaten out,…nailed…and burned,…[and] buried some of the living with the dead," among other actions.[19]

What follows are 120 pages of testimony gathered from some ninety witnesses: officers and enlisted men, doctors at the medical facilities where the wounded had been brought, and civilians who had been present at Fort Pillow in various capacities. Occasionally sprinkled into the mix of deponents are others regarding related subjects, such as the capture of Union City and the raid on Paducah, but the largest portion of testimony relates to what had allegedly happened at Fort Pillow.

The most common theme in the testimony is the murder of people who desired or were attempting to surrender. Most of the wounded who spoke to Wade and Gooch indicated that some of their injuries occurred after they had ceased to resist. Almost all of them seemed to have taken place below the bluff that contained the earthworks, either at the landing, on the riverbank, or in the river itself. Most of these wounds occurred in the context of racial epithets hurled at the victims by their assailants. Interestingly, there seemed to have been among the Confederates who committed these acts few officers present, those being either junior officers who participated or encouraged the slaughter or more-senior-level officers who tried to stop it.

Typical of both the nature and problems of the testimony is that given by Elias Falls, a cook at the fort who was recovering from his wounds at the Mound City hospital when he spoke with investigators. "They killed all the men after they surrendered," he confirmed, before adding, "until orders were given to stop." When asked who gave such orders, Falls replied, based on hearsay, "They told me his name was Forrest." Although the Confederate general obviously benefited from this observation, the black cook did not actually see the general give such commands. What he saw, in addition to men being murdered, was "an officer [of undetermined rank who] told the secesh soldier if he did that again he would arrest him, and he went off."[20]

Another deponent offered a similar picture. "One officer said, 'Boys, I will have you arrested, if you don't quit killing them boys,'" George Shaw explained. Then a Confederate argued that the superior officer should "'[l]et them go on; it isn't our law to take any niggers prisoners; kill every one of them.'"[21] Isaac J. Leadbetter, a member of the 13th Tennessee (U.S.), observed that he "did not see" any officers "until they carried me up on the hill."[22]

Like Falls, some witnesses attributed actions to Bedford Forrest himself. Jacob Thompson, a black cook, offered testimony richly laced with inaccuracies. When asked if he saw any Confederate officers present at the time of the killings, he responded, "Yes, sir; old Forrest was one." "Did you know Forrest?" Gooch inquired. Thompson answered affirmatively and described the over-six-foot-tall Confederate cavalry commander incongruously as "a little bit of a man" before adding with certainty, "I had seen him before at Jackson." Other statements from Thompson are equally suspect, including his admission that some of what he stated he had learned while on board the vessel taking him northward and was based upon what "the gunboat men" told him.[23]

At least one student of Fort Pillow has argued that questioning such testimony is tantamount to presenting a "Confederist" apology for the cruelties and excesses that actually took place. "Curiously," Richard Fuchs explains, "many who condemned the report as a distortion of the true events were not adverse to utilizing selected portions that buttressed their point of view," although this statement suggests that he recognizes that such "portions" exist in the report for the apologists to "utilize."[24] There are ample examples of testimony that can be treated as trustworthy; Thompson's is just not one of them. But all of these accounts have significance as a part of the historical record, both of what happened at Fort Pillow and the nature of the investigation that the Joint Committee carried out to collect those "facts."

A black private, Major Williams, offered the understandable explanation that he did not have a weapon on him when he was shot, stating, "I was an artillery man, and had no arms."[25] As a member of the 6th U.S. Heavy Artillery, his weapon would have been the artillery piece he had abandoned when the Confederates overran the fort. But Daniel Tyler, another member of the 6th, appears to have found a weapon of some type as he fled from Fort Pillow. He explained that when a Confederate approached him below the bluff, the following verbal exchange took place: "'Whose gun are you holding?' I said 'Nobody's.' He said 'God damn you, I will shoot you,' and then he shot me." Tyler then added that he saw no one else shot except himself, and when he pretended to be dead, a Confederate burial team threw him into a mass grave with others. When asked if he said anything to this detail, he replied, "No sir; I did not want to speak to them." Tyler then noted that "one of the secesh" saw that he was still alive and "made a young one dig me out. They dug me out, and I was carried not far off to a fire."[26]

Clark Barteau commanded one of the Confederate units given the responsibility for securing any routes of escape or reinforcement by river. In the aftermath of the fighting, his men engaged in collecting arms and other military equipment that could be appropriated for their use. Although it is impossible to know the exact locations in which these weapons were found, Barteau's men almost certainly would have retrieved the discarded Union arms in the areas in which the Confederates had been fighting: at the base of the bluff and along the river's edge. As it was, the haul of weapons was fairly substantial. Barteau's ordnance officer recorded that the men gathered seventy .58-caliber Enfield rifles and nine .44-caliber "Revolving Pistols" in addition to various accoutrements for cavalry mounts.[27] The captured weaponry seems to give credence to the argument that at least some of the members of the garrison retained their arms in the area below the bluff where the worst of the killings took place.

Fire proved to be notorious in the hands of the Confederates at Fort Pillow. Charred remains caught the notice of the first visitors to the site on the day after the engagement. It was the Southerners' misfortune that among these initial arrivals were two newspaper reporters from rival publications in St. Louis, Missouri. Their observations, and the testimony from witnesses before the Joint Committee investigators, left powerful images in the public mind of the worst kind of demise on or around any battlefield—burning to death. Yet such first impressions might not have proven accurate when other factors could be taken into account.

There were ample opportunities for bodies to be burned in whole or in part through the legitimate activities of war. The Federals had belatedly sought to burn the wooden barracks before the final Confederate assault, and the Southerners had tried mightily to stop them. The defenders succeeded in torching only one row before being driven off by gunfire, a combination that most assuredly caused some of the men to be hit in such a manner as to cause their bodies to be exposed to the flames.

Others may have been the victims of carelessness or indifference. As the main body of Confederates prepared to leave the vicinity, they left behind a small detail with the unenviable duties of burying any remaining bodies and destroying the public property of the fort. These men were certainly less efficient at the first task than they were at the second. Again, as the Federal landing parties attested, bodies remained unburied below the bluff and on the hillsides, while evidence of burned structures was equally abundant.

Forrest, who had no desire to attempt to hold Fort Pillow, certainly would have wanted everything of any military significance that his command could not carry away to be denied the enemy's use. But as Basil Duke, the famed Kentucky raider who was kinsman and comrade to John Hunt Morgan, later explained, "This remarkable accusation could hardly have been credited even by the most prejudiced, for even had Forrest been a cruel man, ... he would certainly never have wasted the time necessary to burn 'niggers' in so elaborate a fashion."

Nathan Bedford Forrest was obviously no saint, but his commonsense approach and the priorities of a battlefield offered no imperative for mass murder. Defeating former slaves would be sufficient to demonstrate their inferiority. To the man who had made his living in the slave trade, such recaptured individuals would be better returned to their masters as prewar national and wartime Confederate policies had provided. Furthermore, ongoing military operations should not be compromised by expending valuable time on sadistic practices when there were enough practical matters left to be accomplished. Duke was surprised that Forrest even gave "notice" to such charges.[28]

Nevertheless, the burning stories stuck. Whenever Fort Pillow received attention, these items were topics for discussion. Shortly after the incidents, a Union soldier confided in his diary, "News of the capture of Fort Pillow, by Forrest, and his massacre and burning of the colored soldiers and their officers."[29] In the third volume of his 1865 *A Youth's History of the Rebellion*, which presents the story of "the dreadful massacre" to young readers, William M. Thayer draws directly on the testimony from the Joint Committee. "They robbed all of the money and every article of value, and burned some of the buildings with the dead and wounded in them," he explains through the device of a conversation with a comrade. "Yes, they even nailed men to the sides of the buildings which they then set on fire, and the bodies were consumed in the flames."[30]

The most serious of such allegations concerns the death of Lieutenant J. C. Ackerstrom, the post quartermaster. His murder by being nailed to a board or door of a structure while it burned down around him is among the most sensational accounts presented, providing the basis for a line of questioning by which Wade and Gooch could provide an unmistakable atrocity against a white officer. Whatever readers of their report might think about the fates of black troops, this horrible story was bound to be one with which they could relate and empathize.

Yet testimony from black deponents is particularly problematic on this issue. Daniel Tyler observed, "I heard one white man was burned alive; I did not see him."[31] John Haskins noted, "They said they burned him in the house."[32] Eli Carlton was more helpful. When asked about the murder, he explained: "I heard so.... I saw them take the quartermaster; they said 'Here is one of our men; let us take him up and fix him.' A white man told me the next day that they burned him." Then asked if the lieutenant was wounded at the time, Carlton replied: "No, sir; he walked right straight. He had three stripes on his arm. I knew him well; I worked with him."[33] Of course, it is possible that he mistook a sergeant for the officer, but his insistence that he "knew him well" opens to question the entirety of Carlton's statements in this matter.

Members of the 13th Tennessee could be expected to know more about the quartermaster and his presumed fate. Second Lieutenant William Clary stated that he had heard that "a man was nailed to a building that was burned." He had also been told that there was a reason the lieutenant's body had not been retrieved and given a decent burial. "Some of the rebels said he was a damned conscript that had run away from Forrest. But I never heard Lieutenant Akerstrom say any such thing."[34] If this were the case, there was certainly reason to believe that the Southerners would want to punish their recalcitrant former comrade and use his gruesome fate as an example to others.

Other testimony on Ackerstrom's fate, from Isaac Leadbetter, Lieutenant Mack Leaming, and John W. Shelton, proved of no assistance.[35] All three could only relate what they had heard about the alleged incident, not what they had actually seen of it. When pressed as to when he heard about the killing, Shelton explained, "After I came up here" to the hospital at Mound City.[36] A civilian concurred with the timing when asked when he heard about the nailing-and-burning incident. "Since we came up here," James McCoy stated plainly.[37]

The honesty of these Tennesseans on this question must have been somewhat unsettling for Wade and Gooch. It confirmed that the men had been talking among themselves about Fort Pillow after the fact, thus a significant portion of their testimony could not help but be shaped by those conversations. It also proved that the investigators did not manipulate all aspects of the report or they would have surely encouraged more useful answers. Nevertheless, as Kenneth Moore points out, "The congressmen formed the questions to elicit certain responses." He concludes that in at least one instance, "Gooch's line of questioning masterfully extracted the anticipated answer."[38]

Undoubtedly, the most troublesome testimony in respect of pinning the horrific Ackerstrom atrocity convincingly on the Confederates at Fort Pillow came from John F. Ray of the 13th Tennessee. "He [the lieutenant] was shot by the side of me," he explained. "Was he killed?" "I thought so at the time; he fell on his face. He was shot in the forehead, and I thought he was killed. I heard afterward that he was not [killed]." When asked about the timing of Ackerstrom's wounding, Ray responded, "About two minutes after the flag of truce went back, during the action."[39]

Uniformly, each of those who had been at the fort when the Confederates attacked reported seeing or hearing members of the garrison and its auxiliaries being killed after the defense had collapsed. Many of them testified that their own wounds resulted from such postcombat abuses. Even where challenges can be made concerning specific recollections, and taking into account the fact that the scope of the investigation was politically motivated, the sheer volume of the testimony suggests that excesses took place at Fort Pillow on a significant scale. Some of the statements are highly questionable, being based on hearsay; others bear the mark of individuals who told truthfully what they knew, or at least believed, to have happened after the fall of the fort.

Author Richard Fuchs admits, "The report does contain some exaggerations and misstatements of fact and was a product of ex parte statements that avoided the scrutiny of rebuttal testimony or cross-examination." He criticizes the investigators' "proformer questioning" and "lack of probing style and searching inquisitiveness" that would not pass muster today.[40] Wade and Gooch certainly inquired in the manner that best suited their purposes, and their style of questioning seems more intent in gaining the desired answer than obtaining objective factual information. But such techniques and the flaws contained in the report itself should not discredit the effort in its entirety.

Coupled with a graphic report on the condition of returned prisoners of war, the Fort Pillow report was bound to evoke a strong response among those who read or heard about it. Secretary of War Stanton expected the cumulative effect to be significant. "The enormity of the crime committed by the rebels towards our prisoners for the last several months is not known or realized by our people," he informed Senator Wade on May 4, "and cannot but fill with horror the civilized world when the facts are fully revealed." As with Fort Pillow, there could be no other explanation in his mind than a pattern of wanton inhumanity on the part of the Confederate government and its representatives. "There appears to have been a deliberate system of savage and barbarous treatment and starvation" toward the captive Federals.[41]

The testimony of Dr. Knowles, serving in a hospital in Baltimore, Maryland, completed the connection between the subjects of the committee's reports. "I think the rebels have determined upon the policy of starving their prisoners, just as much as the murders at Fort Pillow were a part of their policy."[42] The combination of the massacre and the prisoner atrocities made for powerful reading and was bound to shape and influence public opinion and national policy.

The subject of the pending congressional report was clearly on the minds of the president and cabinet officials when they met in early May. Secretary of the Navy Gideon Welles recorded in his diary, "At a Cabinet-meeting the President requested each member to give him an opinion as to what course the Government should pursue in relation to the recent massacre at Fort Pillow." These suggestions would vary to one extent or another, but Welles was uneasy about relying too heavily on what the Joint Committee findings would say. "There must be something in these terrible reports," he concluded, "but I distrust Congressional Committees. They exaggerate."[43]

Lincoln polled the cabinet members in that meeting because it was "quite certain" that a "massacre" of troops had taken place. Secretary of State William Seward urged a moderate approach that affirmed the right of all U.S. soldiers to be treated as prisoners of war while detaining Southern captives as hostages for good behavior on the part of their government and its people. Secretary of the Treasury Chase, Secretary of War Stanton, and Secretary of the Navy Welles concurred with the holding of prisoners but thought they should be Confederate officers only. The latter two cabinet officials preferred to withhold any potential benefits for amnesty or exchange for Forrest, Chalmers, or any other Confederate of rank associated with the massacre.

Postmaster General Montgomery Blair departed from the others in advocating that hostages be taken from among Confederate prisoners. He considered it sufficient to "pursue the actual offenders" and threaten their arrest and severe punishment for the crimes they had committed. Attorney General Edward Bate agreed: punish the guilty, but the government should not engage in retribution for its own sake. As he explained poignantly to his colleagues, "I would have no compact with the enemy for mutual slaughter; no cartel of blood and murder; no stipulation to the effect that if you murder one of my men I will murder one of yours!"

Secretary of the Interior John P. Usher provided the most politic response. Confederate prisoners might be set aside, but nothing should be done until the military events then beginning to unfold in Virginia and elsewhere played out. The last thing the government would need would be to respond to disastrous headlines in the newspapers and have to retract any threats they had felt compelled to make.[44] With Grant set to plunge into the Wilderness of Virginia against Lee and Sherman poised to advance on Atlanta, Georgia, against Joseph Johnston, the best course might be to wait and see how events transpired before committing to any policy in such a controversial area.

As it turned out, that was precisely what happened. Any notion of an official response by the administration got lost in the attention that turned to another man, General Grant, accused in some circles of being a "butcher" due to the high Federal casualties sustained during his Overland Campaign.[45] Lincoln associates John Nicolay and John Hay thought that these "bloody conflicts crowded out of view and consideration a topic so difficult and so hazardous as wholesale retribution for the Fort Pillow barbarity." They concluded, "It does not appear that the Fort Pillow question was ever seriously renewed in the Cabinet or definitely concluded by the President."[46]

But in the aftermath of what had occurred at Fort Pillow, especially as illustrated in the Northern press and reinforced by the congressional investigation, Lincoln still had to take into consideration the least palatable aspect of his 1863 "Order of Retaliation." Consequently, on May 17, 1864, he drafted a message for Secretary of War Stanton that outlined strong measures for responding to the "massacre." The foundation of this response was for "insurgent officers, theretofore, and up to that time, held by said [U.S.] government as prisoners of war," to be "set apart."

Still, if some form of retribution seemed warranted, the president exhibited his powerful reluctance at resorting to it by offering a way out for any Confederate official. Noting that "as blood can not restore blood, and government should not act for revenge," Lincoln hoped to gain "any assurance ... that there shall be no similar massacre, nor any officer or soldier of the United States, whether white or colored, now held, or hereafter captured by the insurgents, shall be treated other than according to the laws of war."[47]

Even for so noble a reason as protecting black Union soldiers from white Confederate abuses, Lincoln abhorred the necessity for retaliation and understood quite well the difference between theory and reality. "The difficulty is not stating the principle," he had recently explained to the audience at the Sanitary Fair in Baltimore, "but in practically applying it."[48] Lincoln had insisted to Frederick Douglass, "Retaliation was a terrible remedy" that promised to spiral out of anyone's ability to control. "[Once] begun, there was no telling where it would end," he observed.[49] That the cycle of violence and reaction might not stop was especially troubling, for atrocity might well build on atrocity in a war that had already reached devastating dimensions for death and destruction.

If he remained hesitant in the spring of 1864 to take every measure at his disposal to secure the lives and welfare of black Union soldiers, Lincoln had nevertheless taken important steps in the progress of a nation in which the governor of Kentucky also insisted that recruiters of slave soldiers from masters in his state would face prosecution. Of course, President Lincoln, who had once argued, "I think it cannot be shown that when I have once taken a position, I have ever retreated from it," could be rightly taken to task for not doing more to protect his black soldiery. In the meantime, although Fort Pillow now threatened to become lost in the maelstrom of war, it would hardly be forgotten as the conflict slowly wound to its conclusion. As one modern writer noted, "Fort Pillow lay abandoned and silent, but the furies loosed there flew far and wide."[50]

CHAPTER 8

# REACTION TO FORT PILLOW

## 1864–1865

Vengeance is mine; I will repay says the Lord.

*Rufus Kinsley, Union soldier, April 18, 1864*

They got what was coming to them.

*Henri Garidel, Confederate ordnance clerk, April 20, 1864*

I regard captured Negroes as I do other captured property, and not as captured soldiers.

*Nathan Bedford Forrest to Cadwallader C. Washburn, June 23, 1864*

From mid-April 1864 forward, Nathan Bedford Forrest was fighting for a reputation he felt that he had fairly won on the field of battle but was losing, and in some circles clearly had lost, in the field of public opinion. The general seemed not to have ever understood precisely why that was the case, but he was well aware of it, and he troubled himself enormously to counteract these negative assessments both during and after the war.[1]

Of course, General Forrest did not have to convince everyone of his position regarding Fort Pillow. Many Confederates and sympathizing civilians who learned of the affair through second- or third-hand reports tended to consider the matter of excessive deaths among the garrison, and particularly among the black troops, as an acceptable outcome. "General Forrest captured Fort Pillow and about six hundred [troops,] the most of them Negroes," soldier Richard White informed a cousin on April 23. "[H]e didn't [take] any of them prisoners [but] killed every one of them[.]" Then the Confederate added blithely, "I think that was the best thing he iver done in his life."[2]

Civilians responded to the news as they understood it too. A Louisianan "exiled" in Richmond inscribed his thoughts in his journal with a hint of sympathy. "The taking of Fort Pillow by the Confederates has been confirmed in today's paper. The details are horrifying. Those Yankees and Negroes have been very badly treated." But Henri Garidel was too strong a Confederate sympathizer to let matters rest there, concluding coldly, "They got what was coming to them."[3]

Diarist George Browder thought the business at Fort Pillow had produced a salutary effect on blacks. "The papers are full of reports of Forrests capturing & killing negro troops," he noted in his April 20 entry. "There is a decided lull in negro enlistments. They *seem* more contented [emphasis his]."[4] Despite such a self-serving assessment, and without offering any further tangible evidence for his conclusion, this white Southerner was nevertheless satisfied that Fort Pillow had provided a necessary object lesson for potential Union enlistees from among the slave population.

Another diarist expressed a similar sentiment from her distant view in the aftermath of the fight. "General Forrest has taken Fort Pillow, put most of the garrison out of harm's way, killed every officer there," Ellen Renshaw House wrote on April 22. But she was hardly troubled by these results. "Good for him. I think he did exactly right."[5] Two weeks later, from Middleburg, Virginia, Mary Cochran confided in her diary her hopes that recent events would prove to be indicators "that results of stupendous magnitude are imminent." Noting that "God has encouraged our hearts by giving us success at various points," she specifically referenced Fort Pillow, which had "fallen before Forrest and his brave men."[6]

A newspaper from southwestern Virginia echoed this latter point. "Forrest's late victory at Fort Pillow has called forth most terrible howls from the Northern press and the Northern people," began a short editorial in the *Abingdon Virginian* on April 29. Citing four hundred out of six hundred deaths among the garrison, alongside another one hundred civilians reported to have perished, the writer observed caustically, "This is all true, perhaps, and the pity is that a single soul escaped." Refusals to accept calls for surrender and the presence of "tories who had sought Yankee protection" rendered the outcome inevitable, and fittingly, these individuals "met the fate they deserved."[7]

Union remarks in the immediate aftermath of the battle were understandably different in tone. In Ringgold, Georgia, James Connolly received word of what had happened at the Tennessee fort rather quickly. "Just now a dispatch has come saying Forrest has captured Fort Pillow on the Mississippi, and massacred some 300 black soldiers who were a part of the garrison," he explained to his wife on April 17. His reaction was swift and sure. "If that be true it will create a hundred fold more sympathy in the army for the negro than ever existed before, and will insure Forrest 'a strong rope and short shrift' if he ever falls into the hands of negro soldiers."[8]

From his posting in Alabama, William Nugen wrote his sister on April 20. "I have just been reading about the fight at Fort Pillow Ky. [sic]," he explained, "what a terrible affair that was. [T]hey used the Colored Soldiers brutally[,] Burying them alive." Nugen added that the people "of this country" considered Forrest "a notorious character."[9] Another concluded his diary entry solemnly with a verse from the book of Romans: "'Vengeance is mine; I will repay says the Lord.'"[10]

From his station "On board U.S. Gunboat Peosta" lying "Off Paducah," Hubert Saunders wrote his mother that Federal forces there were not having any trouble from "the rebs," but "they played the very devil down to fort Pilow, murdering the soldiers after they had taken them prisoner," adding "some of the darky soldiers they made dig their own graves and then buried them a live."[11]

In Memphis, Channing Richards was unequivocal about his feelings concerning what he had learned about Forrest's attack and its aftermath. "There is one event of this month that may yet have an important bearing upon the conduct of the war, and therefore deserves mention," he observed. "The Rebels captured Fort Pillow 20 miles from Memphis on the 5th of April." But if his date was off, his thinking on the significance of the event was unmistakable. "The garrison consisted principally of colored troops, and they were murdered in cold blood after the Fort was taken. [S]uch a violation of all the laws of civilized warfare would disgrace barbarians." While convinced that the Lincoln administration had little choice but to respond, he was only cautiously optimistic. "It remains to be seen whether the Government will take means to protect its soldiers from such inhumanities."[12]

A Union soldier encamped near Ringgold, Georgia, was concerned too that his government take steps to safeguard its troops in the field. Recounting recent events to his sister, Robert Winn explained, "But the most to be remembered is the massacre of our pickets yesterday morning—eight men have been brought in dead, and four wounded, at least three mortally, and a Lieut. (and some more I believe) missing." The Confederates had set a trap and, in the early morning hours, drove the men into it, "where paying no regard to their surrender they murdered them." Winn had not participated in the action but learned of it from one of the mortally wounded victims. The situation seemed to reflect the increasingly difficult and brutal nature of warfare as he saw it, referencing the earlier Calfkiller incident as well as Fort Pillow, in which men died after attempting to surrender. "This upon the heels of the Ft. Pillow slaughters and that upon the Calf Killer affair will certainly rouse the government to some measures calculated to prevent these murders [from] being profitable to the Confederacy, for if it is profitable, it will be persisted in."[13]

The Northern public also had new visual images to sustain the stories of atrocities committed at Fort Pillow. *Harper's Weekly* produced a powerful rendering of the affair on April 30. Capturing the bloodshed as well as the chaos of the fight, *The Massacre at Fort Pillow* leaves no confusion about what had taken place. The portrayal depicts Confederates shooting and bayoneting unarmed, wounded, and defenseless black troops, with a handful of whites as witnesses. One Union officer extends his hand helplessly toward the assailants while two Confederates ghoulishly cut the throat of one black soldier. It is a piece of artwork perfectly designed to capitalize on what Northern newspapers had told their readers had happened at the remote fortification.[14]

Not to be outdone, *Frank Leslie's Illustrated Newspaper* offered its version of the volatile story in a woodcut that emphasized victorious Confederates bludgeoning, hacking, and stabbing a mound of defenseless Federals. Although the constraints of space required the illustrator to compress the fort, one of the ravines, and the landing into much closer proximity than could have been possible, the artistic license allowed the connection of each of the landscape features of the engagement. *Rebel Massacre of the Union Troops after the Capture of Fort Pillow, April 12th, 1864,* proclaims the title attached to the image. Readers would not need to work too diligently to decipher the meaning or register an appropriate emotional response to the horrendous scene.[15]

Further repercussions occurred far and wide in the final full year of the war. In Georgia the sense of anger associated with the incident was not confined to its racial components or victims. The treatment of white Union troops from Tennessee was also not lost on their comrades, and when connected to examples of closer geographical proximity that seemed to be intensifying, the result was palpable. "The Tennessee troops in our Army say they will never take any more prisoners, especially from Rebel Tennessee Regiment[s], because of outrage at Fort Pillow," an Illinois sergeant in the Army of the Cumberland informed his family members in early May. In this case there was no need for further motivation or authorization as to the appropriate response. Ominously, Lyman Widney added, "None of Forrest's command will escape death if captured by our troops, whether an order for retaliation is issued or not."[16]

Rebel Tennesseans or Forrest's troops were not the only ones liable to be subjected to harsh measures by incensed Union soldiers. Any Confederate who was foolish or unfortunate enough to be connected somehow with the massacre, especially in terms of appearing to celebrate it, risked a terrible retribution. At Resaca, Georgia, the Federals captured a Southern artillerist bearing a prominent "Fort Pillow" tattoo on his arm. Enraged troops showed him no mercy, shooting and bayoneting the red-headed Rebel for his temerity.[17] On another occasion, a Union officer related the deaths of five Confederate soldiers. "Had it not been for Ft. Pillow," he wrote, "those 5 men might be alive now. 'Remember Fort Pillow' is getting to be the *feeling* if not the word." Such deaths might be regrettable, but the Federal concluded, "we cannot blame these men much."[18]

The feeling was particularly intense for one Union soldier from Iowa. On May 11 he bluntly informed his father, "I want *no prisoners*. [I]f they raise the Black flag we can fight under it. [T]hey have raised it at Fort Pillow ... and I say give rebbels no quarter, and the feeling is the same throughout the army in the west, *we will retaliate*." The Iowan, based in Little Rock, Arkansas, could hardly contain himself on the subject. "[N]o prisoner will ever be taken by me," he assured his father, "and I ask not to be shown any quarter by a prisoner murdering traitor."[19] Such strong feelings among white Union soldiers indicated that if any participating Confederates thought that their actions at Fort Pillow would intimidate their opponents, they were sorely mistaken.

Ironically, the events in Tennessee of the previous year served to benefit the Confederate cause in other ways. In North Georgia, near Adairsville, Marcus Woodcock of the 9th Kentucky Infantry (U.S.) recorded the appearance of some one hundred Southern deserters, including officers. Two of these explained that many more of their disaffected comrades might have deserted if "they [did] not fear some kind of retaliation for the Fort Pillow massacre[.]"[20]

Nor did such emotions necessarily abate with time. In June 1864 a Vermonter observed, "Sometimes the negroes treat their prisoners rather roughly in remembrance of Fort Pillow, and similar outrages.... Their wrath was especially directed against the officers." Despite pleas from the white Southerners, the black soldiers remained unmoved. "How was it at Fort Pillow?" the writer noted them taunting, "and pay no attention to their entreaties." Finally, Wilbur Fisk explained after citing an example of a Mason in Union uniform saving his Confederate counterpart from being killed, "Such a kind of warfare is too horrible to contemplate, though we cannot blame the negroes under the present circumstances."[21] As these incidents illustrate, this type of ad-hoc retaliation was not uncommon, and reactions to it on the part of white Federal soldiers remained decidedly mixed.[22]

In Confederate circles opinion concerning the possibility of Union retribution was far less tortured. Southern editorialists had a field day with President Lincoln's invocation of the threat of retaliation. The exiled *Memphis Daily Appeal,* with its offices then located in Atlanta, Georgia, repeated a *Richmond Dispatch* editorial that commented how the "Northern Government" seemed to be "quite out of temper about Fort Pillow." The writer observed that much of the "horror" being expressed had to be affected and was certainly disingenuous, given the North's own track record. "A volume could not hold a simple recital of the most atrocious and bloody deeds perpetrated by Lincoln's hordes of mercenaries and cut-throats upon our own people, both soldiers and unoffending, defenseless, and helpless citizens."

The editorial took the unusual tack of suggesting that even if Forrest had carried out "a rule of civilized warfare" and put the garrison to the sword, the effect was a salutary one and thus did not justify threats of retaliation from the Union. "This measure, by which a wholesale lesson and example was given that may save the effusion of blood hereafter, has elicited the threatening of the aforesaid chief of the Federal despotism." If retaliation were to occur, then "let him do his worst." Confederate soldiers would know how to respond.[23]

The Tennessee editor offered no elaboration on the Richmond commentary, perhaps satisfied that his readers could digest for themselves the appropriate interpretation. But he presented his own views on the "Future Character of the War." In this piece he argued that Fort Pillow and other fights illustrated the willingness of Southern troops to wage war "with a determination to do or die in the strife." If these men fought as "demons," then they were likely to continue to do so "until every Northern hireling is driven from Southern soil."

"Wronged, robbed, incensed, and enraged," the writer promised a greater ferocity on the part of the Confederate people against the Union invader. "He has yet to feel the extreme fierceness of Southern ire and the more pointed keenness of Southern steel. He has many severe lessons yet to learn and our soldiers happen to be just now in the best possible mood to teach them." Even so, with Fort Pillow fresh in the readers' minds, he advised that no one misinterpret this ferocity for wanton savagery, although the Confederates would "hereafter fight with their gloves off."[24]

Nevertheless, Bedford Forrest remained on the defensive regarding the subject. To trusted aide David C. Kelley, the general explained "that he was opposed to the killing of negro troops; that it was his policy to capture all he could and return them to their owners."[25] This notion gibed with his prewar avocation. Viewing slaves as commodities to be bought and sold, he would have considered it preferable to restore the formerly enslaved blacks he captured to those who could lay legal claim to them. Forrest reiterated this position in June 1864 in correspondence with Union general Cadwallader Washburn. "I regard captured Negroes as I do other captured property, and not as captured soldiers."[26] Nor was there any indication of an intention to kill some of them first as a deterrent to others.

Forrest thought it important that his position be seen in the context of the government's policy and not as the particular whim of a frontline general, even one of such renown as himself. "It is not the policy nor the interest of the South to destroy the negro—on the contrary, to preserve and protect him—and all who have surrendered to us have received kind and humane treatment."[27] If such a viewpoint contained self-serving delusion or exaggeration, it also reflected the paternalistic framework in which Bedford Forrest lived and operated.

The general was aware of at least some of the implications of Fort Pillow upon his record as a soldier. "You ask me to state whether 'I contemplate either their slaughter or their return to slavery,'" he noted to Washburn. "I answer that I slaughter no man except in open warfare, and that my prisoners, both white and black, are turned over to my Government to be dealt with as it may direct."[28] And his actions adhered to this policy. Following the April 12 engagement, Forrest's provost marshal sent in a brief report designed to facilitate the process. "I accompany herewith [a] list of prisoners captured by Major-General Forrest at Fort Pillow, as also one containing the names and owners and residences of the negroes captured at [the] same place."[29]

"Fort Pillow" became useful as a motivating device or a rallying cry. In early May 1864, as Ulysses Grant slogged his way through the woods, fields, and farm lanes of Central Virginia toward Richmond, Union and Confederate forces clashed with each other in the vicinity of the Harris Farm near the Fredericksburg Road. Heavy fighting on May 19–20 between the Federals and Confederates under Major Generals Robert Rodes and John B. Gordon produced confusion and casualties in equal measure. At one point Union officers began to implore their men "Forward! Remember Fort Pillow!" as incentive. But approaching darkness and the density of the woods before them caused hesitation in the ranks. Afterward a Confederate concluded, "Perhaps they feared the fate of their Fort Pillow comrades and obeyed the order [just] to 'remember' it."[30]

The "Fort Pillow massacre" was becoming a reference point for engagements between white Confederate and black Union troops wherever they took place. Near the end of May, General Braxton Bragg instructed Major General Fitzhugh Lee to proceed against the Federal garrison of Fort Pocahontas, Virginia. U.S. Colored Troops (USCT) under the command of Brigadier General Edward A. Wild had already achieved a level of notoriety in North Carolina and added to that reputation in Virginia with alleged actions of brutality and heavy handedness against white civilians. Bragg wanted the cavalry general to "break up the nest and stop their uncivilized proceedings in the neighborhood."

Lee set out in the late afternoon of May 24 and, despite hard riding, did not reach the Union position until midmorning the next day. Members of the 1st and 10th USCT manned the defenses, supported by a gunboat, the USS *Dawn,* as the Confederate troopers approached the works. The rate of fire suggested that the 2,500 Southern horsemen would not be able to overwhelm the defenders despite having a numerical advantage over their 1,800 opponents.[31] Lee opted to achieve a capitulation of the garrison by demand if possible. "If the surrender of the Federal forces is made," he assured Wild, "the soldiers will be taken to Richmond and treated as prisoners of war." The Confederate quickly added, "But if they do not surrender, Gen. Lee will not be answerable for the consequences." The implication was clear: The Union defenders would take their chances if the Confederates overran the works and, as one Union officer observed as he witnessed the proceedings, "their success and our failure [would have] meant another Fort Pillow massacre."[32] Although the dire consequences were not lost on Wild, he had no intentions of folding under the pressure. "We will try that," Union general Benjamin Butler reported Wild as writing in reply.[33] The Union commander added with authority that the Confederate general could "[t]ake the fort if you can."[34] Of the negotiations, Wild reported simply: "I declined. We then went at it again."[35]

Heavy fighting marked the next phase of the battle as the gray horsemen surged against the Union position in what historian Gordon Rhea has described as "the first major encounter between black troops and the Army of Northern Virginia."[36] Confederate losses were severe in what also became known as the Battle of Wilson's Wharf. Some two hundred men suffered wounds or perished in the attempt, while Wild set his losses in the successful defense at two killed, nineteen wounded, and one missing.[37] In his final assessment of the fighting in Virginia, Wild employed language that Bedford Forrest might have appreciated as ironic when he observed, "We might have slaughtered twice as many of them, but that we were at the time short of artillery ammunition."[38] Fitzhugh Lee had failed to "break up the nest" of the Union command, but in another tragic footnote to the main action, the Confederates killed several black captives for supposedly attempting to escape and returned one individual to his master in the Richmond area.[39]

As the summer of 1864 progressed, the specter of Fort Pillow continued to appear in ways and across distances that few could have anticipated. In Virginia, when Grant's campaign bogged down into siege operations outside Petersburg, a scheme developed to construct a tunnel shaft with vertical chambers that could be packed with black powder beneath a portion of the Confederate lines. Occupying what became known as Elliott's Salient, South Carolinians hunkered down opposite their Union adversaries until a massive explosion ripped through their position in the early hours of July 30. The resulting crater extended 150–200 feet in length and 60 feet across, the explosion scooping out the ground on which they had just been standing to a depth of 30 feet. The remnants of men and equipment lay scattered about or covered in dirt and debris as the Federals unleashed a massive assault aimed at exploiting this breach.

Originally intended to feature black troops trained and prepared specifically for the operation, the order of advance changed when a last-minute decision sent white divisions out in the lead instead. These men had neither the preparation nor the equipment to handle the circumstances, and the attack began to lose focus and thrust almost immediately. It did not help Union chances for success that the Southern forces recovered more quickly than might be expected from the shock. Confederate general William Mahone carried out an effective counterattack with his command, and by the time the black troops arrived, the Crater and the intersecting maze of trenches and traverses had already turned into a seething mass of humanity that essentially had no place else to go.[40]

As with any engagement, the fighting in and around the gaping hole offered every form of combat for its participants to experience. With shouts of "Remember Fort Pillow" to buttress them, small pockets of the first black troops arriving amid the carnage carried out their threat to take no prisoners. One Union lieutenant thought these men deserved "small blame" for harboring these sentiments, but he did not condone their actions and took steps to safeguard Confederate captives.[41]

The circumstances soon reversed as the Southerners scrambled to regain their lost ground. The presence of the black troops now brought forth powerful visceral reactions from these men. A North Carolinian who joined the melee noted simply of his black adversaries, "We were not very particular whether we captured or killed them."[42] Another participant recalled that before they moved up, "General Mahone walked in front of the lines and told us the negroes in the Crater had holloed 'Remember Fort Pillow! No Quarter!'" Only in retrospect the diminutive Virginian saw that his harangue might produce excessive results, and he hastened to admonish his men "not to kill quite all of them."[43]

There would be plenty of gray-clad soldiers who needed no additional incentive to kill such troops. The battle cry of "Remember Fort Pillow!" produced predictable reactions from both blue and gray combatants. One historian has observed, "No one on either side could have mistaken the import of these three words."[44] A member of Mahone's Division recorded: "The Negros hollared No Quarter, Remember Fort Pillow and when our boys charged they took them at their word. At least some did." Not indicating if he was among that number, the writer added, "They killed them with the butts of their muskets," piling the bodies several deep in some places as a result.[45] South Carolinian Milton Barrett wrote family members that the "Nigro Troops ... come yealing like Devels, crying, 'No quarters.'" He explained that some of the attackers "got to the works. Our troops charged them, got back to the works, killed five hundred negroes and took two prisoners and set them to work."[46] Another historian has noted the ways in which both "the general confusion and the 'no quarter' presumption complicated matters."[47]

For those who survived the chaos of combat, the psychological terror was hardly over once they had surrendered. Some of these black Union prisoners tried the expedient of repudiating their service by insisting that they had been coerced into it by the Federals or by offering that they now wished to return to their masters. The reception of these pleas depended upon the individual to whom they were made, even as other Confederates worked through the traverses and bombproofs, searching for men who would perish without even this opportunity for salvation.[48]

Other black prisoners stumbled toward the rear only to meet with groups determined that they not proceed unmolested. Confederate lieutenant colonel William R. J. Pegram thought it "cruel to murder them in cold blood" but found condemnation of the perpetrators difficult. In any event, he recalled the effects of these rear-area deaths graphically. "You could see them lying dead all along the route."[49] Confederate artillerist Edward Porter Alexander noted simply, "Some of the Negro prisoners, who were originally allowed to surrender by some soldiers, were afterward shot by others, & there was, without doubt, a great deal of unnecessary killing of them." For Alexander, this engagement represented the "first occasion on which any of the Army of Northern Virginia came in contact with Negro troops, & the general feeling of the men toward their employment was very bitter." He thought that the use of such troops "as advertisement" for "servile insurrection & massacre throughout the South" caused "the fighting on this occasion [to become] exceedingly fierce & bitter on the part of our men."[50]

William Mahone, William Pegram, and Porter Alexander illustrate the extent to which white Southern commanders were grappling with the issues of race and war in 1864. Robert E. Lee also struggled with the shifting environment that accompanied the introduction of free blacks and slaves into Union uniforms and active combat roles. In October he traded communications with Ulysses Grant over the questions of prisoner exchange and the position of the Confederacy on the treatment of captured black troops. Lee had originally proposed making arrangements for exchanges without specifying any racial classification. Grant wanted to know if these numbers were to include black as well as white soldiers.[51]

Lee's response was instructive. "In my proposition of the 1st instant to exchange prisoners of war belonging to the armies operating in Virginia," he replied, "I intended to include all captured soldiers of the United States of whatever nation and color under my control." But there was a list of excepted persons that he did not accept as legitimate combatants. "Deserters from our service and negroes belonging to our citizens are not considered subjects of exchange and were not included in my proposition."[52]

The onus was now on Grant to express the position upon which he and the Federal government would make their stand. "In answer I have to state that the Government is bound to secure all persons received into her armies of the rights due to soldiers," the Union commander replied.[53] Until such assurances could be given, there was little choice regarding the release of prisoners of war. Any exchange would have to wait until the impasse could be resolved.

Confederate secretary of war James A. Seddon clarified his government's stance to General Lee on October 15. "When among the colored men taken in arms from the enemy are found any who are ascertained by their own confession or due identification to be slaves who have run away or been taken from their owners in the Confederacy, they are considered and treated as recaptured slaves," he explained, "and advertisement is made according to provisions of an act of [the Confederate] Congress to enable the owners to come forward and reclaim them."[54] Seddon seemed to be responding to the criticism leveled at Robert Ould, Confederate commissioner of exchange, from General Butler, who cited a call, put out through the *Richmond Examiner,* for owners of captured black soldiers to come to the camp "and prove their claims."[55]

Seddon also felt obligated to respond to charges that black troops were being made to work on Confederate defenses. He assured Lee, who could then presumably pass along the same information to anyone who inquired, "No orders have been given by this Department to put other than slaves to work on the fortifications, and colored soldiers of the United States when captured have not, by the direction of the Department, been treated otherwise than as prisoners of war, unless identified or claimed to be recaptured slaves." Slaves had been used for such purposes from the start of the conflict, and any captured soldiers deemed to have been slaves and "unreclaimed by their masters, are subject to similar labor." Any other persons placed into these circumstances would have been put there by mistake, and appropriate measures would be taken to rectify the error. But Seddon wanted the point to be perfectly clear, "If slaves, they have been legitimately so employed."[56]

Once again Ben Butler prompted a statement of policy from the Confederates by producing documents from white Southern deserters in which they alleged that black troops were being employed to build earthworks.[57] Secretary Seddon argued in support of the legitimacy of his government's position by reasserting the sense of the enslaved as property. "As slaves taken by violence in war or seduced by the instigations of the enemy, should, on being recaptured, be restored to their former owners is but the plain result of their recognition as property," he maintained. Furthermore, warfare could not alter that condition. He asserted, "even as persons held to previous service, it is difficult to conceive on what principle their previous relations as persons or property can be changed toward their former owners by the violence or seduction of an enemy."[58] The Confederacy was not ready to concede that the acts of their opponents, ranging from confiscation to emancipation, had any bearing on the status of the enslaved.

Lee informed Grant accordingly but initially focused on prisoners whom his government would not have insisted ought to be considered as enslaved anyway. "All negroes in the military or naval service of the United States taken by us who are not identified as the property of citizens or residents of the Confederate States are regarded as prisoners of war, being held to be proper subjects of exchange, as I recently had the honor to inform you." The general reiterated, "No labor is exacted from such persons by the Confederate authorities." Then came the crux of the matter. "Negroes who owe service or labor to citizens or residents of the Confederate States, and who through compulsion, persuasion, or on their own accord, leave their owners and are placed in the military or naval service of the United States, occupy a different position." Lee maintained that this status was unchanged from that which had held in antebellum years. "The right to the service or labor of negro slaves in the Confederate States is the same now as when these States were members of the Federal Union." The Confederacy's premier field general then sounded more like an attorney general when he concluded, "It has been uniformly held that the capture or abduction of a slave does not impair the right of the owner to such slave, but that the right attaches to him immediately upon recapture."[59] Of course, it was precisely the uniformity of such views that was in question here.

On the same day that Lee addressed his position of former slaves as prisoners of war to his Union counterpart, Confederate major general John C. Breckinridge forwarded a message to one of his subordinates, Brigadier General J. C. Vaughn, that applied Lee's viewpoint to their specific situations. "I have no objection to your exchanging prisoners, man for man, free negroes included," Breckinridge noted Lee as instructing. But he again reiterated, "Recaptured slaves of Confederate citizens will not be exchanged."[60]

These communications came amid a flurry of developments in the field that reflected the ways in which a spirit similar to that exhibited at Fort Pillow prevailed later in 1864. In a raid against the salt-making complex at Saltville, Virginia, Union brigadier general Stephen Burbridge suffered a setback on October 1. Among the Federals making the assault were members of the 5th U.S. Colored Cavalry. A stubborn defense by a hodge-podge command of Confederates holding bluffs overlooking the Holston River, coupled with diminishing stocks of ammunition and rising casualties, convinced Burbridge to pull back from his effort to capture and destroy the vital works. This retreat prevented the Federals from removing many of their wounded comrades who lay nearest the Southern lines. It was at this point in the aftermath of the fighting that, as historian William C. Davis notes, "the real horror of Saltville began."

Some of the Confederates sought revenge for their casualties, while others simply exhibited the rage they felt at facing black soldiers. George Mosgrove of the 4th Kentucky witnessed numerous instances of unjustified killing as "the desultory firing" he had been hearing could "at once [be] explained—the Tennesseans were killing negroes." He recorded the events as they unfolded: "I cautiously rode forward and came upon a squad of Tennesseans, mad and excited to the highest degree. They were shooting every wounded negro they could find." Mosgrove could hear the firing continue out of his sight and deduced that similar executions of defenseless prisoners were taking place, later maintaining that anger over having "lost many good men and officers, probably shot by these same negroes," had rendered the Tennesseans "so exasperated that they could not be deterred from their murderous work." A number of "slightly wounded" black troops, "standing about in groups" but presenting no resistance or threat to their assailants, "soon went down before the unerring pistols and rifles of the enraged Tennesseans." The nature of the killing paralleled incidents that had occurred at Fort Pillow. One of the surviving wounded Union white officers offered an explanation that fit the circumstances in West Tennessee as well as they did in southwestern Virginia: "I don't know that anybody had command. They all appeared to be commanding themselves." Only the subsequent appearance of an incensed General Breckinridge brought a temporary cessation to the killing.

Much of what happened at Saltville approached what had occurred at Fort Pillow, but there were some significant differences. If, as Davis observes, "Forrest's men had the faint excuse that they had just finished fighting and were still flushed with battle-fever," the same could not be said of the Saltville Confederates. "They had passed a full night since the battle close[d], were rested ... and surely aware of the conviction current in the army that the Federals had withdrawn during the night." There was no battle to renew or defense to maintain, only the opportunity to finish the work of dispatching wounded and defenseless opponents because it could be done. And at least until General Breckinridge intervened, there was nothing to stop them.[61]

A notorious figure named Champ Ferguson was among the murderous men at Saltville. Although he insisted, "The Saltville Massacre, as it has been termed, was no work of mine," witnesses held him accountable for over a dozen deaths. Breckinridge ordered Ferguson's incarceration in a Wytheville, Virginia, jail pending investigation, but the chaotic events prevented that accounting. Nevertheless, a final verdict for Ferguson came on a Nashville gallows on October 25, 1865.[62]

Robert E. Lee reacted strongly to a report from Breckinridge that noted the killing. "He is much pained to hear of the treatment the negro prisoners are reported to have received, and agrees with you in entirely condemning it." Lee was convinced that at least one "general officer" bore responsibility for "the crime," deserved "his unqualified reprobation," and should be made to answer the charges for the disgraceful and horrific incident. Despite this expression from the Confederate commander, this "general officer" remained formally unidentified.[63]

In such matters Ulysses Grant had already demonstrated a willingness to apply a cold calculus in order to bring the war to a successful conclusion. In August 1864 he had replied to General Butler's request for clarification on the condition of black Union prisoners in Confederate hands: "But do[es] the Government intend to abandon the colored troops?"[64] Although Grant recognized the changing nature of the conflict and hoped to "stop" any forms of Confederate retaliation, larger matters loomed. "On the subject of exchange," he noted, the issue was one of denying the Confederacy soldiers who could return to the ranks to continue fighting. "Every man we hold, when released on parole or otherwise, becomes an active soldier against us at once either directly or indirectly." Even if the decision proved "hard on our men held in Southern prisons not to exchange them," their lingering confinement would have a deleterious effect on the Confederate war effort. "If we hold those [we have] caught they amount to no more than dead men," he concluded.[65]

The status of prisoners of war in a complex and transitional time was not the only issue confronting American society in the fall of 1864. Another incident, widely seen at the time and since as a "massacre," occurred in Colorado Territory. On November 29 Colonel John M. Chivington and some 700 Colorado volunteers under his command descended on a Native American camp under Black Kettle located along Sand Creek. The chief had hoisted a U.S. flag and a white one as an indication of the camp's peaceful intentions, but the column commander and many of his men were disinclined to honor the gesture. In the ensuing engagement only a handful of warriors "managed to offer anything that could be described as an organized defense," according to one historian. "The rest sought safety in frantic flight."[66] Pertaining to Sand Creek, Chivington left little to interpretation when he observed in the aftermath of his attack, resulting in 500–600 individuals being killed, "It may perhaps be unnecessary for me to state that I captured no prisoners."[67]

Just as had been done in the aftermath of Fort Pillow, the Committee on the Conduct of the War undertook an investigation of what came to be known as the Sand Creek Massacre. To his credit, Ben Wade offered a condemnation of Chivington that was as vehement as any he had made against Forrest and employed much of the same terminology. Wade's cover letter noted that the colonel "deliberately planned and executed a foul and dastardly massacre which would have disgraced the veriest savage among those who were the victims of his cruelty." The officer had ignored signs of the "friendly character" of the Native Americans and "took advantage of their inapprehension and defenceless condition to gratify the worst passions that ever cursed the heart of man." The senator attached a political motive to Chivington's actions, believing them to be based upon "pandering to the passions of an excited population" in order to win favor and advancement for himself. In any event, Wade and other committee members called, in the interest "of justice and upholding the honor of the nation," for "prompt and energetic measures . . . to punish, as their crimes deserve, those who have been guilty of these brutal and cowardly acts."[68]

Bedford Forrest could have gained little comfort or satisfaction from the Chivington denunciation, except to note that it was directed at someone other than himself, and continued to feel unduly targeted for the excesses attributed to him. But he was not above using the example of Fort Pillow for his benefit. In November 1864, as the veterans of General John Bell Hood's diminished Army of Tennessee were gathering to invade Tennessee and perhaps liberate Nashville from Union hands, Forrest presented a speech relating his exploits since spring. "I have seen the Mississippi run with blood for two hundred yards," he was supposed to have said in camp, "and I'm gwine to see it again. I've captured seventy-eight pieces of artillery and sixteen thousand Yankees, and buried twenty-five hundred of them." The reference to Fort Pillow was unmistakable, but the reaction of the troops went unrecorded. Forrest obviously meant for the remarks to help motivate his troops in the fighting to come, seemly not recognizing the incongruity of applying Fort Pillow for his own purposes while lamenting the same for his opponents.[69]

The death throes of the Confederate States of America came in early 1865, when little realistic hope remained of establishing an independent nation whose cornerstone was the inviolate institution of slavery. From Tupelo, Mississippi, Confederate lieutenant colonel C. Irvine Walker of the 10th South Carolina Infantry contemplated both the fate of his nation and the institution of slavery within it. "The question of arming the negroes is now being agitated in the Army and Country," he wrote on January 17. "What do you think of it?" he asked rhetorically. "I am totally opposed to it, except as a last resort. It is only better than subjugation. I am very much afraid that it will be done." Reiterating that such an act would represent the most extreme measure for national survival, Walker nevertheless thought that he would support the measure "if the government adopts it." Still, while accommodations might be made to keep white Confederates in the ranks under these circumstances, the lieutenant colonel was skeptical. "As far as I am concerned I would rather be 2nd Lieut. in the 10th S.C. than Lt. Genl. of Negro troops." He was convinced that "with proper discipline they can be made to fight tolerably well" and thought he knew just the individual to accomplish this difficult task. "Forrest says he can make them fight, and I believe him right. If he can make our Cavalry, as it is now organized and commanded, fight he can make anything fight."[70] Indeed, Walker held Forrest in high esteem, having noted only a few weeks earlier, with Hood's army outside Nashville, "However Forrest is there and if any man in the Confederacy can succeed, he is the man for the undertaking."[71]

By January General Robert E. Lee had also reached the point of advocating the use of blacks as soldiers in the Confederate ranks. "I think therefore, we must decide whether slavery shall be extinguished by our enemies, and the slaves used against us, or use them ourselves at the risk of the effects which may be produced upon our social institutions," he explained. "My own opinion is that we should employ them without delay," recognizing that this step could not be taken without "giving immediate freedom to all who enlist," among other possible inducements. The time had arrived from which slavery could not remain as it had been prior to the war, even should the South succeed in securing its independence.[72] President Davis and the Confederate Congress would follow their most famous field commander's lead, but although no one could know with certainty at the time, little could be done in this regard before the quest for Southern independence was over.

In the meantime, soldiers in the field retained responsibility for perpetuating the war effort. Nathan Bedford Forrest still found opportunities to mortify his opponents and remained enigmatic in many ways, not the least when it came to his public perception of the handling of prisoners of war. An exchange between some of his staff and Union officers in the early part of 1865 was supposed to have reflected the general's thoughts on such matters. Although both principal adversaries were removed from direct participation, Brigadier General James H. Wilson forwarded to departmental headquarters an indication of Forrest's views on the approximately 7,000 Federal prisoners being held in Mississippi and Alabama. Of these, 1,600 were "taken by Forrest's command" and "turned over by him to the infantry and subsequently treated very badly." The Confederate foot soldiers' demands for clothing from the prisoners appeared to be the chief culprit for the mistreatment, but Forrest, according to the account, "is represented to be very indignant at this. Says many of the men are nearly naked and all badly in want of clothing, and that he will designate a staff officer and pledge himself for his good faith, if we will send supplies to Rienzi[, Mississippi,] for these prisoners." Forrest offered his "guarantees" of protection for the "trains, men, and stores" forwarded for the use of these captives.[73]

Wilson took advantage of this opportunity to gather information on the Confederates when he sent his provost marshal, Colonel John G. Parkhurst, and an observant aide, Lewis Hosea, to meet with Forrest on the subject.[74] During this mission, Captain Hosea assessed the opposing general carefully, reaping valuable intelligence for his commander at the time and for students of the Confederate cavalryman afterward.

In his operations against Forrest in Alabama in 1865, Wilson had the opportunity for redemption at the Confederate's expense by applying lessons he had learned from his earlier experiences against him near Spring Hill during Hood's Tennessee Campaign in November 1864. Badly outmaneuvered on that occasion, Wilson changed his tactics when he once again tangled with Forrest during the Selma Campaign by using his overwhelming numbers and firepower to keep his opponent's forces divided and off balance through swift and decisive movements of his own. Wilson crushed the Selma defenders on Sunday, April 2, leaving a bloodied Bedford Forrest to scramble away from the city with the shattered remnants of his command.

During the circuitous ride away from Selma, the Confederate general and members of his personal escort engaged in an action that added additional fuel to the anti-Forrest and Fort Pillow Massacre fires. In this instance, some of Forrest's men located and captured a picket post manned by members of the 4th U.S. Cavalry. These captives divulged the presence of other comrades nearby, and the opportunity presented itself for retribution against a unit that these Southerners held responsible for the death of the popular artillerist Sam Freeman in 1862 and other subsequent misdeeds.

Forrest's men determined to use the darkness and the element of surprise to capture the detachment, though realizing a firefight was also likely once their presence became known. They insisted that their commander, who ordinarily would lead them personally, remain with the horseholders in the rear in order to avoid his "unnecessary exposure" if fighting should erupt in the darkness. Still nursing his wounds from Selma, and exhausted from the exertions of the recent battle and his narrow escape, Forrest agreed to remain behind while the others carried out the dangerous enterprise.[75] Without evidence one way or another, it would be no more than speculation as to why, like at Fort Pillow, Forrest allowed the effort to proceed without his direct leadership or personal involvement.

As these men crept forward, some of the Federals became aware that something was amiss and succeeded in firing several warning shots. An "animated fight resulted," but the advantages of surprise and darkness rested with the attackers. Forrest rode forward himself as the firing subsided. The engagement produced thirty-five killed or wounded among the Federals, while the attackers suffered only one man wounded. Although it was unclear if they also had suffered wounds, five of the bluecoats left the scene as captives.[76] The Confederate lieutenant who had led the squad forward and sustained a wound in the fight insisted that "not a single man was killed after he surrendered."[77]

Federal accounts presented the incident in a decidedly different light. In his subsequent report, a Union surgeon maintained that "Forrest, retreating from Selma, came across a party of Federals asleep in a neighboring field, and charged on them, and, refusing to listen to their cries for surrender, killed or wounded the entire party, numbering twenty-five men."[78] Sergeant James Larson of the 4th Cavalry compared the incident to the more notorious action a year earlier, calling it a "repitition of Ft. Pillow."[79] An assessment from a contemporary figure in a biography of Union general George Thomas likened the circumstances to frontier savagery, noting that in the "ferocity" of the attack, Forrest "killed every man" of the Union detachment.[80]

Bedford Forrest had not led the assault but again became associated with an outcome that included a high fatality rate and minimal prisoners among enemy troops with whom his men held a particular grudge. Once more, there was a fine line between the general's responsibility for the actions of his men and his individual, direct involvement in the affair. For the members of the Union unit who survived and their comrades who perished, these factors amounted to a distinction without a difference.

Much later after the war, James H. Wilson recalled the post-Selma incident and observed that the Confederates had "killed the last one" of the surprised party of Federals. He concluded, "Such incidents as this were far too frequent with Forrest." Wilson also understood other aspects of his one-time opponent's personality. "He appears to have had a ruthless temper which impelled him upon every occasion where he had a clear advantage to push his success to a bloody end," he concluded, "and yet he always seemed not only to resent but to have a plausible excuse for the cruel excesses that were charged against him."[81] Forrest offered no official excuse or explanation for this incident, which quickly became lost in the broader sweep of events occurring at the same time and never generated the type of headlines or news coverage that had marked the "Fort Pillow Massacre" a year earlier.

Fort Pillow continued to represent the worst of such "cruel excesses," and some Union soldiers persisted in invoking the event as the war wound to a conclusion. As late as April 9, on the same Sabbath day that Lee met with Grant to seal the fate of the Army of Northern Virginia at Appomattox Court House in Virginia, the Federals prepared for a final assault on the Gulf Coast against Confederate defenses there. William Wiley of the 77th Illinois Infantry recorded aspects of the fighting for Fort Blakeley, Alabama. In addition to the heavy losses among the attackers and the use of torpedoes, or "subterra shells" (buried improvised explosive devices), another element of the battle caught the infantryman's attention. "The colored troops [were] so worked up by the time they got in the fort that their officers couldn't control them," Wiley observed. "They set up [the] yell, Remember Fort Pillow and were determined to do as the rebels had done with the colored troops at Fort Pillow. Kill them, surrender or no surrender!" According to the Illinois infantryman, "They had to bring up a division of white troops to stop them."[82]

The extent to which such killing took place at Fort Blakeley is unclear. But the fact that many of the opposing Southern troops thought that it would occur and feared for their safety is indisputable from the after-action reports. The commander of the USCT units in the engagement, Brigadier General John P. Hawkins, reported, "The prisoners captured amounted to 21 officers and men—a small number, owing to the fact that when we entered [the works] many of the enemy, fearing the conduct of my troops, ran over to where the white troops were entering."[83]

A Union lieutenant described a scene at Blakely as reminiscent of the fall of Fort Pillow, although the affected troops involved in this instance were Confederate. Noting that the Southern defenders "were panic struck," he explained that many of them "jumped into the river and were drowned attempting to cross, or were shot while swimming. Still others threw down their arms and run for their lives over to the white troops on our left, to give themselves up to save being butchered by our niggers[.]" The turnabout in affairs was complete, for the officer noted that "the niggers did not take a prisoner, they killed all they took to a man."[84]

A black schoolteacher-turned-soldier perhaps summarized best what many felt concerning the turbulence of the times. In a letter from his post in South Carolina, Corporal John H. B. Payne contemplated: "I do not wonder at the conduct and disaster that transpired at Fort Pillow. I wonder that we have not had more New York [draft] riots and Fort Pillow massacres." But whatever might occur, he was sure of why he and other black men in blue were enduring such sacrifices. "Liberty is what I am struggling for; and what pulse does not beat high at the very mention of the name."[85]

The final scenes of Lieutenant General Forrest's career contained another example of the complexity of the cavalryman's character. In a postwar appearance before a congressional committee in Washington, he asserted that concerning the slaves that he had taken into the service, he had made the determination to "set them free" based upon their faithfulness "with me" during the war. At the time of his testimony, Forrest recalled that he reached this point of decision more than a year before the conflict closed.

Certainly, Forrest may have begun to contemplate such measures as he recalled and for the reasons he gave regarding loyal service to him. But the clerk who performed the task and generated the appropriate paperwork for the manumissions remembered the circumstances differently. George Cable insisted that these acts of freedom occurred at Gainesville, Alabama, in the final days of the general's part in the war.[86] Forrest had always desired to control whatever process in which he was involved, and only when the end became clear did he take steps to free his remaining slaves to prevent others from doing so instead.

Bedford Forrest's official association with the Confederate States of America ended on May 9, 1865, with the surrender of his forces at Gainesville. He had determined to wage war wholeheartedly but afterward seemed equally anxious to pursue a peaceful course. The general's farewell address to his men mirrored these sentiments. "That we are beaten is a self-evident fact," he began, "and any further resistance on our part would be justly regarded as the very height of folly and rashness." Forrest understood the power of his example and recognized the influence it could have beyond the context of war. "I have never on the field of battle sent you where I was unwilling to go myself, nor would I now advise you to a course which I felt myself unwilling to pursue." He now replicated the tone set earlier in Virginia by Robert E. Lee in that general's final instructions to his men. "You have been good soldiers, you can be good citizens. Obey the laws, preserve your honor, and the government to which you have surrendered can afford to be and will be magnanimous."[87]

Union generals such as Sherman and George Thomas assumed that Forrest would remain in the field indefinitely, or at least until he could be driven out of it. The Ohioan thought Forrest and other "desperadoes" knew no other course to follow.[88] Sherman explained to his wife that he saw guerrilla warfare as the greatest danger left to face and that Forrest would be among those who engaged in it.[89] The Virginian promised that any price exacted for such conduct would not be visited on Forrest alone. By virtue of "such a reckless and bloodthirsty adventure he will be treated thereafter as an outlaw," Thomas asserted, "and the States of Mississippi and Alabama will be so destroyed that they will not recover for fifty years."[90]

Forrest confounded these former adversaries by proving himself to be true to the sentiments he had expressed to his men. Instead of urging irregular warfare or exile, he quietly left his military career behind to return to his plantation properties in an attempt to start anew. As he rejoined civilian circles, Bedford Forrest demonstrated a remarkable flexibility and lack of enmity. Far from remaining antagonistic toward his recent foes, the ex-Confederate was not averse to maintaining contacts with whomever he thought could be helpful to him. Former Union officers soon became partners and compatriots in his enterprises rather than remaining opponents.

A postwar visit illustrated the new state of affairs when, near the end of May, Forrest ventured into Vicksburg and called upon Union general Gouverneur Warren. That officer must have been surprised by the visit. Yet there was camaraderie between the men in one sense. The temperamental Warren had left the Army of the Potomac under a cloud just as his men crushed their opponents at Five Forks at the beginning of April. Forrest labored under the shadow of Fort Pillow with the understandable likelihood that a victorious enemy might yet seek vengeance for what had happened there. Perhaps the Union officer's personal fall from grace made him empathetic to Forrest's circumstances. At any rate, Warren passed along to his wife the Southern horseman's autograph and the quiet observation, "You know, his treatment of the colored soldiers when he captured Ft. Pillow makes him a marked character."[91]

CHAPTER 9

# "Forrest of Fort Pillow"

## 1865–2014

I shan't go away.

*Nathan Bedford Forrest, late 1865*

I am also aware, that I am at this moment regarded in large communities, at the North, with abhorrence, as a detestable monster, ruthless and swift to take life, and guilty of unpardonable crimes in connection with the capture of Fort Pillow.

*Nathan Bedford Forrest to President Johnson, November 25, 1866*

Congress may yet restore Forrest to citizenship & give him a gold medal bearing the mottoe Ft. Pillow!

*Former Union soldier, c. 1867*

Nathan Bedford Forrest's actions prior to and during the war laid the foundations on which he would be judged in the aftermath of the conflict. As a former slave trader and commander of the forces that overwhelmed Fort Pillow in April 1864, he exhibited connections many Northerners found repugnant. Yet the former Confederate general planned to adhere to the instructions he had given his men for returning to a productive civilian life. Even as he traveled back to Memphis, he informed interested citizens at one stop that he was "now as good a Union man as anybody." His next comment reflected the sincerity of his stance and his unmistakable vernacular when he insisted that he understood "the South was whipped."[1]

Forrest's postwar course garnered attention from media and his peers, as could be expected for any man who had proven to be such a fierce and controversial warrior. His activities after the war reflected an intent to settle back into civilian life. The *Macon (Ga.) Daily Telegraph* informed its readers in February 1866: "A gentleman who left General Forrest's plantation, in

Sunflower county, Miss., on the 30th, states that, instead of General Forrest being in full flight to Mexico, as has been reported, he was "quietly at work preparing to plant a large cotton crop."[2] A U.S. Treasury agent in Memphis noted simply in a letter to his wife that "Forrest has been paroled and is on his farm."[3]

As rumors circulated suggesting that former Confederates might be better served to leave the country than to remain in it, Forrest responded with characteristic defiance. He had considered such a resettlement just before he decided to surrender his command, but having rejected that course then, he was not about to pursue it now. "This is my country," he insisted. "I am hard at work upon my plantation, and carefully observing the obligations of my parole." He did not believe that representatives of the U.S. government would come after him under such circumstances but was adamant regardless. "I shan't go away."[4] Indeed, a local newspaper extolled the former soldier's example in peacetime and urged others to follow it.[5]

A return to the peaceful pursuits of civilian life might have appealed to Forrest after four years of hard campaigning, but achieving any measure of solitude would prove problematic for him. His reputation included Fort Pillow, and the events that had occurred there in 1864 were seared into the public consciousness. That the peaceful situation he now found himself in was anomalous with the violence of his past was evident to all who cared to notice. It did not escape the observation of Salmon P. Chase, former secretary of the treasury and now chief justice of the U.S. Supreme Court. On Sunday, June 18, 1865, Chase confided in his journal as he traveled along the Mississippi River, "passed Fort Pillow abt. 9 where the horrible massacre took place—Passenger remarked 'Forrest is on his farm plowing.'"[6]

As perplexing as the postwar status of Bedford Forrest may have been to some in the North, the antipathies that had contributed to the events at Fort Pillow created lingering concern about the future in the minds of Confederates too. Trepidation about the relationship between white Tennessee Unionists and their adversaries continued in the waning days of the war. Obviously, that fear registered greatest with the people who faced defeat and potential retribution at the hands of their disaffected neighbors. From war-ravaged Jackson, Tennessee, Confederate colonel J. F. Newsom posted a communication with a Union counterpart to register this concern and seek some form of relief for the people in his jurisdiction. "In behalf of the citizens I ask that none of the men belonging to the commands of Colonels Hawkins and Hurst be sent here," Newsom asked. He followed with his frank assessment of conditions in the aftermath of bitter internecine warfare in the region. "The feeling that exists between soldiers of these commands and the citizens is such that private malice and private revenge might be more the result of such a policy than the restoration of order."[7]

By June, Fielding Hurst informed Governor William G. Brownlow that he was tendering his resignation "as a representative in the Senatorial Branch of the Legislature of Tenn. from the 21st Dist."[8] But Hurst continued to take an active interest in local political affairs. A couple of days after his resignation, he offered the names of two men for clerk and sheriff, "both of whom I know to be among the most competent and reliable men of this County and the staunchest friends of the Government." More than anything else, he wanted the governor to be assured that these appointments "will give general satisfaction to loyal and good men."[9]

In a subsequent note on the same day, Hurst expressed concern that in the aftermath of hostilities, there might be a return of ex-Confederates to positions of authority: "I understand there have been some appointments made by the bogus County Court of Hardeman" of men who "[are] base Rebels just [back] from the Rebel army."[10] This state of affairs would certainly not do for the soldier who had just spent years combating such men.[11] Traitors, as Hurst saw them, could hardly be allowed back into positions of political power and authority.

Concerns over retribution on the one hand and restoration of the old guard on the other might have been uppermost in other people's thoughts, but Forrest continued to concentrate his efforts on returning his lands to productivity. His absence during the war meant that there was much work to be done. But the social and economic dynamics were certainly different with the demise of slavery, requiring Forrest to demonstrate his adaptability. That he was more successful in adjusting to the new order than many others was reflected in the report of an official from the Bureau of Refugees, Freedmen, and Abandoned Lands, who asserted that the warrior-turned-planter offered labor contracts to freedmen that "range higher than any others I found."[12]

In addition to offering better wages for his workers, Forrest also turned to several former Union officers to assist him. "They got me my hands, and they kept my hands engaged for me," he recalled of this period.[13] Forrest's behavior might have confounded detractors and fellow planters who could not compete with his tactics to obtain sufficient labor, but he demanded, as always, unquestioned acceptance of his authority. Just prior to the favorable assessment of his contracting terms by the Freedmen's Bureau official, he experienced a deadly encounter with one of his workers that threatened the progress he had sought to make in restoring his farm to good working order.

In late March 1866 Forrest was supervising the clearing of drainage on his property in order to combat an outbreak of cholera when a situation that had been building for some time reached a heated climax. A freedman named Thomas Edwards had already clashed over various matters with the plantation manager, former Union officer B. F. Diffenbocker. Contemporary accounts indicate that Edwards had a fierce temper and a tendency toward physical violence. Reproof for an earlier wife-beating incident, on the grounds that the behavior "was against General Forrest's orders for any man to whip his wife on the place," brought the hasty reply, "I do not care a God damn for General Forrest.... If Gen'l Forrest or any other man attempts to interfere with me in the privilege I enjoy as regards whipping her or beating [her], I'll cut his God damn guts out."[14]

Forrest was certainly capable of similar responses to those who did not follow his orders, and when Edwards refused to assist with the work and stormed into his cabin threatening to "whip" his wife for not having a meal prepared, heated language between the men occurred and threats escalated quickly. Forrest later insisted that he "slipped" into the laborer's cabin "and remarked to him that he had already abused his wife too much and that I had frequently requested him to cease his abuses to her, and that he could not whip her, that if he attempted to whip her again I would whip him." Neither man was prepared to back down. Both noticed an ax handle lying nearby, but Forrest reached the implement first as they lunged for it. The former cavalryman subsequently recalled that Edwards "made a lick at me" with a knife, and Forrest swung the ax handle to parry the weapon, striking the freedman "behind the left ear" and "knocking him down, killing him instantly."[15]

The incident unleashed a night of intense emotion on the plantation as news of the freedman's death circulated, but the arrival of a deputy named Wirt Shaw prevented further violence. As had been the case with other controversial moments in Forrest's life, multiple versions of what happened next arose. They ranged from an account that placed the cavalryman at his door, pistols in hand and shouting orders to overawe the angry former slaves, to one in which Forrest was barricaded in his home, prepared to fend off an attack that never materialized.[16]

Whatever transpired over the evening, the next morning the deputy boarded a steamer with Forrest in his custody. The former Confederate quickly learned, to his chagrin, that Federal soldiers filled the vessel and asked that his identity not be revealed. Shaw intended to honor the request, but word leaked out that Forrest was onboard, and the general's celebrity overwhelmed any effort to conceal his presence. Even so, the result was hardly the one the ex-Confederate had expected. Shaw recalled that rather than Forrest being "insulted," the soldiery "lionized" their fellow traveler. By the time the boat reached its destination, only the prisoner's insistence prevented the men from tossing Shaw into the Mississippi River in order to facilitate Forrest's escape.[17]

Bedford Forrest's arrest and arraignment for the death of Thomas Edwards presented a prime opportunity for punishing the man many held responsible for the Fort Pillow killings. Yet there is no evidence that anyone sought to prosecute the case beyond its own merits. After spending the summer months obtaining testimony and preparing their cases, the opposing sides faced each other at trial on October 6. At the close of the formal arguments, the judge's instructions to the jurors included nothing less than manslaughter. The panel's request for the addition of self-defense during their deliberations allowed them to reach that verdict on October 11.[18]

At the same time of the Forrest-Edwards encounter and the subsequent trial, the general faced another ominous situation. Following a spectacular raid into Memphis in 1864, a grand jury had returned an indictment for treason against Forrest, his brothers William and Jesse, and other prominent Memphians who supported the Confederacy.[19] In March 1866, just prior to the Edwards incident, Bedford Forrest posted a $10,000 bond with the expectation of a formal hearing later in the year. An offer of assistance came from a former comrade, which Forrest gratefully accepted. As he indicated in his response to Harvey Walter, who had been a judge advocate in the Army of Tennessee, the general felt that a successful outcome of his "tresen case" might well rest on the reputation garnered by his "milatary career."[20] Far from expecting that his actions in uniform would be held against him, including presumably those at Fort Pillow, the former Confederate seemed to believe that they would help in exonerating him of even a charge of treason. As it turned out, any cause for concern faded—the trial never occurred.

While awaiting his hearing on the Edwards case and anticipating a pending treason trial, Forrest paused in Memphis to communicate with a former wartime associate, Major W. Brent. His letter of September 13, 1866, mixed the ordinary affairs of business and family with other matters that were uppermost in his mind. Key among these was Fort Pillow. "I am making out a full statement of the so called Fort Pillow massacre," he explained, "and so soon as completed I will send it forward to the President as Commander in Chief of the Army and Navy of the United States in which I state that if my explanation is not satisfactory I demand an investigation by a Board of Officers."[21]

Two months later Forrest communicated directly with President Andrew Johnson. In words crafted by another but, as was his practice, reflective of his sentiments, the former Confederate laid out his course in the "nearly eighteen months, since laying down my arms." In those months he had maintained his loyalty and advised others to "give their attention[s] to industrial construction, and the development of our vast material resources, rather than to the discussion of vexations and unprofitable political affairs."

Despite the fact that such efforts had "not been unnoticed, nor unappreciated," he recognized that controversy followed him as well. "Yet, I am also aware," he explained openly to Johnson, "that I am at this moment regarded in large communities, at the North, with abhorrence, as a detestable monster, ruthless and swift to take life, and guilty of unpardonable crimes in connection with the capture of Fort Pillow on the 12th of April 1864." Although he characterized such notions as a "mis-judgment of my conduct and character," Forrest stated that they "should not surprise me" and observed that this type of imputation "pains and mortifies me greatly." He insisted that he could make "perfect justification before the world, of my course as a soldier and commander in the storming of Fort Pillow." In closing, Forrest offered to "waive all immunity from investigation into my conduct at Fort Pillow" in order to restore his name and citizenship.[22]

Understandably, not everyone embraced the idea of reconciliation with and restoration of rights for the former Confederate cavalry commander. One former soldier from Wisconsin observed plainly, "Congress may yet restore Forrest to citizenship & give him a gold medal bearing the mottoe Ft. Pillow!" Such efforts would not merit approval from this veteran or others like him. "May God who has sustained us so long save us now from Disgrace," he concluded.[23]

Bedford Forrest would have his say with the publication of what amounted to an autobiography by Thomas Jordan and J. P. Pryor. The general wrote an endorsement of the work, accepting the authors' conclusions concerning his military career. "Believing it to be proper that there should be a timely and lasting record of the deeds and services of those whom I have been so fortunate as to command, I placed all the facts and papers in my possession or available to me, in the hands of accomplished writers, who have done their part with close and conscientious research, and have endeavored to make up a chronicle neither over-wrought nor over-colored, as I can testify." Regarding the authenticity of this record, Forrest asserted, "For the greater part of the statements of the narrative I am responsible." In this volume Fort Pillow receives ample, and careful, coverage.[24]

The authors set the table in this respect by outlining the "long course of brutal, infamous conduct on the part of Bradford's Battalion toward the non-combatant people of West-Tennessee" that, in part, prompted Forrest to move against and "break up their lair."[25] They note that Major Booth had pickets out and received word early of Forrest's approach. "But, evidently feeling safe against any serious enterprise of any sort," they observe of the Union post commander, "the Federals neglected ordinary military precautions for the defense of the place against just such an assault as the one we have now to narrate."[26]

Jordan and Pryor refute the notion that Forrest's actions in response to the approach of the *Olive Branch* constituted a breach of military ethics. "This clearly legitimate movement constitutes in large part the *gravamen* of the charge ... that Forrest acted in bad faith and violated the flag of truce. Assuredly, no allegation could be more unfounded in this connection."[27] The writers chose their words carefully, remaining silent on the concurrent movements of Confederates against the quartermaster's stores and of Stinnett's advance force to the fort's ditch prior to the final assault.

Of the actions following the collapse of organized Federal resistance, Jordan and Pryor take the position that the Confederates sent to prevent enemy reinforcements were also in the prime location to prevent retreat or escape. "Finding that the succor which they had been promised from the gunboat was not rendered, nor at hand," the writers explain, "they were greatly bewildered. Many threw themselves into the river and were drowned in their mad attempt to swim away from the direful danger they apprehended; a number turning in the direction of Coal Creek, dashed as wildly into that stream and perished; others sought to escape along the river-bank southward, and, persisting in their efforts to get away, were shot or driven back."

The authors offer no description of individual excesses, although they address the argument of massacring prisoners by maintaining that in the "general confusion and tumult, in fact, a dissolution of all organization" that "as always happens in places taken by storm, unquestionably some whites, as well as negroes, who had thrown down their arms, and besought quarter, were shot under the *insania belli* which invariably rages on such occasions." Offering the further exculpatory elements that no formal surrender had taken place and that "[m]any of the prisoners were intoxicated, and few were not, to some degree, under the influence of liquor," the biographers observe that "as soon as he could reach the scene," Forrest became actively engaged in suppressing additional fire and securing the wounded and prisoners "from possible injury."[28]

Such an account features the arguments that Nathan Bedford Forrest most wished to present to the readers and hoped would suffice to relieve him from accusations of perpetrating a massacre. The degree to which the authors, presumably with the former general's blessing, lay out their case through the "Commentaries" that follow the narrative, the footnotes that accompany it, and an appendix that constitutes a "List of Prisoners Captured at Fort Pillow" reflects the desire of pro-Forrest contingents to silence critics. Having completed the task of informing "the candid and those who are capable of accepting the truth," Jordan and Pryor close with their unequivocal assessment that General Forrest's "course, therefore, stands utterly devoid of the essence of outrage or wrong."[29]

Another year passed without satisfaction as the ex-Confederate cavalryman still had not obtained his hearing or a respite from the accusations of perpetuating a massacre at Fort Pillow. In a letter of November 16, 1868, he decried "the charges made against me," labeling them "as false and black as the hearts of the men who made them."[30]

Whatever Forrest's friends may have believed, politics had elevated the passions associated with Fort Pillow during the war and would do so again after it. The election of 1868 between Republican Ulysses S. Grant and Democrat Horatio Seymour (with running mate Frank Blair) promised to be particularly contentious. Forrest began drawing attention for his Fort Pillow notoriety as he grew increasingly visible in his support of the Democratic Party. On his way to the Democratic convention held in New York in June, the Tennessean received word of a boisterous individual who wished to confront the "Butcher of Fort Pillow." Such blowhards failed to impress the backwoods-born former general who had stared down death and danger many times. As the fellow approached Forrest on the train, the ex-cavalryman "bounded from his seat, and demanded to know what the man wanted." The man considered discretion the better part of valor in this instance and fled unceremoniously from the car.

Even when delegate-at-large Forrest reached his destination, he proved to be the source of curiosity among the local citizenry. One matron took it upon herself to learn from him personally if he was indeed responsible for the deaths of so many defenseless black soldiers at Fort Pillow as maintained by the press. Despite whatever irritation he may have felt at having this matter thrust once more at him, Forrest observed dryly: "Yes, madam, I killed the men and women for my soldiers' dinner and ate the babies for myself for breakfast."[31]

The Tennessean's nefarious reputation soared as election rhetoric mounted. The editor of the *White Cloud Kansas Chief* condemned the man he called "Napoleon Bonaparte Forrest" for his part in the "Fort Pillow infamy," though not before referring to him as "one of the most attractive personages at the New York [Democratic Party] Convention." Following a recitation of the usual charges, the writer turned to the political purpose of the piece, referring specifically to the Democratic candidates for president and vice president. "Forrest, the leader and commander of this gang of wholesale murderers, is now the leading supporter of Seymour and Blair—was, in fact, instrumental in having the latter nominated in the New York Convention." The effect of supporting the Democrats, he concluded, would be "to hand over this government, with all its vast interests, to Forest [sic] and such men as he!"[32]

On September 14, 1868, the *New York Times* sought to expose the cavalryman's past transgressions by reprinting a highly charged statement originally composed by then Union major general David S. Stanley on April 21, 1864. Labeled provocatively "Is Forrest a Butcher?—A Little Bit of History," the preface to the letter opened with the observation, "Since Gen. N. B. FORREST has again become active as a member of the Democratic Party, reorganized on a peace footing, it has been denied that, while fighting in the field for that party, he was in any way responsible for the massacre at Fort Pillow." Stanley's letter was now offered as a wartime illustration that "throws some light upon FORREST'S own exploits as a negro-killer."

At the time, Stanley argued, "The late massacre at Fort Pillow, by FORREST, seems to have filled the community with indignation and surprise." The Union general did not count himself among that number. "To those in the front of our armies, who know FORREST," he explained, "there is nothing at all astonishing in his conduct at Fort Pillow." Stanley noted the shooting incident that had occurred during the 1862 Murfreesboro Raid as evidence of Forrest's depravity. "I know that this very much respected Confederate hero has, upon former occasions, condescended to become his own executioner."[33] The account was meant to reinforce the public view of wanton cruelty on the part of Bedford Forrest that would also taint anyone associated with him in the current national political arena.

There has been no record of the Confederate's reaction to Stanley's charge, but he was especially irritated by the accusations that issued forth from former Union cavalry general Judson Kilpatrick. In a published account in which the *New York Times* identified him as "Fort Pillow Forrest," the Tennessean blasted his Union challenger as a "blackguard, a liar, a scoundrel and poltroon." Kilpatrick's utterances came under harsh indictment for being "false and mendacious representations of me," with Forrest simultaneously condemning the Union cavalryman's "criminal capacity for ribald invention" and "his unprincipled and indecent libels."[34]

Nor were such comments meant for public consumption alone. In a letter to an individual who must have written him concerning the touchy subject, Forrest sent a short, blistering reply: "I not only denounce Kilpatrick but any other such a liar who says I ever overstepped the bounds of civilized warfare during my career in the Army."[35] In many ways as he supervised the composition of the response, Forrest must have experienced a sense of déjà vu, for the renewed and obviously unwelcomed publicity over Fort Pillow was occurring at the height of the presidential election of 1868 as it had in the election of 1864.

Basil Duke expressed surprise at the extent to which his former colleague became upset over such incidents. "I sympathized of course with Forrest," he noted, "but was somewhat amused at the indignation he expressed, for I supposed that he had become so accustomed to such attacks as to regard them with indifference."[36] The statement revealed that Duke may have known Bedford Forrest the general, but he did not truly know him as a man. Forrest could not let this kind of derogatory comment go unchallenged. Talk of a duel with Kilpatrick was not empty rhetoric; Forrest was a product of the honor-bound South. Duke supposedly went so far as to help make arrangements for satisfaction with sabers on horseback, a choice befitting the wartime careers of the prospective duelists, but Kilpatrick failed to follow through on the grounds that Forrest was not "a gentleman."[37]

Such a judgment was most ironic for the former Union cavalryman. A philanderer of the worst sort, Kilpatrick engaged in questionable financial and personal dealings, had a penchant for assiduously avoiding the truth, and enjoyed a tarnished reputation among his own compatriots. Of course, it may well have been that while pondering the matter, he also reckoned himself a poor risk against a man who had personally dispatched thirty combatants in wartime.[38] Kilpatrick's verbal assaults amounted to minor inconveniences and irksome diversions. Even Republicans found the former Union horseman difficult to sustain. Secretary of the Navy Welles condemned his compatriot for "making a fool of himself, [by] running all over the country [giving] partisan speeches."[39]

During this period, Forrest's greatest challenge came not so much from the ungainly verbal fumblings of Judson Kilpatrick as from the skillful pen strokes of Thomas Nast. The popular political cartoonist for *Harper's Weekly* proved an exceptionally difficult opponent to overcome for those who found themselves on the wrong side of his work. One historian has labeled these efforts "harsh and uncompromising."[40] Certainly, Forrest would have agreed, for when Nast turned his focus on the Southerner, it was with the ruthlessness of a partisan Republican and the skill of a master at his craft.

In several images Nast unleashed the power of his artistic talents against the former Confederate general. Highlighting the association of the Democratic Party with figures from the Civil War, the cartoonist offered a scathing depiction of *Leaders of the Democratic Party* in 1868. Focusing on "the Rioter Seymour," Nast tarnishes the presidential candidate with connections to the New York City draft riots of 1863 by placing him next to lynched figures on lampposts amid a city engulfed in smoke and flames. In addition, the Democrat's close associates include Raphael Semmes, commander of the commerce raider *Alabama,* as "The Pirate" and former Confederate generals Wade Hampton as "The Hangman" and Forrest as "The Butcher."

The legend below a rabid-looking General Forrest, simultaneously waving a Confederate flag and blasting away at victims with his pistol, specifically invokes Fort Pillow. One quotation, from "May's Official Report," has the cavalryman ranting "No quarter!" "Kill 'em!" and "damn 'em!" A second draws from the language in one of Forrest's postraid reports lauding the behavior of troops under General Chalmers: "HE HAS REASON TO BE PROUD OF THE CONDUCT OF THE OFFICERS AND MEN OF HIS COMMAND," Forrest had written of the campaign that included "the Fort Pillow Massacre."[41]

In September 1868 a cartoon appeared that Nast entitled *This Is a White Man's Government,* prominently featuring Forrest standing over a prostrate black Union soldier. He holds aloft the knife of "The Lost Cause," carries in his back pocket the whip of slavery, and proudly wears the badge of Fort Pillow. Together with the figure of an Irish brute and a wealthy business tycoon, whom Nast delighted in excoriating as ruthless adherents to the Democratic banner, Forrest stands triumphantly over the fallen Federal as he reaches for a ballot-box globe that lies just outside his grasp.[42]

The following month Nast portrayed Bedford Forrest in the company of many other former Confederates and notable Democratic politicians. Although led by party standard-bearers Seymour and Blair, Forrest can be seen prominently in the front ranks behind a flag emblazoned with the terms "slavery," "Fort Pillow," "mob law," and "the Ku Klux Klan." The ex-Confederate cavalryman might seem distracted from the foreground action of the Democratic Party relieving a freed-black "modern Samson" of his strength—his vote—because he is focused on torching a pile of documents that includes the U.S. Constitution.[43]

Nast's considerable talents had helped reelect Abraham Lincoln and would one day assist in bringing down the powerful leader of New York

City's Tammany Hall Democratic machine, William Marcy "Boss" Tweed.[44] For now, his focus remained squarely on men like Forrest as he sought to derail the Democratic presidential ticket in this election year.

Electioneering was not the only activity that put Bedford Forrest's name back in the headlines. His interest and involvement in railroading led to a wide-ranging interview with a reporter from the *Louisville Courier Journal* in March 9, 1869. Reprinted shortly afterward in the *Memphis Daily Appeal*, the discussion included the former Confederate's assessment of planting interests in the South. Asked how the region could be sufficiently repopulated to sustain large-scale agricultural endeavors, Forrest replied: "With negroes. They are the best laborers we have ever had in the South." Insisting that he would not have such persons "enslaved, if I could," Forrest insisted, "My house servants are with me yet in Memphis, and never would leave me." Although not mentioning the remuneration these "house servants" now received for their work, the one-time slave trader and master insisted that he had no animus toward the former slaves, offering a rather surprising historical reference: "I have always felt kind towards them, and have always treated them kindly. Even the 'Fort Pillow massacre' was investigated and the Federal officers to a man, stated that I was not to blame."[45]

In 1873 an international crisis nearly offered Forrest the possibility of further removing himself from the tinge of Fort Pillow by returning to the saddle, this time under Old Glory. A crew of misguided adventurers on a vessel called the *Virginius* fell into Spanish hands at the end of October while engaged in gunrunning on behalf of Cuban insurrectionists. Their captors executed the leaders of the effort, a former Union lieutenant and an ex-Confederate, and a number of their crewmen as pirates, prompting a loud outcry in the United States. Bedford Forrest was among the Civil War veterans who offered to raise regiments for a fight if one came, but neither President Ulysses Grant nor General in Chief William T. Sherman were anxious to go to war over this provocation. In declining his offer, Sherman nevertheless forwarded the request to the War Department, noting, "were it left to me in the event of a war requiring cavalry, I would unhesitatingly accept his services and give him a prominent place." Then Forrest's old antagonist added wryly, "I believe now he would fight against our national enemies as vehemently as he did against us, and that is saying enough."[46]

Despite Forrest's efforts to restore his reputation, and following his flirtation with the Democratic Party in 1868 and his offer of military service in 1873, he found himself increasingly sapped by poor health and beset by financial hardship.

In his last difficult years, while working diligently to restore his financial standing, Forrest continued to exhibit other characteristics that had marked his life. At a "Pole-Bearers" barbeque in 1875, he addressed an audience largely consisting of black Memphians. "I came here with the jeers of some white people, who think I am doing wrong," he explained unapologetically. "I believe I can exert some influence, and do much to assist the people in strengthening fraternal relations, and shall do all in my power to elevate every man—to depress none." Oblivious to his paternalistic tone, Forrest insisted that he would aid anyone in advancing to "wherever you are capable of going." The ex-Confederate recognized that at a minimum such sentiments coming from him must meet with a healthy sense of skepticism. "Many things have been said about me which are wrong," he maintained, "and which white and black persons here, who stood by me through the war, can contradict." The undercurrent was Fort Pillow, and Forrest turned to revisionism to address the incident. "I have been in the heat of battle when colored men asked me to protect them," he noted. "I have placed myself between them and the bullets of my men, and told them they should go unharmed." Forrest closed affirmatively, "Go to work, be industrious, live honestly and act truly, and when you are oppressed I'll come to your relief ... and assure you that I am with you in heart and in hand."[47]

The speech represents in microcosm the difficulties of assessing motive for Forrest. Clearly, he believed himself to be a friend to people of all races, yet there was no question that he maintained his notions of an established social order. Black citizens required "elevation" to progress forward and should "be industrious" in their efforts in order to receive such assistance. They could also anticipate oppression from whites not yet ready to embrace their equality and for whom even the gesture of a speech by one of their own was unwelcome. Then there was the requirement, advanced by Forrest himself, of having had to interpose himself between black Union soldiers and "the bullets of my men" for the sake of the formers' "protection." While it was possible that the situation the general recounted reflected the dangers of combat at Fort Pillow or Brice's Cross Roads, he may well have exposed an admission of the excesses laid against him while hoping to avoid responsibility for them. Forrest's words were open to interpretation, then and since, on the sensitive issues of race, racism, and atrocity.

A more generous tone was not out of keeping with the Bedford Forrest who also turned to the church at about this time. He had always held a fascination for religious ceremonies and recognized his wife's devotion to her faith, but it was only in his last years that he sought conversion for himself.

The former general approached Reverend George Tucker Stainback on the evening of November 14, 1875, to announce his acceptance of the tenets of Christianity. "There was no half way of doing things with Forrest," the preacher recalled, "and this is the way he entered the religious faith."[48] Even then he could not entirely bring himself to turn from his trips to the gaming table or harness the temper that still boiled beneath the surface. Furthermore, the man who contemplated his eternal future was also struggling to recoup his worldly finances and regain the physical strength he had once enjoyed, but which was rapidly slipping away from him. Friends and former comrades who saw him now were appalled by his emaciated appearance. "That Devil Forrest" was clearly no longer the "Wizard of the Saddle," and he was just as obviously declining swiftly. Changes in diet and visits to spas could not stay the deterioration that threatened his life.

In the final days he moved from his home on President's Island outside of Memphis into his brother Jesse's house in the developing city. He accepted a few visitors, prominent among them the former president of the Confederate States of America, Jefferson Davis. But this was not a fight he was going to win. As the end approached, Bedford Forrest turned his thoughts to the most significant aspect of his life. It was not a desire to ask for absolution or to seek forgiveness regarding anything he had done in the fifty-six years of his personal pilgrimage. His last words reflected what had always been most important to him in his adult years: "Call my wife."[49]

Nathan Bedford Forrest's passing on October 29, 1877, prompted Southern newspapers to record the martial deeds of the general and praise his military legacy. Obituaries in Northern newspapers reminded their readers that his death marked the passing of "the Butcher of Fort Pillow." Those in "the border states and the West," according to one historian, "represented a synthesis of southern and northern opinion." Court Carney explains, "Southern newspapers seldom mentioned the massacre at Fort Pillow, and northern newspapers rarely acknowledged Forrest's heroism." For many Northerners of both races, the Tennessean was a figure to be abhorred. "For them, the general personified Confederate villainy, and he became a potent postwar symbol of an aggressive southern Democratic Party and the emergent cult of the Lost Cause."[50]

In the days after the passing of the ex-Confederate cavalry chieftain, the *New York Times* presented a satirical retrospective entitled "In the Light of Conciliation." "Fortune was kind to Gen. FORREST in permitting him to live until the era of conciliation," it began. "Had he died a year ago, the friends of the so-called Union would have recognized his skill and bravery as a soldier, but would have felt compelled to say he fought in behalf of a bad cause and stained his reputation by an atrocious massacre." Instead, Forrest had survived until the spirit of reconciliation made such observations out of place. "The charge that Gen. FORREST massacred the colored defenders of Fort Pillow is, of course, a malignant falsehood," the editorial explained facetiously, providing as evidence the fact that none of those supposed to have been massacred "will testify under oath" against the general and his men. "To suppose that they were literally massacred, is to assume that Gen. FORREST was capable of an atrocious act, and no one who cares anything for conciliation could be capable of such an assumption."[51]

"Fort Pillow" had already become a legacy that promised to outlive Nathan Bedford Forrest. One Union veteran used the incident as a comparison to explain excesses associated with the Confederate victory at Plymouth, North Carolina, at about the same time as Forrest's capture of the Mississippi River fort. The killing of blacks and North Carolina Unionists there prompted former lieutenant Bernard F. Blakeslee of the 6th Connecticut to label it as "the Fort Pillow massacre re-enacted."[52]

Yet just two years after Forrest's death, a defense of Confederate leadership at Fort Pillow emerged from an unlikely source. Dr. Charles Fitch, the Iowa surgeon who had sought Forrest's protection, wrote a letter for the *Southern Historical Society Papers*. Given its distance from the events and the venue in which it appeared, such an account, even generated by a Massachusetts-born Union veteran, might be suspect. If so, Fitch was nevertheless remarkably consistent about what he remembered as having happened fifteen years earlier.

"The greatest slaughter," he reiterated, was "under the bluffs next to the river." Of the few Confederate officers the doctor saw in the immediate area, "none [were] above the ranks of lieutenant and captain." This state of affairs offered little supervision for the men and their activities there. Fitch was clear that the Confederate commander was not among them. "Forrest was up" in the fort itself, "sighting a piece of artillery on the little gunboat up the river," he explained. The doctor was sure that the general was oblivious to other actions going on around him. "I do not think Forrest knew what was going on under the bluffs."

Even with Forrest's verbal order of protection, Fitch was not completely safe from other Confederates. Fortunately, General Chalmers countered these threats with a timely intervention on his behalf. "You cursed them, and put a guard over me," the surgeon recalled gratefully, "giving orders to the guard to shoot down the first one that molested me." Fitch knew that excesses had taken place but was adamant that the ranking Confederates were not directly involved. "I have always thought that neither you [Chalmers] nor Forrest knew anything that was going on at the time under the bluffs. What was done was done very quickly."[53]

Still, if Bedford Forrest and James Chalmers did not lead their men in a massacre of the garrison, excesses did take place for which they, as commanders, bore responsibility. At Fort Pillow Forrest's preference for leading from the front, once he arrived in the fort after its capture, prevented him from exerting greater control over his men and their actions. He had forfeited that control by insisting on aiming an artillery piece himself, rather than detailing that work to others. Although he was willing to delegate tasks, as he had to do whenever he sent out detachments, he retained a tendency to involve himself too minutely in the action on the field rather than to supervise from a broader perspective. He did this when placing sharpshooters after Chalmers had already deployed them effectively. Forrest simply could not help himself from being hands on, which he certainly also would have been had he planned to carry out a complete massacre of the Fort Pillow garrison.

Supporters of the two generals could argue about their responsibilities for what happened along the Mississippi, but Chalmers's subsequent political career ensured that the story would remain relevant. Although he expressed distress for the negative association he had with Fort Pillow, Chalmers also seemed to revel in the notoriety it brought him. Initially seated in Congress from Mississippi in the period 1877–81, the ex-Confederate ran afoul of his old political friends as he sought to establish his footing on new ground.[54]

*The National Republican* of Washington, D.C., provided its readers with the text of a congratulatory telegram the former Confederate sent to a controversial wartime counterpart who had also won election to Congress. "Fort Pillow Chalmers to Beast Butler, greeting," the Mississippian wrote to Benjamin Butler in Massachusetts. "Both in. Shake?" The men could hardly be construed as friends, but Chalmers may have felt that he understood the virulence of public sentiments against both of them, expressing this with a wry sense of humor and irony.[55]

Chalmers was still in the news in the late 1880s, but an interview that appeared in the *Pittsburg Dispatch* focused as much on Fort Pillow as it did on the politics of the day. The writer posited that "some" of the "Southern journals suggest that if you are nominated for Governor, the Republican rally should be [held] at Fort Pillow." Chalmers lamented quietly, "You know they have blamed me even more than General Forrest for that affair at Fort Pillow." Quickly and rather disingenuously, given his arrival at the fort before his commander that day, he added, "I was second in command under Forrest." He then insisted, "There is no truth in the alleged atrocities at Fort Pillow" and recalled asking for an investigation on the matter when he first entered Congress, one that was "not made." The remainder of the interview consisted of a refutation of the main charges and a description of the personality and character of his former chief.[56]

In an attempt to sell tobacco products and capitalize on the twin themes of the late war—nostalgia and reconciliation—W. Duke Sons & Company of Durham, North Carolina, included a series of "short histories" of Union and Confederate figures in cigarette packs. Nathan Bedford Forrest's fifteen-page miniaturized "history" appeared in 1888 and included a section on Fort Pillow that undoubtedly caused Southern purchasers to grimace. The writer or writers of the sketch clearly held that a massacre had occurred and accepted the Joint Committee's testimony as proof. Forrest's alleged contribution was a statement offered that was supposed to be in his own words: "We busted the fort at ninerclock and skatered the nigers. The men is still a cillanem in the woods." The section concluded, "Accounting for some prisoners, he wrote in another report, 'Them as was cotch with spuns and brest-pins and sich was cilled, and the rest of the lot was payrold and tolled to git.'" Of course, this insert contained no citations of sources for verification or substantiation.[57]

While colorful and colloquial, the accuracy of this "short history" is another matter. Forrest's written words indicate genuine limitations in spelling but reflect the way that he talked. He had a tendency to spell "killed" as "kild" in his personal correspondence, not "cilled," thus the attempt at colloquialism in this instance seems more fictional than authentic. Nor is the timeline of events correct. The fort had not been "busted" at nine o'clock in the morning as suggested, although it was about that time when a sharpshooter sighted Major Booth and squeezed his trigger. Forrest himself would not have reached the scene of action until an hour after the fort had fallen, if this account had been accurate. Forrest also had made plain his determination to follow his government's policy toward captured blacks who could be identified as slaves belonging to Southern masters as property to be returned. Others were to be held until such identification could be made and even forced to work on Confederate military defenses at times, though certainly not arbitrarily paroled and told "to git." Taken on its face and in the context of its presentation, this short "history" of General Forrest was clearly meant to increase sales of tobacco products more than it was meant to reflect historical fact.

Another image of Fort Pillow considerably more damning to the general's interpretation emerged in 1892 as part of a series of thirty-six lithographs featuring Civil War battles produced by Louis Kurz and Alexander Allison. *The Fort Pillow Massacre* contains the romantic stylizations common to these depictions, with soldiers far-too-immaculately uniformed for actual warfare and presented in highly formalized poses. But the work also envisions the circumstances of the Joint Committee report, with mostly black men, women, and children falling victim to Confederate butchery. Forrest is seen on high ground overlooking and supervising the action as some of his men storm the fort and overpower the defenders, while the remaining troops systematically slaughter their adversaries along the landing. A handful of individuals, some of them wounded, have already entered the river, while others literally stand at the bank to be shot down by Southern volleys or stabbed to death by individual Confederates. The whole drama is played out beneath a white flag tied to the pole in the fort just behind and slightly above the bulk of the killing as additional Southerners surge forward to join the indiscriminate murder.

Thus, almost thirty years after the events at Fort Pillow, feelings remained strong, at least among some of those capable of influencing public opinion through images. Like the wartime artists of *Harper's Weekly* and *Frank Leslie's Illustrated Newspaper* before them, Kurz and Allison sought to present the war as their primary audience wanted to see it.[58]

Near the end of the nineteenth century, with Nathan Bedford Forrest now gone for better than twenty years and the April 1864 events fading into increasingly distant memory, a woman from Warrenton, Virginia, conducted her own inquiry into Fort Pillow. Corresponding with ex-Confederates such as Bennett H. Young, the raider of St. Albans, Vermont, and John Cussons as well as historian and Forrest biographer John Allan Wyeth, she probed for information concerning the fight.

Cussons could offer "no personal knowledge of the Fort Pillow affair" beyond what some of Forrest's men had related to him. He shared the secondhand knowledge that the black troops "would not throw down their arms; that a number of them who were left on the ground fired into our rear during the pursuit; that a part of our troops went back, shooting all who retained their muskets." It was at that point that the Confederates apparently became aware of deception on the part of some defenders, when "it was then found that many of the Negroes who had dropped to the ground were not disabled—in short that they were treacherously killing our men who had spared them." Cussons concluded, "Of course, every soldier knows what will occur under circumstances such as these."[59]

Young suggested that his correspondent read a piece in the *Confederate Veteran* that contained "a statement from Forrest's Adjt. General, which seemed to me to be very clear and to sustain all that Forrest['s] friends had said in regard to the circumstances and relieving him of any charge of cruelty or atrocity."[60]

But not every voice the writer heard spoke in support of Forrest or in defense of the pro-Confederate version of events. H. G. Wilson offered a more substantial, and decidedly different, answer to her inquiries. In a letter he stated categorically his conclusion that a massacre had indeed occurred. "I can use no other word," he observed.[61]

Dr. Wyeth's associate J. A. Robertson responded to a letter in July that the Forrest biographer was in Europe with his family and could not reply himself until he returned to New York City in the autumn.[62] But when Robertson forwarded the letter to him, Wyeth chose to answer it immediately from Carlsbad, Austria. He explained that his *Life of General Nathan Bedford Forrest* would appear in September. In addition to the treatment of Fort Pillow in the text, he suggested that the publication of an article, "The Storming of Fort Pillow," would "I believe put a quietus on that awful lie."[63] Wyeth could only hope that this would be so.

But any peace on the issue of Forrest and Fort Pillow was to prove elusive. The conflicts associated with America's entrance onto the world imperial stage at the turn of the century created additional context for references to the 1864 engagement. "Heat in the Senate" blared a headline from the *Richmond Dispatch* in April 1902, when comments associated with the suppression of what was then called the Philippine Insurrection reached its readership. Republican senator John C. Spooner of Wisconsin took the floor to wonder rhetorically to the speaker, Democrat Henry Teller of Colorado, "Does the Senator not remember Fort Pillow?" Although the question had not been directed at him, Democratic Tennessee senator Edward Carmack interjected, countering with an inquiry as to what the reference meant. Spooner replied, "I had in mind what has been considered a massacre of colored troops there." As an indication of the emotion still wrought from such references, the contributing writer noted, "Mr. Carmack insisted with some heat that there was no massacre of troops or killing of prisoners at Fort Pillow," and the topic shifted to more-recent events without additional clarification or correction.[64] Newspapers across the country carried the exchange, a San Francisco version labeling the "discussion" as "spirited."[65]

By the early 1900s, a self-anointed committee of the United Confederate Veterans was in place to determine the validity of works of history for Southern classrooms. In 1903, his final year as the chair of that committee, Stephen D. Lee, Forrest's former superior, authorized a report that condemned author Ella Haines Stratton for bias in her *Young People's History of Our Country*. The most significant charge against the book was in respect to its coverage of Fort Pillow. Under the banner of reconciliation, the committee report noted that the members were "pained at this late date to see such paragraphs, breathing all the bad blood of the bitterest war of the centuries," and called upon the writer to have "those paragraphs expunged." For her part, Stratton was utterly unapologetic, and, from the committee's standpoint, uncooperative. She insisted that in the case of Fort Pillow, "[n]o Indian massacre could rival the scene" and recapitulated the litany of atrocities that had appeared in the congressional report and Northern newspaper headlines of the day. "The Confederates won the victory of the war at Fort Pillow," she concluded brusquely, "but Forrest and his men lost the victory of principle and the respect of the whole world." Obviously, from the committee's point of view, this writer's work could have no place in Southern schools, molding the minds of the region's young people in such a distorted fashion.[66]

Interestingly, it was an equestrian statue put in place two years later in Memphis that would have a greater influence on popular thought than any single volume on the general. Sculpted by Charles H. Niehaus, the twenty-foot-tall monument featured Nathan Bedford Forrest on his famed steed, King Philip.[67] The horse had secured renown in some circles for his public displays of disdain for dark uniforms even after the conflict was ended, prompting one Federal soldier to observe that now he understood the secret of the Confederate cavalryman's success in the war.[68] Such tales flourished among those who held the general and his exploits in high esteem, regardless of the mitigating factors of his personality and actions on and off his many battlefields. Forrest was simply larger than life, a fact that the former Confederate cavalryman, a storyteller himself, would have relished.

Ironically, one of the earliest controversies associated with the monument involved the orientation of the statue. Niehaus had placed it so that the figures of the horse and rider faced to the south, prompting some veterans to complain that it appeared as if the general were retreating from his enemies. Over the years, others would assert that Forrest was facing his beloved South and had contemptuously turned his back on those same adversaries. As in all things Forrest, there is no truth to either speculation, for the sculptor had simply wanted to give his work the best light in which to be viewed.[69]

Years later the subject of the work and the changing nature of the surrounding community generated renewed debate concerning their removal to a new site. The reinternment of the remains of General Forrest and his wife, Mary Ann, from Elmwood Cemetery to the base of the statue added further complication for those who wished to have the monument in Forrest Park taken down.

The light that Niehaus coveted for his statue has since shone on it literally and the general's life and military career figuratively with alternate degrees of intensity. To the popular mind, Nathan Bedford Forrest has been at once the great tactician who "got there first with the most" men and the perpetrator of a massacre at Fort Pillow. In reality the battle-scarred warrior with his homespun aphorisms about war was neither the infallible "wizard" nor the senseless "butcher" that some have seemed so intent on making him out to be. He was a product of his time, his heritage, and his life experiences. In one sense Forrest would be distressed that what transpired at Fort Pillow in 1864 was continuing to be laid at his feet; but in another, he would be pleased that he has remained at the heart of a story that continues to be told.

EPILOGUE

# "War Means . . . Killing"

War means fighting and fighting means killing.

*Nathan Bedford Forrest*

Cry havoc and let slip the dogs of war.

*Mark Antony,* Julius Caesar

As far as the knowledge of the Rebellion extends, so far will the affair at Fort Pillow be known.

*William M. Thayer, A* Youth's History of the Rebellion

Connecting a poorly educated American backwoodsman with a European literary giant might seem odd on the surface, but both Nathan Bedford Forrest and William Shakespeare shared at least one ingredient: each understood human nature well. For Forrest, warfare came down to one simple fact: "War means fighting and fighting means killing."[1] He did not shy away from the killing that took place on any field, including Fort Pillow. Death was a fact of war for which no apology or admission of guilt was necessary if those deaths occurred in the legitimate course of combat operations, which he insisted had happened in April 1864. Likewise, the Bard of Stratford-upon-Avon knew the basic elements of war and the consequences they had on the lives of those who experienced them. In *The Tragedy of Julius Caesar,* he put powerful words in the mouth of Mark Antony as that character delivers the assassinated leader's funeral oration. "Cry havoc and let slip the dogs of war," Antony calls out in his anger over Caesar's murder.[2] For those who had experienced the fighting at Fort Pillow, these words could have pertained to that day in April 1864 as well.

Shakespeare's understanding of the warrior mentality could be applied to any age, but in many important ways, the experiences of Americans in the South during the Revolutionary War came closest to predicting elements that would reappear in the Civil War eighty years later. In the chaos of panic and battle on numerous fields in the 1780s, animosities and bloodlust transcended the boundaries of decency and humanity, perhaps best illustrated by the necessity for Colonel William Campbell to ride among his infuriated patriot comrades at Kings Mountain imploring, "For God's sake, quit! It's murder to shoot any more men!"[3]

Charges of "massacre," applied and implied, existed for leaders and soldiery on both the Colonial and British sides of the conflict. At the Battle of the Waxhaws in May 1780, the number of Colonial casualties was significantly higher than the five killed and twelve wounded that Banastre Tarleton's men suffered despite their roles as the attackers. Yet in attempting evenhandedness, historian David Wilson maintains, "A one-sided battle with heavy casualties is not, in and of itself, proof of massacre." He found no direct evidence of Tarleton's refusal to offer quarter and thought the presence of captives "sufficient to indemnify Tarleton of having issued orders to kill everyone." Nevertheless, Wilson concludes, "Even though Tarleton may be innocent of ordering an atrocity, he is certainly guilty of failing to restrain his men once the engagement ceased to be a battle and became a simple slaughter."[4] He could have said the same of Nathan Bedford Forrest at Fort Pillow.

Historian Jim Piecuch argues that under the circumstances that prevailed at the Waxhaws, no massacre had occurred "in the sense that prisoners were systematically killed after being surrendered." He explains: "There was a brief, confused, and violent battle in which the American line was quickly broken. Organization disappeared as some Americans fled, others attempted to surrender, and still others continued to resist."[5]

At San Jacinto during the Texas Revolution, the descriptions of the aftermath of the conventional phase of fighting also mesh closely with those associated with Fort Pillow. Combatants on one side took full advantage of the powerful impulses of outrage and battle fury to seize opportunities for exacting a terrible price from the broken and helpless fighters on the other side.

Although men undisputedly died at Fort Pillow after they had ceased to resist effectively, the description of the circumstances at the Waxhaws, San Jacinto, and elsewhere fit well with the chaotic nature of the Civil War engagement. The panic and raw emotions attendant to each proved deadly for the participants beyond any reasonable boundaries of traditional combat. In the fighting in 1780, British officers, including the notorious Tarleton, proved unsuccessful in reasserting a sense of order after organized resistance had collapsed; the same would happen to Bedford Forrest along the Mississippi River in 1864.[6] Likewise, concerning San Jacinto, at least one historian has argued that Sam Houston "had lost control" of events in the aftermath of the conventional fighting there.[7]

Fort Pillow exhibited battle fury at its worst, with the pandemonium of a collapsing defense aided by the racial and sectional antagonisms that motivated many of the participants. The historical lessons of the Waxhaws and Kings Mountain, San Jacinto and Buena Vista, Little Big Horn and Wounded Knee, and the nature of warfare that has occurred elsewhere suggests that when tactical disintegration occurs, the opportunities for excess accelerate. As one Civil War veteran wrote, "The truth is, when bullets are whacking against tree-trunks and solid shot are cracking skulls like egg-shells, the consuming passion in the breast of the average man is to get out of the way."[8] That some men would take advantage of this tendency in others seemed to be as true at Fort Pillow as it had been and would be elsewhere. Such situations are bound to be made worse when the darker elements of human nature and personal animosities enter the equation.

In his assessment of the psychology of Civil War soldiers under the stresses of combat, Eric T. Dean observes that on the battlefield, "frenzy drove and impelled soldiers to commit acts of violence and cruelty, including shooting down defenseless soldiers."[9] As such, the assertion by Union general Mason Brayman that "these murders came not of sudden heat, consequent upon battle and perpetrated by soldiers whom their officers could not control," is simply incorrect. At Fort Pillow that is exactly what happened, as it had on other battlefields before and after the American Civil War and at other places within that conflict. Forrest's threats of "no quarter" notwithstanding, Brayman and others exaggerated a tactic meant to intimidate opponents to surrender with minimal bloodshed into sinister precursors of "indiscriminate murder." The Union officer concluded, "By the casualty of war the fate intended for Paducah and Columbus fell only upon Fort Pillow."[10] He would have been most correct if he had maintained that through "the casualty of war," Fort Pillow's fate might have been instead like that of Paducah and Columbus, where the garrisons initiated a successful defense, or like Union City, where no excessive casualties occurred when the Union commander there surrendered, even among captives for whom there were similar bitter feelings.

Subsequent historical events have helped shed light for students of warfare on the circumstances in American wars by which the combinations of battle fury, panic, and antipathies of various sorts led to excesses on the battlefield. These also have added to an understanding of what happened at Fort Pillow in 1864. The Philippine War at the beginning of the twentieth century provided numerous instances of vicious encounters between combatants and civilians, which racial antagonisms and the nature of the warfare itself exacerbated.[11]

In his study of race and war in the Pacific theater during World War II, John Dower found ample evidence of excessive behavior toward men who should otherwise have become prisoners of war. He concludes that many motives prompted this reaction from Allied troops toward their Japanese opponents, from the deaths of comrades and the actions of some of the enemy soldiers themselves to the dehumanization of the opponent and the ruthlessness of some participants.[12] The same could be said of Forrest's men at Fort Pillow. Of course, such explanations do not excuse the excesses, diminish their existence, or exonerate Forrest of any responsibility for them, but rather they place them in a context from which they can be examined and better understood.

Likewise in the European theater, surrender and mercy often seemed to become the personal prerogatives of the soldiers and units involved. Men could act with shocking indifference to opponents who had ceased to resist or who otherwise no longer represented a danger to them. Even with the threat of punishment for such transgressions, there was often little commanders could do to prevent them. Near the end of the war, a British soldier observed, "The question of killing does not present itself as a moral problem any more—or as a problem at all." An American officer explained to his family concerning his men: "Slowly it is beginning to dawn on them that the only good German is a dead German. The result is that we're killing more and taking fewer prisoners."[13] Perhaps the modern news correspondent Eric Sevareid captured the dilemma all humans face in warfare when he observed: "War happens inside a man. It happens to one man alone."[14]

At Fort Pillow, Bedford Forrest did not operate in a vacuum. Because he absorbed the culture in which he lived and operated, he could not help but be influenced by it. That world, shaped by the changing nature of warfare and the alterations in social norms, included increasingly darker references. Demands for "the black flag," "no quarter," "retaliation," "retribution," "reprisal," and such characterized the tone of the conflict in greater measure as the fighting persisted. The fact that both the Confederacy and the Union were experiencing these transitions also blurred the lines along which critiques could be made of what was or was not acceptable, especially by those who still clung to the comforts of the old, familiar structure. Forrest's world was changing, and his tendencies toward bluster as well as bluff, his intimidating persona, and his latent desire to conform to the system in which he operated provided him with little assistance in processing the breakdowns in order and discipline at Fort Pillow. Had Forrest's personality allowed him to accept responsibility for failing to control circumstances as they developed, his background and current social framework would have worked against him.

The components of battle and their effect on the soldiers engaged are crucial for understanding what happened at Fort Pillow, as were the transitions being wrought in the combatants' societies, but the personality that has loomed largest in the story has remained Nathan Bedford Forrest. His presence and personal history have created the conditions by which judgment is most often passed. At Fort Pillow the Confederate commander demonstrated two important traits: his common-sense approach to warfare and his dogged determination to see an engagement to a successful conclusion. These factors influenced his actions and attitudes while on that field.

Ironically, given his reputation, the Confederate cavalryman seems to have held two personality characteristics in check. No account suggests that Forrest's temper ran amuck against his opponents as it was wont to do on other occasions, and the general did not lead his men personally in overrunning the fort. In the first instance, the closest Forrest came to exhibiting his anger came toward men in his own command who were looting Federal stores. In the second, he had taken steps to delegate key elements of the fighting to subordinates and allow them to carry out the larger plan while he watched. Geographic separation and his own preoccupations also prevented more-effective personal leadership once the defense collapsed, threatening his ability to exercise command and control.

Although he arrived after the initial contact and the first disposition of his troops, Forrest held undisputed authority in his role as Confederate commander at Fort Pillow. The handling of deployments was largely the work of his lieutenants, but as a hands-on commander himself, Forrest remained in the saddle, as much as enemy fire would allow him to do so, to supervise and station men and units as he saw fit. By examining the ground himself, he became familiar with the terrain features and defensive configurations that his men would confront in trying to capture the fort. This approach, and his willingness to consult freely with his subordinates, enabled Forrest to improve his positions so that if, or when, a final push became necessary, his men would have as many advantages and face as few disadvantages as possible. His active, if diminished, role as well as his responsibility as commander also meant that he could not distance himself entirely from the actions his men took for good or ill in waging combat and in its aftermath.

Of course, if Forrest could normally identify the important elements of a battle, this ability would have been worthless without translating his observations into practice. He could do that too, as the Union garrison realized when screaming Southerners came dashing over the earthworks, firing into the stunned defenders and overwhelming them. The final assault was a culmination of decisions Forrest employed to make victory as inevitable as possible, from pinning the defenders to the parapet wall with covering fire to using the unburned barracks and the nature of the geographic features to get his men as close as possible before ordering them forward. He used psychology with the men too, although tellingly not employing race as a factor, but rather states' rights to encourage them in the grim task they faced.

Forrest liked to use intimidation, which he nurtured so assiduously to his advantage in other circumstances by bluffing an opponent into submission. That such a tactic did not work at Fort Pillow, indeed may have backfired on him, did not prevent him from seeking victory. A bloodless success could be savored as much as any other because it emanated from his fertile mind and not the blades or barrels of his weapons. But if the general could not say that he had bested this adversary with his brain, he would not avoid applying brawn out of any concern for appearances. The brutality of war was an acceptable risk if forced to commit to battle.

As a rule, Bedford Forrest exhibited clarity of vision on the battlefield and naturally seemed to take into account and quickly digest diverse situations as they developed. Circumstances at the closing stages of the fighting challenged his usually effective approach, but neither Lionel Booth nor William Bradford appeared to match their opponent in such command flexibility or creative reflex. They remained enshrouded in the fog of war, and this limitation adversely affected the outcome for their men. But Forrest's choices on the field created their own set of limitations for him as well.

As the battle reached its violent denouement, the general's actions appeared to contradict his usual practices. The testimony of Dr. Fitch offers a picture of Forrest as displaying an obsession with a Union gunboat and the river from which other assistance might appear. This prevented the Confederate leader from exercising his proper command responsibility and thereby diminished his ability to exert greater control over his men. For a soldier who normally exhibited a capacity to handle complex situations as they unfolded, or in more modern terminology, one who often multitasked successfully, Bedford Forrest's insistence upon playing the artillerist betrayed him in this instance. It is perhaps understandable that he considered the Union threat from the river to remain viable, having experienced the setback at Paducah largely due to the firepower of two Federal vessels located there; from that perspective his decision to abrogate higher-command obligations made sense. Indeed, he would indulge in this activity later in 1864 at Johnsonville, where personally serving as a cannoneer could not affect the larger demands of command and control. But he could not afford to succumb to such temptation at Fort Pillow.

If Forrest failed to understand what was happening on the landing below the fort or became preoccupied with the possibility of Union succor from the river, his lapse in leadership had implications both on that field and afterward. Commanders ought to be expected to demonstrate awareness and flexibility in every circumstance they encounter in warfare, a challenge that nevertheless has plagued generals great and small, including William T. Sherman and Ulysses S. Grant at Shiloh and Robert E. Lee at Gettysburg.

The plausibility that Forrest could allow himself to be diverted from broader supervision of the battlefield could be seen elsewhere in the actions of other generals as well. At Chattanooga Union general Gordon Granger merited criticism for neglecting his larger duties as a division commander to engage in artillery target practice against Confederate positions at Missionary Ridge. "Pay more attention to your corps, sir!" his superior George Thomas snapped appropriately on that occasion.[15] But there was no one in a similar position to insist that Forrest alter his behavior at Fort Pillow.

The difference in vantage points for men on the front line and officers in the rear, where Forrest had placed himself, also complicated matters for the general. In an assessment of survival in combat, sociologist Frederick J. Kviz, identifies distinctions between formal military organization and the men who desired to emerge from their experiences in battle. "This conflict has its roots in the different perspectives from which the commander and the ordinary soldier view combat," he explains. "While the commander approaches combat from a 'win/lose' aspect, the individual soldier conceives of it as a matter of personal survival, and the further the commander is removed from the combat scene the less will be his influence upon the combat soldier's behavior."[16]

Once the fighting was over, Forrest failed himself further with personality traits he could not subjugate. One of these was his desire for storytelling and exaggeration. It had always been important for him to be at the center of the story and for it to be a crackling good tale at that. Regarding Fort Pillow, exuberance was not the wisest of emotions for him to feature concerning the fates of garrison members at the hands of at least some of his troops. Rivers had run red before and would do so again with the blood of the slain in combat, but Forrest would have helped himself by not appearing to take such perverse pleasure in such a scene. More problematic for the general was his indulgence in a lifelong penchant for exaggeration in describing the operation once the fighting was over. Whether in the company of other generals or in his interactions with public citizens and figures of authority, Bedford Forrest could not help but exhibit a latent desire to establish his credentials, whether or not he actually "got there first with the most men," for instance, as he often liked to assert.

Likewise, Forrest did himself no favors with his habit of defending or explaining away his actions when he felt obliged to do so. Even in the case of victory or defeat on a given battlefield, the horseman could ride roughshod over facts that might indicate different conclusions. For instance, in a brief meeting at Cahaba, Alabama, after the fall of Selma, the general remarked to his Union opponent, James H. Wilson, that he had been the only enemy commander "I did not get away with, first or last."[17] Whether Forrest meant this in terms of Wilson being solely responsible for the Confederate defeat or in some other regard, he appears to have conveniently forgotten earlier setbacks at Dover and Parker's Crossroads in 1862 and at Harrisburg/Tupelo in 1864.

The general's educational limitations could not be used to absolve him from the words he employed in his surrender demands or his afteraction reports simply because they were not literally his own. Using clerks to craft his language did not prevent Forrest from expressing what he wanted said the way he wanted it when the occasion arose. He had taught himself enough to know the context of what anyone was writing on his behalf. Consequently, when his letter requesting a presidential pardon arrived on Andrew Johnson's desk in November 1866, Forrest felt secure in the declaration made therein concerning Fort Pillow that "all fair minded people" would join him "in complete refutation of the *exparte* proceedings of the Congressional Committee, with their manifestly leading questions, and willing witnesses whose prompted evidence should, thenceforward, mislead no one."[18]

Another characteristic that complicated matters for Forrest was his tendency for saying things as they came to him, without the subtlety and nuance that might have deflected some of the reaction they would invoke. On one occasion he chose awkward language and themes to express his gratitude for the gift of a horse. "Fellow-citizens, I'm really obliged to all of you that have had a hand in presenting me this nag," he explained. "I promise to ride him to the front, an' I wish I could take some of you along with me. Too many of you are wearing citizens clothes—black coats and boiled shirts." The cavalry commander then added, "That's what's ruin' us, an' I must say—tho I don't want to hurt nobody's feelings—that as for the men who shirk the fight and refuse to bear their honest part in it, hoss or no hoss, I've got no self-respect for 'em whatsoever.'" The crowd responded with applause, and Forrest was left with the sense that he had made a favorable impression, whether there was any underlying resentment for the tone of his remarks or not.[19]

No hostile reaction occurred based upon these inflammatory public utterances. Yet Forrest's violent confrontations with Confederate lieutenant Andrew Wills Gould at Columbia and former slave Thomas Edwards after the war demonstrate that his noncombat encounters could become deadly. Bedford Forrest was capable of killing without much hesitation, and those who failed to take that element of his personality into account did so at their peril.

Nevertheless, it is equally clear that, for a man personally credited with the combat deaths of thirty enemy soldiers, killing was not all that he was about. There was more substance to Forrest than simply dealing death to those who opposed him. He appreciated bluff as well as the application of the blade to accomplish his preferred outcome; there was also no fear of wielding the sword viciously and decisively if necessary. Still, it must be noted that had Bedford Forrest wanted the garrison of Fort Pillow truly massacred—that is, wiped out to the man, or as close to it as he could make humanly possible—he would have done so. The fact remains that he did not. He took prisoners that day, even turning wounded Federals over to the care of their own forces. The Confederate commander was content to demonstrate superiority over these opponents by defeating them, not by turning as many of them into martyrs as possible merely because he could.

Even so, the argument could be made that Forrest turned his back on what he knew was taking place, or had every reason to believe might be taking place, in order to preserve plausible deniability later. It is impossible to rule out a high level of calculation in the general's thinking. Forrest was noted for sophistication in planning. A staff officer observed that the general "was deliberate in the formation of his plans, with a rare faculty of estimating his chances." That officer also noted that "once formed, with each detail marked out clearly in his mind," Forrest "lost no time in the execution—to which he brought the terrible energy and enthusiasm of his whole soul."[20] Later in the war, Lieutenant General Richard Taylor arrived at a similar conclusion about his subordinate's abilities to ask questions, obtain answers and information, and then mold the whole into a meticulous plan of action. Although Taylor initially harbored doubts—"I began to think he had no stomach for the work"—he watched as Forrest "isolated the chances of success from the causes of failure with the care of a chemist experimenting in his laboratory" and launched himself into action.[21] But at Fort Pillow, neither Forrest nor anyone who served with him indicated that part of the established plan of battle was to let the men have free rein to do as they wished with impunity, even for a prescribed period of time or with some form of tacit approval.

It was always possible that an enraged Bedford Forrest, incensed at the mere presence of black troops arrayed against his men, could have wanted them all to perish as an example for the world to see. Yet the general could accomplish a demonstration of white superiority simply by defeating them, and he had a very practical incentive for taking any former slaves captive. The ex-slave trader adhered to his government's policy of returning runaways to masters who could lay claim to them. He might have been wiser to demonstrate that he understood how much society and the world around him had changed, but slavery was not yet a dead letter for him or the Confederate South. Such an attitude made him a product of his time and place, not of any other, when sensibilities had changed and social morays were different.

By the same token, the existence of Union soldiers from Tennessee, whom the men under Forrest, at least, seemed to think were responsible for egregious wrongs aimed at their pro-Confederate neighbors, might appear sufficient to warrant severe punishment. But once more, Forrest could obtain the same effect with a victory over these troops. Indiscriminate killing would hardly allow the general the standing he believed he held over men like Fielding Hurst and William Bradford, however much he might think they deserved a summary fate. In attempting to cultivate public and official opinion for his recriminations against his opponents' excesses, Forrest would not have wanted to undermine or neutralize the effectiveness of his arguments.

Nor did the existence of excesses on other battlefields or at other times provide Forrest or his command any justification for engaging in similar activities themselves. As historian James I. Robertson, Jr., notes, "there can be no doubt that captured, unarmed, and sometimes wounded black soldiers at Fort Pillow, Tennessee, Poison Spring, Arkansas, Petersburg, Virginia, and Saltville, Virginia, were murdered by wrathful Confederates."[22] Regardless of actual provocations or any the attackers at Fort Pillow believed to have existed, none could legitimize the deaths of prisoners or those who could no longer resist. Racial and sectional antipathy, or even battle rage, could not exonerate those who demonstrated unbridled mercilessness against defenseless opponents. Yet if Forrest could not be expected to anticipate all of the actions others took in the wake of the assault, he was, as commander of the troops involved, ultimately answerable for them.

Many factors contributed to the situation that developed on the banks of the Mississippi River in April 1864. Fort Pillow should have been abandoned as per Sherman's earlier orders but was not by an officer who benefited from retaining a garrison there despite being unable to guarantee it adequate support. Forrest lost control of the battle by remaining in the rear during the assault and then in its aftermath by focusing on the gunboat after the garrison's defeat. In that vacuum of authority, individuals sought their own opportunities for retribution on any enemy they despised. Forrest, by virtue of his own circumstances, became powerless to stop them for a time, even if he had wished to do so.

There is no doubt that when it comes to a recounting of the events at Fort Pillow in April 1864, those who have studied the engagement have had to struggle with biases in presenting evidence to support their arguments. For those who offered their positions in the years immediately following the attack, there was the almost insurmountable problem of being too close to the subject to grasp objectivity. For these examiners, it was simply too difficult to divorce themselves from the events to which, in the main, they had participated or helped shape and interpret.

When it came to the "Fort Pillow massacre," the "quietus" that John Allen Wyeth had thought would come at the end of the nineteenth century failed to occur. It remains to this day. Almost immediately, individuals on both sides staked out extreme positions as if in so doing they could silence those who would challenge and stand in contrast to them.

Along this line, author Richard Fuchs maintains, "Only the ghosts of the attacking Confederatists would hold to a different conclusion." Assailing contrary interpretations, he argues, "Again, the demons of sophistry are doing a semantic tape [sic] dance to avoid having to fault Forrest for the Fort Pillow atrocities."[23] This is the type of diatribe that would have pleased both Bedford Forrest and Ben Wade. Forrest would have appreciated the use of assault to obscure the weakness of one's own position; Wade would have applauded the vehemence of the attack. Even so, the author admits, "Concededly, much of the evidence against General Forrest is circumstantial and ex parte, as is similarly the case with rebuttal proof offered by Confederates."[24] Nevertheless, he concludes, "The evidence preponderates with acknowledgments of Forrest's misfeasance."[25]

Did Forrest's performance at Fort Pillow amount to "misfeasance" in that he, or his command, engaged in the acceptable and legally recognized activity of warfare against enemy combatants, though in an unlawful (that is, murderous) manner when they killed people incapable or unwilling to resist any longer? Did his men exhibit an uncontrolled, perhaps uncontrollable, bloodlust in the heat of combat? Did they follow the instructions of their commander, behave as they assumed he expected them to do, or act on their own in ways that he might or might not have approved personally?

The answers have remained elusive, particularly when taking differing interpretations into account. "There must have been some individual atrocities," historian Clement Eaton observes, "but Forrest should be acquitted of the charge of ordering a brutal murder of the Federal garrison without quarter."[26] Indeed, it can be said with a high degree of certainty that while Nathan Bedford Forrest did not exercise his customary control over the situation—during which, due to the chaos, heat of battle, and accompanying racial and sectional hostility, men died who should not have—he did not deliberately perpetuate a massacre, in whole or in part, at Fort Pillow.

The chaotic nature of retreat and resistance, and the disintegration that occurred as the defense broke down, blurred the distinction between a battle that had ended and one that was continuing on an ad-hoc basis. Union leadership was insufficient to the demands of the moment, including relying so heavily on the promise of aid from a gunboat that simply could not provide such assistance at the critical moment. But Forrest's inability to secure the battlefield and his troops tarnished his victory and allowed him to be labeled the "butcher of Fort Pillow." Even though this stigma remained with him for the rest of his life, Bedford Forrest endured far less than those Union men who perished unnecessarily that day.

To be sure, there are always universal rights and wrongs. But even these can have malleability over time, when what one society has tolerated in the name of national security or in defense of the homeland can be condemned in another time in history as excessive or inhumane. Fort Pillow cannot be expunged from Forrest's record. The unnecessary deaths that occurred there cannot be justified. But putting what happened in western Tennessee on April 12, 1864, into context is not the same as condoning those actions or asserting apologetic explanations or defenses for them. Bedford Forrest was not innocent of the blood shed at Fort Pillow any more than he was responsible for designing or executing a deliberate massacre there.

As usual, history is not to be explained by one simple, all-pervasive, and unanimously agreed-upon answer. In the case of this confrontation between Confederates and Federals in West Tennessee, "the dogs of war" created a "havoc" that has endured for generations and shows no signs of abating. Perhaps a contemporary observer captured the sentiment best in 1865, while the events of the conflict were still fresh in his mind: "As far as the knowledge of the Rebellion extends, so far will the affair at Fort Pillow be known."[27]

# APPENDIX A

*Organization of Confederate Troops during the West Tennessee Campaign, March–April 1864*

**Major General Nathan Bedford Forrest**

**Chalmers's Division, Brigadier General James R. Chalmers**

*First Brigade, Colonel James J. Neely*
7th Tennessee Cavalry, Colonel William L. Duckworth
12th Tennessee Cavalry, Lieutenant Colonel John U. Green
14th Tennessee Cavalry, Colonel James J. Neely
15th Tennessee Cavalry, Colonel Francis M. Stewart

*Second Brigade, Colonel Robert McCulloch*
2nd Missouri Cavalry, Lieutenant Colonel Robert A. McCulloch
Willis's Texas Cavalry Battalion, Lieutenant Colonel Leo Willis
1st Mississippi Partisans, Major J. M. Parks
5th Mississippi Cavalry, Major W. B. Peery
19th Mississippi Cavalry Battalion, Lieutenant Colonel W. L. Duff
18th Mississippi Cavalry Battalion, Lieutenant Colonel A. H. Chalmers
McDonald's Cavalry Battalion, Lieutenant Colonel James R. Crews

**Buford's Division, Brigadier General Abraham Buford**

*Third Brigade, Colonel A. P. Thompson (1,200/1,004)*
3rd Kentucky Cavalry, Lieutenant Colonel G. A. C. Holt
7th Kentucky Cavalry, Colonel Edward Crossland
8th Kentucky Cavalry, Colonel Hylon B. Lyon
12th Kentucky Cavalry, Colonel W. W. Faulkner
Jeffrey Forrest's Regiment, Lieutenant Colonel D. M. Wisdom

*Fourth Brigade, General Tyree H. Bell (1,600/1,254)*
20th Tennessee Cavalry, Colonel Robert M. Russell
21st Tennessee Cavalry, (also called the 16th Tennessee), Colonel Andrew N. Wilson
22nd Tennessee Cavalry, (also called the 2nd Tennessee), Colonel Clark R. Barteau

---

The first number in parentheses is for rank and file (including officers), the second for the effective enlisted men. Jordan and Pryor, 404. See also Tennesseans in the Civil War, 1:59, 68, 70, 80, 82, 85, 87, 89, 97, 98, 99, 102, 103–104.

# APPENDIX B

## *Federal Officers at Fort Pillow, April 12, 1864*

Major Lionel F. Booth (killed by sharpshooters during the battle)
Major William F. Bradford (killed days after the battle)
Captain Theodore F. Bradford (killed while signaling USS *New Era* after the battle)
Captain Delos Carson
Captain Charles J. Epeneter (wounded by sharpshooters during the battle)
Captain Carl D. Lamburg (absent from Fort Pillow)
Captain John L. Poston
Captain W. T. Smith (absent from Fort Pillow)
Captain J. F. Young
Lieutenant J. C. Ackerstrom
Lieutenant John C. Barr (killed by sharpshooters during the battle)
Lieutenant Peter R. Bischoff
Lieutenant William Cleary (absent from Fort Pillow)
Lieutenant John D. Hill (killed by sharpshooters during the battle)
Lieutenant A. M. Hunter
Lieutenant Mack J. Leaming (wounded after the battle)
Lieutenant Henry Lippett
Lieutenant N. D. Logan
Lieutenant P. H. McBride
Lieutenant Thomas W. McClure
Lieutenant John H. Porter (mortally wounded by sharpshooters during the battle)
Lieutenant Cord Revelle
Lieutenant F. A. Smith (absent from Fort Pillow)
Lieutenant Daniel Van Horn
Lieutenant James Wilson (killed by sharpshooters during the battle)
Surgeon Charles Fitch
Surgeon Chapman Underwood

---

List compiled from reports regarding the action at Fort Pillow, U.S. War Department, *War of the Rebellion,* 32(1):554–72.

# NOTES

### Abbreviations

| | |
|---|---|
| *CWTI* | *Civil War Times Illustrated* |
| DU | Perkins Library, Duke University, Durham, N.C. |
| FL | Filson Library, Louisville, Ky. |
| FP-NCA | Nathan Bedford Forrest Papers, Pearce Civil War Collection, Navarro College Archives, Corsicana, Tex. |
| JCCW | Joint Committee on the Conduct of the War |
| NA | National Archives, Washington, D.C. |
| OR | *The Official Records of the Union and Confederate Armies in the War of Rebellion* |
| ORN | *Official Records of the Union and Confederate Navies* |
| RJCCW | *Report of the Joint Committee on the Conduct of the War,* vol. 7 |
| SHC-UNC | Southern Historical Collection, University of North Carolina, Chapel Hill |
| *TennVet* | Dyer and Moore, *Tennessee Civil War Veterans Questionnaires* |
| TSLA | Tennessee State Library and Archives, Nashville |
| VHS | Virginia Historical Society, Richmond |

### Preface

1. Castel, "Fort Pillow Massacre," 38.
2. Steiner, *Medical-Military Portraits of Union and Confederate Generals,* 322.
3. In *A Battle from the Start,* the chapter on Fort Pillow concludes: "For a variety of reasons, Fort Pillow became a collective release of pent-up anger and hatred. It became, in clinical terms, a group catharsis. And as the overall commander of the troops on the scene, some of whom carried out these acts, Nathan Bedford Forrest was responsible" (196).
4. Ambrose, "My Lai," 191.
5. Burkhardt, *Confederate Rage, Yankee Wrath,* 245.

### Introduction

1. "Andersonville" has arguably been the single word from the American Civil War that has generated the most negative reactions in the popular mind.
2. Henry, *"First with the Most" Forrest,* 248 (emphasis in original).
3. Eaton, *History of the Southern Confederacy,* 263.
4. Burkhardt, *Confederate Rage, Yankee Wrath,* 105.
5. Ashdown and Caudill, *Myth of Nathan Bedford Forrest,* 71.
6. Ward, *River Run Red,* xv.

7. Gregory J. W. Urwin, "Introduction: Warfare, Race, and the Civil War in American Memory," in *Black Flag over Dixie*, 1–18 (quotes on 5, 6, 7, 8, 11).
8. Gregory J. W. Urwin, "'We Cannot Treat Negroes ... as Prisoners of War': Racial Atrocities and Reprisals in Civil War Arkansas," in ibid., 143.
9. Davis, "Some Themes of Counter-Subversion," 205.
10. Ambrose, "My Lai," 191.
11. Morrill, *Southern Campaigns of the American Revolution*, 77.
12. Piecuch, *Blood Be upon Your Head*, 27.
13. Ibid., 39.
14. Wilson, *Southern Strategy*, 257.
15. Piecuch, *Blood Be upon Your Head*, 9, 31.
16. Quoted in Morrill, *Southern Campaigns of the American Revolution*, 104–105.
17. Quoted in John S. Pancake, *This Destructive War: The British Campaign in the Carolinas, 1780–1782* (University: University of Alabama Press, 1985), 120.
18. Morrill, *Southern Campaigns of the American Revolution*, 110.
19. De Bruhl, *Sword of San Jacinto*, 210.
20. Mexican casualties at San Jacinto amounted to over 600 "dead and dying," with some 700 captured. Ibid., 211.
21. Haley, *Sam Houston*, 151.
22. W. H. L. Wallace to Dear George, Mar. 1, 1847, Camp Taylor, 20 miles south of Saltillo, Mexico, in Wallace, *Life and Letters*, 48.
23. Ibid., 49–50.
24. Chambers Diary, "Wednesday, March the 9th: Affair at Suffolk, Va.," Henry A. Chambers Papers, NCDHA. For the broader context of these incidents, see Wills, *War Hits Home*, 213–20.
25. Quoted in Suderow, "Suffolk Slaughter," 38–39.
26. Angus McDonald to Mother, Mar. 11, 1864, Franklin Depot, Va., Eleanor S. Brockenbrough Library, Museum of the Confederacy, Richmond, Va.
27. Quoted in Suderow, "Suffolk Slaughter," 38–39.
28. Weymouth T. Jordan, Jr., and Gerald W. Thomas, "Massacre at Plymouth: April 20, 1864," in Urwin, *Black Flag over Dixie*, 172.
29. Quoted in Wert, *Custer*, 277. See also ibid., 273–80 (for Washita) and 340–55 (for Little Big Horn).
30. Fox, *Archaeology, History, and Custer's Last Battle*, 49.
31. Gump, *Dust Rose like Smoke*, 115.
32. Pakenham, *Scramble for Africa*, 104–105.
33. Ibid., 67–68.
34. Morris, *Washing of the Spears*, 567–73.
35. Pakenham, *Scramble for Africa*, 610–15.
36. Perret, *Country Made by War*, 295. A description of the "water cure" can be found in Miller, *"Benevolent Assimilation,"* 251.
37. Quoted in Miller, *"Benevolent Assimilation,"* 188. The author chronicles numerous examples of such activity.
38. Quoted in Linn, *Philippine War*, 124.
39. Sexton, *Soldiers in the Sun*, 271. For the entire incident at Balangiga and the U.S. response, see ibid., 269–74.
40. Quoted in Keegan, *Face of Battle*, 49–50.

41. bid., 52.
42. Quoted in Ambrose, *D-Day,* 351. Perhaps the most telling popular indicator to a modern audience that all wars produce such horrific moments may be found in the Steven Spielberg motion picture *Saving Private Ryan* (1998). In the period after the slaughter on Omaha Beach, so graphically and dramatically depicted onscreen, the U.S. soldiers who had survived the ordeal sought individual ways of responding to what they had just survived. In the film these scenes include the shooting of at least one German soldier who was attempting to surrender.
43. Ambrose notes that the soldier had endured consecutive days of combat and significant sleep deprivation prior to the incident. "My Lai," 199.
44. Dower, *War without Mercy,* 66.
45. Greeley, *American Conflict,* 2:620.
46. Davis endorsement, Aug. 10, 1864, *OR,* 32(1):617.
47. Davis, *Short History,* 416–17.

## 1. Warrior in an Uncivil War

1. The standard biographies of Forrest include Henry, *"First with the Most" Forrest;* Hurst, *Nathan Bedford Forrest;* Lytle, *Bedford Forrest and His Critter Company;* Maness, *Untutored Genius;* Mathes, *General Forrest;* and Wills, *Battle from the Start.* The closest that Forrest had to an autobiography, and which certainly serves as an authorized biography, is Jordan and Pryor, *Campaigns of Lieut.-Gen. N. B. Forrest.* Of less use for historical purposes are Eckenrode, *Life of Nathan B. Forrest,* and Sheppard, *Bedford Forrest.*
2. Morton, *Artillery of Nathan Bedford Forrest's Cavalry,* 181.
3. Quoted in Imboden, "Stonewall Jackson in the Shenandoah," 297.
4. Quoted in Wyeth, *Life of General Nathan Bedford Forrest,* 569.
5. Quoted in ibid., 198.
6. Quoted in Bearss, *Forrest at Brice's Cross Roads,* 71. See also Wyeth, *Life of General Nathan Bedford Forrest,* 404.
7. For instance, Forrest used this phrase with a Union officer in 1865 as he prepared to meet James H. Wilson at Selma, Alabama. Lewis M. Hosea letter, Feb. 26, 1865, Monroe Cockrell Papers, TSLA. See also Wilson, *Southern Strategy,* 184–85.
8. Coahoma County Circuit Court, *Final Record,* Book E, Clarksdale, Miss., 355–56.
9. "General Forrest," *Cincinnati Daily Enquirer,* June 28, 1866.
10. Maury, *Recollections of a Virginian,* 206.
11. "General Forrest," *Cincinnati Daily Enquirer,* June 28, 1866.
12. Kviz, "Survival in Combat," 224.
13. Bradley, *Forrest's Escort and Staff,* 179.
14. Morton, *Artillery of Nathan Bedford Forrest's Cavalry,* 178.
15. Forrest exchanged heated words with Earl Van Dorn, Joseph Wheeler, Braxton Bragg, and Benjamin Franklin Cheatham, among others. Of lesser ranks, the cavalryman's temper fell on numerous individuals who failed to act properly or effectively in a variety of settings, ranging from severe tongue lashings to literal physical blows. See, for example, Wills, *Battle from the Start,* 102, 104, 107,

114, 145–47, 154–55, 161, 214, 259–60, 290. For the rare instance when a subordinate responded strongly to a tirade and thereby won Forrest's grudging respect, see ibid., 256–57; and Morton, *Artillery of Nathan Bedford Forrest's Cavalry*, 239–40.
16. Wills, *Battle from the Start*, 122–27. See also F. H. Smith, "Forrest-Gould Affair," 32–36; and H. H. Smith, "Reminiscences," 14–15.
17. Wyeth, *Life of General Nathan Bedford Forrest*, 226.
18. Jordan and Pryor, *Campaigns of Lieut.-Gen. N. B. Forrest*, 23–24; Wyeth, *Life of General Nathan Bedford Forrest*, 18.
19. Wills, *Battle from the Start*, 26; Probate Court, *Final Record Book*, 1845–46, Hernando, Miss., 218–19.
20. Quoted in Henry, *"First with the Most" Forrest*, 25.
21. Quoted in Bradley, *Forrest's Escort and Staff*, 179.
22. Letter quoted in Eckenrode, *Life of Nathan B. Forrest*, 169–70.
23. Jordan and Pryor, *Campaigns of Lieut.-Gen. N. B. Forrest*, 26.
24. "General Forrest," *Cincinnati Daily Enquirer*, June 28, 1866.
25. Wyeth, *Life of General Nathan Bedford Forrest*, 629.
26. Mathes, *General Forrest*, 357; Lytle, *Bedford Forrest and His Critter Company*, 20.
27. Wyeth, *Life of General Nathan Bedford Forrest*, 629.
28. See, for example, Henry, *"First with the Most" Forrest*, 26. For a fuller discussion of Forrest's prewar slave-trading experiences and persona, see Wills, *Battle from the Start*, 27, 29–37.
29. Cable, "Recollections," 224–25.
30. Wyeth, *Life of General Nathan Bedford Forrest*, 21.
31. Quoted in ibid., 629.
32. Hearn, *Occidental Gleanings*, 145, 148.
33. "A Sketch of Gen. Forrest," *Mobile Daily Advertiser and Register*, June 25, 1864.
34. Forrest's two terms as alderman ran from July 1858 to July 1860. Jordan and Pryor, *Campaigns of Lieut.-Gen. N. B. Forrest*, 33.
35. Jordan and Pryor suggest that "a heavy blow in the face" caused the weapon to discharge and kill the victim. *Campaigns of Lieut.-Gen. N. B. Forrest*, 29. William Fitzgerald drew upon local newspaper accounts to conclude that the shooting was more deliberate. "Did Nathan Bedford Forrest Really Rescue John Able?," 18.
36. Jordan and Pryor, *Campaigns of Lieut.-Gen. N. B. Forrest*, 31–33.
37. Fitzgerald effectively debunks the Forrest/Able story with firsthand accounts and offers several possible explanations, but he does not settle on any one of them. "Did Nathan Bedford Forrest Really Rescue John Able?," 16–26. Frederic Bancroft suggests that Forrest's biographers wanted to elevate their subject by perpetuating the story. *Slave-Trading in the Old South*, 259–68.
38. Maury, "Recollections of Nathan Bedford Forrest," 142–43, 144.
39. N. B. Forrest testimony, in JCCW, *Ku Klux Conspiracy*, 20, 32–35.
40. Quoted in Henry, *"First with the Most" Forrest*, 82.
41. Jordan and Pryor, *Campaigns of Lieut.-Gen. N. B. Forrest*, 40; Henry, *"First with the Most" Forrest*, 30.
42. William Richardson Hunt to J. P. Benjamin, Mar. 3, 1862, *OR*, ser. 2, 1:965.
43. Duke, *Reminiscences*, 345.

44. Forrest report, n.d., *OR*, 7:429–31.
45. Duke, *Reminiscences*, 345.
46. Wyeth, *Life of General Nathan Bedford Forrest*, 77.
47. Ashdown and Caudill, *Myth of Nathan Bedford Forrest*, 16.
48. Jordan and Pryor, *Campaigns of Lieut.-Gen. N. B. Forrest*, ix.
49. Wills, *Battle from the Start*, 75; Charles F. Bryan, "'I Mean to Have Them All': Forrest's Murfreesboro Raid," *CWTI* 12 (July 1974): 31.
50. Parkhurst report, n.d., *OR*, 16(1):805.
51. Forrest report, [?] 1862, ibid., 811.
52. Wyeth, *Life of General Nathan Bedford Forrest*, 77–78.
53. Jordan and Pryor, *Campaigns of Lieut.-Gen. N. B. Forrest*, 169–70.
54. D. S. Stanley, "Is Forrest a Butcher?—A Little Bit of History," *New York Times*, Sept. 14, 1868.
55. Tennessee Cavalry, Fourth Regiment, Folder 13, Military Units, Confederate Collection, Civil War Collection, Box 17, TSLA.
56. Richardson, *Messages and Papers of the Confederacy*, 1:337–38.
57. Wyeth, *Life of General Nathan Bedford Forrest*, 150.
58. By this point in the war, Forrest was becoming quite newsworthy. Newspaper editor George Adair, who would be an important chronicler of the 1864 West Tennessee campaign, took a special train to Rome, Georgia, to interview his friend Forrest about Streight's Raid. Andrews, *South Reports the Civil War*, 341.
59. "General Forrest," FL.
60. Quoted in Maury, *Recollections of a Virginian*, 209. See also Longacre, "All's Fair in Love and War," 40.
61. Quoted in Longacre, "All's Fair in Love and War," 40.
62. "A Sketch of Gen. Forrest," *Mobile Daily Advertiser and Register*, June 25, 1864.
63. Powell, *Failure in the Saddle*, 206. Powell maintains that Forrest would have been better served by more "effective use of his chain of command." Ibid., 206–207.
64. Ibid., 212.
65. The Confederate Congress offered Forrest a second resolution of thanks on February 17, 1864, "especially for the daring skill and perseverance exhibited in the pursuit and capture of the largely superior forces of the enemy near Rome, Georgia, in May last; for gallant conduct at Chickamauga, and for his recent brilliant services in West Tennessee." Richardson, *Messages and Papers of the Confederacy*, 1:433–34.
66. William T. Howard to Father, Oct. 6, 1862, CWTI Collection, Lionel Baxter Collection, U.S. Army Military History Institute, Carlisle Barracks, Pa.
67. "McAlister, Robert Milton," *TennVet*, 4:1408–1409.
68. "H. C. Coles," ibid., 2:538–39.
69. R. E. Corry to Dear Wife, Nov. 21, 1863, Camp near Okalona, Miss., Robert E. Corry Papers, Auburn University Papers, Auburn, Ala.
70. R. E. Corry to My dear Lizzie, Nov. 25, 1863, Camp near Okalona, Miss., ibid. Lonnie Speer describes the Alton facility as "an abandoned penitentiary" that by February 1862 was already "overcrowded." *Portals to Hell*, 67.
71. James Ramage notes that already Morgan was being compared to Revolutionary War heroes, hailed as "the [Francis] Marion of the war." *Rebel Raider*, 64–65.

72. Duke, *Reminiscences*, 345–46.
73. Compton, "Atlanta Paper, No. 8," 239.
74. Wilson, *Under the Old Flag*, 2:184.
75. Maury, *Recollections of a Virginian*, 206.
76. "From Mississippi," *Augusta [Ga.] Chronicle & Sentinel*, Apr. 13, 1864.
77. Quoted in Wyeth, *Life of General Nathan Bedford Forrest*, 134–35.

## 2. Fighting for Freedom

1. Lincoln quoted in Schuyler Hamilton to McDowell, July 16, 1861, Washington, D.C., *OR*, ser. 2, 1:760.
2. Report, July 30, 1861, in Butler, *Private and Official Correspondence*, 1:185–87. "Contraband" became a commonly used term for African Americans, particularly those who sought refuge within Union lines.
3. Foner, *Fiery Trial*, 175.
4. Frémont proclamation, Aug. 30, 1861, St. Louis, *OR*, ser. 2, 1:221–22.
5. Abraham Lincoln was uncharacteristically discourteous when he met with Jessie Frémont after she had traveled to Washington to present her husband's case in person. Lincoln biographer David Donald recounted that the president was quite terse with her. "You are quite a female politician," he asserted before explaining that the main object of the war was the Union and not slavery. *Lincoln*, 315.
6. Lincoln to John C. Frémont, Sept. 2, 1861, Washington, D.C., *Collected Works*, 4:506. See also Foner, *Fiery Trial*, 108–109.
7. Lincoln to Orville H. Browning, Sept. 22, 1861, Washington, D.C., *Collected Works*, 531–32.
8. Annual Message to Congress, Dec. 3, 1861, ibid., 5:48; Message to Congress, Mar. 6, 1862, ibid., 145.
9. Lincoln to Henry J. Raymond, Mar. 9, 1862, Washington, D.C., ibid., 153. Raymond responded to the suggestion from the president for "another article" on the subject with the assurance that he had instructed "the office to sustain the measure *without qualifications or cavil*, and I believe the paper has done so since [emphasis in original]." Raymond to Lincoln, Mar. 15, 1862, ibid.
10. McPherson, *Crossroads of Freedom*, 65.
11. General Orders No. 7, Apr. 13, 1862, Fort Pulaski, Cockspur Island, Ga., *OR*, 14:333.
12. General Orders No. 11, May 9, 1862, Hilton Head, Port Royal, S.C., ibid., 341.
13. Lincoln, "Proclamation Revoking General Hunter's Order of Military Emancipation of May 9, 1862," May 19, 1862, *Collected Works*, 5:222–23.
14. Lincoln to the Senate and House of Representatives, May 26, 1862, ibid., 240–41.
15. Lincoln, "Remarks to a Delegation of Progressive Friends," June 20, 1862, ibid., 278.
16. Huggins, *Slave and Citizen*, 81; Franklin, *Emancipation Proclamation*, 19.
17. Lincoln, Emancipation Proclamation draft, *Collected Works*, 5:336–37.
18. Lincoln to Reverdy Johnson, July 26, 1862, Washington, D.C., ibid., 343. See also McPherson, "How Lincoln Won the War with Metaphor," 98.

19. Lincoln to August Belmont, July 31, 1862, *Collected Works*, 5:350.
20. Lincoln, "Message to Congress in Special Session, July 4, 1861," ibid., 4:427.
21. "Horace Greeley and Abraham Lincoln on Emancipation, August 19 and 22, 1862," in *Great Issues of American History*, ed. Richard Hofstadter, 3 vols. (New York: Vintage, 1958), 1:406–10.
22. Lincoln to Horace Greeley, Aug. 22, 1862, Washington, D.C., *Collected Works*, 5:388. The president's response was to a published letter by Horace Greeley. See "The Prayer of Twenty Millions," *New York Tribune*, Aug. 20, 1862.
23. McPherson, *Drawn with the Sword*, 63.
24. Ibid.
25. Quoted in ibid., 77.
26. W. T. Sherman to My dear Sir, Aug. 24, 1862, Memphis, *Sherman's Civil War*, 285.
27. W. T. Sherman to John Sherman, Sept. 3, 1862, Memphis, ibid., 293.
28. Proclamation of M. Jeff Thompson, Sept. 2, 1861, Camp Hunter, *OR*, ser. 2, 1:181.
29. Speer, *War of Vengeance*, xi–xii.
30. Davis to Robert E. Lee, Aug. 1, 1862, Richmond, Va., *OR*, ser. 2, 4:835.
31. General Orders No. 48, Aug. 21, 1862, Richmond, Va., *OR*, 14:599.
32. Lincoln, "Reply to Emancipation Memorial Presented by Chicago Christians of All Denominations," Sept. 13, 1862, *Collected Works*, 5:419–25.
33. Historian James McPherson has declared Antietam as "one of the war's great turning points" for its role in laying the groundwork for the Emancipation Proclamation. *Battle Cry of Freedom*, 545. For a full treatment of the Maryland Campaign, see Sears, *Landscape turned Red*. See also McPherson, *Crossroads of Freedom*.
34. Lincoln, "Annual Message to Congress," Dec. 1, 1862, *Collected Works*, 5:529–30.
35. Frye, *September Suspense*, 193–94.
36. For an excellent treatment of these conditions, see Mountcastle, *Punitive War*.
37. Alvin M. Josephy, Jr., *The Civil War in the American West* (New York: Knopf, 1991), 135–38. The 3rd Minnesota, which had suffered a humiliation at the hands of Forrest in the previous July, heard the cry "Remember Murfreesboro" raised during the critical engagement of Wood Lake (September 23). Ibid., 135.
38. Quoted in Davis, *Lincoln's Men*, 73.
39. Historian Charles Roland sets the figures at 179,000 blacks, slave and free, in the Union army and 20,000 in the navy. *American Iliad*, 100.
40. Trudeau, "'Kill the Last Damn One of Them,'" 384.
41. General Orders No. 12, Jan. 29, 1863, New Orleans, *OR*, 15:666–67.
42. For a full examination, see McFeely, *Frederick Douglass*.
43. D. P. Crook notes in his 1974 study of Civil War diplomacy that the "traditional historical view" of the Emancipation Proclamation was as "a watershed in the international history of the Civil War" but that subsequent research "has diminished the popularity of such interpretations." *North, the South, and the Powers*, 236–37.
44. Quoted in Jones, *Abraham Lincoln*, 116. See also Jones, "History and Mythology," 45.
45. Quoted in Adams, *Great Britain and the American Civil War*, 101.
46. Smith, *Lines Are Drawn*, 74.

47. George H. Thomas letter to War Department, Nov. 18, 1863, quoted in Cleaves, *Rock of Chickamauga*, 204.
48. Lincoln, "Order of Retaliation," July 30, 1863, Washington, D.C., *Collected Works*, 6:357.
49. For treatments of these experiences and the circumstances surrounding them, see Bernstein, *New York City Draft Riots*, and Spann, *Gotham at War.*
50. Holmes, *Diary*, 283 (July 17, 1863).
51. Quoted in McPherson, *Tried by War*, 203.
52. Lincoln to General Banks, Aug. 5, 1863, Washington, D.C., *Collected Works*, 6:365.
53. Lincoln to General Grant, Aug. 9, 1863, Washington, D.C., ibid., 374.
54. Grant to Lincoln, Aug. 23, 1863, Cairo, Ill., ibid., 374–75.
55. See Thomas, *Confederate Nation*, 63–64. Thomas includes the Constitution of the Confederate States of America in an appendix. Ibid., 307–22. Chief among the protections provided for slavery are Article I, Section 9(4), which prohibited Congress from passing any law "denying or impairing the right of property in negro slaves," and Article IV, Section 2, which guaranteed the right of citizens to "transit and sojourn in any State of this Confederacy, with their slaves and other property; and the right of property in said slaves shall not be thereby impaired." Ibid., 313, 319.
56. Stephens, "Cornerstone Speech," 55.
57. S. Cooper, General Orders No. 60, Aug. 21, 1862, Richmond, Va., *OR*, ser. 2, 4:857.
58. John A. Seddon to G. T. Beauregard, Nov. 30, 1862, Richmond, Va., ibid., 954.
59. General Orders No. 111, Proclamation of Pres. Jefferson Davis, Dec. 24, 1862, ibid., 5:797.
60. Extract from President's Message, Jan. 12, 1863, ibid., 5:808.
61. Jefferson Davis, "A Proclamation to the Soldiers of the Confederate States," Aug. 1, 1863, in Richardson, *Messages and Papers of the Confederacy*, 1:329.
62. Holmes, *Diary*, 296 (Aug. 17, 1863).
63. Jones, *Rebel War Clerk's Diary*, 219.
64. Cleburne Memorial, [Jan. 2, 1864], *OR*, 52(2):589–92.
65. Craig L. Symonds, *Stonewall of the West: Patrick Cleburne and the Civil War* (Lawrence: University Press of Kansas, 1997), 194–95.
66. Davis, *Jefferson Davis*, 541.
67. William Nugent to "My darling Nellie," Aug. 15, 1863, Okolona, Miss., *My Dear Nellie: The Civil War Letters of William L. Nugent to Eleanor Smith Nugent*, ed. William M. Cash and Lucy Somerville Howorth (Jackson: University Press of Mississippi, 1977), 125.
68. William Nugent to "My own darling wife," Aug. 27, 1863, Okolona, Miss., ibid., 129.
69. Forrest to John H. Winder, Oct. 22, 1863, Dalton, Ga., *OR*, ser. 2, 6:415.

### 3. "Attending" to Fort Pillow

1. Quoted in Hurst, *Nathan Bedford Forrest*, 115–16.
2. Jordan and Pryor, *Campaigns of Lieut.-Gen. N. B. Forrest*, 247.
3. Ibid.
4. "General Forrest," FL.
5. Forrest to Jack, Mar. 21, 1864, *OR*, 32(3):664.
6. Blankinship, "Colonel Fielding Hurst and the Hurst Nation," 74.

7. Hurst, *Nathan Bedford Forrest*, 158.
8. Blankinship, "Colonel Fielding Hurst and the Hurst Nation," 81.
9. Quoted in ibid., 76.
10. Tennessee Civil War Centennial Commission, *Tennesseans in the Civil War*, 1:334.
11. Special Orders No. 264, Oct. 26, 1863, *OR*, 31(1):750–51.
12. John D. Stevenson to Hurlbut, Nov. 7, 1863, ibid., 31(3):82.
13. Hurlbut to Stevenson, Nov. 7, 1863, ibid.
14. Blankinship, "Colonel Fielding Hurst and the Hurst Nation," 81–82.
15. S. L. Woodward to Hurst, Jan. 11, 1864, *OR*, 32(2):66.
16. Ibid., 67.
17. S. L. Woodward to Hurst, Jan. 20, 1864, ibid., 156.
18. William Sooy Smith to Grant, Jan. 17, 1864, ibid., 124.
19. Forrest to Buckland, Mar. 22, 1864, ibid., 32(3):117.
20. Blankinship, "Colonel Fielding Hurst and the Hurst Nation," 83.
21. T. C. Hindman to Sherman, Sept. 23, 1862, Little Rock, *OR*, ser. 2, 4:574.
22. Sherman to S. R. Curtis, Sept. 29, 1862, Memphis, ibid., 572–73.
23. Sherman to T. C. Hindman, Sept. 28, 1862, Memphis, *Sherman's Civil War*, 308–309.
24. Ibid. Hindman had expressed regret for not teaching the Federals lessons of appropriate warfare, which prompted Sherman to chide, "The idea of your comments on the failure of your efforts to induce our army to conform to the usages of civilized warfare excites a smile; indeed you should not indulge in such language in official letters." Ibid., 308.
25. Sherman to Hindman, Oct. 17, 1862, Memphis, ibid., 316–17.
26. Forrest to Samuel Cooper, Aug. 9, 1863, *OR*, 30(4):508.
27. Bragg endorsement, Aug. 14, 1863, ibid., 509.
28. Forrest to Davis, Aug. 19, 1863, ibid., 507. The file includes the earlier Forrest correspondence and Bragg's response.
29. J. Davis endorsement, ibid., 508.
30. J. Davis, fifth endorsement, ibid.
31. For a less flattering critique, see Powell, *Failure in the Saddle*.
32. Wyeth, *Life of General Nathan Bedford Forrest*, 242.
33. Quoted in ibid., 264–66.
34. Quoted in Henry, *"First with the Most" Forrest*, 199.
35. Both Forrest and Bragg became exasperated with each other in the aftermath of Chickamauga. At one point Bragg stormed: "[L]ook at Forrest. . . . The man is ignorant, and does not know anything of cooperation. He is nothing more than a good raider." Quoted in McDonough, *Chattanooga*, 32. For his part, Forrest confronted Bragg directly with a long and pointed diatribe. Bragg agreed to the subsequent transfer after stating his reluctance to do so, but he thought it might be done now "without injury to the public interests in this quarter." Bragg to S. D. Lee, Oct. 13, 1863, *OR*, 31(3):604.
36. Forrest to Buckland, Mar. 22, 1864, *OR*, 32(3):117.
37. Reed to Strange, Mar. 21, 1864, ibid., 118–19; Forrest report, Mar. 22, 1864, ibid., 119.
38. Forrest report, Mar. 22, 1864.

39. Forrest to Jack, Mar. 21, 1864, *OR,* 32(3):664.
40. Forrest to C. A. White, Nov. 16, 1868, Memphis, FP-NCA.
41. Stokes report, Feb. 24, 1864, *OR,* 32(1):416. For a fuller account of this aspect of the war, see J. B. Jones, Jr., "Fevers Ran High."
42. Tennessee Civil War Centennial Commission, *Tennesseans in the Civil War,* 1:353–54.
43. Wm. Sooy Smith to Major Bradford, Feb. 1, 1864, Memphis, *OR,* 32(2):311.
44. Macaluso, *Fort Pillow Massacre,* 48.
45. Witherspoon, *Reminiscences,* 101.
46. Ibid., 102.
47. Special Orders No. 26, Feb. 27, 1864, Starkeville, Miss., in Leroy Moncure Nutt Papers, SHC-UNC.
48. Sherman to Thomas, Apr. 13, 1864, *RJCCW,* 32.
49. Sherman to Rawlins, Apr. 14, 1864, ibid., 31.
50. Lonnie Maness set the total of Confederates at 475. "A Ruse That Worked," 94.
51. Beatty report, Apr. 12, 1864, *OR,* 32(1):543–44; Gray report, Apr. 4, 1864, ibid., 544.
52. Witherspoon, *Reminiscences,* 103.
53. Beatty report, Apr. 12, 1864, 543–44; Gray report, Apr. 4, 1864, 544.
54. Wyeth, *Life of General Nathan Bedford Forrest,* 110–14.
55. Capt. T. P. Gray placed the first flag of truce and notice at 9:30 A.M. Lt. Robert W. Helmer stated the time as 9:00. See Gray report, Apr. 4, 1864, 544; and Helmer report, Mar. 31, 1864, *OR,* 32(1):545.
56. Wills, *Battle from the Start,* 174; Henry, *"First with the Most" Forrest,* 239; Wyeth, *Life of General Nathan Bedford Forrest,* 328.
57. Hurst, *Nathan Bedford Forrest,* 160.
58. Beatty report, Apr. 12, 1864, 543. Lieutenant Helmer noted that four captains and nine lieutenants met as a council of war to consider the Confederate demand and offer Hawkins their advice. "Out of the above number of officers," he wrote, "2 captains opposed the surrender; the lieutenants were not asked to express themselves, but were generally in favor of fighting." Helmer report, Mar. 31, 1864, 545–46.
59. Beatty report, Apr. 12, 1864, 543.
60. Forrest put the number of captured Union City Federals at 450 and horses at "about 200." Captain Beatty established the Federal prisoners at "16 officers and about 500 enlisted men." Captain Gray recorded 481 prisoners on March 26, two days after the battle. General Brayman placed the number at "probably 500," with "about 300 mounted." An undetermined number of the Tennessee bluecoats seem to have escaped their captors in the interim. Forrest report, Mar. 27, 1864, *OR,* 32(1):607; Beatty report, Apr. 12, 1864, 542–43; Gray report, Apr. 4, 1864, 545; Brayman report, Mar. 24, 1864, *OR,* 32(1):503; Helmer report, Mar. 31, 1864, 546.
61. Beatty report, Apr. 12, 1864, 543–44.
62. Brayman report, Mar. 24, 1864, 503.
63. Charles L. Lufkin, "West Tennessee Unionists in the Civil War," *Tennessee Historical Quarterly* 46 (Spring 1987): 33.

NOTES TO PAGES 77–83    231

64. The facility at Salisbury, North Carolina, surpassed Andersonville in percentage of deaths at 34 percent to Andersonville's 29 percent, although the number of deaths in the Georgia prison was far greater. McPherson, *Battle Cry of Freedom*, 797. Lonnie Spear notes 12,919 dead at Andersonville and 3,700 at Salisbury. *Portals to Hell*, 332, 338.
65. Holley, "Seventh Tennessee Volunteer Cavalry," 51.
66. Wyeth, *Life of General Nathan Bedford Forrest*, 626–27.
67. Andrews, *South Reports the Civil War*, 39.
68. *Augusta [Ga.] Chronicle & Sentinel*, Jan. 6, Feb. 19, 1864.
69. G.W.A., "From Gen. Forrest's Command," Apr. 27, 1864, Jackson, Tenn., in *Memphis Daily Appeal*, May 13, 1864. Although Colonel Adair was not immediately identified as such in the letter, he was well acquainted with Forrest from prewar years and lived in Atlanta after the war. Wyeth, *Life of General Nathan Bedford Forrest*, 18, 556–57.
70. The log books of the two gunboats differ slightly as to when news of the Confederate approach reached these vessels. The captain of the *Peosta* was ashore and returned at 3:05 P.M., "having learned that our pickets were being driven in by a force of the Rebels," while the *Paw Paw* received instructions to "drop down to the fort" at 2:15, recording the first action as taking place some thirty minutes later. Deck log of the *Peosta*, Mar. 25, 1864, RG 24, NA; deck log of the *Paw Paw*, Mar. 25, 1864, ibid.
71. Hicks report, Apr. 16, 1864, *OR*, 32(1):547. See also Huch, "Fort Pillow Massacre," 65.
72. G.W.A., "From Gen. Forrest's Command."
73. Wyeth, *Life of General Nathan Bedford Forrest*, 330.
74. J. W. Greif, "Forrest's Raid on Paducah," *Confederate Veteran* 5 (May 1897): 212.
75. Operator to Lieutenant Mason, Mar. 26, 1864, "North of the River," Paducah, *OR*, 32(1):506.
76. G.W.A., "From Gen. Forrest's Command."
77. James F. Chapman report, Mar. 29, 1864, Paducah, *OR*, 32(1):551.
78. Wyeth, *Life of General Nathan Bedford Forrest*, 330. In his veteran questionnaire, Samuel Crisp Odom simply wrote, "Main battles were Puducah Kentucky where one (1) my brothers was killed[.]" "Odom, Samuel Crisp," *TennVet*, 4:1649–50.
79. Deck log of the *Peosta*, Mar. 25, 1864, RG 24, NA.
80. Deck log of the *Paw Paw*, Mar. 25, 1864, ibid.
81. Wyeth, *Life of General Nathan Bedford Forrest*, 305.
82. Hicks report, Apr. 16, 1864, 547.
83. Ibid.
84. Deck log of the *Peosta*, Mar. 25, 1864, RG 24, NA.
85. Ibid.; deck log of the *Paw Paw*, Mar. 25, 1864, ibid.
86. Forrest report, Mar. 27, 1864, 607.
87. G.W.A., "From Gen. Forrest's Command."
88. Huch, "Fort Pillow Massacre," 68–69, 70.
89. Forrest report, Mar. 27, 1864, 607.
90. G.W.A., "From Gen. Forrest's Command."

91. "Bondurant, Benjamin T.," *TennVet*, 1:344.
92. Chalmers address, Apr. 20, 1864, *OR*, 32(1):623.
93. G.W.A., "From Gen. Forrest's Command."
94. Forrest established the Union losses in this skirmish as "six killed and fifteen or twenty wounded and three prisoners." Forrest report, Apr. 4, 1864, *OR*, 32(1):608. Adair said the action occurred on April 5, but this apparently was a typographical error in the newspaper's publication of his letter. G.W.A., "From Gen. Forrest's Command."
95. Forrest report, Apr. 4, 1864, 608–609.
96. Forrest report, Mar. 27, 1864, 607.
97. James F. Chapman report, Mar. 29, 1864, *OR*, 32(1): 551–52.
98. Forrest report, Apr. 4, 1864, 608–609.
99. "Crofford, John Alexander," *TennVet*, 2:594.
100. Huch, "Fort Pillow Massacre," 70.
101. Gorgas, *Journals*, 97.

### 4. "Will He Fight or Surrender?"

1. Sherman to McPherson, Mar. 7, 1864, *RJCCW*, 9.
2. Derek W. Frisby, "'Remember Fort Pillow!': Politics, Atrocity Propaganda, and the Evolution of Hard War," in Urwin, *Black Flag over Dixie*, 107, 116. See also Sherman to Grant, Apr. 15, 1864 (received at 2:30 P.M.), *OR*, 32(3):367.
3. Trudeau, "'Kill the Last Damn One of Them,'" 382.
4. Ibid., 387.
5. See, for example, deck log of the *New Era*, Feb. 26, 27, Mar. 16, 17, 1864, RG 24, NA. The Federals placed three prisoners in irons on March 16.
6. Ibid., Apr. 10, 1864. Regarding provisions, on April 2 the gunboat took on "corn for the Garrison at Fort Pillow." Ibid.
7. Ibid.
8. The log for the next day indicates only standard river traffic and notices of the weather. There are no statements concerning imminent enemy action. Ibid., Apr. 11, 1864.
9. Hollis, "Diary," 96.
10. Alex M. Jones to Dear wife and children, Apr. 15, 1864, Jones-Black Family Papers, University of Memphis Archives.
11. Vidette, "Letter from West Tennessee, General Forrest's Latest Campaign, April 15, 1864," *Mobile Daily Advertiser and Register*, Apr. 30, 1864.
12. Jordan and Pryor, *Campaigns of Lieut.-Gen. N. B. Forrest*, 425.
13. Wyeth, *Life of General Nathan Bedford Forrest*, 339.
14. Tyree Bell Reminiscences, DU, 45. See also Hughes, *Tyree H. Bell*, 122.
15. Vidette, "Letter from West Tennessee."
16. Capt. James Marshall testimony, in JCCW, *Fort Pillow Massacre*, 86. See also Marshall report, Apr. 15, 1864, *ORN*, ser. 1, 26:219 (all citations to series 1 unless otherwise indicated).
17. Marshall report, Apr. 15, 1864, 219.
18. Edward Benton testimony, in JCCW, *Fort Pillow Massacre*, 119.
19. Jacob Thompson testimony, in ibid., 30; James R. Brigham statement, in ibid., 108; Ward, *River Run Red*, 83–84, 159.

NOTES TO PAGES 89–96    233

20. Jones to Dear wife and children, Apr. 15, 1864.
21. Bell Reminiscences, 45. See also Hughes, *Tyree H. Bell*, 122.
22. Marshall testimony, 86.
23. Wills, *Battle from the Start*, 50–51, 59–60.
24. G.W.A., "From Gen. Forrest's Command," Apr. 27, 1864, Jackson, Tenn., in *Memphis Daily Appeal*, May 13, 1864.
25. Jones to Dear wife and children, Apr. 15, 1864.
26. Wyeth, *Life of General Nathan Bedford Forrest*, 310.
27. Revelle testimony, *OR*, 32(1):528; Gaylord testimony, ibid., 535.
28. Gaylord testimony, 535.
29. Mack J. Leaming report, Jan. 17, 1865, *OR*, 32(1):559.
30. Weaver testimony, ibid., 538.
31. Anderson, "True Story of Fort Pillow," 322.
32. Tyree Bell set Forrest's arrival much later than other accounts. "It took until about 12 o'clock to get that position," he explained. "Gen. Forrest had not yet got to us." Then he added, "About one or two o'clock that night [afternoon], Gen. Forrest got there." Wyeth noted the time at 11:00. A.M., supported by documentation he had in his possession. Adair said that Forrest "reached the battlefield … at half past nine o'clock." Jordan and Pryor explain, "It was about nine o'clock as General Forrest reached the ground." Bell Reminiscences, 45, 46; Hughes, *Tyree H. Bell*, 122; Wyeth, *Life of General Nathan Bedford Forrest*, 316; G.W.A., "From Gen. Forrest's Command"; Jordan and Pryor, *Campaigns of Lieut.-Gen. N. B. Forrest*, 429.
33. G.W.A., "From Gen. Forrest's Command."
34. Whitlow did not offer any other opinion or statement on what he had seen or experienced at Fort Pillow that day. Quoted in Cartwright, "'Better Confederates Did Not Live,'" 108.
35. Wyeth, *Life of General Nathan Bedford Forrest*, 342. See also Henry, *"First with the Most" Forrest*, 252.
36. G.W.A., "From Gen. Forrest's Command."
37. "The Rumor of the Death of Forrest," *Memphis Daily Appeal*, Apr. 20, 1864. Two days later the paper published "Forrest Still Lives," confirmed in a letter by the general's artillery chief, John Morton, to his father: "Gen. Forrest is not killed; heard from him last night." Ibid., Apr. 22, 1864. See also "Forrest's Death Contradicted," *[Atlanta, Ga.] Daily Intelligencer*, Apr. 21, 1864.
38. Marshall testimony, 86.
39. Marshall to Lt. Cmdr. S. Ledyard Phelps, addendum to report, Apr. 15, 1864, *ORN*, 26:220–21.
40. T. T. Hopkins, May 12, 1864, Camp of McCulloch's Brigade, Forrest's Cavalry, Tupelo, in *Mobile Daily Advertiser and Register*, May 18, 1864. The officer was Albion Throckmorton Ryon. Notice accompanying Hopkins letter, ibid.
41. Bell Reminiscences, 45; Hughes, *Tyree H. Bell*, 122.
42. Jordan and Pryor, *Campaigns of Lieut.-Gen. N. B. Forrest*, 427–28.
43. G.W.A., "From Gen. Forrest's Command." Jordan and Pryor note that "move up" was "Forrest's favorite phrase, in such affairs." *Campaigns of Lieut.-Gen. N. B. Forrest*, 429.
44. Wyeth, *Life of General Nathan Bedford Forrest*, 341.

45. Thomas Adison testimony, in JCCW, *Fort Pillow Massacre*, 21.
46. Leaming report, Jan. 17, 1865, *OR*, 32(1):559–60.
47. Quoted in Maury, *Recollections of a Virginian*, 206.
48. Bell Reminiscences, 46–47; Hughes, *Tyree H. Bell*, 122.
49. Marshall report, Apr. 15, 1864, 219–20.
50. Marshall testimony, 86.
51. Fort, "Journal of a Civil War 'Commando,'" 19.
52. Jones to Dear wife and children, Apr. 15, 1864.
53. Washburn enclosures, *OR*, 32(1):596.
54. Ibid.
55. Parkhurst report, n.d., *OR*, 16(1):805.
56. Jordan and Pryor, *Campaigns of Lieut.-Gen. N. B. Forrest*, 273; Wyeth, *Life of General Nathan Bedford Forrest*, 217–18.
57. N. B. Forrest to John H. Winder, Oct. 22, 1863, Dalton, Ga., *OR*, ser. 2, 6:415. Winder was himself notorious for his alleged mistreatment of Union prisoners, although his biographer Arch Frederic Blakey presents a more balanced account of an individual who sought humane treatment for the prisoners of war, black and white, under his charge. For Winder's attitude and actions toward black Union captives, see *General John H. Winder*, 43, 159, 166.
58. Chalmers, "Forrest and His Campaigns," 471.
59. "General Forrest," FL.
60. G. W. Cable to My Dear Mother, Apr. 16, 1865, Gainesville, Ala., in Cable, *Life and Letters*, 23.
61. Cable, "Recollections," 224–25.
62. A variation of this saying is found in Wyeth, *Life of General Nathan Bedford Forrest*, 374.
63. Bradley, "Lieutenant General Nathan Bedford Forrest," 16.
64. "General Forrest," FL.
65. Chalmers, "Forrest and His Campaigns," 486.
66. Anderson, "True Story of Fort Pillow," 323. A slightly different version appears in Wyeth, *Life of General Nathan Bedford Forrest*, 351 and 386.
67. Jordan and Pryor, *Campaigns of Lieut.-Gen. N. B. Forrest*, 432–33.
68. Shepley report, *OR*, 32(1):572–73.
69. Quoted in Wyeth, *Life of General Nathan Bedford Forrest*, 385.
70. Ibid., 384, 389.
71. Hubbard, *Notes of a Private*, 101–102.
72. Bell Reminiscences, 47–48.
73. Marshall testimony, 86.
74. James McCoy testimony, in JCCW, *Fort Pillow Massacre*, 48.
75. Ibid.
76. Maury, "Recollections of Nathan Bedford Forrest," 146. No official records appear to corroborate such shootings by the general in this instance.
77. Quoted in Jordan and Pryor, *Campaigns of Lieut.-Gen. N. B. Forrest*, 435.
78. Forrest report, Apr. 26, 1864, *OR*, 32(1):614.
79. Minor discrepancies exist in the phraseology employed in this exchange of notes. For instance, one version of this last note uses the pronoun "I," while Forrest's copy apparently contains the pronoun "We." Washburn enclosures,

597. See also G.W.A., "From Gen. Forrest's Command," *Memphis Daily Appeal,* May 13, 1864.
80. Jordan and Pryor note, "Jacob Gaus was the name of his [Forrest's] favorite orderly bugler." *Campaigns of Lieut.-Gen. N. B. Forrest,* 396.

## 5. "The Slaughter Was Awful"

1. Forrest report, Apr. 26, 1864, *OR,* 32(1):615.
2. Mimosa, "Forrest's Late Expedition, April 21, 1864," *Mobile Daily Advertiser and Register,* Apr. 28, 1864.
3. Accounts exist that put Forrest at the head of at least a portion of the charging Confederates, but the overwhelming evidence points to his remaining on the secondary line until the attackers had carried the main defenses. One of the accounts indicates, "Gen. Forrest led the charge of one brigade, and Gen. Chalmers the other." Vidette, "Letter from West Tennessee, General Forrest's Latest Campaign, April 15, 1864," *Mobile Daily Advertiser and Register,* Apr. 30, 1864. Capt. H. A. M. Henderson notes, "Gen. Forrest at the head of his escort, *mounted* [emphasis in original], charged into the fort, creating great terror among the garrison." "Letter from Capt. Henderson, May 5th, 1864," *Mobile Daily Advertiser and Register,* May 8, 1864.
4. Forrest report, Apr. 15, 1864, *OR,* 32(1):610.
5. Elsewhere I have speculated that the general may "have sensed what was about to happen and wished to distance himself from it." Such a motivation is among the many possibilities, however remote, for Forrest as he confronted the fort and its garrison. Another author seized on this suggestion as "curious" in support of his own thesis that Forrest carried out a massacre at Fort Pillow. Such an interpretation of my words is at least a misreading by one who clearly has an agenda in his assessment of the events on April 12, 1864. Wills, *Battle from the Start,* 185; Fuchs, *Unerring Fire,* 138.
6. G.W.A., "From Gen. Forrest's Command," Apr. 27, 1864, Jackson, Tenn., in *Memphis Daily Appeal,* May 13, 1864. Reed "was wounded by Minnie [sic] balls, which struck him almost simultaneously in the shoulder, ankle and spine," sustained as he carried the regimental colors. "Lieut-Col. Reid," *Memphis Daily Appeal,* Apr. 29, 1864. Although Reed was grievously wounded with what were thought initially to be mortal injuries, his compatriots began to believe that he might recover before the officer took a turn for the worst and succumbed just after midnight on May 1, 1864. Anderson, "Col. Wiley M. Reed," 102.
7. Jordan and Pryor, *Campaigns of Lieut.-Gen. N. B. Forrest,* 441–42.
8. Memphis, "Movements of Gen. Forrest, Details of the Capture of Fort Pillow, April 18, 1864," *Memphis Daily Appeal,* May 2, 1864.
9. Vidette, "Letter from West Tennessee."
10. Alex M. Jones to Dear wife and children, Apr. 15, 1864, Memphis, Jones-Black Family Papers, University of Memphis Archives.
11. Fox, *Archaeology, History, and Custer's Last Battle,* 49.
12. Vidette, "Letter from West Tennessee."
13. Memphis, "Movements of Gen. Forrest."
14. Marion, "Gen. Forrest's Expedition, April 20th, 1864," *Mobile Daily Advertiser and Register,* Apr. 26, 1864.

236 NOTES TO PAGES 109–20

15. Memphis,"Movements of Gen. Forrest."
16. Robinson,"Fort Pillow 'Massacre,' Observations of a Minnesotan," 188.
17. Capt. James Marshall testimony, in JCCW, *Fort Pillow Massacre*, 86.
18. Marshall report, Apr. 15, 1864, *ORN*, 26:220.
19. Marshall testimony, 86.
20. Marshall to Phelps, addendum to Marshall report, Apr. 15, 1864, *ORN*, 26:220–21.
21. Lamberg reports, Apr. 20, Apr. 27, 1864, *OR*, 32(1):566, 567.
22. Robinson,"Fort Pillow 'Massacre,' Observations of a Minnesotan," 188.
23. Clark to sisters, Apr. 14, 1864, Achilles V. Clark Letters, Confederate Collection, TSLA; Cimprich and Mainfort,"Fort Pillow Revisited," 279–99.
24. Tyree Bell Reminiscences, DU, 47–48.
25. Samuel H. Caldwell letter, Apr. 15, 1864, in Cimprich and Mainfort,"Fort Pillow Revisited," 300–301.
26. Wiley, *Johnny Reb*, 314.
27. Robertson, *Soldiers Blue and Gray*, 35.
28. Anderson,"True Story of Fort Pillow," 323.
29. Robinson, "Fort Pillow 'Massacre,' Observations of a Minnesotan," 188–89. Subsequently, the Confederates released Robinson. Ibid., 190. Years later his daughter recalled that when he spoke to her of the incident, he observed of his close encounter with death,"Why the blamed little cuss would have blown me to pieces if his ammunition hadn't given out." Transcription notes, Mrs. Peter S. Burghart to Bell I. Wiley, Dec. 5, 1949, Wiley Papers, Emory University, Atlanta, Ga.
30. Quoted in Cimprich and Mainfort,"Dr. Fitch's Report," 36–37.
31. Bell Reminiscences, 48.
32. Maury,"Recollections of Nathan Bedford Forrest," 146.
33. Cimprich and Mainfort,"Fort Pillow Massacre," 835–37.
34. Forrest reports, Apr. 15, 1864, 609, 610, 612; Apr. 26, 1864, 616.
35. Chalmers report, May 7, 1864, *OR*, 32(1):621.
36. J.W.R.,"An Interview with Gen. Forrest," *Memphis Daily Appeal*, Mar. 12, 1869.
37. Forrest report, Apr. 15, 1864, 609.
38. Ibid., 610.
39. Brands, *Lone Star Nation*, 452–55; De Bruhl, *Sword of San Jacinto*, 210.
40. Washburn to Forrest, *OR*, 32(1):603–604.
41. Quoted in Morrill, *Southern Campaigns of the American Revolution*, 94.
42. A. P. Hill report, *OR*, 19(1):982.
43. Historian Ed Bearss has used this quotation,"War to the knife and knife to the hilt," which he attributes to Bedford Forrest on numerous occasions.
44. Forrest report, Apr. 15, 1864, 610–11.
45. Forrest to Davis, Apr. 15, 1864, *OR*, 32(1):611–12. See also the letter as reproduced in Davis, *Papers*, 10:342–44. This illustrates the editorial changes made in the original that differ slightly from the version that appears in the *Official Records*, reflected in brackets in the Davis text.

### 6. "Remember Fort Pillow"

1. Alex M. Jones to Dear wife and children, Apr. 15, 1864, Memphis, Jones-Black Family Papers, University of Memphis Archives.

NOTES TO PAGES 120–29    237

2. Anderson to Ferguson, Apr. 13, 1864, *OR*, 32(1):599.
3. Ferguson report, Apr. 14, 1864, ibid., 571; Ferguson report, Apr. 14, 1864, *ORN*, 26:231.
4. Ferguson report, Apr. 13, 1864, *ORN*, 26:234.
5. Attachment to communication of Charles W. Anderson, Apr. 13, 1864, ibid., 224.
6. Tyree Bell Reminiscences, DU, 48.
7. Washburn to Forrest, June 19, 1864, *OR*, 32(1):589; McLagan statement, n.d., ibid., 557; McLagan testimony, 101–103.
8. Forrest to Washburn, June 23, 1864, *OR*, 32(1):592.
9. Macaluso, *Fort Pillow Massacre*, 46. The author notes that white prisoners from Fort Pillow wound up at Andersonville Prison in Georgia, "where more than half died during their captivity." He explains that the black prisoners ended up in Mobile, Alabama, where they worked on the city's defenses." Ibid., 34.
10. Wyeth, *Life of General Nathan Bedford Forrest*, 631.
11. Anderson, "Gen. Forrest among Civilians," 106.
12. Lawrence report, Apr. 13, 1864, *OR*, 32(1):553.
13. Hicks report, Apr. 20, 1864, ibid., 549–50.
14. Compiled Service Report, "From April 21st to 29th," 7th Tennessee Cavalry, RG 393, NA.
15. "Rebel Account, Claim of G. M. Baber, Filed June 13, 1868," Miscellaneous Documents, 1847–1911, Ms. 9032, Alderman Library, University of Virginia, Charlottesville.
16. Fielding Hurst to Andrew Johnson, Apr. 29, 1864, Headquarters 6th Tenn. Cavalry, Memphis, Andrew Johnson Papers, Box 1, Folder 4, 1864, TSLA (emphasis in original).
17. *Miner and Workman's Advocate [London]*, Apr. 30, 1864.
18. *Memphis Daily Appeal*, May 2, 1864.
19. Ashdown and Caudill, *Myth of Nathan Bedford Forrest*, 81.
20. "The Black Flag," *New York Times*, Apr. 16, 1864.
21. For example, see "From Washington," ibid., Apr. 18, 1864; "The Massacre at Fort Pillow," ibid., Apr. 20, 1864; and "The Massacre at Fort Pillow," ibid., Apr. 22, 1864.
22. "Shocking from the Mississippi," *New York Tribune*, Apr. 16, 1864.
23. "The Fort Pillow Massacre," *Army and Navy Journal*, Apr. 23, 1864.
24. "The Butcher Forrest and His Family," *Chicago Tribune*, May 4, 1864.
25. "A Parallel," *Knoxville Whig and Rebel Ventilator*, May 14, 1864.
26. "Additional from the North," *Mobile Advertiser and Register*, May 6, 1864.
27. "Losses in Chalmers' Division," ibid., May 11, 1864.
28. John M. Porter Diary, Apr. 16, 1864, FL.
29. Cheairs to My Dear Sister, May 1, 1864, Prison No. 2, Camp Chase, Ohio, *I'll Sing If I Can*, 101.
30. Ibid., 6–7.
31. Ibid., 101. The editor of the Cheairs letters mentions censorship at Camp Chase. See ibid., iii.
32. Forrest to S. D. Lee, May 16, 1864, *ORN*, 26:234–35.
33. Young to Forrest, May 19, 1864, ibid., 235.
34. "Massacre at Fort Pillow," Apr. 20, 1864.

35. Fuchs, *Unerring Fire*, 82.
36. Speer, *Portals to Hell*, 255–59. Ironically, the Confederates attempted to close Cahaba and transfer the prisoners to Andersonville but had to reconsider when the Georgia prison camp became woefully overcrowded. Ibid., 257. See also Bryant, *Cahaba Prison and the Sultana Disaster.* Bryant notes that Cahaba "remained a collecting station for men en route to Andersonville." Ibid., 1.
37. For Sherman's activities in this period and the incorporation of Fort Pillow in the larger strategic equations, see Castel, *Decision in the West*, 90–99.
38. Sherman to Rawlins, Apr. 14, 1864, *RJCCW,* 31. See also *OR,* 32(3):351.
39. Sherman to McPherson, Mar. 7, 1864, *RJCCW,* 9.
40. Sherman to Stanton, June 15, 1864—6:30 P.M., *OR,* 39(2):121.
41. Brayman to Sherman, Apr. 14, 1864, *OR,* 32(3):361.
42. Sherman to Brayman, Apr. 14, 1864, ibid., 362. Sherman began his Meridian Campaign on February 5 and withdrew from the area on February 20 after wrecking the Mississippi rail junction. William Sooy Smith was supposed to have joined in the operation, but his defeat by Forrest at Okolona on February 22 prevented this.
43. Sherman to Grant, Apr. 15, 1864 (received at 2:30 P.M.), ibid., 367.
44. Sherman to McPherson, Apr. 15, 1864, ibid., 373.
45. Sherman to Grant, Apr. 15, 1864 (received at 2:30 P.M.), 367.
46. Grant to Sherman, Apr. 15, 1864, 8:00 P.M., *OR,* 32(3):366.
47. Sherman to Grant, Apr. 16, 1864, 10:30 A.M., ibid., 382.
48. Sherman to John Sherman, Apr. 22, 1864, Nashville, quoted in Stanley P. Hirshson, *The White Tecumseh: A Biography of General William T. Sherman* (New York: J. Wiley, 1997), 188.
49. Sherman to Rawlins, Apr. 19, 1864, *OR,* 32(3):411.
50. Sherman to Washburn, Apr. 21, 1864, ibid., 441.
51. Sherman to Washburn, Apr. 24, 1864, ibid., 485.
52. Sherman to Washburn, Apr. 28, 1864, ibid., 527.
53. Georgia governor Joseph Brown engaged in a biting exchange with President Davis over such issues but failed to convince the Confederate chief executive of the efficacy of his views. In June he asked Davis, "Could not Forrest ... do more now for our cause in Sherman's rear than anywhere else?" The president was unmoved. "Most men in your position," he rejoined, "would not assume to decide on the value of the service to be rendered by troops in distant positions." Brown to Davis, June 28, 1864, *OR,* 52(2):680–81; Davis to Brown, June 29, 1864, ibid., 681. See also Brown to Davis, July 5, 1864, *OR,* 39(2):688; Davis to Brown, July 5, 1864, ibid.; and Brown to Davis, July 7, 1864, *OR,* 52(2):687. Steven Woodworth notes the failure of the "Confederate departmental system," calling Forrest's retention in Mississippi "sheer folly for the Confederacy, for whom Mississippi had become a backwater and Georgia the scene of life-and-death struggle." *Davis and His Generals,* 278. This point echoes the conclusions reached in Connelly and Jones, *Politics of Command,* 166–67.
54. Henry, *"First with the Most" Forrest,* 282–83.
55. "Brantley, Solomon Norman," *TennVet,* 1:375.

56. Agnew, "Battle of Tishomingo Creek," 402.
57. Witherspoon, *Reminiscences*, 123–25.
58. D. C. Jones to Bettie, June 13, 1864, in Jones, "Memoirs and Letters," 12.
59. "Brantley, Solomon Norman," *TennVet*, 1:375. Brantley made the point that these soldiers discarded their uniforms and successfully escaped to Memphis.
60. Recent historians have assessed the psychological value stories of Fort Pillow offered to the public in the North. George Burkhardt observes: "Neither Forrest nor his men knew that Fort Pillow would become a cause célèbre, a bitter controversy reverberating for many years after their attack. Assuredly, they never dreamed that it would create a great propaganda coup for the North or a benchmark for Civil War atrocities, light the fuse for a private war, or provide a chilling battle cry." *Confederate Rage, Yankee Wrath*, 105.

## 7. An Election Year Gets "Massacred"

1. Davis report, May 8, 1863, *OR*, 18:273.
2. Marvel, *Great Task Remaining*, 325.
3. "First Debate with Stephen A. Douglas at Ottawa, Ill., Aug. 21, 1858," in Lincoln, *Collected Works*, 3:27.
4. Lincoln, "Address at Sanitary Fair, Baltimore, Md.," Apr. 18, 1864, ibid., 7:302–303.
5. Urwin, "Introduction: Warfare, Race, and the Civil War in American Memory," in *Black Flag over Dixie*, 13.
6. Trefousse, *Benjamin Franklin Wade*, 214.
7. JCCW, *Fort Pillow Massacre*, 1.
8. The Joint Committee on the Conduct of the War consisted of five Republicans and two Democrats in both the Thirty-Seventh and Thirty-Eighth Congresses. Benjamin Wade served as chairman. Andrew Johnson began his service as the only member from a state that had seceded but was replaced in 1862, when he became military governor of Tennessee. Despite its role in critiquing the military leaders and operations of the United States, committee members held only limited direct experience of the military. For a full treatment of this committee, see Tap, *Over Lincoln's Shoulder*.
9. Trefousse, *Benjamin Franklin Wade*.
10. H. Williams, "Benjamin Wade and Atrocity Propaganda," 34.
11. Ibid., 40.
12. Dale Baum, "Gooch, Daniel Wheelwright," in Hubbell and Geary, *Biographical Dictionary of the Union*, 202–203.
13. Tap, *Over Lincoln's Shoulder*, 28–29, 32.
14. Edwin M. Stanton, Apr. 18, 1864, *OR*, ser. 2, 7:64.
15. Ibid., 64–65.
16. Frisby, "'Remember Fort Pillow!'" in Urwin, *Black Flag over Dixie*, 125.
17. Tap, *Over Lincoln's Shoulder*, 193.
18. JCCW, *Fort Pillow Massacre*, 1–2.
19. Ibid., 4–5.
20. Elias Falls testimony, ibid., 15.
21. George Shaw testimony, ibid., 25–26.
22. Isaac J. Leadbetter testimony, ibid., 35.

23. Jacob Thompson testimony, ibid., 30, 31.
24. Fuchs, *Unerring Fire*, 105.
25. Major Williams testimony, in JCCW, *Fort Pillow Massacre*, 27.
26. Daniel Tyler testimony, ibid., 18. *Harper's Weekly* popularized Tyler's story in May in a piece entitled "Buried Alive." See Ashdown and Caudill, *Myth of Nathan Bedford Forrest*, 126–27.
27. "Statement of Ordnance and Ordnance Stores taken up by Col. C. R. Barteau, Comdg. 2nd Regt. Tenn. Cavalry on the 12th day of April 1864, on the Battlefield at Fort Pillow, Tenn.," Compiled Service Reports, 2nd Tennessee Cavalry, RG 393, NA.
28. Duke, *Reminiscences*, 350.
29. Kinsley, *Diary of a Christian Soldier*, 146.
30. Thayer, *Youth's History of the Rebellion*, 3:287, 293. See also ibid., 295–96, 297, 298, 300.
31. Tyler testimony, 19.
32. John Haskins testimony, in JCCW, *Fort Pillow Massacre*, 20.
33. Eli Carlton testimony, ibid., 29.
34. Lt. William Clary testimony, ibid., 53. Clary observed that he had learned about Akerstrom's fate from "Mrs. Ruffin, the wife of Thomas Ruffin." The committee took statements from several civilians, including two women, but either Mrs. Ruffin was unavailable or unwilling to testify. See Mrs. Rosa Johnson testimony and Mrs. Rebecca Williams testimony, ibid., 75–76.
35. Leadbetter testimony, 35; Lt. Mc. J. Leming [sic] testimony, in JCCW, *Fort Pillow Massacre*, 40–41; John W. Shelton testimony, ibid., 50.
36. Shelton testimony, 50.
37. James McCoy testimony, in JCCW, *Fort Pillow Massacre*, 48.
38. Moore, "Fort Pillow, Forrest, and the United States Colored Troops," 114–15.
39. John F. Ray testimony, in JCCW, *Fort Pillow Massacre*, 50–51.
40. Fuchs, *Unerring Fire*, 104–105.
41. Stanton to Wade, May 4, 1864, in "Returned Prisoners" report in JCCW, *Fort Pillow Massacre*, 4.
42. Knowles testimony, ibid., 28.
43. Welles, *Diary*, 2:23.
44. Nicolay and Hay, *Abraham Lincoln*, 6:481–83. For Stanton's recommendations to the president, see Stanton to Lincoln, May 5, 1864, *OR*, ser. 2, 7:113–14. For an examination of the issue of hostages during the war, see Garrison, *Civil War Hostages*.
45. Brooks Simpson counters the view of Grant as "a bloodthirsty butcher" in *Ulysses S. Grant*, 463–64.
46. Nicolay and Hay, *Abraham Lincoln*, 6:483–84. Modern historians have concurred in the general conclusion that no follow-up occurred on these delicate matters. James McPherson notes, "The Lincoln administration never did execute a Confederate soldier or place any of them at hard labor." *Tried by War*, 205.
47. Lincoln to Edwin M. Stanton, May 17, 1864, Washington, D.C., *Collected Works*, 7:345–46.
48. Lincoln, "Address at Sanitary Fair," 302.

49. Quoted in McPherson, *Tried by War,* 204.
50. Burkhardt, *Confederate Rage, Yankee Wrath,* 118.

## 8. Reaction to Fort Pillow

1. Wills, *Battle from the Start.*
2. Quoted in Mitchell, *Civil War Soldiers,* 193.
3. Garidel, *Exile in Richmond,* 119.
4. Browder, *Heavens Are Weeping,* 176.
5. House, *A Very Violent Rebel,* 130.
6. Cochran Diary, May 1, 1864, FL.
7. "The News," *Abingdon Virginian,* Apr. 29, 1864.
8. Your husband to Dear wife, Apr. 17, 1864, Ringgold, Ga., in Connolly, *Three Years in the Army of the Cumberland,* 191–92.
9. William H. Nugen to Sister Mary, Apr. 20, 1864, William H. Nugen Papers, DU.
10. Kinsley, *Diary of a Christian Soldier,* 146.
11. Hubert Saunders to Dear Mother, Apr. 19, 1864, Hubert Saunders Papers, DU.
12. Document, Apr. 21, 1864, Memphis, Channing Richards Papers, FL.
13. Robert Winn to Dear Sister, Apr. 24, 1864, Camp near Ringgold, Catoosa Co., Ga., Winn-Cook Family Papers, FL.
14. *The Massacre at Fort Pillow, Harper's Weekly,* Apr. 30, 1864.
15. *Massacre of the Federal Troops after the Capture of Fort Pillow, April 12th, 1864, Frank Leslie's Illustrated Newspaper,* May 7, 1864.
16. Lyman to Dear Parents and Brother, May 1, 1864, camp near Rossville, Ga., Lyman S. Widney Letters, Kennesaw Mountain National Battlefield Park, Kennesaw, Ga.
17. Mitchell, *Civil War Soldiers,* 193.
18. Quoted in Glatthaar, *Forged in Battle,* 157 (emphasis in original).
19. Musser, *Soldier Boy,* 127 (emphasis in original).
20. Woodcock, *A Southern Boy in Blue,* 286.
21. Fisk, *Hard Marching Every Day,* 231.
22. Ibid., 157–58.
23. "Northern Retaliation," *Memphis Daily Appeal,* May 5, 1864.
24. "Future Character of the War," ibid.
25. Quoted in Wyeth, *Life of General Nathan Bedford Forrest,* 390.
26. Forrest to Washburn, June 23, 1864, *OR,* 32(1):590.
27. Ibid., 591, 593.
28. Ibid.
29. Goodwin report, *OR,* 32(1):619.
30. Quoted in Rhea, *To the North Anna River,* 184. Union losses were high for the fighting, at approximately 1,500 men. Ibid., 188.
31. Butler report, May 25, 1864, 11:00 A.M., *OR,* 36(2):269–70.
32. Quoted in Rhea, *To the North Anna River,* 366.
33. Butler report, May 25, 1864, 7:30 A.M., *OR,* 36(2):269.
34. Quoted in Rhea, *To the North Anna River,* 366.
35. Wild report, May 25, 1864, Wilson's Wharf, Va., *OR,* 36(2):270.
36. Rhea, *To the North Anna River,* 366.
37. Wild report, May 25, 1864, 271.

38. Ibid.
39. Rhea, *To the North Anna River,* 366.
40. Recent treatments of the Crater include Axelrod, *Horrid Pit;* Cavanaugh and Marvel, *Battle of the Crater;* Hess, *Into the Crater;* and Slotkin, *No Quarter.*
41. Quoted in Hess, *Into the Crater,* 128.
42. Ibid., 155–56, 164 (quote).
43. Phillips, "Wilcox's Alabamians in Virginia," 490.
44. Axelrod, *Horrid Pit,* 177.
45. Quoted in Suderow, "Battle of the Crater," 222.
46. Milton Barrett to Dear Brother and Sister, Aug. 1, 1864, Camp on the south side of the James River, Va., in Heller and Heller, *Confederacy Is on Her Way up the Spout,* 123.
47. Slotkin, *No Quarter,* 292.
48. Hess, *Into the Crater,* 192–93.
49. Quoted in Carmichael, *Lee's Young Artillerist,* 130–31.
50. Alexander, *Fighting for the Confederacy,* 462.
51. Lee to Grant, Oct. 1, 1864, *OR,* ser. 2, 7:906–907; Grant to Lee, Oct. 2, 1864, ibid., 909.
52. Lee to Grant, Oct. 3, 1864, ibid., 914.
53. Grant to Lee, Oct. 3, 1864, ibid.
54. Seddon to Lee, Oct. 15, 1864, Richmond, Va., ibid., 991.
55. Quoted in Butler to Ould, Oct. 12, 1864, In the Field, ibid., 970.
56. Seddon to Lee, Oct. 15, 1864, 991.
57. See enclosures, Butler to Ould, Oct. 12, 1864, 967–69.
58. Seddon to Lee, Oct. 15, 1864, 991.
59. Lee to Grant, Oct. 19, 1864, *OR,* ser. 2, 7:1010–11.
60. Lee communication in Breckinridge to J. C. Vaughn, Oct. 19, 1864, Wytheville, Va., *OR,* 39(3):830.
61. Davis, "Massacre at Saltville," 4–11, 43–48. According to Burkhardt, "Saltville became the war's last large-scale slaughter of black soldiers, not for lack of will or rage, but because the proper conditions never obtained again." *Confederate Rage, Yankee Wrath,* 201.
62. For a full treatment of Ferguson, see McKnight, *Confederate Outlaw.*
63. Davis speculates that the "general officer" in question was most likely to be Felix Huston Robertson. "Massacre at Saltville," 47.
64. Butler to Hitchcock, Aug. 18, 1864, "In the Field," [Va.], *OR,* ser. 2, 7:606.
65. Grant to Butler, Aug. 18, 1864, City Point, Va., ibid., 606–607.
66. Utley, *Frontiersmen in Blue,* 295.
67. Quoted in Long, *Civil War Day by Day,* 602.
68. "Massacre of Cheyenne Indians," *RJCCW.* Bruce Tap mentions the Chivington investigation briefly but notes that the committee's actions kept the matter in the public sphere and had a deleterious effect on the officer's political aspirations. *Over Lincoln's Shoulder,* 232.
69. Quoted in Andrews, *South Reports the Civil War,* 474.
70. Letter, Jan. 17, 1865, Hd. Qrs. 10th S.C. Regt., Tupelo, Miss., in Walker, *Great Things,* 164.
71. Letter, Dec. 14, 1864, Hd. Qrs. 10th S.C. Regt., in front of Nashville, Tenn., in ibid., 150.

72. Quoted in Thomas, *Lee*, 347.
73. J. H. Wilson to William D. Whipple, Feb. 14, 1865, Gravelly Springs, Ala., *OR*, 49(1):710.
74. Henry, *"First with the Most" Forrest*, 423.
75. Wyeth, *Life of General Nathan Bedford Forrest*, 607.
76. Jordan and Pryor, *Campaigns of Lieut.-Gen. N. B. Forrest*, 676–77. Jordan and Pryor argue that the Union troops had been engaged in plundering local civilians.
77. Lt. George Cowan quoted in Henry, *"First with the Most" Forrest*, 433. Wyeth adds the affirmation, "and any statements to this effect are wholly untrue." *Life of General Nathan Bedford Forrest*, 609.
78. Francis Salter report, n.d., *OR*, 49(1):406.
79. Quoted in J. P. Jones, *Yankee Blitzkrieg*, 97.
80. Piatt and Boynton, *General George H. Thomas*, 614.
81. Wilson, *Under the Old Flag*, 2:240.
82. Wiley, *Civil War Diary of a Common Soldier*, 150. See also Canby report, June 1, 1865, *OR*, 49(1):98; and statement on Union casualties, ibid., 102. Of the total losses attributed to the fighting at Fort Blakeley, the USCT units suffered 31 killed and 285 wounded. Ibid.
83. Hawkins report, Apr. 16, 1865, *OR*, 49(1):287. For an account that employs similar language to explain the capture of 22 officers and 208 men, see Hawkins to J. F. Lacey, Apr. 9, 1865, *OR*, 49(2):306. The white units reported the remainder of the 3,700 officers and men who became prisoners of war on April 9. See Canby report, June 1, 1865, 98; Veatch report, Apr. 18, 1865, *OR*, 49(1):157; Andrews report, Apr. 10, 1865, ibid., 201–202; and Gerrard report, Apr. 11, 1865, ibid., 247.
84. Quoted in Glatthaar, *Forged in Battle*, 158.
85. John H. B. Payne letter, May 24, 1864, quoted in Redkey, *Grand Army of Black Men*, 210.
86. Cable, "Recollections," 244[?].
87. Quoted in Henry, *"First with the Most" Forrest*, 438.
88. Sherman to Grant, Apr. 25, 1865, *OR*, 47(3):303.
89. Sherman, *Home Letters*, 346.
90. Thomas to Hatch, May 2, 1865, George H. Thomas Papers, DU.
91. Quoted in Jordan, *"Happiness Is Not My Companion,"* 242. On Warren's relief from duty with the Army of the Potomac, see ibid., 232–34.

### 9. "Forrest of Fort Pillow"

1. Quoted in Henry, *"First with the Most" Forrest*, 439.
2. *Macon [Ga.] Daily Telegraph*, Feb. 9, 1866.
3. W. R. Hackley to wife, May 28, 1865, "Letters," 104.
4. Quoted in Maury, *Recollections of a Virginian*, 222–23.
5. *Friar's Point (Miss.) Coahomian*, Nov. 10, 1865.
6. Chase, *Papers*, 1:575.
7. J. F. Newsom to Meredith, May 10, 1865, *OR*, 49(2):712.
8. Fielding Hurst to His Excellency W. G. Brownlow, June 25, 1865, Memphis, William G. Brownlow Papers, TSLA.

244   NOTES TO PAGES 186–91

9. Hurst to Brownlow, June 27, 1865, Memphis, ibid.
10. Ibid.
11. Fielding Hurst also struggled with postwar realities, and although he obtained an appointment as a judge, he became financially and physically broken. Bedford Forrest's wartime nemesis, Hurst outlived the Confederate by some five years, dying on April 3, 1882. Blakinship, "Colonel Fielding Hurst and the Hurst Nation," 85–86.
12. George Corliss to Lt. Stuart Eldridge, Apr. 9, 1866, Bureau of Refugees, Freedmen, and Abandoned Lands, NA, roll 13.
13. N. B. Forrest testimony, in JCCW, *Ku Klux Conspiracy*, 24.
14. Edwards made this statement to the plantation's white carpenter, who testified to it before investigating officers of the Freedmen's Bureau. Statement of Lewis G. Jones, in Corliss to Eldridge, Apr. 9, 1866.
15. Statement of N. B. Forrest, ibid. Statements by Sarah Edwards, Thomas's wife, and Hannah Powell, who lived in the cabin with the couple, conflicted with regard to the alleged abuse but generally corroborated Forrest's statement about the initial interactions between the men. They were less clear as to the nature of the violent confrontation that followed. Statements of Mrs. Sarah Jane Edwards and Hannah Powell, ibid.
16. In the first instance, Forrest was supposed to have issued commands that the laborers, many of whom were former Union soldiers, felt obliged to obey. With the bravado that had made him famous, he ordered peremptorily, "Now men, get out of this yard or I will shoot the heads off every one of you." Mathes, *General Forrest*, 359–60. A second version feature a standoff between a heavily armed Forrest and angry freedmen blocking his escape. Forrest only gave way when the sheriff appeared and identified himself. He then allegedly declared, "It's alright, you've got me. Come in," turning himself over to the deputy's authority. Sherard interview, July 22, 1936, Carnegie Public Library, Clarksdale, Miss., 15–17.
17. Sherard interview, July 22, 1936, 15–17.
18. Coahoma County Circuit Court, *Final Record*, Book E, Clarksdale, Miss., 453–55.
19. Monroe Cockrell Papers, TSLA.
20. Forrest to Walter, Aug. 14, 1866, Harvey W. Walter Papers, SHC-UNC.
21. Forrest to Maj. W. Brent, Sept. 13, 1866, Memphis, FP-NCA.
22. Forrest to Johnson, Nov. 25, 1866, Memphis, Nathan Bedford Forrest Papers, DU.
23. Quoted in Burkhardt, *Confederate Rage, Yankee Wrath*, 245.
24. N. B. Forrest, Oct. 3, 1867, Memphis, Tenn., in Jordan and Pryor, *Campaigns of Lieut.-Gen. N. B. Forrest*, viii.
25. Ibid., 424.
26. Ibid., 426.
27. Ibid., 433 (emphasis in original).
28. Ibid., 438–40.
29. Ibid., 453. The "Commentaries" run on pages 445–53.
30. Forrest to C. A. White, Nov. 16, 1868, Memphis, FP-NCA.
31. Quoted in Davison and Foxx, *Nathan Bedford Forrest*, 442.

32. "The Massacre of Fort Pillow," *White Cloud Kansas Chief,* Aug. 20, 1868.
33. D. S. Stanley, "Is Forrest a Butcher?—A Little Bit of History," *New York Times,* Sept. 14, 1868.
34. "Fort Pillow Forrest's Independent Challenge to Gen. Kilpatrick," ibid., Nov. 3, 1868.
35. Forrest to C. A. White, Nov. 16, 1868.
36. Duke, *Reminiscences,* 351–54.
37. Ibid.
38. Samuel Martin's portrait of Judson Kilpatrick is scathing, with strong indictments of his subject's arrogance, untruthfulness, womanizing, and rampant corruption. Martin, "*Kill-Cavalry,*" 33, 37, 62, 67, 128–29, 131, 199, 201, 204, 208, 211, 217–18, 221–22, 226, 230–31, 233, 236, 238–39, 241–42, 247–48, 252.
39. Welles, *Diary,* 3:437.
40. Thompson, *Image of War,* 90.
41. *Leaders of the Democratic Party, Harper's Weekly,* ca. 1868.
42. *This Is a White Man's Government, Harper's Weekly,* Sept. 5, 1868. The business figure is meant to portray August Belmont, the financier and organizer who remained active in the Democratic Party through the Civil War. Frank R. Levstik, "Belmont, August," in Hubbell and Geary, *Biographical Dictionary of the Union,* 34.
43. *The Modern Sampson, Harper's Weekly,* Oct. 3, 1868.
44. Thompson, *Image of War,* 176–78. See also Hess and Northrup, *Drawn & Quartered.*
45. J.W.R., "An Interview with Gen. Forrest," *Memphis Daily Appeal,* Mar. 12, 1869.
46. Quoted in *New York Times,* Dec. 9, 1873. For an assessment of this incident, see Bradford, *The* Virginius *Affair.*
47. Quoted in Davison and Foxx, *Nathan Bedford Forrest,* 476.
48. Quoted in Henry, *"First with the Most" Forrest,* 459–60.
49. Note of Minor Meriwether, Forrest to Meriwether, May 26, 1875, Meriwether Family Papers, University of Memphis Archives.
50. Carney, "Contested Image," 603–607.
51. "In the Light of Conciliation," *New York Times,* Oct. 31, 1877.
52. Quoted in Jordan and Thomas, "Massacre at Plymouth," in Urwin, *Black Flag over Dixie,* 174.
53. Fitch, "Capture of Fort Pillow," 40–41.
54. "Chalmers," in *Biographical Dictionary of Congress,* 803.
55. Letter, "Chalmers Sends Greeting to Butler," Nov. 9, 1882, *National Republican,* Nov. 17, 1882. Many white Southerners reviled Butler for his wartime actions toward women in New Orleans, his heavy-handed approach toward Confederate sympathizers, and his outspoken defense of African American rights.
56. Sophie Sparkle, "Chat with Chalmers," *Pittsburg Dispatch,* Aug. 31, 1889.
57. *Short History of Gen. N. B. Forrest,* Alderman Library, University of Virginia, Charlottesville, 14.
58. The prints are all reproduced in *Battles of the Civil War, 1861–1865,* with text by various authors and presented in the chronological order of the battles themselves. The pages are unnumbered.

59. John Cussons to My dear Miss Rowland, June 30, 1899, Glen Allen, Va., VHS.
60. Bennett H. Young to My Dear Miss Rowland, June 30, 1899, Louisville, VHS.
61. H. W. Wilson to Dear Madam, May 17, 1899, London, England, VHS.
62. J. A. Robertson to Dear Madam, July 10, 1899, New York City, VHS.
63. John A. Wyeth to Dear Madam, July 22, 1899, Carlsbad, Austria, VHS.
64. "Heat in the Senate," *Richmond Dispatch,* Apr. 30, 1902.
65. "General MacArthur Takes All the Responsibility for the Capture of Aguinaldo," *San Francisco Call,* Apr. 30, 1902.
66. Quoted in Hattaway, *General Stephen D. Lee,* 222–23.
67. "Forrest Monument Unveiled amid Cheering Thousands," *Memphis News-Scimitar,* May 16, 1905.
68. James Dinkins, *1861 to 1865, by an Old Johnnie: Personal Recollections and Experiences in the Confederate Army* (Cincinnati: R. Clarke, 1897), 265–67. When a servant protected the horse, which had rushed at and kicked at the soldiers, one of the men observed to Forrest, "General, I can now account for your success; your negroes fight for you and your horses fight for you." Ibid., 267.
69. Niehaus also wanted to keep other memorials and monuments out of the park so as not to overshadow or otherwise diminish his work. Carney, "Contested Image," 614–15. See also Ashdown and Caudill, *Myth of Nathan Bedford Forrest,* 178–79.

## Epilogue

1. Chalmers, "Forrest and His Campaigns," 454.
2. Shakespeare, *Tragedy of Julius Caesar,* 102.
3. Quoted in C. Ward, *War of the Revolution,* 744.
4. Wilson, *Southern Strategy,* 259. Wilson extends culpability for British excesses to Lord Cornwallis for failing to restrain or punish Tarleton for "the atrocities that Tarleton's men committed." Ibid.
5. Piecuch, *Blood Be upon Your Head,* 27.
6. Ibid., 39.
7. De Bruhl, *Sword of San Jacinto,* 210.
8. Thompson, "With Burnside at Antietam," 662.
9. Dean, *Shook over Hell,* 58–59.
10. Brayman to Edwin M. Stanton, Apr. 28, 1864, *OR,* 32(1):519.
11. See, for example, G. Jones, *Honor in the Dust.*
12. Dower, *War without Mercy,* 61–71.
13. Quoted in Atkinson, *Guns at Last Light,* 526. Atkinson notes excesses among combatants on both sides toward those who had ceased to resist. See ibid., 95–96, 167, 424–25, 525–27, 581–82.
14. Quoted in ibid., 335.
15. Quoted in Wills, *As True as Steel,* 230.
16. Kviz, "Survival in Combat," 229.
17. Wilson, *Under the Old Flag,* 2:241–43; Longacre, *From Union Stars to Top Hat,* 209–10. Forrest held Joseph Wheeler and Stephen D. Lee responsible for the defeats at Dover and Harrisburg/Tupelo, respectively.
18. Forrest to Johnson, Nov. 25, 1865, Memphis, Nathan Bedford Forrest Papers, DU.

19. "General Forrest," FL.
20. "A Sketch of Gen. Forrest," *Daily Dispatch,* June 15, 1864.
21. Taylor, *Destruction and Reconstruction,* 242–43.
22. Robertson, *Soldiers Blue and Gray,* 35.
23. Fuchs, *Unerring Fire,* 9–10.
24. Ibid., 138.
25. Ibid., 139.
26. Eaton, *History of the Southern Confederacy,* 264.
27. Thayer, *Youth's History of the Rebellion,* 3:304.

# BIBLIOGRAPHY

### Primary Sources
#### Manuscripts
Alderman Library, University of Virginia, Charlottesville
    "Rebel Account, Claim of G. M. Baber, Filed June 13, 1868," Miscellaneous Documents, 1847–1911. Ms. 9032.
    *A Short History of Gen. N. B. Forrest.* Park Place, N.Y.: Knapp, 1888. Produced for W. Duke Sons & Company, Durham, North Carolina.
Auburn University Papers, Auburn, Alabama
    Robert E. Corry Papers.
Coahoma County Court, Clarksdale, Mississippi
    *Final Record,* Book E.
Eleanor S. Brockenbrough Library, Museum of the Confederacy, Richmond, Virginia
    Angus McDonald Letter.
Filson Library, Louisville, Kentucky
    Mary Catherine Noland Cochran Diary.
    "General Forrest," newspaper clipping.
    John M. Porter Diary.
    Channing Richards Papers.
    Winn-Cook Family Papers.
Kennesaw Mountain National Battlefield Park, Kennesaw, Georgia
    Lyman S. Widney Letters.
National Archives, Washington, D.C.
    General Orders and Circulars, Bureau of Refugees, Freedmen, and Abandoned Lands.
        USS *New Era* Deck Log, RG 24.
        USS *Paw Paw* Deck Log, RG 24.
        USS *Peosta* Deck Log, RG 24.
Navarro College Archives, Corsicana, Texas
    Nathan Bedford Forrest Papers. Pearce Civil War Collection.
North Carolina Department of History and Archives, Raleigh
    Henry A. Chambers Papers.
Robert W. Woodruff Library, Emory University, Atlanta, Georgia
    Bell I Wiley Papers.
Southern Historical Collection, University of North Carolina, Chapel Hill
    Jason Niles Diary.
    Leroy Moncure Nutt Papers.
    Harvey W. Walter Papers.
Tennessee State Library and Archives, Nashville
    William G. Brownlow Papers.
    Achilles V. Clark Letters. Confederate Collection.

Nathan Bedford Forrest—Monroe Cockrell Papers.
Andrew Johnson Papers.
Tennessee Cavalry, Fourth Regiment, Folder 13, Military Units. Confederate Collection, Civil War Collection, Box 17.
University of Memphis Archives, Memphis, Tennessee
Jones-Black Family Papers.
Meriwether Family Papers.
Virginia Historical Society, Richmond
Nathan Bedford Forrest Papers.
William R. Perkins Library, Duke University, Durham, North Carolina
Tyree Bell Reminiscences.
Nathan Bedford Forrest Papers.
William H. Nugen Papers.
Hubert Saunders Papers.
George H. Thomas Papers.

## Government Publications

*Biographical Dictionary of the United States Congress, 1774–2005.* Washington, D.C.: Government Printing Office, 2005.
U.S. Congress. Joint Committee on the Conduct of the War. *Fort Pillow Massacre.* 38th Cong., 1st sess., 1864. H. Rep. 65.
———. *Ku Klux Conspiracy: Report of the Joint Select Committee to Inquire into the Condition of Affairs in the Late Insurrectionary States.* 42nd Cong., 2nd sess., 1872. S. Rep. 41, vol. 13.
———. *Reports of the Joint Committee on the Conduct of the War.* Volume 7. Wilmington, N.C.: Broadfoot, 2002.
U.S. Department of the Army. *The Medal of Honor of the United States Army.* Washington, D.C.: Government Printing Office, 1948.
U.S. Department of the Navy. *Official Records of the Union and Confederate Navies in the War of the Rebellion.* 30 vols. Washington, D.C.: Government Printing Office, 1894–1922.
U.S. War Department. *Atlas to Accompany the Official Records of the Union and Confederate Armies.* 2 vols. Washington, D.C.: Government Printing Office, 1891–95.
———. *The War of the Rebellion: A Compilation of the Official Records of the Union and Confederate Armies.* 70 vols. in 127 parts and index. Washington, D.C.: Government Printing Office, 1880–95.

## Newspapers

*Army and Navy Journal [New York].*
*[Atlanta, Ga.] Daily Intelligencer.*
*Augusta [Ga.] Chronicle & Sentinel.*
*Brownlow's Knoxville Whig and Rebel Ventilator.*
*Charleston Mercury.*
*Frank Leslie's Illustrated Newspaper.*
*Friar's Point [Miss.] Coahomian.*
*Harper's Weekly.*

*Macon [Ga.] Daily Telegraph.*
*Memphis Daily Appeal.*
*Memphis News-Scimitar.*
*Miner and Workman's Advocate [London].*
*Mobile Daily Advertiser and Register.*
*National Republican [Washington, D.C.].*
*New York Times.*
*New York Tribune.*
*Pittsburg Dispatch.*
*Richmond Daily Dispatch.*
*Richmond Daily Enquirer.*
*Richmond Daily Examiner.*
*Richmond Dispatch.*
*Richmond Sentinel.*
*Richmond Whig.*
*San Francisco Call.*
*White Cloud Kansas Chief.*

## Books

Alexander, Edward Porter. *Fighting for the Confederacy: The Personal Recollections of General Edward Porter Alexander.* Edited by Gary W. Gallagher. Chapel Hill: University of North Carolina Press, 1989.

*Battles of the Civil War, 1861–1865: A Pictorial Presentation, the Complete Kurz & Allison Prints.* Little Rock, Ark.: Pioneer—Civil War Publications, 1960.

Berlin, Ira, Joseph P. Reidy, and Leslie S. Rowland, eds. *Freedom: A Documentary History of Emancipation, 1861–1867.* Series 2. Cambridge: Cambridge University Press, 1982.

Browder, George Richard. *The Heavens Are Weeping: The Diaries of George Richard Browder, 1852–1886.* Edited by Richard L. Troutman. Grand Rapids, Mich.: Zondervan, 1987.

Butler, Benjamin. *Private and Official Correspondence of General Benjamin F. Butler during the Period of the Civil War.* Edited by Jessie A. Marshall. 5 vols. Norwood, Mass., 1917.

Cable, Lucy Leffingwell Bikle. *George W. Cable: His Life and Letters.* New York: Russell and Russell, 1967.

Chase, Salmon P. *The Salmon P. Chase Papers.* Edited by John Niven. 5 vols. Kent, Ohio: Kent State University Press, 1993.

Cheairs, Nathaniel F. *I'll Sing if I Can: The Life and Prison Letters of Major N. F. Cheairs, C.S.A.* Edited by Nathaniel Cheairs Hughes, Jr. Signal Mountain, Tenn.: Mountain, 1998.

Chestnut, Mary Boykin. *Mary Chestnut's Civil War.* Edited by C. Vann Woodward. New Haven, Conn.: Yale University Press, 1981.

Connolly, James A. *Three Years in the Army of the Cumberland: The Letters and Diary of Major James A. Connolly.* Edited by Paul M. Angle. Bloomington: Indiana University Press, 1959.

Davis, Jefferson. *The Papers of Jefferson Davis.* Edited by Lynda Lasswell Crist. Baton Rouge: Louisiana State University Press, 1999,

———. *A Short History of the Confederate States of America.* New York: Belford, 1890.

Duke, Basil W. *Reminiscences of General Basil W. Duke, C.S.A.* Garden City, N.Y.: Doubleday, Page, 1911.

Duncan, Thomas D. *Recollections of Thomas D. Duncan: A Confederate Soldier.* Nashville, Tenn.: McQuiddy, 1922.

Dyer, Gustavus W., and John Trotwood Moore, comps. *Tennessee Civil War Veterans Questionnaires.* 5 vols. Easley, S.C.: Southern Historical Press, 1985.

Edmonston, Catherine Ann Devereux. *"Journal of a Secesh Lady": The Diary of Catherine Ann Devereux Edmonston, 1869–1866.* Edited by Beth G. Crabtree and James W. Patton. Raleigh, N.C.: Division of Archives and History, 1979.

Fisk, Wilbur. *Hard Marching Every Day: The Civil War Letters of Private Wilbur Fisk, 1861–1865.* Edited by Emil and Ruth Rosenblatt. Lawrence: University Press of Kansas, 1992.

Garidel, Henri. *Exile in Richmond: The Confederate Journal of Henri Garidel.* Edited by Michael Bedout Chesson and Leslie Jean Roberts. Charlottesville: University Press of Virginia, 2001.

Gorgas, Josiah. *The Journals of Josiah Gorgas, 1857–1878.* Edited by Sarah Woolfork Williams. Foreword by Frank E. Vandiver. Tuscaloosa: University of Alabama Press, 1995.

Greeley, Horace. *The American Conflict: A History of the Great Rebellion in the United States of America, 1860–'65.* 2 vols. Hartford, Conn.: Case, 1867.

Hearn, Lafcadio. *Occidental Gleanings.* New York: Dodd, Mead, 1925.

Heller, J. Roderick, III, and Carolyn Ayres Heller, eds. *The Confederacy Is on Her Way up the Spout: Letters to South Carolina, 1861–1864.* Athens: University of Georgia Press, 1992.

Holmes, Emma. *The Diary of Miss Emma Holmes, 1861–1866.* Edited by John F. Marszalek. Baton Rouge: Louisiana State University Press, 1994.

Hood, John Bell. *Advance and Retreat: Personal Experiences in the United States and Confederate States Armies.* Philadelphia: Press of Burk and M'Fetridge, 1880.

House, Ellen Renshaw. *A Very Violent Rebel: The Civil War Diary of Ellen Renshaw House.* Edited by Daniel E. Sutherland. Knoxville: University of Tennessee Press, 1996.

Hubbard, John Milton. *Notes of a Private.* St. Louis: Nixon-Jones, 1911.

Johnston, Joseph E. *Narrative of Military Operations, Directed, during the Late War between the States, by Joseph E. Johnston.* New York: D. Appleton, 1874.

Jones, John Beauchamp. *A Rebel War Clerk's Diary at the Confederate States Capital.* Edited by Earl Schenck Miers. New York: A. S. Barnes, 1961.

Kean, Robert Garlick Hill. *Inside the Confederate Government: The Diary of Robert Garlick Hill Kean.* Edited by Edward Younger. New York: Oxford University Press, 1957.

Kinsley, Rufus. *Diary of a Christian Soldier: Rufus Kinsley and the Civil War.* Edited by David C. Rankin. Cambridge: Cambridge University Press, 2004.

Lee, Robert E. *Recollections and Letters of General Robert E. Lee.* Garden City, N.Y.: Garden City Publishing, 1926.

Lincoln, Abraham. *The Collected Works of Abraham Lincoln.* Edited by Roy P. Basler. 9 vols. New Brunswick, N.J.: Rutgers University Press, 1953.

Maury, Dabney Herndon. *Recollections of a Virginian in the Mexican, Indian, and Civil Wars.* New York: Charles Scribner's Sons, 1894.

Moore, Frank, ed. *The Rebellion Record: A Diary of American Events, with Documents, Narratives, Illustrative Incidents, Poetry, etc.* New York: D. Van Nostrand, 1867.

Morton, John Watson. *The Artillery of Nathan Bedford Forrest's Cavalry.* Nashville, Tenn.: Publishing House of the M.E. Church South, 1905.

Musser, Charles O. *Soldier Boy: The Civil War Letters of Charles O. Musser, 29th Iowa.* Edited by Barry Popchock. Iowa City: University of Iowa Press, 1995.

Nugent, William L. *My Dear Nellie: The Civil War Letters of William L. Nugent to Eleanor Smith Nugent.* Edited by William M. Cash and Lucy Somerville Howorth. Jackson: University Press of Mississippi, 1977.

Redkey, Edwin S., ed. *A Grand Army of Black Men: Letters from African-American Soldiers in the Union Army, 1861–1865.* New York: Cambridge University Press, 1992.

Richardson, James D., comp. *A Compilation of the Messages and Papers of the Confederacy, including the Diplomatic Correspondence, 1861–1865.* 2 vols. Nashville, Tenn.: U.S. Publishing, 1906.

Shakespeare, William. *The Tragedy of Julius Caesar.* Edited by Lawrence Mason. New Haven, Conn.: Yale University Library, 1919.

Sherman, William T. *Home Letters of General Sherman.* Edited by M. A. DeWolfe Howe. New York: Charles Scribner's Sons, 1909.

———. *Memoirs of General William T. Sherman.* New York: Charles L. Webster, 1892.

———. *Sherman's Civil War: Selected Correspondence of William T. Sherman, 1860–1865.* Edited by Brooks D. Simpson and Jean V. Berlin. Chapel Hill: University of North Carolina Press, 1999.

Taylor, Richard. *Destruction and Reconstruction: Personal Experiences of the Late War.* New York: D. Appleton, 1879.

Walker, C. Irvine. *Great Things Are Expected of Us: The Letters of Colonel C. Irvine Walker, 10th South Carolina Infantry, C.S.A.* Edited by William Lee White and Charles Denny Runion. Knoxville: University of Tennessee Press, 2009.

Wallace, Isabel. *Life and Letters of General W. H. L. Wallace.* Chicago, R. R. Donnelley, 1909.

Welles, Gideon. *Diary of Gideon Welles, Secretary of the Navy under Lincoln and Johnson.* 3 vols. Boston: Houghton-Mifflin, 1911.

Wiley, William. *The Civil War Diary of a Common Soldier: William Wiley of the 77th Illinois Infantry.* Edited by Terrence J. Winschel. Baton Rouge: Louisiana State University Press, 2001.

Wilson, James Harrison. *Under the Old Flag: Recollections of Military Operations in the War for the Union, the Spanish War, the Boxer Rebellion, etc.* 2 vols. New York: D. Appleton, 1912.

Witherspoon, William. *Reminiscences of a Scout, Spy, and Soldier of Forrest's Cavalry.* Jackson, Tenn.: McCowat-Mercer, 1910. In *As They Saw Forrest: Some Recollections and Comments of Contemporaries.* Edited by Robert Selph Henry, 66–136. Wilmington, N.C.: Broadfoot, 1987.

Woodcock, Marcus. *A Southern Boy in Blue: The Memoir of Marcus Woodcock, 9th Kentucky Infantry (U.S.A.).* Edited by Kenneth W. Noe. Knoxville: University of Tennessee Press, 1996.

## Articles

Agnew, Samuel A. "Battle of Tishomingo Creek." *Confederate Veteran* 8 (1900): 401–403.
Anderson, Charles W. "Col. Wiley M. Reed." *Confederate Veteran* 5 (March 1897): 101–102.
———. "Gen. Forrest among Civilians." *Confederate Veteran* 5 (April 1897): 106.
———. "The True Story of Fort Pillow." *Confederate Veteran* 3 (November 1895): 322-326.
Cable, George W. "George W. Cable's Recollections of General Forrest." Edited by Arlin Turner. *Journal of Southern History* 21 (May 1955): 224–28.
Chalmers, James R. "Forrest and His Campaigns." In "Meeting at the White Sulphur Springs." *Southern Historical Society Papers* 7 (October 1879): 449–86.
Clark, Achilles V. "A Letter of Account." Edited by Dan E. Pomeroy. *Civil War Times Illustrated* 24, no. 4 (June 1985): 24–25.
Compton, James. "Atlanta Paper, No. 8, the Second Division of the 16th Army Corps, in the Atlanta Campaign." In *The Atlanta Papers,* edited by Stanley C. Kerksis, 235–57. Dayton, Ohio: Morningside, 1980.
Fitch, C. "Capture of Fort Pillow—Vindication of General Chalmers by a Federal Officer." *Southern Historical Society Papers* 7 (1879): 439–41.
Fort, DeWitt Clinton. "The Journal of a Civil War 'Commando,' DeWitt Clinton Fort." Edited by Lois D. Bejach. *West Tennessee Historical Society Papers* 2 (1948): 5–32.
Hackley, William Beverley Randolph. "The Letters of William Beverley Randolph Hackley: Treasury Agent in West Tennessee, 1863–1866." Edited by Walter J. Fraser, Jr., and Mrs. Pat C. Clark. *West Tennessee Historical Society Papers* 25 (1971): 90–107.
Hollis, Elisha Tompkin. "The Diary of Captain Elisha Tompkin Hollis." Edited by William W. Chester. *West Tennessee Historical Society Papers* 39 (December 1985): 82–118.
Imboden, John D. "Stonewall Jackson in the Shenandoah." In *Battles and Leaders of the Civil War,* edited by Robert U. Johnson and Clarence C. Buel, 2:282–98. Reprint, New York: Thomas Yoseloff, 1956.
Jones, Daniel Curd. "The Memoirs and Letters of D. C. Jones, 2nd Lieutenant, Rice's Battery." *Confederate Chronicles of Tennessee* 4 (1994): 1–37.
Kelly, D. C. "General Nathan Bedford Forrest." *Methodist Review* 49 (March–April 1900): 220–35.
Maury, Dabney H. "Recollections of Nathan Bedford Forrest." In *Battles and Leaders of the Civil War, Volume 5,* edited by Peter Cozzens, 139–52. Urbana: University of Illinois Press, 2002.
Phillips, B. F. "Wilcox's Alabamians in Virginia." *Confederate Veteran* 15 (November 1907): 490.
Robinson, Charles. "Fort Pillow 'Massacre,' Observations of a Minnesotan." Edited by George Bodnia. *Minnesota History* 43 (Spring 1973): 186–90.
Smith, Frank H. "The Forrest-Gould Affair." *Civil War Times Illustrated* 9 (November 1970): 32–37.
Smith, Henry H. "Reminiscences of Capt. Henry H. Smith." *Confederate Veteran* 8 (January 1900): 14–15.

Stephens, Alexander H. "Cornerstone Speech." In *America's War: Talking about the Civil War and Emancipation on Their 150th Anniversaries,* edited by Edward L. Ayers, 51–57. Washington, D.C.: American Library Association and the National Endowment for the Humanities, 2012.

Suderow, Bruce. "The Suffolk Slaughter: 'We Did Not Take Any Prisoners.'" *Civil War Times Illustrated* 23, no. 3 (May 1984): 37–39.

Thompson, David L. "With Burnside at Antietam." In *Battles and Leaders of the Civil War,* edited by Robert U. Johnson and Clarence C. Buel, 2:660–62. Reprint, New York: Thomas Yoseloff, 1956.

Tullos, Thomas R. "When Capt. Sam Freeman Was Killed." *Confederate Veteran* 21 (August 1913): 407.

## Secondary Sources

### Books

Adams, E. D. *Great Britain and the American Civil War.* New York: Russell and Russell, n.d.

Ambrose, Stephen E. *D-Day, June 6, 1944: The Climate Battle of World War II.* New York: Simon and Schuster, 1994.

Andrews, J. Cutler. *The South Reports the Civil War.* Princeton, N.J.: Princeton University Press, 1970.

Ash, Stephen V. *When the Yankees Came: Conflict & Chaos in the Occupied South, 1861–1865.* Chapel Hill: University of North Carolina Press, 1995.

Ashdown, Paul, and Edward Caudill. *The Myth of Nathan Bedford Forrest.* Lanham, Md.: Rowman and Littlefield, 2005.

Atkinson, Rick. *The Guns at Last Light: The War in Western Europe, 1944–1945.* New York: Henry Holt, 2013.

Axelrod, Alan. *The Horrid Pit: The Battle of the Crater, the Civil War's Cruelest Mission.* New York: Carroll and Graf, 2007.

Bancroft, Frederic. *Slave-Trading in the Old South.* Baltimore: J. H. Furst, 1931.

Baum, Dale. *The Civil War Party System: The Case of Massachusetts, 1848–1876.* Chapel Hill: University of North Carolina Press, 1984.

Bearss, Edwin C. *Forrest at Brice's Cross Roads and in North Mississippi in 1864.* Dayton, Ohio: Morningside, 1979.

Bernstein, Iver. *The New York City Draft Riots: Their Significance for American Society and Politics in the Age of the Civil War.* New York: Oxford University Press, 1990.

Black, Robert C., III. *The Railroads of the Confederacy.* Chapel Hill: University of North Carolina Press, 1952.

Blakey, Arch Frderic. *General John H. Winder, C.S.A.* Gainesville: University Press of Florida, 1990.

Bradford, Richard H. *The* Virginius *Affair.* Boulder: Colorado Associated University Press, 1980.

Bradley, Michael R. *Nathan Bedford Forrest's Escort and Staff.* Gretna, La.: Pelican, 2006.

Brands, H. W. *Lone Star Nation: How a Ragged Army of Volunteers Won the Battle for Texas Independence—and Changed America.* New York: Doubleday, 2004.

Bruce, Dickson D., Jr. *Violence and Culture in the Antebellum South.* Austin: University of Texas Press, 1979.
Burkhardt, George S. *Confederate Rage, Yankee Wrath: No Quarter in the Civil War.* Carbondale: Southern Illinois University Press, 2007.
Carmichael, Peter. *Lee's Young Artillerist: William R. J. Pegram.* Charlottesville: University Press of Virginia, 1995.
Carter, Dan T. *When the War Was Over: The Failure of Self-Reconstruction in the South, 1865–1867.* Baton Rouge: Louisiana State University Press, 1985.
Castel, Albert. *Decision in the West: The Atlanta Campaign of 1864.* Lawrence: University Press of Kansas, 1992.
Cavanaugh, Michael A., and William Marvel. *The Battle of the Crater: "The Horrid Pit," June 25–August 6, 1864.* Lynchburg, Va.: H. E. Howard, 1989.
Cleaves, Freeman. *Rock of Chickamauga: The Life of George H. Thomas.* Norman: University of Oklahoma Press, 1948.
Connelly, Thomas L. *Autumn of Glory: The Army of Tennessee, 1862–1865.* Baton Rouge: Louisiana State University Press, 1967.
Connelly, Thomas L., and Archer Jones. *The Politics of Command: Factions and Ideas in Confederate Strategy.* Baton Rouge: Louisiana State University Press, 1973.
Cornish, Dudley Taylor. *The Sable Arm: Negro Troops in the Union Army, 1861–1865.* New York: W. W. Norton, 1956.
Crook, D. P. *The North, the South, and the Powers, 1861–1865.* New York: John Wiley and Sons, 1974.
Cullum, George W. *Biographical Register of the Officers and Graduates of the U.S. Military Academy at West Point, N.Y., from Its Establishment, in 1802 and 1890, with the Early History of the United States Military Academy.* 2 vols. Boston: Houghton Mifflin, 1891.
Davis, William C. *Jefferson Davis: The Man and His Hour.* New York: HarperCollins, 1991.
———. *Lincoln's Men: How President Lincoln became Father to an Army and a Nation.* New York: Free Press, 1999.
Davison, Eddy W., and Daniel Foxx. *Nathan Bedford Forrest: In Search of the Enigma.* Gretna, La.: Pelican, 2007.
Dean, Eric T., Jr. *Shook over Hell: Post-Traumatic Stress, Vietnam, and the Civil War.* Cambridge, Mass.: Harvard University Press, 1997.
De Bruhl, Marshall. *The Sword of San Jacinto: A Life of Sam Houston.* New York: Random House, 1993.
Denny, Robert E. *Civil War Prisons & Escapes: A Day-by-Day Chronicle.* New York: Sterling, 1993.
Donald, David Herbert. *Lincoln.* New York: Simon and Schuster, 1995.
Dower, John W. *War without Mercy: Race and Power in the Pacific War.* New York: Pantheon Books, 1986.
Eaton, Clement. *A History of the Southern Confederacy.* New York: Free Press, 1954.
Eckenrode, H. J. *Life of Nathan B. Forrest.* Richmond, Va.: B. F. Johnson, 1918.
Foner, Eric. *The Fiery Trial: Abraham Lincoln and American Slavery.* New York: W. W. Norton, 2010.
———. *Free Soil, Free Labor, Free Men: The Ideology of the Republican Party Before the Civil War.* New York: Oxford University Press, 1970.

———. *Nothing but Freedom: Emancipation and Its Legacy.* Baton Rouge: Louisiana State University Press, 1983.

———. *Reconstruction: America's Unfinished Revolution, 1863–1877.* New York: Harper and Row, 1988.

Fox, Richard Allan, Jr. *Archaeology, History, and Custer's Last Battle: The Little Big Horn Reexamined.* Norman: University of Oklahoma Press, 1993.

Franklin, John Hope. *The Emancipation Proclamation.* Garden City, N.Y.: Doubleday, 1963.

Freeman, Douglas Southall. *R. E. Lee: A Biography.* 4 vols. New York: Charles Scribner's Sons, 1934–35.

Frye, Dennis E. *September Suspense: Lincoln's Union in Peril.* Harpers Ferry, W.V.: Antietam Rest Publishing, 2012.

Fuchs, Richard L. *An Unerring Fire: The Massacre at Fort Pillow.* Mechanicsburg, Pa.: Stackpole, 2002.

Garrison, Webb. *Civil War Hostages: Hostage Taking in the Civil War.* Shippensburg, Pa: White Mane, 2000.

Gauss, John. *Black Flag! Black Flag!: The Battle at Fort Pillow.* Lanham, Md.: University Press of America, 2003.

Glatthaar, Joseph T. *Forged in Battle: The Civil War Alliance of Black Soldiers and White Officers.* New York: Free Press, 1971.

Grimsley, Mark. *The Hard Hand of War: Union Military Policy toward Southern Civilians, 1861–1865.* Cambridge: Cambridge University Press, 1995.

Gump, James O. *The Dust Rose like Smoke: The Subjugation of the Zulu and the Sioux.* Lincoln: University of Nebraska Press, 1994.

Haley, James L. *Sam Houston.* Norman: University of Oklahoma Press, 2002.

Hattaway, Herman. *General Stephen D. Lee.* Jackson: University Press of Mississippi, 1976.

Henry, Robert Selph. *"First with the Most" Forrest.* Indianapolis: Bobbs-Merrill, 1944.

Hess, Earl J. *Into the Crater: The Mine Attack at Petersburg.* Columbia: University of South Carolina Press, 2010.

Hess, Stephen, and Sandy Northrup. *Drawn & Quartered: The History of the American Political Cartoon.* Montgomery, Ala.: Elliott and Clark, 1996.

Huggins, Nathan Irvin. *Slave and Citizen: The Life of Frederick Douglass.* New York: Little, Brown, 1980.

Hughes, Nathaniel Cheairs, Jr., with Connie Walton Moretti and James Michael Browne. *Brigadier General Tyree H. Bell, C.S.A.: Forrest's Fighting Lieutenant.* Knoxville: University of Tennessee Press, 2004.

Hurst, Jack. *Nathan Bedford Forrest.* New York: Alfred A. Knopf, 1993.

Jones, Gregg. *Honor in the Dust: Theodore Roosevelt, War in the Philippines, and the Rise and Fall of America's Imperial Dream.* New York: New American Library, 2012.

Jones, Howard. *Abraham Lincoln and a New Birth of Freedom: The Union and Slavery in the Diplomacy of the Civil War.* Lincoln: University of Nebraska Press, 1999.

Jones, James Pickett. *Yankee Blitzkrieg: Wilson's Raid through Alabama and Georgia.* Athens: University of Georgia Press, 1976.

Jordan, David M. *"Happiness Is Not My Companion": The Life of General G. K. Warren.* Bloomington: Indiana University Press, 2001.

Jordan, Ervin L., Jr. *Black Confederates and Afro-Yankees in Civil War Virginia.* Charlottesville: University Press of Virginia, 1995.

Jordan, Thomas, and J. P. Pryor. *The Campaigns of Lieut.-Gen. N. B. Forrest, and of Forrest's Cavalry.* New Orleans: Blelock, 1868.

Keegan, John. *The Face of Battle.* New York: Viking, 1976.

Lash, Jeffrey N. *A Politician turned General: The Civil War Career of Stephen Augustus Hurlbut.* Kent, Ohio: Kent State University Press, 2003.

Linn, Brian McAllister. *The Philippine War, 1899–1902.* Lawrence: University Press of Kansas, 2000.

Long, E. B. *The Civil War Day by Day: An Almanac, 1861–1865.* Garden City, N.Y.: Doubleday, 1971.

Longacre, Edward. *From Union Stars to Top Hat: A Biography of the Extraordinary General James Harrison Wilson.* Harrisburg, Pa.: Stackpole, 1972.

Lytle, Andrew Nelson. *Bedford Forrest and His Critter Company.* New York: G. P. Putnam's Sons, 1931.

Macaluso, Gregory J. *The Fort Pillow Massacre: The Reason Why.* New York: Vantage, 1989.

Maness, Lonnie. *An Untutored Genius: The Military Career of General Nathan Bedford Forrest.* Oxford, Miss.: Guild Bindery, 1990.

Martin, Samuel J. *"Kill-Cavalry," Sherman's Merchant of Terror: The Life of Union General Hugh Judson Kilpatrick.* Madison, Wis.: Fairleigh Dickinson University Press, 1996.

Marvel, William. *The Great Task Remaining: The Third Year of Lincoln's War.* Boston: Houghton Mifflin Harcourt, 2010.

Mathes, J. Harvey. *General Forrest.* New York: D. Appleton, 1902.

McDonough, James Lee. *Chattanooga: A Death Grip on the Confederacy.* Knoxville: University of Tennessee Press, 1984.

McFeely, William S. *Frederick Douglass.* New York: Norton, 1991.

———. *Yankee Stepfather: General O. O. Howard and the Freedmen.* New Haven, Conn.: Yale University Press, 1968.

McKnight, Brian D. *Confederate Outlaw: Champ Ferguson and the Civil War in Appalachia.* Baton Rouge: Louisiana State University Press, 2011.

McPherson, James M. *Battle Cry of Freedom: The Civil War Era.* New York: Oxford University Press, 1988.

———. *Crossroads of Freedom: Antietam.* New York: Oxford University Press, 2002.

———. *Drawn with the Sword: Reflections on the American Civil War.* New York: Oxford University Press, 1996.

———. *For Cause and Comrades: Why Men Fought in the Civil War.* New York: Oxford University Press, 1997.

———. *The Negro's Civil War: How American Negroes Felt and Acted during the War for the Union.* New York: Pantheon, 1965.

———. *Tried by War: Abraham Lincoln as Commander in Chief.* New York: Penguin, 2008.

Miller, Stuart Creighton. *"Benevolent Assimilation": The American Conquest of the Philippines, 1899–1903.* New Haven, Conn.: Yale University Press, 1982.

Mitchell, Reid. *Civil War Soldiers: Their Expectations and Their Experiences.* New York: Viking, 1988.

Morrill, Dan L. *Southern Campaigns of the American Revolution.* Baltimore, Md.: Nautical and Aviation, 1993.

Morris, Donald R. *The Washing of the Spears: A History of the Rise of the Zulu Nation under Shaka and Its Fall in the Zulu War of 1879.* New York: Simon and Schuster, 1965.

Mountcastle, Clay. *Punitive War: Confederate Guerrillas and Union Reprisals.* Lawrence: University Press of Kansas, 2009.

Nicolay, John G., and John Hay. *Abraham Lincoln: A History.* 10 Vols. New York: Century, 1890.

Owens, Harry P., and James J. Cooke, eds. *The Old South in the Crucible of War.* Jackson: University Press of Mississippi, 1983.

Pakenham, Thomas. *The Scramble for Africa: The White Man's Conquest of the Dark Continent from 1876 to 1912.* New York: Random House, 1991.

Perret, Geoffrey. *A Country Made by War, from the Revolution to Vietnam: The Story of America's Rise to Power.* New York: Random House, 1989.

Piatt, Don, and Henry V. Boynton. *General George H. Thomas: A Critical Biography.* Cincinnati: Robert Clarke, 1893.

Piecuch, Jim. *The Blood Be upon Your Head: Tarleton and the Myth of Buford's Massacre, the Battle of the Waxhaws, May 29, 1780.* Lugoff, S.C.: Southern Campaigns of the American Revolution, 2010.

Powell, David A. *Failure in the Saddle: Nathan Bedford Forrest, Joseph Wheeler, and the Confederate Cavalry in the Chickamauga Campaign.* New York: Savas Beatie, 2010.

Quarles, Benjamin. *The Negro in the Civil War.* Boston: Little, Brown, 1953.

Ramage, James. *Rebel Raider: The Life of General John Hunt Morgan.* Lexington: University Press of Kentucky, 1986.

Rhea, Gordon C. *To the North Anna River: Grant and Lee, May 13–25, 1864.* Baton Rouge: Louisiana State University Press, 2000.

Robertson, James I., Jr. *Soldiers Blue and Gray.* Columbia: University of South Carolina Press, 1988.

Roland, Charles P. *An American Iliad: The Story of the Civil War.* New York: McGraw-Hill, 1991.

Sears, Stephen W. *Landscape turned Red: The Battle of Antietam.* New Haven, Conn.: Ticknor and Fields, 1983.

Sexton, William Thaddeus. *Soldiers in the Sun: An Adventure in Imperialism.* Harrisburg, Pa.: Military Service Publishers, 1939. Reprint, Freeport, N.Y.: Books for Libraries Press, 1971.

Sheppard, Eric William. *Bedford Forrest: The Confederacy's Greatest Cavalryman.* New York: Dial, 1930.

Simpson, Brooks D. *Ulysses S. Grant: Triumph over Adversity, 1822–1865.* Boston: Houghton-Mifflin, 2000.

Slotkin, Richard. *No Quarter: The Battle of the Crater, 1864.* New York: Random House, 2009.

Smith, Kristen M., ed. *The Lines Are Drawn: Political Cartoons of the Civil War.* Athens, Ga.: Hill Street, 1999.

Spann, Edward K. *Gotham at War: New York City, 1860–1865.* Wilmington, Del.: Scholarly Resources, 2002.

Speer, Lonnie R. *Portals to Hell: Military Prisons of the Civil War.* Mechanicsburg, Pa.: Stackpole, 1997.
———. *War of Vengeance: Acts of Retaliation against Civil War POWs.* Mechanicsburg, Pa.: Stackpole, 2002.
Steiner, Paul E. *Medical-Military Portraits of Union and Confederate Generals.* Philadelphia: Whitmore, 1968.
Tap, Bruce. *Over Lincoln's Shoulder: The Committee on the Conduct of the War.* Lawrence: University Press of Kansas, 1998.
Tennessee Civil War Centennial Commission. *Tennesseans in the Civil War: A Military History of Confederate and Union Units with Available Rosters of Personnel.* 2 vols. Nashville: Tennessee Civil War Centennial Commission, 1964.
Thayer, William M. *A Youth's History of the Rebellion: From the Battle of Murfreesboro to the Massacre at Fort Pillow.* 3 vols. New York: John W. Lovell, 1865.
Thomas, Emory M. *The Confederacy as a Revolutionary Experience.* Englewood Cliffs, N.J.: Prentice-Hall, 1971.
———. *The Confederate Nation, 1861–1865.* New York: Harper and Row, 1979.
———. *Robert E. Lee: A Biography.* New York: W.W. Norton, 1995.
Thompson, W. Fletcher, Jr. *The Image of War: The Pictorial Reporting of the American Civil War.* New York: Thomas Yoseloff, 1960.
Trefousse, Hans L. *Benjamin Franklin Wade: Radical Republican from Ohio.* New York: Twayne, 1963.
Trudeau, Noah Andre. *Like Men of War: Black Troops in the Civil War, 1862–1865.* Boston: Little, Brown, 1998.
Urwin, Gregory J.W., ed. *Black Flag over Dixie: Racial Atrocities and Reprisals in the Civil War.* Carbondale: Southern Illinois University Press, 2004.
Utley, Robert M. *Frontiersmen in Blue: The United States Army and the Indian, 1848–1865.* New York: Macmillan, 1967.
Ward, Andrew. *River Run Red: The Fort Pillow Massacre in the Civil War.* New York: Viking, 2005.
Ward, Christopher. *War of the Revolution.* New York: Macmillan, 1952.
Warner, Ezra J. *Generals in Blue: Lives of Union Commanders.* Baton Rouge: Louisiana State University Press, 1964.
———. *Generals in Gray: Lives of Confederate Commanders.* Baton Rouge: Louisiana State University Press, 1959.
Waugh, John C. *The Class of 1846: From West Point to Appomattox: Stonewall Jackson, George McClellan, and Their Brothers.* New York: Warner Books, 1994.
Wert, Jeffry D. *Custer: The Controversial Life of George Armstrong Custer.* New York: Simon and Schuster, 1996.
———. *General James Longstreet: The Confederacy's Most Controversial Soldier: A Biography.* New York: Simon and Schuster, 1993.
Wiley, Bell I. *Johnny Reb: The Common Soldier of the Confederacy.* Baton Rouge: Louisiana State University Press, 1978.
———. *The Road to Appomattox.* Memphis: Memphis State College Press, 1956.
———. *Southern Negroes, 1861–1865.* Baton Rouge: Louisiana State University Press, 1965.

Williams, George W. *History of the Negro Race in America, 1619–1880.* 2 vols. New York, 1883.
Williams, Kenneth P. *Lincoln Finds a General: A Military Study of the Civil War.* 5 vols. New York: Macmillan, 1949–59.
Wills, Brian Steel. *A Battle from the Start: The Life of Nathan Bedford Forrest.* New York: HarperCollins, 1992.
———. *George Henry Thomas: As True as Steel.* Lawrence: University Press of Kansas, 2012.
———. *The War Hits Home: The Civil War in Southeastern Virginia.* Charlottesville: University Press of Virginia, 2001.
Wilson, David K. *The Southern Strategy: Britain's Conquest of South Carolina and Georgia, 1775–1780.* Columbia: University of South Carolina Press, 2005.
Womack, Bob. *Call Forth the Mighty Men.* Bessemer, Ala.: Colonial, 1987.
Woodworth, Steven. *Jefferson Davis and His Generals: The Failure of Confederate Command in the West.* Lawrence: University Press of Kansas, 1990.
Wyatt-Brown, Bertram. *Southern Honor: Ethics & Behavior in the Old South.* New York: Oxford University Press, 1982.
Wyeth, John Allan. *Life of General Nathan Bedford Forrest.* New York: Harper and Brothers, 1899.

## Articles

Ambrose, Stephen E. "My Lai: Atrocities in Historical Perspective." In *Americans at War,* 191–202. Jackson: University Press of Mississippi, 1997.
Blankinship, Gary. "Colonel Fielding Hurst and the Hurst Nation." *West Tennessee Historical Society Papers* 34 (October 1980): 71–87.
Bradley, Mary Forrest. "Lieutenant General Nathan Bedford Forrest." *Southern Magazine* 3 (July 1936): 15–16, 42.
Carney, Court. "The Contested Image of Nathan Bedford Forrest." *Journal of Southern History* 67 (August 2001): 601–30.
Cartwright, Thomas Y. "'Better Confederates Did Not Live': Black Southerners in Nathan Bedford Forrest's Command." In *Black Southerners in Gray,* edited by Richard Rollins, 95–120. *Journal of Confederate History* Series 11. Murfreesboro, Tenn.: Southern Heritage, 1994.
Castel, Albert. "Fort Pillow: Victory or Massacre?" *American History Illustrated* 9 (1974): 4–10, 46–48.
———. "The Fort Pillow Massacre: A Fresh Examination of the Evidence." *Civil War History* 4 (1958): 37–50.
Cimprich, John. "The Fort Pillow Massacre: Assessing the Evidence." In *Black Soldiers in Blue: African American Troops in the Civil War Era,* edited by John David Smith, 150–68. Chapel Hill: University of North Carolina Press, 2002.
Cimprich, John, and Robert C. Mainfort, Jr. "Dr. Fitch's Report on the Fort Pillow Massacre." *Tennessee Historical Quarterly* 44 (Spring 1985): 27–39.
———. "The Fort Pillow Massacre: A Statistical Note." *Journal of American History* 76 (December 1989): 830–37.
———. "Fort Pillow Revisited: New Evidence about an Old Controversy." *Civil War History* 28 (December 1982): 293–306.

Davis, David Brion. "Some Themes of Counter-Subversion: An Analysis of Anti-Mason, Anti-Catholic, and Anti-Mormon Literature." *Mississippi Valley Historical Review* 47 (September 1960): 205–24.

Davis, William C. "The Massacre at Saltville." *Civil War Times Illustrated* 9 (February 1971): 4–11, 43–48.

Fitzgerald, William S. "Did Nathan Bedford Forrest Really Rescue John Able?" *Tennessee Historical Quarterly* 39 (Spring 1980): 16–26.

Gorn, Elliott J. "'Gouge and Bite, Pull Hair and Scratch': The Social Significance of Fighting in the Southern Backcountry." *American Historical Review* 90 (February 1985): 18–32.

Holley, Peggy Scott. "The Seventh Tennessee Volunteer Cavalry: West Tennessee Unionists in Andersonville Prison." *West Tennessee Historical Society Papers* 42 (December 1988): 39–55.

Hubbell, John T., and James W. Geary, eds. *Biographical Dictionary of the Union: Northern Leaders of the Civil War.* Westport, Conn.: Greenwood, 1995.

Huch, Ronald K. "The Fort Pillow Massacre: The Aftermath of Paducah." *Journal of the Illinois State Historical Society* 66 (Spring 1973): 62–70.

Jones, Howard. "History and Mythology: The Crisis over British Intervention in the Civil War." In *The Union, the Confederacy, and the Atlantic Rim,* edited by Robert E. May, 29–67. West Lafayette, Ind.: Perdue University Press, 1995.

Jones, James B., Jr. "'Fevers Ran High': The Civil War in the Cumberland." In *Rural Life and Culture in the Upper Cumberland,* edited by Michael E. Birdwell and W. Calvin Dickson, 73–104. Lexington: University Press of Kentucky, 2004.

Jordan, John L. "Was There a Massacre at Fort Pillow?" *Tennessee Historical Quarterly* 6 (June 1947): 99–133.

Kviz, Frederick J. "Survival in Combat as a Collective Exchange Process." *Journal of Political and Military Sociology* 6 (Fall 1978): 219–32.

Lockett, James D. "The Lynching Massacre of Black and White Soldiers at Fort Pillow, Tennessee, April 12, 1864." *Western Journal of Black Studies* 22 (Summer 1998): 84–93.

Longacre, Edward G. "All's Fair in Love and War." *Civil War Times Illustrated* 8 (June 1969): 32–40.

Lovett, Bobby L. "The West Tennessee Colored Troops in Civil War Combat." *West Tennessee Historical Society Papers* 34 (October 1980): 53–70.

Lufkin, Charles L. "'Not Heard from since April 12, 1864': The Thirteenth Tennessee, Cavalry, U.S.A." *Tennessee Historical Quarterly* 45 (Spring 1986): 133–49.

Maness, Lonnie E. "The Fort Pillow Massacre: Fact or Fiction." *Tennessee Historical Quarterly* 45 (Spring 1986): 287–315.

———. "Fort Pillow under Confederate and Union Control." *West Tennessee Historical Society Papers* 38 (December 1984): 84–98.

———. "A Ruse That Worked: The Capture of Union City in 1864." *West Tennessee Historical Society Papers* 30 (October 1976): 91–103.

McPherson, James M. "How Lincoln Won the War with Metaphor." In *With My Face to the Enemy: Perspectives on the Civil War,* edited by Robert Cowley, 87–102. New York: G. P. Putnam's Sons, 2001.

Moneyhon, Carl H. "White Society and African-American Soldiers." In *"All Cut to Pieces and Gone to Hell": The Civil War, Race Relations, and the Battle of*

*Poison Spring,* edited by Mark K. Christ, 31–57. Little Rock: August House, 2003.

Moore, Kenneth Bancroft. "Fort Pillow, Forrest, and the United States Colored Troops in 1864." *Tennessee Historical Quarterly* 54 (Summer 1995): 112–23.

Morris, Jr., Roy. "Fort Pillow: Massacre or Madness?" *America's Civil War* (November 2000): 26–32.

Suderow, Bryce A. "The Battle of the Crater: The Civil War's Worst Massacre." *Civil War History* 43 (September 1997): 219–24.

Tap, Bruce. "'These Devils Are Not Fit to Live on God's Earth': War Crimes and the Committee on the Conduct of the War, 1861–1865." *Civil War History* 42 (June 1996): 116–32.

Trudeau, Noah Andre. "'Kill the Last Damn One of Them': The Fort Pillow Massacre." In *With My Face to the Enemy: Perspectives on the Civil War,* edited by Robert Cowley, 382–94. New York: G. P. Putnam's Sons, 2001.

Williams, Edward F., III. "Confederate Victories at Fort Pillow." Memphis: Nathan Bedford Forrest Trail Committee, Historical Hiking Trails, 1973.

Williams, Harry. "Benjamin F. Wade and the Atrocity Propaganda of the Civil War." *Ohio State Archaeological and Historical Quarterly* 47 (January 1939): 33–43.

# INDEX

*References to illustrations are in italic type. Numbered entries for military groups are in numerical, rather than alphabetical, order.*

1st Kentucky Heavy Artillery (U.S.), 78
2nd West Tennessee Cavalry (U.S.), 75
4th Kentucky Infantry (U.S.), 174
5th Tennessee Cavalry (U.S.), 72
6th Connecticut Infantry, 198
6th Tennessee Cavalry (U.S.) 65, 66, 124
7th Tennessee Cavalry (C.S.), 74
7th Tennessee Cavalry (U.S.), 66, 74
9th Kentucky Infantry (U.S.), 166
10th South Carolina Infantry, 177
13th Tennessee Cavalry (U.S.), 104, 121, 154, 157, 158
16th Kentucky Cavalry (U.S.), 78
16th Tennessee Infantry (C.S.), 96
20th Tennessee Cavalry (C.S.), 88
22nd Michigan Infantry, 31
25th Tennessee Infantry (C.S.), 73
49th North Carolina Infantry, 10
54th Massachusetts Infantry, 53
77th Illinois Infantry, 180
101st Airborne Division, 15
122nd Illinois Infantry, 78

"Abe Lincoln's Last Card; Or Rouge-Et-Noir," 54
*Abingdon Virginian*, 163
Able, John, 23–24, 113, 116
Ackerstrom, John C., 103, 157, 158
Adair, George W., 78, 81, 90, 92, 93, 95, 225n58
Adairsville, Ga., 166
Adison, Thomas, 96
Africa, 13, 38
African Americans (blacks), 5, 16, 23, 36–37, 38, 39, 52, 55, 82, 83, 125, 196, 201, 226n2, 246n55; attitudes of Confederate civilians toward, 49, 56–58, 59, 162–63; attitudes of Confederate soldiers toward, 111, 127, 132–33, 170, 171, 172,
174, 201, 214, 234n57, 241n61; as Confederate soldiers, 56, 59, 178; at Fort Pillow, 60, 82, 163, 191, 214; Lincoln and black Union soldiers, 55–56, 149, 161; at Paducah, 78, 82; as Union soldiers, 4–5, 10, 12, 30, 36–37, 52, 53, 54, 55, 60, 78, 79, 82, 84, 85, 87, 109, 115, 130, 131, *144*, 152, 153, 154, 157, 161, 165, 166, 168, 173, 175, 181, 194, 198. *See also various units under United States Colored Troops (USCT)/African American troops*
Alabama, 19, 62, 99, 164, 178, 179, 182
*Alabama*, 194
Alamo, The, 9, 126
Alexander, Edward Porter, 171, 172
Allison, Alexander, 201
Alton Prison, Ill., 34
Ambrose, Stephen, 6
Anderson, Charles W., 61, 92, 97, 101, 112, 120, 123, 128, *136*
Andersonville Prison, 77, 129, 221n1, 231n64, 237n9, 238n36
Antagonism (racial/sectional), 4, 5, 6, 10, 15, 55, 72, 79, 82, 97, 116, 123, 150, 207, 214, 216
Antietam (Sharpsburg), Battle of, 50, 227n33
Antietam Creek, 50
Antony, Mark, 205
Appomattox Court House, Va., 180
Arkansas, 5
*Army and Navy Journal*, 126
Army of Northern Virginia, 50, 169, 171, 180
Army of Tennessee, 63, 69, 70, 177, 188
Army of the Cumberland, 165
Army of the Potomac, 183
Ashdown, Paul, 4, 17, 27, 125

265

## 266　INDEX

Atlanta, Ga., 61, 87, 125, 160, 167
*Atlanta Southern Confederacy*, 78
Atrocity, 3, 6, 67, 103, 110–13, 121, 150–59 passim, 161, 196, 202, 206, 237n29
*Augusta (Ga.) Chronicle & Sentinel*, 78

Ball's Bluff, Va., 118
Baltimore, Md., 149, 159, 161
Banks, Nathaniel Prentiss, 53, 56
Barrett, Milton, 171
Barteau, Clark S., 101, 155
Bate, William Brimage, 160
Beatty, John W., 77
Beauregard, Pierre Gustave Toutant, 51, 57
Bedford County, Tenn., 73
Bell, Tyree Harris, 83, 89, 90, 94, 96, 103, 105, 111, 114, 121, *137*
Belmont, August, 44, 246n42
Benjamin, Judah, 25
Benton, Edward, 89
Benton County, 124
Black Kettle, 176
Blair, Francis "Frank," *146*, 191, 192, 194
Blair, Montgomery, 44, 159
Blakeslee, Bernard F., 198
Blankinship, Gary, 65
"Bloody Tarleton," 8
Boer, 13
Bolivar, 83, 127
Bondurant, Benjamin, 93
Booth, Lionel F., 87, 89, 91, 97, 104, 117, 190, 200, 210
Boston, Mass., 151
*Boston Post*, 125
Bouton, Edward, 132
Bradford, Theodore (Theodorick), 121
Bradford, William F., 72, 73, 87, 92, 104, 109, 110, 114, 119, 190, 210, 214; death of, 121–22
Bragg, Braxton, 33, 51, 63, 69, 70, 169, 223n15, 230n35
Brantley, Solomon, 132, 133
Brayman, Mason, 130, 207
Breckinridge, John Cabell, 51, 174, 175
Brent, W., 188
Brice's Cross Roads, Miss., 19, 20, 35, 63, 131, 132, 133, 196

Brigham, James R., 89
Browder, George, 163
Brown, John, 43, 57
Brown, Joseph E., 239n53
Brownfield, Robert, 7
Browning, Orville, 40
Brownlow, William Gannaway "Parson," 126, 186
Brownsville, Tenn., 88, 120
Buckner, Simon Bolivar, 26
Buena Vista, Mexico, Battle of, 10, 108, 207
"Buffaloes," 12
Buford, Abraham (Revolution), 7, 8, 9
Buford, Abraham, 63, 78, 123, 124, *137*
"Buford's Massacre," 8
Bull Run, Va. *See* Manassas, Va.
Burbridge, Stephen, 174
Bureau of Refugees, Freedmen, and Abandoned Lands, 186
Burkhardt, George, 3
Butler, Benjamin Franklin, "Beast," 39, 169, 172, 173, 175, 199, 246n55

Cable, George, 100, 182
Cahaba, Ala., 128, 129, 212, 238n36
Cairo, Ill., 68, 102, 128, 130, 151
Caldwell, Samuel H., 111
Calfkiller incident, 164–65
Calfkiller River, 72
Calley, William, 6
Camden, S.C., 118
Cameron, Simon, 43
Campbell, William, 206
Camp Chase, 127
Camp Sumter. *See* Andersonville Prison
Carlsbad, Austria, 202
Carlton, Eli, 157
Carmack, Edward, 202
Carney, Court, 197
Caudill, Edward, 4, 17, 27, 125
Chalmers, James Ronald, 83, 87, 89, 90, 92, 94, 99, 100, 116, 127, *136*, 159, 194, 198–99
Chambers, Henry, 10, 11
Chapel Hill, Tenn., 18
Charleston, S.C., 7, 53, 55
Charleston Harbor, 25

Chase, Salmon Portland, 44, 159, 185
Chattanooga, Tenn., 61, 129, 211
Cheairs, Nathaniel F., 127, 128
Cheatham, Benjamin Franklin, 223n15
Chelmsford, Lord (Frederic Thesiger), 13
Chesapeake Bay, 38
Cheyenne, 12
Chicago, Ill., 49
*Chicago Tribune*, 126
Chickamauga, Battle of, 33, 35, 69, 113, 225n65, 230n35
Chivington, John, 12, 176, 177
Cimprich, John, 115
Civil War, 6, 10, 17, 19, 38, 48, 51, 108, 115, 118, 150, 194, 201, 205, 206, 207
Clark, Achilles V., 110, 111, 113
Clary, William, 157
Cleburne, Patrick Ronayne, 58, 59
*Cleveland Herald*, 126
Coahoma County, Miss., 47
Coal (Cold) Creek, 90, 190
Cochran, Mary, 163
Cockspur Island, Ga., 42
Coles, H. C., 34
Colfax, Schuyler, *146*
Colorado, 202
Colorado Territory, 12, 176
Columbia, Tenn., 21, 213
Columbus, Ky., 78, 123, 124, 207
Compromise of 1850, 39
Confederate States of America (Confederacy), 17, 25, 36, 38, 39, 46, 48, 56, 58, 59, 71, 77, 165, 172, 173, 174, 177, 178, 182, 188, 197, 214; congress of, 30, 57, 172, 178, 225n65, 228n55; constitution of, 56
*Confederate Veteran*, 201
Confiscation Acts, 47, 54; First, 39, 40; Second, 43
Connolly, James, 163
Constitution. *See* United States Constitution
"Contraband," or "Contraband of War," 39
Cooper, Samuel, 57, 68
"Copperhead," 148
Corinth, Miss., 27, 51

"Cornerstone of the Confederacy," 57
Cornwallis, Lord Charles, 247n4
Corry, Robert E., 34
Cowan, J. B., 70
Cowan, Samuel, 21
Crafts, George Washington, 89
Crampton's Gap, 50
"Crater, The." *See* Petersburg, Va.
Crews, James R., 83
Cuba, 195
Cumberland River, 26
Curtis, Samuel, 68
Cussons, John, 201
Custer, George Armstrong, 12

*Dacotah*, 81
Dakotas, 51
Dalton, Ga., 60
Dartmouth College, 151
Davis, David Brion, 6
Davis, Jefferson, 16, 48, 49, 54, 57, 58, 59, 69, 70, 119, 178, 197, 239n53
Davis, William C., 174, 175
*Dawn*, 169
Dean, Eric T., 207
Delaware, 41
Democratic Party (Democrats), 46, 148, 151, 191, 194, 195, 197, 202, 246n42; National Convention of (1868), 191, 192
Demopolis, 85
Department of the Gulf, 53
Department of the West, 39
De Peyster, Abraham, 8
Diffenbocker, B. F., 187
District of Columbia, 41, 42
Division of the Mississippi, 129
Dodds, Willis, 71
Douglas, Stephen A., "Little Giant," 149
Douglass, Frederick, 38, 53, 56, 161
Douglass, Lewis, 53
Dover, Tenn., 113, 212, 247n17
Dower, John, 15, 208
Dresden, Tenn., 82
Duckworth, William L., 75, 76, 77, 80, 123, 124, 127
Duke, Basil Wilson, 26, 34, 156, 192
Dunham, N.C., 200

Eaton, Clement, 3, 216
Edwards, Sarah Jane, 245n15
Edwards, Thomas, 187, 188, 213
Election of 1860, 24–25
Election of 1868, 191, 193, 195
Election of 1864, 3, 4, 15, 119, 134, 148, 193
Elliott's Salient, 170
Elmwood Cemetery, 204
Emancipation Proclamation, 50, 52, 53, 54, 56, 57, 148, 227n33, 228n43
Epeneter, Charles J., 92

Fallen Timbers, 27
Falls, Elias, 153, 154
Faulkner, W.W., 78
Ferguson, Champ, 175
Ferguson, Patrick, 8
Ferguson, William, 120, 121
First Cumberland Presbyterian Church, 107
Fisk, Wilbur, 166
Fitch, Charles, 113, 114, 198, 210
Five Forks, Va., 183
Florida, 42
Floyd, John Buchanan, 26
"Fog of War," 210
Foner, Eric, 39
Forrest, Jeffrey E. (brother), 61, 62, 63
Forrest, Jesse (brother), 188, 197
Forrest, Jonathan (uncle), 21
Forrest, Mary Ann Montgomery (wife), 21, 197, 204
"Forrest Myth," 17
Forrest, Nathan Bedford, 6, 17, 18, 47, 53, 59, 60, 61, *135*, *143*, *144*, *145*, *147*; appearance and habits of, 22–23, 33, 95–96; attitudes concerning legitimate warfare, 65, 66–67, 71–72; attitudes toward blacks as Union soldiers, 59, 82, 98, 99, 120, 123, 167–68, 191, 196, 200, 214; birth and early life, 18–19; and bluff, 28, 31–32, 36, 67, 75, 104, 118, 208, 210, 213; as the "Butcher of Fort Pillow," 4, 191, 197, 204, 216; death of, 197; education of, 77, 99–100, 212; at fall of Fort Pillow, 113–15, 116; and gambling, 20; maxims of, 19–20, 28, 31, 34–35, 97, 212; as "Napoleon Bonaparte Forrest," 192; official reports of, 126–28, 162–63; and postwar period, 184–85, 186–97 passim; and slavery, 25, 168, 214; as a slave trader, 22, 156, 184, 195, 214; storytelling by, 24–31–33, 36, 211–12; style of fighting, 25, 26, 71, 74, 83, 106, 116, 193, 205, 213; surrender demands by, 28, 36, 98–101; surrender of, 182; temper of, 21, 69–70; as "That Devil Forrest," 4, 197; use of intimidation/bluster, 23, 26, 30, 31, 67, 208, 210; as the "Wizard of the Saddle," 4, 88, 197, 204
Forrest, William H. (brother), 97, 188
Forrest, William "Willie" Montgomery (son), 25
Forrest Park, 204
Fort, DeWitt Clinton, 98
Fort Anderson, Ky., 78, 79, 82, 84, 99
Fort Blakeley, Ala., 180, 181
Fort Donelson, Tenn., 25, 26, 90, 128
Fort Pillow, Tenn., 18, 36, 37, 63, 70, 72, 73, 82, 84, 85, 87, 124, 156, 161, 185, 214, 233n6; actions during truce at, 101–104; Battle of, 89–115 passim; and memory, 4, 17; and propaganda, 17, 119, 150, 151, 239–40n60; casualties from, 115; Confederate advance on, 88–89; dimensions of, 86; final assault on, 105–10; Forrest's appearance before, 92–93, 233n32; Lincoln and 149–50, 159–61; Northern reaction to, 125–26, 163–66; Southern reaction to, 126–27, 162–63; Sherman and, 87, 130–31, 215, 238n37; witness testimony on, 153–55, 157–58
"Fort Pillow Massacre," 5, 84, 134, 166, 168, 169, 179, 180, 181, 188, 194, 195, 198, 201, 215, 236n5

Fort Pocahontas, Va., 169
Fort Pulaski, Ga., 42
Fort Sumter, S.C., 43, 45, 52
Fort Wagner, S.C., 53
France, 54
*Frank Leslie's Illustrated Newspaper*, *141*, 165, 201
Franklin, Tenn., 61
Frederick, Md., 50
Fredericksburg, Va., 58
Fredericksburg Road, 168
Freedmen's Bureau,
Freeman, Samuel L., 61, 62, 63, 179
Frémont, Jessie, 226n5
Frémont, John C., 39, 40, 48
Frisby, Derek, 151
Frye, Dennis, 51
Fuchs, Richard, 129, 154, 158, 215

Gainesville, Ala., 182
Garidel, Henri, 163
Gaus, Jacob, 106, 107
Gaylesville, Ala., 31
Gaylord, Wilbur, 92
Georgia, 42, 70, 77, 129, 131, 132, 165, 166
German (Germans), 13, 14, 15, 208, 223n42
Gettysburg, Battle of, 55, 58, 211
Gibbons, James S., 52
Goliad, 9
Gooch, Daniel Wheelwright, *139*, 150, 151, 152, 153, 154, 157, 158
Gordon, John Brown, 168
Gorgas, Josiah, 84
Gould, Andrew Wills, 21, 113, 213
Granger, Gordon, 211
Grant, Ulysses S., 26, 27, 30, 56, 66, 129, 130, 131, *146*, 160, 168, 170, 172, 173, 175, 180, 191, 195, 211
Great Britain (England), 7, 9, 13, 54, 125
Greeley, Horace, 15, 45, 46
Grierson, Benjamin Henry, 83, 125, 130
Guerrillas (guerrilla warfare), 13, 14, 51, 67, 73, 182
Gulf Coast, 180

Haley, James, 9
Hampton, Wade, *145*, 194
Hardeman County, 186
"Hard War," 151
Harpers Ferry, Va., 50, 57
*Harper's Weekly*, *140*, *142*, 165, 193, 201
Harpeth River, 31
Harris, Isham, 25
Harrisburg (Tupelo), Battle of, 35, 131, 212, 247n17
Harris Farm, 168
Haskins, John, 157
Hawkins, Isaac R., 75, 76, 77, 88, 109, 119, 185, 231n58
Hawkins, John P., 181
Hay, John, 160
Hearn, Lafcadio, 23
Henderson County, Tenn., 71
Henry, Robert Selph, 3
Herero, 13
Hernando, Miss., 21
Hickman, 78
Hicks, Samuel G., 78, 80, 109, 124, 125
Hill, Ambrose Powell, 118
Hindman, Thomas, 67, 68, 229n24
Hollis, Elisha, 88
Holly Springs, Miss., 30
Holmes, Emma, 55, 58
Holston River, 174
Hood, John Bell, 177, 179
Hooker, Joseph "Fighting Joe," 58
Hopkins, T.T., 94
Hosea, Lewis, 178
House, Ellen Renshaw, 163
Houston, Sam, 9, 206
Howard, William T., 33
Hubbard, John M., 103
Huch, Ronald, 82, 84
Hughs, John M., 73
Hunter, David, 42, 48, 49
Hunter, Lieutenant, 92
Hurlbut, Stephen Augustus, 66, 87, 122, 130, 131
Hurst, Fielding, 65, 66, 67, 71, 72, 73, 83, 119, 122, 124, 125, 185, 186, 214, 244–45n11
Hurst, William, 67

## 270  INDEX

Illinois, 34, 38, 40, 149, 165, 181
Ingersoll, Robert G., 75
Iowa, 114, 166, 198
"Irish Guards," 14
Isandlwana (Isandhlwana), 13
Iuka, Miss., 51

Jackson, Tenn., 65, 66, 67, 87, 117, 185
Jackson, Thomas Jonathan "Stonewall," 19, 50
Japan (Japanese), 15
Johnson, Andrew, 124, 189, 212, 240n8
Johnson, Reverdy, 44
Johnson's Island, Ohio, 127
Johnsonville, Tenn., 211
Johnston, Joseph Eggleston, 131, 160
Jones, Alex, 89, 120
Jones, John Beauchamp, 58
Jones, Sallie, 120
Jordan, Thomas, 22, 24, 29, 62, 88, 101, 189, 190, 191
Josephy, Alvin, 52

Kansas, 71
Keegan, John, 14
Kelley, David C., 20, 167
Kentucky (Kentuckians), 34, 40, 41, 51, 63, 71, 75, 78, 83, 90, 122, 125, 156, 161
Kilpatrick, Hugh Judson, 192, 193
King Philip, 203
Kings Mountain, 8, 108, 206, 207
Kirby Smith, Edmund. *See* Smith, Edmund Kirby
Knowles, Dr., 159
Knoxville, Tenn., 126
*Knoxville Whig & Rebel Ventilator*, 126
Ku Klux Klan, 3, 194
Kurz, Louis, 201
Kviz, Frederick J., 211

Larson, James, 180
Lawrence, Kans., 126
Leadbetter, Isaac J., 154, 157
Leaming, Mack J., 92, 121, 122, 157
Lee, Fitzhugh, 169
Lee, Robert Edward, 49, 50, 51, 118, 160, 175, 178, 180, 182, 211; and exchange with Grant over prisoners, 172–74
Lee, Stephen Dill, 72, 128, 202, 247n17
Lexington, Tenn., 75
*Liberty*, 102
*Life of General Nathan Bedford Forrest*, 202
Lincoln, Abraham, 15, 25, 51, 52, 53, 54, 57, 59, 125, 148, 149, 150, 159, 160, 161, 167, 194, 226n5; and black Union troops, 55, 56; and gradual emancipation, 38–43; reply to Greeley, 45–46; shift to expanded emancipation, 44–50 passim
Lipsett, Henry, 121
Little Big Horn, 12, 207
Little Rock, Ark., 68, 166
London, England, 54
Lord, William Blair, 151
Lord Charles Cornwallis, 247n4
Lord Chelmsford (Frederic Thesiger), 13
"Lost Cause," 194, 197
Louisiana, 53, 102
*(Louisville) Courier-Journal*, 125, 195
Loyalists (Tories), 7, 8, 9

Macaluso, Gregory, 73, 122
*Macon (Ga.) Daily Telegraph*, 184
Mahone, William, 170, 171, 172
Maine, 151
Mainfort, Robert, Jr., 115
Majuba Hill, 13
Manassas, Va., 39
Mankato, Minn., 51
Mark Antony, 205
Marks's Mills, Ark., 5
Marshall, James, 89, 90, 93, 97, 103, 109
Marvel, William, 149
Maryland, 40, 41, 50, 51
Mason (Masonry), 166
Massachusetts, 131, 150, 198, 199
Maury, Dabney Herndon, 24, 35, 115
McAlister, Robert Milton, 34
McClellan, George Brinton, 50
McCoy, James, 104, 157

McCulloch, Robert ("Black Bob"), 90, 96, 105
McDonald, Angus, 11
McLaglen, W. R., 121
McNairy County, Tenn., 65
McPherson, James Birdseye, 86, 129, 130
McPherson, James M., 42, 46, 227n33
Memphis, Tenn., 3, 22, 23, 47, 60, 68, 69, 73, 83, 85, 86, 87, 116, 122, 130, 131, 132, 151, 164, 184, 185, 188, 195, 196, 197, 203
*Memphis Daily Appeal*, 78, 125, 167, 195
Meridian, Miss., 130, 239n42
Mexican-American War, 10, 108
Mexico (Mexicans), 117, 126, 185
Middleburg, Va., 163
Middle Tennessee, 31, 33, 34, 132
*Miner and Workman's Advocate*, 125
Minnesota (Minnesotans), 51
Missionary Ridge, 211
Mississippi, 51, 58, 59, 62, 63, 106, 129, 132, 178, 182, 199
Mississippi River, 3, 4, 17, 34, 52, 68, 70, 85, 86, 101, 116, 124, 125, 132, 149, 151, 163, 177, 185, 188, 198, 199, 206, 210, 215
Missouri, 40, 41, 48, 71, 106
*Missouri Democrat*, 128
Mobile, Ala., 237n9
*Mobile Advertiser and Register*, 88, 126–27
Montgomery, Ala., 43
Moore, Kenneth, 158
Morgan, John Hunt, 34, 35, 156
Morrill, Dan, 7
Morrison, Col., 30
Morton, John W., 21
Mosgrove, George, 174
Mound City, 90, 153, 157
Munfordville, Ky., 51
Murfreesboro, Tenn., 27, 28, 29, 30, 35, 36, 99, 118, 192
My Lai, 6

Napoleon, 35
Nashville, Tenn., 26, 31, 74, 107, 129, 175, 177
Nast, Thomas, 193, 194
*National Republican*, 199
Neely, James J., 83, 127
Nelson, John, 89
*New Era*, 87, 88, 89, 90, 92, 93, 94, 97, 101, 102, 103, 107, 109, 114
New Orleans, La., 44, 53, 102, 246n55
Newsom, J. F., 185
New York, 8, 12, 41, 44
New York City, 125, 126, 127, 149, 191, 192, 194–95, 202; 1863 Draft riots in, 55, 181, 194
*New York Times*, 41, 125, 128, 192, 197
*New York Tribune*, 15, 45, 125, 126
Nicolay, John, 160
Niehaus, Charles H., 203, 204
Normandy, 15, 223n42
North Carolina, 7, 8, 169, 170
Nugen, William, 164
Nugent, William, 59

Odon, Samuel Crisp, 232n78
Ohio, 150, 151
Ohio River, 78, 151
Okolona, Miss., 36, 61, 62, 74, 239n42
*Olive Branch*, 102, 190
Ottawa, Ill., 149
Ould, Robert, 172
Overland Campaign, Va., 160
Oxford, Miss., 127

Pacific theater of operations, 15, 208
Paducah, Ky., 88, 93, 94, 99, 105, 119, 123, 124, 153, 164, 207, 210; Battle at, 78–84 passim, 232n78
Parker's Crossroads, Tenn., 31, 36, 97, 113, 212
Parkhurst, John G., 99, 178
Patrick, Marsena, 58
Patriots (Colonials, Whigs), 7, 8, 9, 206
*Paw Paw*, 78, 80, 81, 231n70
Payne, John H. B., 181
Pegram, William R. J., 171, 172
*Peosta*, 78, 80, 81, 164, 231n70
Perryville, Ky., 51
Petersburg, Va., 170, 214; the Crater at, 171

Philippines, 13, 14, 202, 207
Piecuch, James, 7, 206
Pillow, Gideon, 26
*Pittsburg Dispatch*, 199
Plymouth, N.C., 12, 198
Poison Spring, Ark., 5, 214
Polk, Leonidas, 82, 117, 119
Pope, John, 48
Porter, John H., 121, 122
Porter, John M., 127
Potomac River, 118
Powell, David, 33, 113
Powell, Hannah, 245n15
"Prayer of Twenty Millions, The," 45
Price, Sterling, 51
Pryor, J. P., 22, 24, 29, 62, 88, 101, 189, 190, 191
*Punch* (London), 54
Purdy, Tenn., 122

Quantrill, William Clarke, 126

Race and war, 29, 60, 172, 208
Raleigh, Tenn., 83
Randolph, Tenn., 68
Ransom, Robert, 11
Rappahannock River, 58
Rawlins, John Aaron, 74, 129
Ray, John F., 158
Raymond, Henry Jarvis, 41
Reconstruction, 3
Reed, Wiley M., 107, 236n6
"Remember Fort Pillow!," 126, 132, 166, 168, 170, 171, 181, 202
"Remember the Alamo!," 118, 126
Republicans (Republican Party), 150, 151, 152, 191, 193, 194; radicals, 50, 151
Resaca, Ga., 166
Retaliation/reprisal, 4, 5, 48–49, 51, 55, 59, 60, 67, 68, 82, 86, 87, 130, 132, 150, 159–61, 165–66, 167, 176, 208, 241n46
Revenge/vengeance/hatred, 8, 10, 13, 28, 48, 62, 72, 82, 83, 106, 122, 132, 160, 164, 174, 183, 186, 221n3
Revolutionary War, 7, 9, 10, 46, 108, 205

Rhea, Gordon, 169
Richards, Channing, 164
Richmond, Ky., 51
Richmond, Va., 48, 84, 99, 162, 167, 168, 170
Richmond *Daily Dispatch*, 167, 202
Richmond *Examiner*, 172
Rienzi, Miss., 178
Ringgold, Ga., 163, 164
Ripley, Miss., 124
Robertson, J. A., 202
Robertson, James I., Jr., 111, 214
Robinson, Charles, "Charley," 89, 112, 113, 237n29
Rodes, Robert, 168
Rome, Ga., 31, 225n58 and 65
Rosecrans, William Starke, 51
Rowland, Miss (researcher), 201–202
Rucker, Dr., 30
Rutherford County, Tenn., 30

Sacramento, Ky., 26
Salisbury, N.C., 231n64
Saltville, Va., 174, 175, 214, 243n61
Sand Creek, 12, 176
San Francisco, Calif., 202
Sanitary Fair, 149, 161
San Jacinto, Battle of, 9, 14, 108, 117, 118, 126, 206, 207
Santa Anna, Antonio Lopez de, 117
Saunders, Hubert, 164
*Saving Private Ryan*, 223n42
Sayler's Creek (Sailor's Creek), Va., 12
Scruggs, P. T., 128
Seddon, James A., 16, 57, 172, 173
Selma, Ala., 179, 180, 212
Semmes, Raphael, *145*, 194
Sevareid, Eric, 208
Seward, William H., 44, 159
Seymour, Horatio, *145*, *146*, 191, 192, 194
Shakespeare, William, 205
Sharpsburg, Md., 50
Shaw, George, 154
Shaw, Robert Gould, 53, 55
Shaw, Wirt, 187, 188
Shaw, W. J., 88
Shelby, Isaac, 8

Shelton, John M., 157
Shepherdstown, 118
Shepley, George F., 102
Sherman, John, 48, 131
Sherman, William Tecumseh, 63, 67, 68, 74, 86, 129, 132, 160, 182, 195, 211, 215, 229n24; and emancipation, 47–48; and Fort Pillow, 87, 130–31
Shiloh (Pittsburg Landing), Battle of, 26, 27, 211
*Short History of the Confederate States of America, A*, 16
*Silver Cloud*, 120
Sioux, 13
Slavery, 38–59 passim, 177, 178, 186, 194, 214, 226n5, 229n55
Smith, Andrew Jackson, 131
Smith, Edmund Kirby, 51
Smith, William Sooy, 66, 73, 239n42
Somerville, Tenn., 66
Somerville Road, 83
Somme, Battle of, 14
South Carolina, 8, 42, 58, 170, 171, 181
*Southern Historical Society Papers*, 198
South Mountain, 50
Spanish-American War, 13
Speer, Lonnie, 48
Spielberg, Steven, 223n42
Spooner, John C., 202
Springfield, Ill., 149
Spring Hill, Tenn., 179
St. Albans, Vt., 201
St. Louis, Mo., 40, 155
Stainback, George Tucker, 197
Stanley, David Sloane, 30, 61, 192
Stanton, Edwin McMasters, 151, 158, 159, 160
Stephens, Alexander H., 56
Stevenson, John D., 65
Stinnett, James, 96, 97, 102, 190
Stokes, William B., 72, 73
Stratton, Ella Haines, 203
Streight, Abel D., 31–33, 60, 99
Streight's Raid, 21, 59, 225n58
Sturgis, Samuel D., 131, 132
Suffolk, Va., 10, 11, 12
Sunflower County, Miss., 185

Tap, Bruce, 151, 152
Tarleton, Banastre, 7, 118, 206, 247n4
"Tarleton's Quarter," 7, 8
Taylor, Richard, 213
Teller, Henry, 202
Tennessee (Tennesseans), 17, 18, 53, 65, 71, 78, 93, 106, 124, 125, 128, 130, 163, 166, 174, 175, 179, 202; Unionists, 66–67, 71, 73, 122, 124, 163, 165, 185, 214, 231n60, 244n76
Tennessee River, 26, 34, 124, 129
Tenniel, Sir John, 54
Texas, 10
Texas War for Independence, 94, 108, 117, 126, 206
Thayer, William M., 156
Thomas, George Henry, 54, 74, 129, 180, 182, 211
Thompson, A. P., 78, 79, 80, 81, 94
Thompson, Jacob, 89, 154
Thompson, M. Jeff, 48
*Times* (London), 54
*Tragedy of Julius Caesar, The*, 205
Trefousse, Hans, 150
Trenton, Tenn., 75
Trudeau, Noah Andre, 53, 87
Tullahoma Campaign, 33
Tupelo, Miss., 128, 177
Tweed, William Marcy "Boss," 195
Tyler, Daniel, 155, 157
Tyler, Henry A., 80, 123, 124

Ulundi, 13
Union City, Tenn., 74, 75, 77, 78, 80, 84, 127, 153, 207, 213n60
United Confederate Veterans, 202
United States of America, 36, 40, 42, 44, 46
United States Colored Troops (USCT)/African American troops, 169, 181; 1st U.S. Colored Troops, 169; 2nd U.S. Colored Light Artillery, 87; 5th U.S. Colored Cavalry, 174; 6th U.S. Colored Heavy Artillery, 87, 96, 121, 154, 155; 10th U.S. Colored Troops, 169

United States Congress, 25, 39, 41, 43, 50, 134, 151, 189; House of Representatives, 199, 200; Joint Committee of, 5, 105, 150, 152, 154, 155, 156, 159, 176, 200, 201, 212, 240n8; Senate, 149, 202
United States Constitution, 39, 43, 45, 47, 194
United States Regular Army, 4th U.S. Cavalry, 62, 179, 180
Urwin, Gregory J.W., 4–5, 150
Usher, John P., 160

Van Camp, Eugene, 89
Van Dorn, Earl, 30, 51, 223n15
Vaughn, J.C., 174
Vermont, 166
Verona, Miss., 103
Vicksburg, Miss., 30, 56, 68, 183
Vietnam Conflict, 6
Virginia, 19, 45, 50, 54, 71, 129, 130, 160, 163, 169, 170, 171, 175, 182; peninsula of, 39
*Virginius*, 195
Von Trotha, Lothar, 13

Wade, Benjamin Franklin, *139*, 150, 151, 152, 153, 157, 158, 159, 176, 215, 240n8
Walker, C. Irvine, 177
Wallace, William Harvey Lamb, 10
Walter, Harvey, 188
Ward, Andrew, 4
Warren, Gouverneur Kemble, 183
Warrenton, Va., 201
Washburn, Cadwallader Coldan, 117, 121, 130, 131, 168
Washington, D.C., 48, 54, 181, 199, 226n5
Washita River, 12
"Water Cure," 14
Waxhaws, S.C., 7, 108, 206, 207
W. Duke Sons & Company, 200

Weaver, Henry, 92
Welles, Gideon, 159, 193
Wessells, Henry W., 12
Western and Atlantic Railroad, 31
West Tennessee, 36, 63, 65, 66, 70, 73, 75, 83, 84, 114, 119, 124, 127, 175, 190, 216, 225n58, 225n65
Wheeler, Joseph, 223n15, 247n17
White, Richard, 162
*White Cloud Kansas Chief*, 191
Whitlow, Wright, 93
Widney, Lyman, 165
Wild, Edward A., 169
Wilderness, 160
Wiley, Bell I., 111
Wiley, William, 180, 181
Williams, Major, 154
Williams, T. Harry, 151
Wilson, David, 206
Wilson, H.G., 202
Wilson, James Harrison, 35, 178, 179, 180, 212
Wilson's Wharf, Va., 169
Winder, John H., 59–60, 99, 234n57
Winn, Robert, 164
Wisconsin, 189, 202
Woodcock, Marcus, 166
World War I, 14
World War II, 14, 15, 208
Wounded Knee, 13, 207
Wyeth, John Allan, 93, 201, 202, 215
Wytheville, Va., 175

Young, Bennett H., 201
Young, John T., 128, 129
*Young People's History of Our Country*, 203
*Youth's History of the Rebellion, A*, 156
Ypres, Third Battle of, 14

Zulus, 13